Loompanics Unlimited Conquers The Universe

Articles and Features from
The Best Book Catalog
In The World

Loompanics Unlimited Conquers The Universe

Articles and Features from The Best Book Catalog In The World

Edited by Michael Hoy

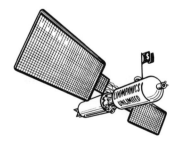

Loompanics Unlimited
Port Townsend, Washington

LOOMPANICS CONQUERS THE UNIVERSE
Edited by Michael Hoy
© 1998 by Loompanics Unlimited

Published by:
Loompanics Unlimited
PO Box 1197
Port Townsend, WA 98368
Loompanics Unlimited is a division of Loompanics Enterprises, Inc.
1-360-385-5087
e-mail: loompanx@olympus.net
Web site: www.loompanics.com

Cover artwork by Rick Altergott

ISBN 1-55950-173-1
Library of Congress Card Catalog 97-81346

Contents

Loompanics Conquers the Universe

Introduction by Claire Wolfe

The only thing more stimulating than writing for Loompanics is reading what others write for Loompanics.

Over the years, my fellow Loompanicians have written about everything from "How to Save the World" to "How to Get Laid." Maybe even "How to Get Laid While Saving the World... While High on Peyote Harvested from Your Backyard." Or "With Nerve Gas Manufactured in Your Very Own Kitchen." Who knows? The possibilities are endless.

Some of the possibilities, I admit, are pretty gross. And maybe not *quite* endless, either. You won't find any love letters to Phyllis Schlafly in any Loompanics collection. Or joyful paeans to state capitalism. No praises for Janet Reno. No celebrations of the history of chastity belts. (Thoughts of Janet Reno render chastity belts redundant, but that's another story.)

Now, in *Loompanics Unlimited Conquers the Universe*, these writers have produced a collection that's vast, mouthy, insolent, intelligent, scholarly, historic, modern, wild, satiric, logical, scatological, eschatological, fanciful, factual, obscure, titillating, effervescent and irreverent. Don't like one essay? No problem. The next will send you off on gales of laughter, or leave you stunned at some abomination your history teacher never told you about.

You never know what you're going to find at the turn of the next page — only that it's likely to be information you never knew before. Some of these essays are a kind of shock camp/cold turkey cure for mental blindness.

I've never been bored reading Loompanics articles or comix. Not once. But this stuff isn't always fun to read, either.

It isn't "fun" to learn about a young Israeli going mad in confinement ("Israel's Anti-Nuclear Prisoner-of-Conscience," page 157) or about barbaric surgeries committed to control women's behavior ("Dr. Ripper: The Rise of Gynecological Surgery," page 24). It isn't fun to read about how one famous underground writer vengefully brought a drug bust down upon another ("Way Beneath the Underground," page 57). The bastard!

It's scary to read about the prison "industry" growing and lobbying for bigger budgets, harsher laws and more convict labor ("America's Private Gulag," page 189, "Prison Economics," page 116, and "Feasting on the Convicted Class," page 92).

It's grotesque to consider the barbarities perpetrated in the name of mental health ("This is Your Lobotomy," page 120 and "Repressed Memory: Junk Science in the Courts," page 202).

Yet...

Even when you're learning something you'd rather not know... even when you're grossed out... even when you're mad as hell and don't want to take it for one more minute, there's something exhilarating about the Mad Hatter's ride through reality that these writers give you.

I've been taking that ride since 1979 or thereabouts. I've got a lifetime pass.

Capital L-ife

If you like life safe, easy and neat, don't read this book.

This stuff is for people who prefer the facts, even when they hit like Black Talons. If you have a taste for Reality with a big red R scrawled in blood, you're in the right place. This is reading for people who want to know what's really going on, even when what's going on isn't pretty. It's for people whose sense of humor is so black it's got an event horizon around it and sucks in passing space ships.

If your tolerance for the politically correct, the hypocritically polite or the superficially sweet is about a millimeter deep and two seconds long — welcome.

If you want to see not only what's on the surface, but what's underneath the makeup — enjoy.

These essays don't just shine another spotlight on center stage; they give you infrared vision into the dark corners where a deformed little stagehand is toiling alone or the prop manager is copulating with the assistant director.

If the high wire isn't risky enough for you — if you want to walk on the flippin' *electric lines* just to see what it's like up there — you were born for Loompanics. (But of course, you're also sensible enough to wear your insulated shoes on those wires, aren't you now?)

The way I've always envisioned it, Loompanics readers demand, no, *take* freedom, wherever and however they find it. *Carpe diem. Carpe Libertas.* If you can't find freedom, you create it. If you can't create it, you'll monkeywrench or outwit whatever gets in your way. Anybody who tries to take freedom from you had better beware.

Because, after all, you read Loompanics works. You have the knowledge, the tools and the spirit to stop the freedom-snatching bastards.

Freedom is offensive

Loompanics has been called "The First Amendment in action." It's that and several other amendments, too. Second. Fourth. Check any Loompanics catalog and you're likely to find somewhere near all 10. Maybe even that obscure one about no quartering of soldiers.

These writings are freedom personified. And that means, inevitably, that the things you'll read here, or in Loompanics books, are sometimes offensive. Not just offensive to prudes, conventional thinkers, safety fascists and control freaks, but sometimes even to thee and me.

Heck, every time I look at a Loompanics catalog, I find *something* that bugs me. Something that leaves me going, "Oh, gah-rosss!" And I love every minute of it.

I love it because it reminds me the world is a bigger, vaster, more interesting place than I might otherwise think. I love it because that little pain of having my mind stretched is as healthy as the little pain of having my muscles stretched when I exercise. I love it because I'm thrilled to know (in this world of diminishing freedom) that people are still free enough to read things I don't like and do things I don't approve of.

That means *I'm* still free to read things others might not like and do things they might not approve of. It means there's still room to breathe and think on this increasingly stifling small planet.

I love it because it's the wild ideas, the dangerous notions, the exploration of the forbidden... that keeps the human race evolving. When our prejudices are being challenged, when our "common wisdom" gets turned on its self-satisfied fat little head, when something we learn sends a chill of unease down our spines — we know we're out there on the edge of the future. Careening toward the destiny of the human race.

To me, the most exciting thing in the world is to be offended and awakened by the unusual, by the mentally challenging. Goddess save us from the stagnation of the safe and familiar!

For every Loompanics essay that's a complete and total gross-out, there's another that leaves me gaping, "Damn! That's important. Why haven't I ever heard that anywhere else?" That's the way I felt about "Shays' Rebellion and the Battle for the American Jubilee" (page 194). You mean even the inscription on the Liberty Bell has been twisted to mean something other than what it really meant? Well, that's what Michael Hoffman implies. And he's now got me curious enough to do some more digging on my own.

You can't read these things and not get your eyes opened unless you've stapled your eyes shut by a perverse determination to remain ignorant. And it goes beyond the single thing you're reading. Hey, if they lied about the Liberty Bell and Shays' Rebellion, what's the real scoop on the Whiskey Rebellion or the Emancipation Proclamation or Pearl Harbor or Waco or the headlines in tomorrow's paper?

All the news, whether or not it's fit to print

This book has articles that are just plain uselessly fascinating... other articles that put usefully subversive information into your hands articles that forge new intellectual territory and some that just defy classification.

▶ What was going on when Dennis P. Eichhorn and his friend witnessed "Shit in the Woods" (page 5)? Strange stuff

▶ John Perry Barlow's "Declaration of the Independence of Cyberspace" (page 42) is as stirring and defiant as its historic namesake. Any congressthing or bureaucrap trying to put the Internet in chains is going to have to reckon with John Perry, and with a few million freedom-seekers, besides.

▶ "Cannabis Cookie Breakthrough" (page 55) and "Pot-Club Patois" (page 106) are healthy antidotes to the tragically absurd demonization of a useful drug.

▶ "In The Beginning" (page 1) is a simple hoot. (But believe me, I've seen Dennis' office and it's never been that neat.)

▶ "Sneak and Peek Warrants" (page 131) is *still* the only explanation I've ever heard of a new type of search warrant that makes a mockery out of the Fourth Amendment. Why aren't our daily newspapers writing editorials against this outrage? Where are the TV commentators? Where's the ACLU, for God's sake? Why did nobody but Loompanics see this article when it originally appeared in the FBI's own, publicly available, publication?

▶ "The Economy of Ideas" suggests a new definition of intellectual property in an age when information runs free. It's about copyright and that sort of thing. Ho-hum. But it covers aspects of copyright the mainstream media don't want to touch. New concepts upset their little applecarts. God forbid, this article might make them think.

▶ "A New Approach to Group Therapy" (page 29) well, it's just strange. Offensive? You decide.

When it comes right down to it, what *is* offensive, anyway? Get 100 people in a room, hand them all copies of this book, and you'd get 100 different answers. Louis Freeh and Janet Reno would no doubt be offended at the recipe for marijuana cookies or the hard questions asked in Adam Parfrey's "Oklahoma City: Cui Bono?" (page 45).

The American Association of Advertising Agencies would froth at "Adding the Blemish of Truth" (page 73), a how-to for defacing billboards. Prudes and religious bigots can prepare to go apoplectic over "Hail Priapus: A Selection of Swinging Sex Gods" (page 161) and "Western Sect Freedonianism: Have a Little Freedom with Your Religion" (page 169). They might be doubly ticked that the Loompanics gang chose to print both those essays in a Christmas catalog.

I think it's pretty darned offensive to learn how brutally members of the "One Big Union" were treated at the beginning century. ("Wobbly Reverie," page 177) I wouldn't have agreed with the Wobblies' goals. but the jingoistic mindlessness of their attackers was worse. Worse yet, this kind of thing still goes on; demonize a group and you can commit any atrocity upon them — Wobblies, Jews, militias. You bet I'm offended — but it isn't Loompanics that's offended me.

Ultimately, the most offensive and dangerous thing in the universe is *the truth that is painful to know.* But it's also the most important thing. It's the thing that lets you make smart choices instead of stumbling blindly into stupid ones. It's the thing that keeps you from being taken advantage of by con artists — the freelance kind, the ones who write the news, and *especially* the ones in political office. It's the thing, as that old cliché goes, that'll set you free.

So if you have to put up with a few offenses and gross-outs along the way, well, that's a darned small price for enlightenment.

In the wrong hands

Mike Hoy, the publisher of this book, is often asked, "What if Loompanics' information fell into the wrong hands?" That question betrays a superstitious animism on the part of the questioner. It assumes the written word can somehow "make" people behave dangerously. And of course, that belief is errant nonsense.

More people have committed outrages in the name of the Bible than in the name of Loompanics, Paladin, Lysias, Javelin and all the "dangerous" publishers of the world combined. (See "God Made Me Do It!" page 144.) The Bible didn't "make" anyone "do it," and neither did Paladin's *Hit Man* (page 75) or anything Loompanics ever put into print.

As the folks at Loompanics point out, you can make bombs from information in the *Encyclopædia Britannica,* as well as in Loompanics books. But none of Mike's questioners would ask, "What if the *Encyclopædia Britannica* fell into the wrong hands?" Nope. Those same people would proudly buy *that* bomb-making instruction manual for their children, while clucking their tongues over the Loompanics catalog.

For what it's worth, there are no bomb-making instructions in this book. But there are things that blow everyday concepts sky high.

And maybe more people are beginning to understand the value of both literal and intellectual explosives in the hands of free people.

Recently a reporter asked me a question like the one Mike always gets. But this one had a twist. The "wrong hands" he meant were those of the FBI. He wasn't afraid the FBI might learn how to make bombs via Loompanics (though I suppose they could). No, he wondered what harm might befall us if the government cracked down on the free exchange of information.

The reporter knew the value of The Uncensored Idea.

I recently heard another interesting comment from a vendor whose products I'd mentioned in a Loompanics book. He said, "We sometimes get orders from people who are a little strange. You know, who are still fighting the Civil War, or who have some close-minded attitudes. But the people who've called from your book are different. They seem to have more open minds, an interest in the bigger historical picture. Nice people, too."

I don't think it's just my book he's talking about. I think he's observing an attitude I've found in Loompanics readers all around the world. They're *thinkers*. Explorers. Pioneers.

But for a while after I heard the vendor's comments I worried that we might also be becoming *respectable*. Loompanics? Respectable? But (whew!) I don't think so. We're not changing our nature; but others are. And writings like the ones in this book have something to do with it.

Eyes are opening. Ears are hearing. They're hearing that every word out of the mouth of every government official is a lie. They're seeing that government and its whole cozy clan of media, schools, "public-private partnerships," kiss-my-ass-&-I'll-kiss-yours corporations, non-profit organizations, "donors," yadayadayada is just a self-serving, people-tromping, blackmailing, soul-selling, using, abusing, effluvious blob of animated excrement, rolling across the country, sucking up everything it touches and stinking up every place it goes.

What's the alternative to this mass and morass of "respectable" lies and "respectable" corruption? Us.

I see it in this collection. I see it in my heap of old Loompanics catalogs. I see it in the hundreds of Loompanics customers I've met, and in the comments I've been hearing from people everywhere I go. People are ready to hear hard truths, and truths spoken in raw, blunt language.

Given that, I'm not at all surprised to learn that Loompanics Unlimited aims to conquer the universe.

One mind at a time.

Which is really, when you think about it, the only way it can be done.

Claire Wolfe is the author of *101 Things To Do 'Til The Revolution: Ideas and resources for self-liberation, monkey wrenching and preparedness.*

My companion and I were living near Golden Gate Park at the time, and I desperately wanted to be a writer.

This Bukowski guy is really a great writer, Love Doll... if only I could be half as honest in my work.

You will, Denny, you will... it just takes time, that's all.

Then one day I discovered PUNK magazine!

My God!

What is it?

This PUNK is the trippiest thing I've read since the early MAD magazines!

CITY LIGHTS BOOKS

I'm going to be published in PUNK if it's the LAST thing I do!

That's the spirit!

PUNK

I wasted no time in firing off a letter to PUNK...

...and soon received a terse reply.

SO YOU WANT TO WRITE FOR PUNK? WHY DON'T YOU INTERVIEW THE CRIME BAND RIGHT THERE IN SAN FRANCISCO? THEY'VE BEEN BUGGING US FOR A WRITE-UP.

All right!

I called the CRIME band and arranged a visit...

I'll see you at six P.M.!

DON'T BE LATE, MAN!

... and then contacted Tim Page, world-famous photographer.

I'll pick you up at five, Tim... and bring lots of film!

Jolly good... if YOU bring lots of DOPE!

FOSTER'S ALE

SLAUGHTER FIRST CLASS

SUPERVISOR

by JOHN MARR

Illustration by Nick Bougas

© 1996 by John Marr

Pity the poor postal worker. Nobly they make their appointed rounds despite being universal targets of abuse. Blue-haired widows sick their ill-mannered poodles on innocent letter carriers. Used hypodermic syringes "found loose in the mails" tear the flesh of unwitting mail handlers. Frenzied SSI recipients lunge at general-delivery counter clerks quivering behind barriers of bullet-proof glass. And everyone, from senior senators to corner bar drunks, rants and raves when stamps go up a few cents.

Yet, these external threats pale next to the danger within. Over the last 15 years, postal workers, using everything from AK-47s to samurai swords, have made mailrooms the killing fields of American industry. Blood has soaked the mails from San Diego to Boston as berserk postal workers have

sought vengeance for real or imagined slights.

It started inauspiciously enough in 1980 when a rookie New Orleans postal worker shot and killed his supervisor for not giving him the evening off. Over the next few years, four more postal workers died at their comrades' hands in separate incidents throughout the South and Midwest. The first multicide came in 1985, when a mentally-unbalanced sorter fatally shot two comrades in an Atlanta mailroom.

But when most people think of postal massacres, a certain town in Oklahoma springs to mind. And for good reason. Not only does Patrick Sherrill's 1986 rampage through the Edmond post office remain the pinnacle of massacres, it's also the worst workplace shooting in US history. The incident has

(Continued on next page)

resonated through the rank and file ever since. "Edmond, Oklahoma" is the mantra of disgruntled postmen everywhere.

At 44, Patrick Sherrill epitomized the disaffected postal worker. He was about to be fired. A surviving letter carrier recalled "he couldn't even find the Wal-Mart, and that's the biggest store in town." Friendless and never married, he lived alone in a house without an extra chair for visitors. His only source of pride was a two-year stint in the Marines. He liked to tell tales of his Vietnam exploits, although USMC records show he never left the continental United States. His only social activity was a National Guard marksmanship team.

For the first time, the elements of the classic postal massacre converged: military experience, guns, impending dismissal, and an anti-social employee muttering, "They'll be sorry. They'll be sorry and everyone's going to know about it."

Sherrill showed up at work with three target pistols in his mailbag and burst into the post office with both guns blazing. For the next 15 minutes, workers were gunned down indiscriminately, whether they fled, huddled in cubicles, or begged for mercy. One supervisor took three bullets after fruitlessly ordering, "Get out of here, you crazy son of bitch." The survivors either feigned death or hid in the stamp vault.

Sherrill ended the slaughter in the lunchroom by shooting himself in the head. Besides himself, 14 postal workers were dead, and another seven injured — some 20% of the Edmond postal staff. Ironically, Sherrill's supervisor was late and missed the massacre.

Postal violence became almost common over the next few years, with shootings reported in New Orleans, Chelsea, and Boston. The last was by far the most sensational, as disgruntled mail-handler Alfred Hunter stole a plane and attempted to strafe a postal facility with an AK-47. No one was injured in the aerial attack, though not from any lack of effort on Hunter's part.

The next major incident broke the pattern. John Taylor didn't fit the postal-killer profile. The 27-year veteran Escondido, California, letter carrier was happily married and a stellar worker. He was so dedicated he would skip lunch to complete his route on time. Yet even this model employee cracked and began to make lighthearted Pat Sherrill

jokes in August 1989. Only days later, he was completely gone. He shot his wife and showed up at work toting a pistol instead of a bag lunch.

Outside, he killed two letter carriers, both good friends. Inside, Taylor peppered the mailroom with an estimated 20 shots. His marksmanship was poor. His fusillade only injured one clerk. At one point, he even had a bead on a clerk before telling him, "I'm not going to shoot you." Taylor ended his spree a few minutes later with a classic single bullet to the head. In a suicide note, he compounded the mystery by writing he had "...just done what I've had to do."

Comparative calm reigned in the mail rooms for the next two years. But the cycle hadn't ended. These public servants were just gathering their resolve for an orgy of violence that would birth the phrase "going postal."

Ridgewood, New Jersey, a quiet New York suburb, is one of the safest places to *live* in the country. Work is another matter — especially at the local post office.

In 1989, Carol Ott, a Ridgewood post-office supervisor, did the most dangerous thing a postal supervisor can do: she fired mail sorter Joseph Harris. She had cause. Harris was sullen and unfriendly, and harassed other workers. Survivors described his relations with Ott as "...like oil and water..."

Harris declined the union's offer to file a grievance. As one union official recalled, "He said he would take care of things his own way."

Eighteen months later, according to police reports, Harris broke into Ott's home in nearby Wayne, New Jersey, slashing her to death with a samurai sword and fatally shooting her boyfriend. A few hours later, an intruder dressed in black fatigues and a ninja hood and armed with an Uzi, a samurai sword, and several grenades, broke into the Ridgewood post office and put into motion a plan apparently designed to slaughter most of the 120-strong staff.

The intruder shot and killed the first two mail handlers to show up at work at 2 AM. His next intended victim, a truck driver, was more fortunate. While looking for the normal work crew, he came across the masked man lurking in the basement. The black-garbed figure's shot missed. The truck driver fled and called the police. A pair of

(Continued on next page)

explosions drove the first contingent of police back. The ensuing five-hour standoff, however, was quiet. Police arrested Harris at the scene.

After defusing a bomb wired to the door, police searched Harris's apartment where they allegedly found a note by Harris complaining about his unfair treatment, complete with Edmond, Oklahoma, references. According to the county prosecutor, the letter "basically indicated that these people are going to pay." Subsequently, Harris was convicted and sentenced to death for the "Ninja Killing," the 1988 murder of a New Jersey investment banker with whom Harris had had unsuccessful financial dealings. Harris is currently awaiting trial on charges related to the Ridgewood rampage.

Barely a month later, a second discharged postal worker avenged himself against management. The increasingly-familiar story began with Royal Oak, Michigan, letter carrier Thomas "Mackie" McIlvane's firing in July 1990 for "insubordination." Among other sins, he had been fighting with the customers on his route.

Everything about McIlvane practically screamed, "give this man a mailbag and he'll fill it with guns." An ex-Marine, he'd settled a score with a fellow leatherneck by crushing the guy's car with a tank. He was a black belt martial artist, former pro kickboxer, and winner of the Detroit "Tough Man" contest. And he was known as having a "short fuse."

Unlike Harris, McIlvane had faith in the grievance process. He restrained himself for almost two years waiting out his appeals. He was convinced he would be reinstated. If not, he vowed that it would be a "sad day in Royal Oak." Invoking patron saint Patrick Sherrill, he also promised "to make Edmond look like a tea party." The stage was set.

The other Royal Oak workers weren't completely unprepared. Even before McIlvane, labor/-management relations at the Royal Oak post office were so poor, the Senate was investigating. Disgruntled workers had thrown phones through the windows and threatened supervisors with knives. And management wasn't turning the other cheek.

Everyone knew about McIlvane's threats. They had orders to keep him out. Many mentally planned out escape routes "just in case." But plans

and precautions were for naught. The day after McIlvane lost his last appeal, he strolled in through the loading dock, armed with a sawed-off semi-automatic rifle and a full measure of postal wrath.

Fortunately for the rank and file, Mackie's ire — and fire — was directed at management. In his six-minute spree, McIlvane killed four and injured four. The dead were all supervisors. At one point, McIlvane had his gun at a woman's head before he informed her "you're not the one I want," and went hunting more supervisors. With his mission presumably accomplished, McIlvane ended his rampage the usual way with a shot to the head.

The violence kicked into yet a higher gear on May 6, 1993. In an unprecedented display of mailroom mayhem, rampaging postal workers — one in Michigan, one in California — struck almost simultaneously, leaving four dead in their wake. The unrelated attacks mark the first postal "daily double" slayings.

"Bloody Thursday" dawned in the Detroit suburb of Dearborn. Around 8:45 AM, mechanic Larry Jasion brought his 24-year USPS career to a dramatic close. Shouting, "It's time to educate the supervisors!" he opened fire in the garage where he had worked for so many years, killing a mechanic. In another area, he injured two other workers: his boss, dubbed "Dictator" by the union newsletter, and a woman who had beaten him out for a coveted transfer. Jasion himself ended his brief rampage with the traditional bullet to the head.

A former Dearborn postmaster recalled, "If you ask any employee there, 99% of them would say if something like this was going to happen, it would be Larry Jasion..." He lived alone in a house cluttered with guns and ammunition, and ordnance manuals, but with only one setting of silverware and no functional oven. His windows were walled shut; his response to a friendly "Good morning" was, "What's so good about it?" After the Edmond shootings, he started playfully pointing his finger at his then-supervisor and making machine gun noises. The supervisor wisely took early retirement.

By 1992, Jaison was at the end of this rope. At work, the pace was relentless. His mother, a retired disgruntled postal worker, died. He lost the transfer. His closest friend retired. And his co-workers blasted rock music on the garage radio,

(Continued on next page)

turning it up every time he complained. Something was bound to give. And it did.

Postmaster General Marvin Rayburn was attending a meeting in Baltimore when he heard the news. He immediately set out for this latest USPS hot spot. But before he could board a plane to Michigan, another postal worker cracked in California.

More than 2,400 miles away in Dana Point, California, a different but no less familiar postal drama reached a tragic climax. Mark Hilbun was a lonely man. The Air Force veteran lived by himself in an apartment with windows covered by newspaper. But he had a dream — true love. For a year, he wooed a fellow letter carrier. She spurned him. Even roses, late night phone calls, and photos of him kayaking with lewd messages scrawled on the back failed to lure her away from her boyfriend.

In September, he was diagnosed as manic-depressive and fired a few months later as "not fit for duty." Although upset, Hilbun kept the mash notes coming even as he pursued reinstatement. A final note warned, "I love you. I'm going to kill us both and take us both to hell." His intended victim planned to get a restraining order on her next payday — the day after "Bloody Thursday."

Hilbun allegedly started the day by killing his mother and her pet dog. And at 9:30 AM, only hours after Jasion fired his last shot in Dearborn, he sneaked into the post office through a loading dock with a pistol.

According to witnesses, he ordered everyone to get down, called out for his beloved, and opened fire. She managed to hide; however, bullets killed one worker and injured another. Ironically, the dead mailman was Hilbun's closest workplace friend.

According to witnesses, Hilbun then fled. Tensions ran high the next two days as, according to police reports, Hilbun injured at least four more people in stickups around Orange County. Mail deliveries were suspended and armed guards patrolled the post office. He was finally arrested early Saturday in a Huntington Beach sports bar shortly after allegedly wounding two more people in an ATM stickup. At last word, Hilbun had pled innocent by reason of insanity to two counts of murder and six counts of attempted murder. In the wake of the shootings, NBC was forced to pull ads for a *Cheers* episode wherein a letter carrier was suspected of killing his mother.

The violence showed no signs of abating in 1995. As of September, post offices had already played host to at least three attacks, with postal workers the prime suspects. In March, an ex-postal worker allegedly shot and killed two clerks and two customers and injured another while robbing his former workplace in Montclair, New Jersey. Another postal worker was arrested in July in connection with the fatal shooting of his supervisor at a mail-processing facility in the City of Industry, California. And less than two months later, according to police reports, a mail sorter shot and injured two of his closest friends on the job at a Palatine, Illinois, mail-processing center.

One can only sympathize with the plight of the USPS vice president of labor relations. "We cannot fire people who have a tendency to wear camouflage jackets or a fascination with gunfire. You fire someone and they go away — and they come back." Simple bureaucratic obstacles cannot stay postal workers as they diligently complete their appointed rounds of slaughter. It's only a matter of time — and bullets — before some enterprising, nameless mailman dethrones Patrick Sherrill as the reigning champion of mailroom multicide. •

Adapted from a series of articles in *Murder Can Be Fun*, a fanzine dedicated to the morbid, unusual and weird in fact and fiction. Copies of the current issue, dedicated to "Zoo Deaths," are available for $2 from:

John Marr
PO Box 640111
San Francisco, CA 94164.

GI RESISTANCE IN THE VIETNAM ERA
MUTINY AT THE OUTPOSTS OF EMPIRE

by Rob Blurton

Thirty years ago, the most powerful military colossus ever assembled, its triumphant legions spread throughout the world, committed an expeditionary force of its best troops to the Asian mainland. "The American Army of 1965," wrote an admiring historian, "was headstrong with confidence, sharply honed to a lethal fighting edge... [and] eager to test its newly acquired wings of air mobility."[1] In other words, it felt invincible. Battalions dispatched to Indochina were told that the local communist guerrilla-bandits were politically isolated and would quickly succumb to their superior might, but instead they found themselves locked in desperate battle with a determined adversary enjoying massive popular support. This expeditionary force gradually became a gigantic field army of over half a million men, and the lightning war turned into a meatgrinder.

As America's involvement in Vietnam deepened, political and social turbulence at home reached proportions unimaginable in 1965, and the magnificent army started falling apart. Low morale and outright rebellion eroded its combat effectiveness, and the malaise began spreading beyond Southeast Asia to brigades garrisoning more vital imperial frontiers, especially Central Europe.

A startling development took place among the children of the men who dutifully fought the Second World War in theaters around the globe. Their conscripted sons came to see not Asian communists but the United States military machine as the real enemy.

Hundreds of thousands voted against the war with their feet by deserting before their hitches were up. Marines and soldiers murdered their officers. Sailors sabotaged powerful warships, and bomber pilots refused to fly missions.

Mutinies broke out on isolated jungle trails all over Vietnam, forcing troop leaders to "work it out" with the men. Stockades and brigs were rocked by uprisings. GI antiwar organizations and newspapers spontaneously proliferated at U.S. military bases worldwide as soldiers finished with their one-year tour in Vietnam spread the contagion.

The evidence indicates that troop rebellions — contrary to most conventional histories of war — were not merely background blare to the central drama of decisions by politicians and generals. They were instead a critical factor that hindered the expeditionary army's fighting ability, and the snowballing process of decay hastened American withdrawal from the battlefield.

After the U.S. invasion of South Vietnam, draft resistance was the first activity directed against the war effort. Many of those successfully conscripted, though, also became a problem for the armed forces as they learned about the military and the war through experience. Desertion sky-rocketed during peak years of the ground fighting, steadily rising from a rate of 15 incidents per thousand in the 1966 Army to a staggering 74 per thousand by 1971.[2]

This outdid even the Second World War maximum of 63 per thousand during the grueling land combat of 1944. (Army generals found this figure so upsetting that, as an example to others, they actually carried out the firing squad execution in France of one unlucky GI from Detroit who had gone over the hill.) It should be noted that unlike

After taking casualties for days when ordered to repeatedly assault a mountain bunker complex, mutinous U.S. soldiers in South Vietnam face down their battalion commander, September 1969. At home and abroad during this turbulent era, African-Americans stood in the front ranks of struggle against the U.S. empire.

World War II, most Vietnam-era desertions took place away from the combat zone, indicating disgust rather than fear as a primary motivating factor.

Abbie Hoffman once quipped at a demonstration outside the gates of Fort Meade, Maryland, "Behind every GI haircut lies a Samson."[3] By 1967, the peace movement recognized the immense value of antiwar feeling in the ranks, and intensified organizing efforts.

So-called GI coffeehouses were set up by activists outside military posts in the U.S., providing a space where soldiers and civilians could congregate free of the repressive atmosphere that prevailed on-base. These establishments came under legal attack from both military and local city officials. Coffeehouse organizers responded with a "Summer of Support" project in 1968, successfully raising funds to keep the soldiers'

meeting places open.

That year, one could realize the increasing magnitude of military dissent through the nascent GI "underground" press which eventually grew to include hundreds of papers. The most famous of these, *FTA* (short for "Free The Army," but usually translated as a more coarse comment on soldiering), was first published in 1968 at Fort Knox, Kentucky. *The Bond*, from New York City, became the voice of the influential American Servicemen's Union and during the big years of the ground war, this paper was distributed to tens of thousands of GIs worldwide.

Stories revealing on-base incidents that army control kept from the civilian press began to appear in these soldier newspapers. A 1967 *Bond* article, for example, described rioting that erupted at Fort Hood, Texas, when the 198th Infantry

Brigade vented its unhappiness at receiving Vietnam orders.[4]

Another story, published during the 1968 Tet Offensive, reported, "In a highly significant event not noted by the national press, GIs at Fort Jackson, South Carolina, tried to hold a meeting on the post against the war, but the MPs broke it up... Their bitterness is certainly shared by soldiers on other bases."[5]

The civilian antiwar movement's enthusiasm for military resistance had by 1969 reached a point where some teenage members of the Young Socialist Alliance were allowing themselves to be drafted without resistance when they came of age, then immediately agitating from within upon induction.[6]

Over There

It was in Southeast Asia, though, where military units really began to unravel. Fragging, the deliberate murder of unpopular officers and non-commissioned officers, using fragmentation hand grenades (to avoid ballistic detection) became a popular form of resistance among infantry platoons. By 1967, soldiers in the Mekong Delta were offering bounties raised by the men for combat executions of dangerously gung-ho officers.[7]

One droll GI wrote back to the underground newspaper at Camp Pendleton, the sprawling California home of the 1st Marine Division: "After months of assiduous care and maintenance of my M-16, it failed to function at a critical moment, endangering my life and the lives of other men in this company. Last night, at 0300 hours I had a clear, unobstructed shot at the captain. To my chagrin, the weapon misfired. It may be weeks before I get another crack at the bastard and in the meantime I am subject to the ridicule of my associates and can kiss goodbye the $2000 in the company pool."[8]

The murder of overzealous commanders during battle was hardly unknown in earlier American wars, but in Indochina, the practice — and even more, the hesitancy that this constantly implied threat induced in the entire officer corps — mushroomed out of control as the war stalemated. Such ruthless correctives to excessive officer ambition were restricted to life-and-death combat situations in previous conflicts, but by 1970, the phenomenon leapt from the front lines to rear areas and even to bases in Germany.[9] Vietnam was beginning to have a corrosive effect on the U.S. Army far beyond the Asian battlefields.

Fighting The White Man's War

Mirroring turbulent civil society, militant activism among young African-American men was in the forefront of the GI movement. An early example occurred in July 1967 (at the same time of the Detroit

riot/rebellion), when two Camp Pendleton marines called a meeting on the base to question whether "black men should fight white men's wars." To air these concerns, they and twelve other marines requested a Captain's Mast with their commanding officer, which is naval parlance for the military judicial right given troops to redress grievances. Instead, the original two were arrested and charged with insubordination and promoting disloyalty. In November, both were found guilty and sentenced to several years in the brig.[10]

On August 23, 1968, over 100 black soldiers from troubled Fort Hood met to discuss orders for duty in Chicago, where Army units would be used during the Democratic national convention to suppress civilian demonstrations. After allowing an all-night discussion, Army MPs arrested 43 "ringleaders" as the meeting broke up.[11]

The April 1970 invasion of Cambodia provided further impetus to military resistance, paralleling the outrage it generated in the civilian peace movement. Expanded fighting in Asia assured the success of previously scheduled "Armed Forces Day" demonstrat-ions held on May 16, the national Armed Forces Day holiday, which in-cluded over a dozen large rallies and marches at military posts across the country.

The reaction of Army brass at Fort Ord, California (just two weeks after Ohio reserve soldiers shot down unarmed students at Kent State), shows how frightened some were by the protests. When civilians demonstrated outside the gates of the base, post commanders had security forces erect razor wire, set up M-60 machine guns on nearby rooftops, and main-tain riot control troops on alert. The reliability of this contingency unit was so suspect, however, that they were not issued ammunition

Soldiers of the 198th Infantry Brigade wear black armbands while on patrol near Chu Lai to show support for the Moratorium antiwar demonstrations back home, October 1969.

Troopers of the once elite 1st Air Cavalry hang out in Cambodia, May 1970. That year, the division reported thirty-five incidents of combat refusal, some involving entire units.

Without cooperation from the hands ondeck, planes cannot fly: Overworked enlisted carrier sailors during flight operations off the Vietnamese coast.

German and Russian soldiers fraternize on the Eastern Front during the First World War. In June, 1917, these troops simply stopped fighting each other, something no general likes to see.

and were kept aboard trucks lest they fraternize with the demonstrators.[12]

Other manifestations of civilian unrest were matched in the military, including prison rebellion and polarization among blacks and whites. In the summer of 1968, the two largest of many stockade uprisings in Vietnam occurred, both led by black GIs. During the weekend of August 16, marine inmates took over part of the brig outside Da Nang, the Marines' main in-country staging base. The prisoners held out for 20 hours against armed guards, resulting in several injuries.

Two weeks later, at the huge and overcrowded Army facility at Long Binh, the bloodiest revolt in a U.S. military prison in recent times took place. For hours, hundreds of inmates fought a running battle with MPs, and much of the stockade was de-stroyed by fire. Five guards and 58 prisoners were injured, 23 seriously. One GI inmate died.[13]

Another unfortunate symptom of the general breakdown underway was the fracture of unit solidarity along color lines. Confrontations between blacks and whites were pandemic in Vietnam, and in some instances became a war within a war. Perhaps the worst unrest took place at the Camp Baxter Marine post near the demilitarized zone separating North and South Vietnam.

In early 1971, a major racial clash took place that left at least one black GI dead. MPs investigating afterwards discovered that many of the marines were carrying illegal arms, and several caches of ammunition, grenades, and machine guns had been assembled by both sides, ostensibly in preparation for more trouble.[14]

By the turn of the decade, the volume of soldiers balking at orders in war zones had required an Army designation for the rot: "combat refusal." U.S. military operations were crippled by both actual incidents and the generalized atmosphere of battle evasion that restricted military options for unit commanders. For every defiant refusal, dozens more would "search and avoid," or fake their night patrols by stopping 100 meters beyond the perimeter wire to wait out the darkness, radioing in that they were passing the appropriate checkpoints at the appropriate times.

The declining combat ability of the Army was obvious to its troop leaders during the 1970 expansion of ground fighting in Cambodia. While maneuvering across the Cambodian border, many infantry companies avoided battle or were hesitant in moving out to new locations. The 4th Infantry Division, the "Fighting Fourth" of World War II fame, was renamed the "Funky Fourth" by cynical Army officers after it repeatedly lapsed into combat paralysis in Cambodia upon encountering any resistance.[15]

The Brink of Collapse

Historically, armies have gone to the verge of collapse and beyond numerous times. During the First World War alone, the tsarist army of Russia fell apart in 1917, and the French and Italian armies nearly followed suit. In 1918, the German and Austrian armies dis-solved, and even the British had serious problems for a time. (Mutinies among United Kingdom troops actually increased after the shooting stopped. Thousand of survivors of the trenches died in squalid army "demobil-ization centers" in England, a situation which generated riots and rebellions.)[16]

Events in Vietnam — made up of pervasive minor incidents and a substantial number of larger, more formal events of mass insubordin-ation — never constituted a complete physical disin-tegration of the America's military table of organi-zation. In many ways, the situation instead mirrored the more limited Nivelle mutinies by weary French troops in 1917 after the failure of a bloody and ill-advised Western Front offensive. For a period of time in the Reims salient northeast of Paris, tens of thousands of soldiers would defend themselves if attacked, but no longer advance to a pointless death. The tactic was somewhat successful: French generals carried out several firing squad executions, yet left this portion of the line in a basically defensive post-ure for a year until the final campaign of the war,

no doubt sparing some of the mutineers' lives.

Faced with meaningless sacrifice in stalemated wars, tired veterans in both the trenches of France and the jungles of Southeast Asia refused to conduct aggressive patrolling beyond forward positions, though they would still guard their own ramparts. The problem in South Vietnam was so widespread that punishment became impossible, causing the Army to downplay the incidents as much as circumstances allowed.

MAJOR MUTINIES AMONG GROUND FORCES IN VIETNAM INCLUDED:

September 1969: 60 men of the Americal Division refuse to charge bunkers after days of grueling combat near Queson.

November 1969: 21 GIs, all hardened veterans nearing the end of their tours, refuse to advance into enemy-held ground at Cu Chi near the Cambodian border.

April 1970: News correspondent John Laurence and the nation's television viewing audience watch as a squad leader on patrol in War Zone C flatly refuses his captain's reckless command to advance down a hazardous road, and successfully negotiates for an alternate route.

May 1970: During the Cambodian invasion, 16 soldiers from Firebase Washington will not advance with their units across the frontier, and a small group of 4th Division GIs refuse to board helicopters bound for Cambodia.

December 1970: A company commander in the 101st Airborne Division refuses his colonel's directive to move at night after talking the order over with his men and deciding it too dangerous.

March 1971: During the invasion of Laos by South Vietnamese troops, two supporting platoons of American soldiers under enemy fire refuse orders to advance and recover a damaged armored vehicle.

October 1971: A refusal of 6 GIs to patrol outside Firebase Pace near the Laotian border sparks wider mutiny in a company of the 1st Air Calvary Division. 65 men sign a petition to be sent to U.S. Senator Ted Kennedy, requesting protection from what they consider needless danger.

April 1972: In the final reported in-country mutiny, about 100 GIs of the 196th Infantry Brigade refuse an order to mount trucks for an advance into enemy territory near Phu Bai.

Contemporary media did not completely ignore the crisis. Among the miles of column-inches devoted to the actions of politicians and can-do military managers, hints of trouble percolating within the ranks slipped through. By the summer of 1969, a reporter who first came to Vietnam before the American buildup noted that, "rumors of troops quitting in combat were every-where, but nothing could be verified — newsmen never happened to be in the right place at the right time."[17] That August, a *New York Times* story described disill-usioned soldiers "who lack an ideological com-mitment to the war."[18]

In September, the press finally got their verifiable incident when a company of the morale-plagued Americal Division that had suffered heavy casualties during four days of continuous assaults against North Vietnamese bunkers refused to attack on the fifth day. Though high-ranking officers shrugged off the affair, it attracted so much attention that even the official Army paper, *Stars and Stripes*, covered the story.

During one of the October-November 1969 antiwar "Moratoriums" observed nationwide in the U.S., fifteen GIs on patrol near Chu Lai wore black armbands in solidarity with the demon-strators back home. "Before the day was out," *The New York Times* grimly noted, "four of the protesting soldiers had been wounded by Vietcong booby traps."[19]

In April 1970, one veteran company of grunts refused outright a direct order from their inexperienced commanding officer to advance down a dangerous open road, all in front of a CBS television crew.

The following month, a *Newsweek* article on the Cambodian invasion mentioned the growing effect of combat refusals, and concluded that "the current crop of U.S. troops — many of them draftees who make no bones about their opposition to the war — bears little resemblance to the aggressive, gung-ho units that saw action two or three years ago."[20]

Media evidence of growing discontent also emerged back in the States that summer. A crippled marine sergeant told a Senate committee that his injuries had been caused by his own men throwing a hand grenade underneath his bunk after he clamped down on their marijuana use, and CBS broadcast a clip of troopers from the First Air Calvary smoking pot through the barrel of a shotgun.

None of these "liberal media," who certain segments of the population today credit with gutting public support for the war, could manage to put together the mutiny puzzle pieces. It was instead Robert Heinl, a conservative analyst writing in 1971 for a journal of military professionals, who sounded the alarm. To alert his colleagues to the danger, he tied the seemingly unrelated outbursts into a larger fabric of disintegration. No examination of this subject is complete without quoting the former marine combat officer's opening sentences of this extremely influential article that still explode like an artillery shell:

"The morale, discipline, and battle-worthiness of the U.S. Armed Forces are, with a few salient exceptions, lower and worse than at any time in this century and possibly in the history of the United States. By every conceivable indicator, our army that now remains in Vietnam is in a state approaching collapse, with individual units avoiding or having refused combat, murdering their officers and noncommissioned officers, drug-rid-den and dispirited where not near-mutinous. Elsewhere than Vietnam, the situation is nearly as serious."[21] (See Winter 1990-91 *Fifth Estate* for reprint of this article.)

Such frank disclosures by frightened military men soon affected governmental policy discourse. It was no exaggeration to assert as fact the degradation of the Army's fighting ability; by the spring of 1972, even *Foreign Affairs,* an influential journal of the ruling elites, could report: "In the United States, the military establishment, and especially its ground forces, are experiencing a profound crisis in legitimacy due to the impact of Vietnam, internal race tension, corruption, extensive drug abuse, *disintegration of command and operational effectiveness,* and widespread anti-military sentiment." (My emphasis.)[22]

In 1970, the Cambodian debacle and changing political climate allowed a formerly hawkish *Newsweek* columnist to warn that "it might be a good idea to accelerate the rate of withdrawal from Vietnam very sharply... [because] discipline and morale are deteriorating very seriously... Is it any wonder that those who know the score are beginning to think about pulling this non-fighting army out of Vietnam in a hurry?... It is time to take those bitter draftees in our crumbling Army out of Vietnam — and the sooner the better."[23]

These incidents represent only the tip of the iceberg. How many rebellions by tired veterans in remote jungle gorges were "worked out" by the compromises of realistic officers we can never know.

The military cancer of Vietnam came home with the returning vets. Disciplinary problems such as desertion and drug abuse increased substantially in Stateside garrisons with the influx of former occupiers of South Vietnam. Among ground forces back in the U.S., continued resistance to the Indochina war took its most ominous and intriguing turn during antiwar events held in Washington, D.C., in April and May of 1971.

Thousands of protesters there were disillusioned Vietnam veterans, and when an ex-soldier encampment on the Mall was threatened with forcible removal, 82nd Airborne Division troopers dispatched to the capital on riot duty (with many combat returnees in their ranks) told demonstrators they would refuse any orders to interfere with their brother vets. Their commanders wisely did not press the issue.

Sympathetic GIs in other outfits relayed troop-movement information to protest organizers, allowing them to find out in advance which units were being prepared for civil duty, and to leaflet the affected bases with information on the aims of the demonstrations. Fortunately for the nervous bases, D.C. cops aided by nearby county and state police forces were able to contain the unrest, thus not forcing a showdown over the troops' questionable obedience.[24]

In Southeast Asia, the war continued despite protests. To cover major U.S. ground force reductions of 1970-71, the air war had to be racheted up substantially. This intensified resistance in the Navy and Air Force, where it had previously simmered at a lower flame while American land fighting predominated. Antiwar organizing efforts in the U.S. Seventh Fleet increased in direct response to the stepped up bombing.

The Movement for a Democratic Military surfaced in Southern California in early 1970 and drew its greatest strength from the immense San Diego naval base, home port to the aircraft carriers of the Pacific fleet. Rebellion took many forms, but the most effective in curtailing the Navy's warmaking ability was sabotage. 488 "investigations on damage or attempted damage" were noted in fiscal 1971, and the widespread tactic of literally throwing a wrench into the gears of the war machine became the technology-intensive (and thus vulnerable) Navy's nightmare.[25]

The situation reached crisis in 1972. The North Vietnamese Army, emboldened by the rapid withdrawal of American troops, attempted a large scale conventional invasion of the South in April. The "Easter Offensive" was halted only by massive U.S. bombing of NVA troop formations, and air attacks on the major North Vietnamese cities of Hanoi and Haiphong.

Naval air forces were stretched to their breaking point. For the rest of the year, as many as four carriers were stationed in the Tonkin Gulf, with an equal number committed to the area to provide rotation capability. Normal U.S. fleet routine was completely disrupted; nearly all the Pacific fleet, and many ships usually assigned to the Atlantic, sailed west into the fray.

For crew members, the escalation brought severe handicaps. Carrier operations demanded an incredible 100-hour work week, and deployment lasted as long as 45 days, straining crews to the very limits of human endurance. Forced to remain at sea beyond their rotation schedule, and thrust suddenly into the center of an unpopular war, sailor-rebels responded.

In July, at the main Atlantic base in Norfolk, Virginia, a crew member aboard the *Forrestal* torched the carrier's officer berthing areas, causing seven million dollars worth of damage and delaying the ship's

May 1971: GIs arrive in Washington, DC to support local law enforcement during the mass arrests of thousands at a Mayday antiwar demonstration. Regional police forces were able to suppress the protests, and the questionable loyalty of these troops was never tested.

deployment to the Pacific for over two months.[26]

Later that month, a militant deckhand inserted two bolts and a paint scraper in the carrier *Ranger's* number-four engine reduction gears, necessitating a three month layover for one million dollars in repairs. This was the culmination of a wave of sabotage by *Ranger* sailors in direct response to the Easter Offensive escalation of the air war. In May and June alone, over two dozen incidents of willful destruction took place, including cut firehoses, bomb threats, a plugged fire main, fuel in the freshwater supply, a flooded compartment, and assorted damage to generators and oil pumps.[27]

Carrier sabotage compelled the *Kitty Hawk*, in the Tonkin Gulf, to remain on station for months. Shipboard racial tensions already on edge then exploded in a series of violent incidents, necessitating its rotation out of the war zone. Thus, the disablement of one floating airbase after another severely hampered the Navy's ability to conduct bombing operations during

the second half of 1972. Sailor dissent was only suppressed by withdrawal of the carrier task forces from Vietnamese waters by the end of the year, and mass discharge of over 6,000 "troublemakers" in 1972-73.[28]

Airmen Join the Rebellion

With its relaxed discipline and low ratio of actual involvement by members in direct fighting, the Air Force had managed to avoid much of the discontent affecting other services before 1971. Early that year, only ten GI papers circulated among U.S. air bases; by the spring of 1972, there were more than thirty. A Congressional panel, the House Internal Security Committee, recognized a clear pattern: "The trend towards organizing among Air Force personnel, in line with U.S. continued air activities in Indochina, is quite obvious."[29]

Intensified bombing in 1972 brought protests to Air Force installations around the world. The swell of resistance receded as bombing operations declined in the fall, but surged sharply again as a disgusted response to the Christmas B-52 attacks on central Hanoi. That December, two combat pilots from the U Tapao base in Thailand refused to fly bombing missions over Vietnam, beginning the last chapter of GI resistance to America's Indochinese slaughter.

Morale in the Pacific air command deteriorated dramatically throughout 1972, but during the relentless bombing of inner Cambodia in 1973, it plunged to critical levels. Four B-52 pilots stationed in Guam joined with a congresswoman's legal suit challenging the constitutionality of the Cambodian bombing; three were relieved from duty and the forth refused to fly missions after this action against his comrades.[30]

In a more subtle form of rebellion, ground crews left certain operational maintenance undone, which caused increasing numbers of sorties to be aborted shortly after takeoff. Demoralized bomber crews were only too happy to use such excuses, and rates of equipment "failures" increased.[31]

Though the Pentagon claimed its 40% reduction in B-52 missions over Cambodia in May 1973 was due to budget cuts, a *Washington Post* correspondent reported that "despite official assertions, there are indications that the Air Force is facing a deepening morale crisis among pilots and especially among crews of B-52s... High ranking Defense Department sources say the morale situation at Guam has been poor for some time now... these sources say the morale problem at U Tapao in Thailand is also growing worse daily."[32] Despite the highly professional and officer-heavy structure of the air service, resistance to the Cambodian raids certainly affected the U.S. military options.

Today, "mainstream" analysis of these pivotal events in America's Vietnam adventure, other than mention of fragging, that word the war added to our vocabulary, is nearly nonexistent. Why have so many historians ignored the significance of the GI movement? Perhaps because the implications of such a multi-class social movement in an army whose loyalty had been beyond question in the century since the Civil War are scarcely conceivable to scholars steeped in the assumptions of current ideology.

GI activism also contradicts dominant historical notions that interpret the antiwar movement among youth almost entirely as a middle-class student affair, eschewed by the sons of America's working class.

Marcus Raskin mentions this point in his introduction to David Cortright's definitive 1975 study, *Soldiers In Revolt*: "From time to time, incidents were noted in the media, but for the most part these incidents were seen by civilian society as sporadic... [however] the struggle against the war in Indochina moved from the campus and was continued within the military itself by children of all classes — the poor, working, and middle classes. This is an important political fact... unrecorded among journalists, academics, and politicians. To be aware of this fact is to be relieved of the comfortable belief that the armed forces are a quiet, apolitical group."[33]

Awareness of this socially broad movement of war resistance in the military inherently challenges a popular mythology that only lack of political will (the "one-hand-tied-behind-our-back" theory) kept the boys from taking Hanoi, and turning Uncle Ho out. In actuality, the risk of further civil disorder in America and complete collapse of the field army in Asia precluded large offensive operations, as the invasion of Cambodia indicated.

Eventually, there was even concern about the reliability of American troops in riot control operations at home. When the dependability of soldiers to follow orders can even be questioned, the situation is already intolerable for ruling elites. Without loyal armed retainers to back them, the leaders of any state simply shout orders at the wind. "Policy makers" and the military brass realized that the game in Southeast Asia was clearly no longer worth the candle in what was not a life-or-death struggle for the motherland, so the world's mightiest armed force cut its losses and accepted defeat.

However, a mythology of noble unvanquished warriors, even in the ranks of beaten armies, can take root. Defeated soldiers are not useful instruments of state power, and in a government's worst scenario, disillusioned veterans can even turn upon the state they served. Avoiding or shedding the stigma of defeat is crucial to restoring a fighting attitude to demoralized troops.

It Happened Before

A historical example in this century of such successful recovery of a beaten army occurred in Europe after the November 1918 cease fire that ended World War I. Ordered by their admirals to sail into hopeless destruction as a face-saving glorious end, German sailors of the Baltic Fleet instead mutinied and declared that naval power would henceforth reside in enlisted-man councils. Demobilized soldiers returning from the trenches joined them and uprisings flared throughout Germany for over a year, the most famous being the 1919 Berlin *Spartakus* insurrection.

The revolutionary wave of 1918-20 was channeled into a Western-style parliamentary government by leftist politicians and viciously suppressed by their temporary allies, the *Freikorps* militia. This right-wing death squad organization of future Nazis and professional soldiers scourged the nation with counter-revolutionary terror.

During the Weimar Republic years that followed, Hitler's increasingly popular "national socialism" enshrined militarist trappings, and a legend grew that Prussian arms had never been conquered in the field during the Great War. Revised historical interpretation absolved the generals and viewed the armistice as a "stab-in-the-back" delivered by treacherous politicians.

This shibboleth is familiar to anyone living in post-Vietnam America, right down to "in-the-back" imagery that reflects not only phrasing but mood. Such rhetoric proved an effective aid in rehabilitating the disgraced German military machine to blitzkrieg Poland and France only two decades after its soldiers and sailors suppressed not the people but their officers, and ignited a revolution.

It is pertinent to consider this history when assessing the resurgence of militaristic values in 1980s America, and to contrast the Desert Storm troopers of 1991 with the insolent and cynical mutineers pulled out of Vietnam twenty years earlier.

The author spent four years in the Marine Corps, from 1979-1983.

Footnotes

1. Shelby L. Stanton, *Rise and Fall of An American Army: U.S. Ground Forces in Vietnam, 1965-73* (Presidio, 1985) p. 364.
2. David Cortright, *Soldiers In Revolt: The American Military Today* (Anchor, 1975) p. 11-13.
3. Cortright, p. 68
4. *The Bond*, Nov. 3, 1967.
5. *The Bond*, Feb.18, 1968.
6. *1972 House Internal Security Committee Report*, Vol. I, p. 6584.
7. Eugene Linden, "Fragging and Other Withdrawal Symptoms" *Saturday Review*, Jan. 8, 1972, p. 12-17. This excellent article examines race, drugs, and mutiny in a lost army far from home.
8. *All Ready On The Left*, Camp Pendleton, CA, September 1970.
9. Juan Cameron, "Our Gravest Military Problem Is Manpower" *Fortune*, April 1971, p. 138.
10. Adam Yarmolinksy, *The Military Establishment* (Harper and Row, 1971) p. 361-362.
11. Cortright, p. 56-57; *The Bond*, Oct. 16, 1968.
12. Larry G. Waterhouse and Mariann G. Wizard, *Turning the Guns Around: Notes on the GI Movement* (Praeger, 1971) p. 11-13.
13. Jail rebellions: *The New York Times,* Aug. 19, 1968, p. 5; Oct. 1, 1968, p. 3,; Jan. 8, 1969, p. 12.
14. Donald Kirk, "Who Wants To Be the Last American Killed in Vietnam?" *The New York Times Magazine*, Sept. 19, 1971, p. 68.
15. Stanton, p. 330, 440-441.
16. WWI army collapses: Gwynne Dyer, *War* (Stoddart, 1985) p. 86-87, p. 151-54. British demobilization rebellions: Dave Lamb, *Mutinies: 1917-1920* (Solidarity, no copyright date).
17. Richard Boyle, *Flower of the Dragon: The Breakdown of the U.S. Army in Vietnam* (Ramparts Press, 1972) p. 85.
18. *The New York Times,* Aug. 4, 1969, p. 3.
19. *The New York Times,* Oct. 16, 1969, p. 22.
20. "Cambodia: 'We're Cache Counters'" *Newsweek*, Nov. 25, 1970, p. 45.
21. Robert D. Heinl, Jr. (Col. USMC, Ret.) "The Collapse of the Armed Forces" *Armed Forces Journal,* June 7, 1971, p. 30.
22. Morris Janowitz, "Volunteer Armed Forces and Military Purpose" *Foreign Affairs*, April 1972, p. 428.
23. Stewart Alsop, "Vietnam: Out Faster" *Newsweek*, Dec. 7, 1970, p. 104.
24. Cortright, p. 80-83.
25. *HISC*, Vol. II, p. 7051.
26. *The New York Times,* Nov. 28, 1972, p. 18; Dec. 8, 1972, p. 18.
27. *The New York Times,* June 13, 1973, p. 5.
28. Carrier racial unrest: John Jekabson, "The Demoralization of the U.S. Navy" *Alternate Features Service,* #76, Jan. 5, 1973. Mass discharges: *The New York Times*, Feb. 2, 1973, p. 1.
29. "Staff Analysis of Recent Trends in GI Movement Organizing Activities, Dec. 1971-April 1972" in HISC files.
30. *The New York Times*, June 6, 1973, p. 10.
31. *Camp News*, newsletter of the Chicago Area Military Project, Vol. IV, #6, June 15, 1973, p. 3.
32. Michael Getter, *The Washington Post,* May 31, 1973, p. 1 and 9.
33. Cortright, from the introduction, p. xii.

The Labadie Collection, located in the Graduate Library at the University of Michigan in Ann Arbor, is an excellent archive of the Vietnam-era GI press.

This article is reprinted from the Summer 1995 issue of Fifth Estate, a cooperative, nonprofit project, publishing since 1965. The people who produce it are a group of friends who do so neither to secure wages nor as an investment in the newspaper industry, but to encourage resistance and rebellion to this society. Send $2.00 for a sample issue to:
Fifth Estate
4632 Second Avenue
Detroit, MI 48201

DR. RIPPER • THE RISE OF GYNECOLOGICAL SURGERY

by Thom Metzger

Illustration by Nick Bougas © 1996

"While the gynecologists wielded their knives on respectable women, the Ripper applied his knife to the generative tracts of the fallen, actually stealing the womb from the body of one of his victims. No wonder most of London assumed him to be a doctor gone mad." (Caputi, 12).

In "The Fetishes of Sex-Crimes," Jane Caputi goes so far as to argue that Jack the Ripper — the first celebrity sex criminal, granddaddy of all the world's Son of Sams and Jeffrey Dahmers — would never have committed his crimes if it weren't for the rise of gynecological and obstetric surgery. His knives and backstreet operations, his preying on poor women and gloating over his "extirpated" female organs were all, according to Caputi, a shadowy reflection of the more acceptable butchershop medicine taking place in hospitals and private clinics.

In a century when womanhood was deemed untouchable (or "occult" in its original sense: the hidden), pure, childlike, and without sexual desire, medical science found itself pulled one way and pushed the other: to touch or not to touch, to look or

merely to probe and palpate the hidden recesses of the female body, to leave her a sealed vessel or to open her wide and excise the strange glistening organs that — so it was assumed — posed such a threat to the body politic.

Looking closely at the rise of gynecological surgery and the concomitant fall of midwifery, we find a mania for cutting and mechanically-enhanced voyeurism — gleaming knife edges and strange patented, viewing contraptions — that if it were not part of an accepted medical doctrine, would have surely warranted a place in any Sex Criminals Hall of Fame. Disaffected teenagers would now be wearing T-shirts bearing the faces of Drs. Battey and Sims and Baker Brown and not Ed Gein or Charles Manson.

Though the surgical removal of the ovaries had been performed as early as 1809 in America, the operation was rare until the advent of anesthesia. By the mid 1860s, the surgical excision of the ovaries (called ovariotomy or later, oophorectomy) was being performed by dozens of surgeons.

(Continued on next page)

However, it was Dr. Robert Battey who popularized, or one might say crusaded for, the operation.

After gaining invaluable practical experience as a battlefield surgeon during the American Civil War, Battey returned to his native Georgia to establish a private practice. A founding member of the American Gynecological Society and later its president, he excised his first ovary in 1869, to remove a thirty pound cyst. Three years later, he did his first so-called normal ovariotomy, eliminating the organs not because they were in any way diseased, but in hopes of preventing certain psychological maladies or "female problems." Within a few years, due to Battey's publications and self-promotion, ovariotomy was being used to treat epilepsy, neurosis, neuralgia, "cussedness," menstrual disorders, nymphomania, "moral insanity," melancholy, marital unfaithfulness, hysterical mania, lunacy and general unhappiness.

Battey and "Battey's operation," had their detractors; some called the process "spaying," "castration," "desexing," and "unsexing." Results of the operation were often disappointing and mortality rates quite high. But until Battey's death in 1895, the use of his operation was very common. In 1906, it was estimated that 150,000 ovaries had been removed in the U.S. (Van de Warker, 371). At first Battey approached the ovaries through the vagina, "traveling through the dark passage," with his knives and scissors. But in keeping with the ideology of science as revealer of mysteries, uncoverer-of-unknown-treasures, he soon switched to the abdominal approach. Just as those hoping to harvest the earth's mineral treasures shifted when possible from deep dark shafts to strip-mining operations, so Dr. Battey found he had more satisfying results by opening the belly, "harvesting" the organs, and then closing the wound with silk sutures. "It was Dr. Battey," one of his admirers wrote, "who invaded the hidden recesses of the female organism and snatched from its appointed place those delicate little glandular bodies whose mysteries and wonderful functions are of such high interest to the human race."

High interest is perhaps an understatement, as one writer describes gynecologists passing ovaries "around at medical society meetings on plates like trophies." (Baker-Benfield, "Spermatic Economy.")

Battey's operation, though it fell out of favor at the turn of the century and was soon written out of medical history and ignored in surgical text books, was one of the most significant in the history of medicine. For nineteenth century surgeons, the ability to extirpate ovaries was a necessary skill, in effect a test of mettle to enter the ranks of the brotherhood. Its status as "the" operation derives in part from the perception that Battey's procedure was "the first battlefield whereon abdominal engagements were found and won... it was in ovariotomies that the first triumphs were gained" (Dally, 155).

Dr. Robert Barnes used a different metaphor: "It is vivi-section of the noblest kind... the surgeon learns, the subject gains life in health" (Dally, 145).

Ann Dally, a hundred years later, gives a less fanciful explanation: "All abdominal operations derive from it. So much was learned from doing and practicing this operation that it can be argued that all surgery is based on it" (Dally, 135).

An illustration from the 1880s shows three surgeons performing Battey's operation. Though the men wear placid expressions, the postures make the procedure look like nothing so much as gang rape. The man at the patient's head holds her hands down and the one at the other end sits with the woman straddling his groin, legs splayed over him as he wields the knife on her naked and distended belly.

(Continued on next page)

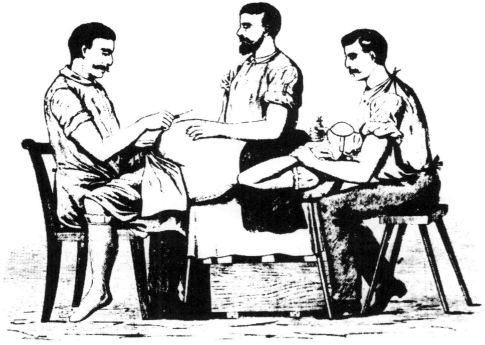

Three male surgeons, c. 1880, performing an ovariotomy on a patient with a large cyst.

Equally important in the surgical exploration of the hidden realms of the female body was Dr. J. Marion Sims, called "The Architect of the Vagina." Esteemed and execrated, benefactor of womankind and sadistic egomaniac, a man who bought slaves for the express purpose of having a ready stable of surgical guinea pigs, yet who also founded the first hospital in the world devoted to women's health — Sims is impossible to pigeonhole. It is fashionable of late to condemn his work as racist barbarism and woman-hating butchery, and certainly Sims was a man with serious flaws. He thought very highly of himself and was quite comfortable battling to keep his dominance in the field — using helpless female subjects to inflate his reputation and gain great wealth. However, Sims also made invaluable contributions to medical science and indeed relieved a great deal of suffering.

A southerner like Battey, Sims entered medical school in 1833. Eleven years later he was confronted by a case which was to be the turning point in his career. A young woman with a severe hare lip begged him to operate to repair the defect she'd lived with since birth. He did so, and according to his autobiography, the result was her transformation into a "very presentable person indeed, and really a pretty woman." The next year he was presented with another distressing case, a slave girl named Anarcha who, after childbirth, suffered a vesico-vaginal fistula, the gangrenous death of tissue which creates a hole through which urine and feces leak into the vagina. A dreadful condition, causing much pain, suffering and humiliation, fistulas of this type were quite common among women with poor obstetric care.

"If there was anything I hated, it was investigating the organs of the female pelvis," Sims wrote later. Nonetheless, he triumphed over his revulsion, or perhaps used it to fuel decades of research and clinical practice. He dedicated the rest of his life to the study of female sex organs, inventing numerous tools and techniques for the repair and "investigation" of the subject he claimed to hate.

In the case of Anarcha, he was to operate thirty times in four years, all without anesthesia. After discovering an examination posture that allowed better access to the fistula (patient on hands and knees, her behind high in the air) and designing a special catheter and speculum to get at the problem area more readily, Sims hit on the idea of using silver sutures introduced by silk thread. And the thirtieth time he operated, she was finally cured.

Sims collected slave women with similar problems — sometimes buying them outright, sometimes borrowing them — he housed his subjects in a small building in his yard, giving him a ready supply for the work he called throughout his career, "experiments."

In 1853, Sims sold his practice and moved to New York City, where greater fame and far greater fortune awaited, and where he found competition among surgeons far more fierce.

In 1855 Sims combined public and private funds to open the first women's hospital in the world. Here, his experiments continued, not with slave women but on extremely poor immigrants. Like the southern slaves, his urban subjects were in such a wretched state that he was able to keep them in his establishment as long as he liked, sometimes for years. Mary Smith, whose bladder, urethra, vulva and vagina had been decimated by primitive medicine in her native Ireland, came to Sims and after thirty operations between 1856 and 1859 Sims had repaired her sex organs enough that she could work as an orderly in his hospital.

Though there was some opposition to his work, Sims, at the time of his death in 1883, was famous in Europe as well as the U.S., and was one of the richest doctors in America (taking the knowledge he gained from experimenting on destitute women and applying it to the wives and daughters of the wealthy). Devoting himself to the hitherto unexplored regions of the female sex organs, Sims patented a number of instruments and procedures, and was called, even by his rival, T.A. Emmett, the "father of American gynecology," and his sole book was deemed "the turning point of Modern Gynecology" (Barker-Benfield, *Half-Known Life*, 91).

His life work was nominally about the increase of fertility, restoring women to their rightful, "God-given" role as producers of offspring. He spoke of emulating "the finger of God" in regard to his digital examinations of the genitals and the surgical repair of organs. He had, according to one biographer, a "magic wand" with which he could return women to their true, divinely-appointed procreative state.

Child-bearing was seen as the foundation of the social order, of the state itself: essential to the perpetuation of names, descent of property and the performance of government. Dr. Ely Van de Warker declared in 1906: "A woman's ovaries belong to the commonwealth; she is simply their custodian" (371). Rudolf Virchow, one of the greatest pathologists of the nineteenth century, wrote: "Woman is a pair of ovaries with a human being attached; whereas man is a human being furnished with a pair of testes" (Dally, 110).

Sims' efforts must be seen within this conceptual framework.

Cutting with his experimental tools, "splitting up the neck of the womb," using his new device — the uterine guillotine, dissecting and resecting female organs, Sims has been seen as both an agent of divine power and a culturally-approved version of Jack the Ripper.

But besides his obsession with cutting and exploring female flesh, another motive becomes clear in his work. He was obsessed not only with dissecting and reshaping, but with looking as well.

"The day which made [Sims] great was the day when the idea of his speculum first dawned on him — that day when he first conceived the thought of throwing an abundance of light into the vagina and around the womb, and at the same time obtaining ample space to work and apply his instruments." Here Sims' obituary writer makes a clear connection between seeing and the skillful, near-magical, use of tools. The speculum — which means "mirror" — was the symbol and instrument of Sims' greatness, the device with which he "...raised himself from obscurity to the dazzle of success by

(Continued on next page)

the elevation of woman's organs from darkness to light" (Barker-Benfield, *Half-Known Life*, 92).

Odd metaphors were applied to the invention. "Sims' speculum had been to diseases of the womb... what the compass is to the mariner," as though the female body was some great lost continent. Sims himself stated: "I saw everything as no man had ever seen before... I felt like an explorer in medicine who first views a new and important territory" (*Half-Known Life*, 95).

Doctor as explorer (locating the new world with his sex-sextant, cutting through the female jungle with his machete/scalpel), physician as pioneer; these metaphors might seem ridiculous but they resonate to the present day. Medicine as a form of "elevated sight," a visual apotheosis — this model continues to inform the way we see the human body and those entrusted with its care.

Oddly, it was Columbus (Renaldus though, not Christopher) who claimed to have "discovered" the clitoris, as though it were some anatomical Atlantis just risen from its watery hiding place. In 1559, Columbus wrote: "Since no one had discerned these projections and their workings, if it is permissible to give names to things discovered by men, it should be called the Love or Sweetness of Venus" (Laqueur, 64). Obviously, humans had been aware of the clitoris long before 1559, but to define it, to single it out and name it as a distinct organ, was for Columbus the equivalent of discovery. Sims has been called the "Architect of the Vagina," as though his investigations and operations were the same as design or creation. In his case, to see was to make, to uncover was to invent.

It was not only looking and naming, but also showing that defined his so-called genius. It's not a coincidence that a surgeon "performs" an operation and that it occurs in a "theater." A great admirer of P.T. Barnum, Sims would pack dozens of spectators into his theater for the latest surgical show. In fact, he was so enamored of displaying his skills that he was eventually expelled from the hospital he founded for repeatedly breaking the rule that limited the number of viewers to fifteen per operation.

Sims' greatest invention, his speculum, was a mirror that reflected as much of the operator as the subject. By flooding with light hitherto occult regions, Sims achieved a kind of self-illumination, glowing brightly in the firmament of surgical stars. He made spectacle of surgery — not merely flamboyant show, but a ritualized incursion of scientific numen to numb or hypnotize the subjects of his bloody work.

A curious corollary of this dynamic was Sims' use of anesthesia to treat vaginismus — the spasming of the vagina that produces a state in which "the virile power of the husband was unusually strong, but yet powerless to overcome." (*Half-Known Life*, 113). Sims etherized women so that their husbands could enter them more easily in order to impregnate them. And in at least one case the doctor would go to the patient's house three times a week to facilitate this quasi-necrophile sex he called "ethereal copulation." One can only imagine the possibilities it provided for "exploration" and "investigation."

Isaac Baker Brown, popularizer of clitoridectomy, can be seen as the third figure (alongside Sims and Battey) in a nineteenth century gyno-surgical triumvirate. Obsessed with female masturbation, which he called "peripheral excitation," Baker Brown concocted a bizarre theory that mandated the surgical removal (or at times the cauterizing) of the clitoris for symptoms as diverse as epilepsy, rebelliousness, loss of appetite, "the inability to look one in the face," nymphomania, "quivering eye lids," hysteria, and non-specific vision problems. He founded the London Surgical Home, a special clinic where his brand of medical mayhem could be administered undisturbed, removing or mutilating the clitorises of an unknown number of women and girls (some as young as ten). In one case, he operated on a young woman because she was disobedient to her mother, sent too many visiting cards to male acquaintances and spent "much time in serious reading." Like many of Baker Brown's subjects, she was soon afterward married and pregnant. In at least five cases, the doctor's subjects were attempting to gain freedom from their husbands under the new divorce law of 1857. All of these women were found to be docile and obedient after the excision of the offending part.

Preferring the scissors to the knife or cautery, Baker Brown went about his grisly work for years, until he was expelled from the British Obstetrical Society in 1867. It's important to note that his fellow surgeons didn't banish him for erroneous science or unnecessary mutilation, but for breaking professional protocol. The other doctors didn't censure him for the belief that excision of the clitoris would prevent nymphomania or cure epilepsy; they removed him because he performed the operation too often and would resort to trickery or threats (the madhouse) to gain consent to remove the locus of "peripheral excitation."

Clitoridectomy was discredited in Britain, but Baker Brown's crusade merely went to the U.S. where it found a more conducive atmosphere. Well into the twentieth century, clitoridectomy was being practiced in America. As late as 1936, medical texts recommended "circumcision" or cauterization for unmanageable girls. As with ovariotomy, the period 1870-1900 was the Golden Age of clitoral excision. And even more so than with Battey's operation, clitoridectomy has been written out of the medical history, an ugly chapter most physicians would prefer to pretend never happened.

However, looking squarely at the gynecological butchery of the late nineteenth century would serve not only as an important humbling experience for the profession, but would also be truly useful for those who wish to understand where medical practice has come from and how medical theory has evolved.

Patriarchy is usually blamed for the gross excesses of gynecological surgeons. And while clearly male dominance of and hatred toward women drove much of the mutilation, it's more useful to look at the abuses of the period not just to assign blame but as a way of understanding current medicine.

(Continued on next page)

Clitoridectomy and ovariotomy were not anomalies. They were mainstream practice, the logical outcome of the doctrines that rule the profession to this day. They are links (some would prefer them to stay missing links) between prescientific medicine ("magic") and that of today ("rational" praxis). Certainly magical thinking was at work in the men who hacked women to pieces, but techniques and knowledge were gained which led to the "humane" and "sane" methods of today. Wish fulfillment and bizarre versions of voyeurism paraded as objective science. Misogyny and obsession-for-control motivated many of the doctors, but without these, we would not have medical science as we know it today. This is not to excuse the barbarous abuses, only to say that we couldn't have had one without the other. The knife and the eye as the supreme tools of medicine, the rigid hierarchy of doctor-patient relationships, the mechanistic view of the body which has given us so many advances in healing — all of these were brought to the fore, exploited and exalted by the gynecological surgeons of the nineteenth century.

Two more cases of medical mania remain to be touched on. More peculiar, certainly more suppressed, these cases might seem merely freakish or ridiculous. But there is value in considering even these episodes as integrally-related to current medicine — black sheep of the family, but blood relatives nonetheless.

Dr. John Scoffern, a vocal dissenter from Baker Brown's expulsion, went so far as to compare him with Christ, quoting the New Testament: "If thy right hand offend thee, cut it off." Making the clitoridectomist into a kind of latter day savior, Scoffern continues: "It remained for Mr. Baker Brown to give the precept effect" (Dally, 157). Inspired by Baker Brown's operations, Scoffern attempted to cure women "of voluble speech and evil tongue" by the use of the knife.

> The patient being under the effect of chloroform, a very fine knife is run quite through the tongue and rapidly withdrawn. The result is that certain muscular fibers are cut; the mobility of the organ is in some measure impaired — to the extent, namely, of making continuous and violent objurgation impossible, but not of interfering with any temperate conversation. (Dally, 158)

Similarly, he devised operations to cure kleptomania — "partially dividing" the muscles and tendons of the hand with a "fine small knife" — and even "gyromania, the disordered rage for waltzing." This last surgical procedure consisted of inserting a knife into the buttocks and calves of women who had a "morbid desire to spin round and round, her waist encircled by a male arm" (Dally, 159). One doesn't need to be a strict Freudian to see the fetishistic content of sticking scalpels — the sole property of the surgical profession — into women's buttocks and tongues.

And finally the Orifical Surgical Society stands perhaps as the pinnacle and debacle of this long tradition. Operating primarily on women, producing a journal from 1890 until 1925, the society can best be described as a cross between a crypto-erotic cult and a secret medical brotherhood. Their doctrine was a mishmash of mystic religion, sexual perversion and quack science — for instance treating an attractive young woman's headache with "rectal dilation" and chronic schizophrenia with clitoridectomy. That the members of the Orifical Society were out for easy money is inarguable, but their psycho-sexual obsessions — probing and manipulating female orifices — can not be written off as mere charlatanry in pursuit of wealth. All successful scams are based on a certain leap of faith. On some level they believed the doctrines they inflicted on others, just as Battey and Sims and Baker Brown believed they were not only curing women of their ills but in some way acting as the agents of God on earth: the knife, the eye, the examining finger imbued with divine power.

Physicians today seldom think in these terms, but the ideology remains a foundation for current medicine. In sterile environments, in white suits and anonymous masks, surgeons have come a long way since London's backstreet operations of 1888. However, Jack's specter still haunts the surgical theaters — demon, angel, unacknowledged avatar.

Works Cited

Barker-Benfield, G.J., *The Horrors of the Half-Known Life*. NY: Harper and Row, 1976.

Barker-Benfield, G.J., "The Spermatic Economy," *Feminist Studies*, No. 1, Summer 1972.

Caputi, Jane E., "The Fetishes of Sex-Crime," *Objects of Special Devotion*. Ed. Ray B. Browne. Bowling Green, OH: The Popular Press, 1982.

Dally, Ann. *Women Under the Knife*. NY: Routledge, 1992.

Laqueur, Thomas. *Making Sex*. Cambridge: Harvard UP, 1990.

Van de Warker, Ely. "The Fetich [sic] of the Ovary," *American Journal of Obstetrics*, 54, July-December, 1906.

This is a message from the original publishers of *Horseshit Magazine* — *The Offensive Review!* The following teleplay is reprinted from the most popular (and most banned) underground publication of the 1960s, *Horseshit Magazine*, The Offensive Review. We still have a limited number of copies of all the original four issues of *Horseshit*. Guess what? It still offends most people! We like that. And it is still banned in many countries. We like that too. You can order all four issues for $30 postpaid. Mailed in a plain, sealed envelope. Or we have a special offer — Each issue signed by the writer and artist for only $40. Send to: Uncommon Books, PO Box 465, Huntington Beach, CA 92648.

Most people go into a state of shock when they first open a copy of *Horseshit*. Then they go about halfway through, reading and looking at the pictures, and they have to put it down and try to get their breath back again. When they've rested up, they go through the rest of the magazine. Then they put it down and they don't know what to think. The next day they read it again and decide they like it. The day after that they decide it's GREAT! They show it to their friends. Then they have to sit there and listen while their friends yell and shout with laughter and point out things they particularly like. Soon, other friends come over, dozens of them. "We want to see THAT magazine," they say. Finally, some bastard steals their *Horseshit*. Then there's nothing left to do but order back issues from us. Be ready for a shock.

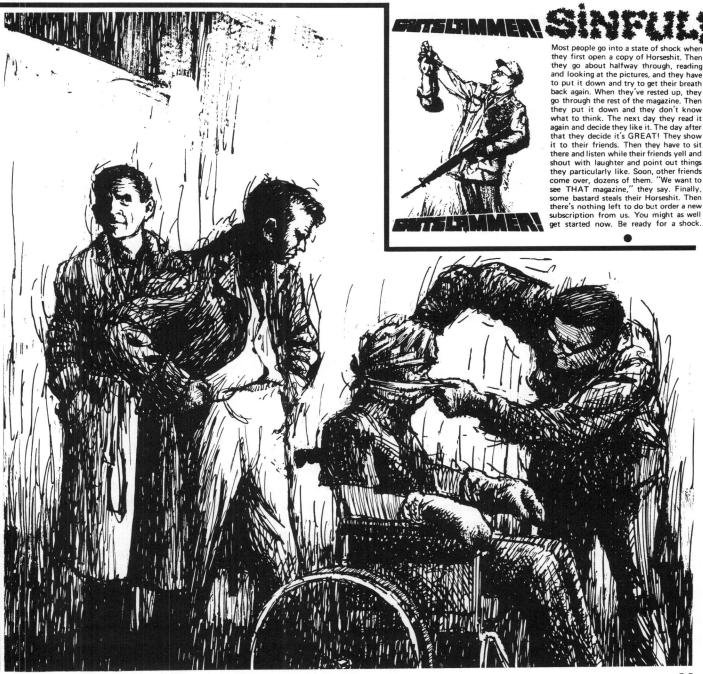

GUTSLAMMER! SINFUL!

Most people go into a state of shock when they first open a copy of Horseshit. Then they go about halfway through, reading and looking at the pictures, and they have to put it down and try to get their breath back again. When they've rested up, they go through the rest of the magazine. Then they put it down and they don't know what to think. The next day they read it again and decide they like it. The day after that they decide it's GREAT! They show it to their friends. Then they have to sit there and listen while their friends yell and shout with laughter and point out things they particularly like. Soon, other friends come over, dozens of them. "We want to see THAT magazine," they say. Finally, some bastard steals their Horseshit. Then there's nothing left to do but order a new subscription from us. You might as well get started now. Be ready for a shock.

GUTSLAMMER!

a new approach to
GROUP THERAPY

A television play by Tom Dunker

Characters:	Crangle, a character
	Various aides.
Moss, an alcoholic	
Hegan, an amputee	TIME: The Present Time
Reslick, a nurse	PLACE: A Hospital
Leach, a doctor	
Scheiner, a psychologist	Presented with no interruptions for commercials.

FADE IN: INTERIOR — TWO BED HOSPITAL ROOM — (DAY)

We see two men, Frank Moss and Marty Hegan, sitting on the edge of their beds, smoking. Both are dressed in hospital pajamas and robes. Hegan has only one leg. Moss looks at bedside clock.

MOSS: It's 8:35. We'd better put these out.

Both men carefully stub out cigarettes and put the butts in their pockets. Moss goes to window and opens it.

HEGAN: I don't know why you bother opening that. Old Reslick must know that we smoke in here.

MOSS: Of course she knows but it's all part of the game. If we're not careful and she catches us, then she has to turn us in. But that's easy enough to avoid. Like all nurses, she's a creature of habit. In just thirty seconds she will stick her muzzy head in that door and say, "Mr. Moss, Mr. Hegan. Time for your appointment with Dr. Scheiner."

Nurse appears at door.

NURSE: Mr. Moss, Mr. Hegan. Time for your appointment with Dr. Scheiner.

Nurse withdraws.

HEGAN: Hey, she forgot...

Nurse reappears.

NURSE: And don't forget to wear your artificial leg, Mr. Hegan. And walk on it. Don't use a crutch.

Nurse withdraws.

HEGAN (Resignedly): She didn't forget. She not only looks like an elephant, she's got a memory like one.

Hegan gets out an artificial leg and straps it on.

MOSS: Can I help you with that?

HEGAN (*Sharply*): No! I got it.

Moss reaches under his pillow and takes out a flat half-pint bottle. He goes to door, looks up and down hall, then comes back and takes a drink.

HEGAN: Hey Moss! You shouldn't be drinking before we see Scheiner. He'll smell it.

MOSS: It's vodka. He can't smell it. Anyway, he's the

(Continued on next page)

reason I have to have a shot. I'm all right otherwise but when I have to go down and listen to his psychological bunk on why I drink, it nearly kills me. What can I do with this bottle? I don't dare leave it here. Can you hide it in there?

HEGAN: Well, yeah, I guess so.

Hegan takes bottle, slips it into artificial leg, and then continues strapping it on.

HEGAN: Boy, I'd like to have that crutch along but I'll never get it past the nurses' station.

MOSS: Sure, you can. I'll go first and start complaining to Reslick about our radiator not working.

HEGAN: What good will that do? We've been complaining about that for three weeks and nothing has been done about it.

MOSS: That's what I mean. Come on.

Hegan takes crutch and follows Moss out door. Moss goes ahead and stops by glass enclosed nurses' station. Mrs. Reslick is bent over desk, filling out forms.

MOSS: Do you want me to take Old Man Crangle down to physical therapy today?

NURSE: *Mister* Crangle has already been taken to his appointments.

MOSS: Oh okay. Mrs. Reslick, the radiator in our room still hasn't been fixed.

NURSE: I've called maintenance about that, Mr. Moss.

MOSS: Yeah, but couldn't you call them again?

Nurse doesn't look up from papers.

NURSE: I'll make a note of it, Mr. Moss.

Moss waves to Hegan, who quietly goes behind him past the station.

MOSS: At night it just gets colder than the dickens in there. You wouldn't believe how cold it gets.

NURSE: Yes, I know. We'll take care of it.

MOSS: And in the daytime it gets hot. Especially when one of the mattresses catches on fire like mine just did.

Nurse is still absorbed in papers.

NURSE: These things take time, Mr. Moss. There's a great deal to be done around this hospital.

MOSS: Well, it seemed to be burning pretty lively when I left. I think the whole wing is on fire now.

NURSE: Perhaps they can get around to it this afternoon, Mr. Moss. Shouldn't you be at your appointments?

MOSS: Yeah, I guess it's that time. See if you can get something done about that though, if you would, please.

NURSE: I'll tell Mr. Corcoran when he comes around.

Moss goes down hall and catches up with Hegan, who is waiting for him.

HEGAN: That worked real good. What were you talking to her about?

MOSS: I just told her that the building was on fire.

HEGAN (*Unbelievingly*): Ahhh, come on. What was it about?

MOSS: Yeah, really. She said she would make a note of it. Surely you realize by now that none of the staff ever listen to what a patient says. When they want us to do something, they talk to us like we're responsible, rational people but if we ask them for something, all of a sudden, we've turned into a bunch of nuts.

HEGAN: I remember the time... Oh, oh. Here comes Dr. Leach. He will give me a bad time for using this crutch.

MOSS: No sweat. Give it here.

Moss takes crutch and tucks it under his arm and starts to swing along. Hegan limps along beside him.

HEGAN: Good morning, Dr. Leach.

LEACH: Oh, good morning to you, ahhh . .

HEGAN: Hegan.

LEACH: Yes, Hegan. You're walking on that artificial leg all the time now, aren't you?

HEGAN: Well, I've tried to, but it gets so sore...

LEACH: Naturally, Hegan, you're going to have some difficulty at first but I don't think that we're asking for very much when we expect you to have a little perseverance.

HEGAN: But, Doctor, I've...

LEACH: I don't see how we can help you if you're not willing to help yourself. Take a few steps there and let me see how much you have learned.

Hegan takes a few steps, making an effort not to limp, while Leach and Moss watch.

LEACH: What's that noise I hear? It sounds like it's coming from your leg.

MOSS: Oh no, that's me, Doc. I'm so nervous I keep bouncing this crutch on the floor.

Moss bounces crutch's rubber tip on floor.

LEACH: It sounded to me more like some kind of liquid...

MOSS: I've been jumpy ever since this morning. I got up and I had these bright flashes in front of my eyes and then this pain hit me right in the small of the back. What would cause something like that, Doc?

LEACH: Well, you'd better speak to your ward doctor about that.

MOSS: But you *are* my ward doctor.

LEACH: Oh. How long have you been on 3-B?

MOSS: This time I've been there about two months.

LEACH: Oh well, no wonder I didn't know you.

MOSS: Anyway, this pain started moving up to the base of my skull and then...

LEACH: I have to be going now. See me on this when I'm making ward rounds, okay?

Leach hurries off.

MOSS: Okay, Doc. (*To Hegan*) These docs get so sick of listening to people's symptoms that they'll do almost

(Continued on next page)

anything to avoid hearing any more of them.

Moss gives Hegan his crutch and they move off down the hall.

HEGAN: Boy, that guy makes me mad. When I came in the hospital this time, I showed him this leg and he said, "It's been two years now and you say you still have some discomfort?" And I said, "Nah, I didn't say anything about discomfort. I said it hurts like hell."

MOSS: Yeah, that's pretty good. Your amputated leg hurts and so they send you to a psychologist. I suppose Scheiner tells you it's all in your head.

HEGAN: He doesn't come right out and say so but you can tell that's what he's thinking.

MOSS: What I like about these psychologists is somebody like you is sent to them and you tell him your leg hurts. He never considers whether your leg might really hurt, instead he looks at you and says, "Now what experience in this man's childhood could cause him to make a statement like that?"

HEGAN: Ahh, they're all nuts. You just have to humor them.

DISSOLVE TO: INTERIOR. DR. SCHEINER'S OFFICE.
The office is empty and the door is open. Moss and Hegan appear in doorway.

HEGAN: He's not here yet. These doctors got a soft life.

MOSS: He just likes to be called Doctor, he's not really one. He's a psychologist and he's going to cure me of my alcoholism. I know he can do it because he's already cured me twice in the past five years.

Hegan sits down heavily. Moss wanders restlessly around the office.

HEGAN: Just walking from the ward to here has made this leg start throbbing.

MOSS: Dig that bottle out. A drink won't stop your leg from throbbing but after a while you'll enjoy the throbbing.

HEGAN: I'll tell you what makes me mad and that's being put there on 3-B. It's nothing but a nut ward. I mean, you know, you're all right and Smitty but some of those guys are out of their heads. Why you tell somebody you're from 3-B and they start looking for the strait jacket.

Hegan has been unstrapping leg and gets out bottle and hands it to Moss.

MOSS: Yeah, it's all part of the new plan. If you're not actually bleeding, then your troubles must be mental rather than physical, so they stick everybody on the same ward and send us all to the psychologist. Two years ago, it was group therapy, before that it was something else.

Moss takes large swig from bottle, hands it back to Hegan. Hegan takes drink.

HEGAN: Uhhh, this stuff tastes terrible by itself.

MOSS: That's where we differ. It tastes good to me. Everything with alcohol in it tastes good. Maybe I'm not an alcoholic but just have unusual taste buds, do you suppose?

Moss is wandering around the office. Behind the door, he finds a long white doctor's coat. He takes it off the hook and puts it on. Then he sits down behind desk.

HEGAN: Hey, that's pretty good. Can you make your face twitch like Scheiner's does?

MOSS: I'm not nervous enough to be a psychologist. Give me another drink.

Hegan hands him the bottle and Moss takes a drink.

MOSS: Does this look like Scheiner's disgruntled bird act?

Moss shrugs his shoulders and putting his head back, rubs the back of his neck against his collar while shaking his head back and forth.

HEGAN: That's just like him. Now you ought to have his wife call him and chew him out and you say, "Yes, dear. If you say so, hon." And then you have to run to the bathroom.

MOSS: Right, and when I come back I say something nasty to you about your not really wanting to get better.

HEGAN: Yeah. You're a coward. You don't really try. You're afraid to walk on that leg. You want to be taken care of.

MOSS: He thinks if he gets you mad, you'll want to go out and lick your problems. The only thing he ever made me want to do was push his face in. Finish that up so we can get rid of the bottle.

Hegan takes bottle and empties it and looks around for some place to put it.

HEGAN: What am I going to do with this? We can't just dump it in the wastebasket.

Moss takes crumpled brown paper sack out of wastebasket and opens it.

MOSS: Let me have it. I'll put it in here.

There is a knock on the side of the open door and two aides appear. Moss moves so that he is standing behind desk.

1st AIDE: Excuse me, Doctor, but have you seen a patient named Crangle? He's supposed to be down at physical therapy only we can't find him.

Moss, surprised, just stares at aides.

HEGAN: Look in the dirty laundry room. Crangle doesn't like PT and he hides in there whenever he gets a chance.

1st AIDE: Oh, okay. Sorry to bother you, Doctor.

MOSS: That's all right. Say, if you're going by Dr. Leach's office, drop this sample off for me, will you?

Moss hands 1st Aide the paper sack containing the empty bottle.

(Continued on next page)

1st AIDE: Yes sir. I'll do that.

MOSS: I don't think he's there so just put it on his desk. And be careful with it. That's the only one I've got.

Aides go out, 1st Aide carefully carrying paper sack.

HEGAN: What did you do that for?

MOSS: Well, we had to get rid of it. Besides it'll give Leach something to think about. He's too wrapped up in that chesty nurse of his. Say, now that I'm a doctor, do you suppose they'll give me a nurse of my own?

HEGAN: Those aides are just new on this section. That's why they didn't know you from Scheiner.

MOSS: Well, I think I could do a better job than some we've got around here.

HEGAN: That Crangle is something, ain't he? He sure hates PT. How come he wears that mask and bandages and stuff?

MOSS: He's got some kind of a nervous condition and just scratches his face until it's all bleeding and sore unless they put those mittens on him.

HEGAN: Uhhahh. It's not nice of me but I just don't like being around him. I suppose I'm afraid that I bother other people the way he bothers me.

MOSS: Nah, you're not like him. Besides when Scheincr gets through with you, you'll be glad you lost that leg. I know that being around him has made me happy that I'm an alcoholic and not a psychologist.

HEGAN: Do you suppose that's why they hired him? To make us feel good in comparison?

MOSS: I wouldn't be surprised, after all if... There's Crangle out in the hall now.

Crangle comes hacking into room in wheelchair. pushing it with his feet since he has mittens on his hands, his face and head are covered with a mask and bandages.

MOSS: What are you doing, Crangle? Hiding out from the aides?

HEGAN: I'd better go tell them he's in here.

MOSS: No, don't do that. Let them worry about finding him. Well, Mr. Crangle, you've come to Old Doc Moss to have your problems solved, haven't you?

Crangle shakes head no.

HEGAN: Hah, he knows better than that. Old Doc Moss would fix up his problems with old liquor. Seven year old scotch, six year old bourbon.

Crangle nods head yes.

MOSS (laughing): See, Crangle knows what's good for him. If they would let me dispense that kind of medicine, I'd fix up everybody in the hospital. I might even be able to do Scheiner some good.

HEGAN: It'd be all right if you dispensed the stuff and didn't drink it all yourself. You know it wouldn't be very funny if Scheiner walked in on us right now.

MOSS: Ah, don't worry about it. I'm going to give this patient, who has come to me for aid and comfort, my best professional advice.

Hegan has been strapping leg on again.

HEGAN: I better keep an eye out in the hall for Scheiner.

MOSS: Mr. Crangle, your problem is very simple. You're over-sexed. You think about women all the time. Now, I think about women all the time, too, but that's all right because I'm a doctor. With you, it's not all right because you're a patient.

Hegan gets up and starts for door.

MOSS: When I have thoughts along this line, it's a normal outgrowth of my healthy, well-adjusted personality. When you think about women, you're encroaching on the province of the medical . . .

Scheiner comes in door and bumps into Hegan. Scheiner is small, quick,nervous man.

SCHEINER: What's going on here? (*To Hegan*) What are you doing?

HEGAN: I was just going down the hall to tell the aides that Crangle is here. They were looking for him.

Hegan goes out.

SCHEINER: And what do you think you're doing, Moss?

MOSS: Me? I was just explaining to Crangle here the nature of the traditional doctor-patient relationship.

Scheiner moves around Crangle and faces Moss. who is still seated behind desk. Crangle backs up to give him room and keeps on going, right out the door.

SCHEINER: Oh you were, were you? While wearing my coat! Moss, I've had a lot of trouble with you. You've always acted as though you really know more than I do.

MOSS: That's true.

SCHEINER: What?!!

MOSS: That's the way I've acted all right.

SCHEINER: Well, I've had just about enough of your insolence. Your disregard of authority. Your jokes, like pretending to be a doctor.

MOSS: I've never pretended to be a doctor, I just...

SCHEINER: You've got my coat on and you're sitting at my desk. I want you to stay right here in this office until I can get Dr. Harbison here and we can see about some sort of disciplinary action.

MOSS: Oh, come on, Doc, I haven't done anything. Take the psychological aspects...

SCHEINER: Don't tell me about psychology! Whatever I say to you, you want to argue. I never want to hear you argue with a member of the staff *again!*

MOSS: Even when they're wrong? Even when they say something stupid?

SCHEINER: That's just what I mean. You think you know more than anyone else. Did it ever occur to you that those of us that run this section have had some training in our work? Isn't it possible that even though

(Continued on next page)

you don't understand something, there may be a good reason for it?

MOSS: Sure, but sometimes anyone can tell that something is being done the wrong way.

Scheiner is taking off his coat and tie and hanging them behind the door.

SCHEINER: From now on, you just let us worry about how this hospital is run. Now give me my coat.

Scheiner is standing in front of desk and Moss stands up to take off coat when the same two aides enter.

1st AIDE: One of the patients just told us that Crangle was here in your office, Doctor, so we came to pick him up.

SCHEINER: He was here a minute ago. Maybe he ducked out into the hall.

Scheiner, after looking around office, starts to go between the two aides into the hall. Aides catch hold of him from either side.

SECOND AIDE: Where do you think you're going?

SCHEINER: Get your hands off me!

1st AIDE: We've been chasing you all morning. Now don't give us any trouble.

SCHEINER: This is ridiculous! I'm Dr. Scheiner.

1st AIDE: Sure you are and I'm the President of the United States. Now let's go to PT.

SCHEINER: I don't know where you men are from that you don't know who I am but Moss will tell you. Moss, tell them they've got the wrong man!

MOSS: You want me to argue with a member of the staff?

All this time the aides are trying to ease Scheiner toward the door and he is resisting them.

SECOND AIDE: You're taking up everybody's time. Come on now.

SCHEINER: Ask him! Just ask him if I'm not a doctor!

1st AIDE: If we ask him just this one question, will you stop fighting us?

SCHEINER: Yes! Tell the truth now, Moss!

1st AIDE *(To Moss):* Is he a doctor?

MOSS: Well no, actually, but...

1st AIDE: That's all we wanted to know. Let's get him out of here, Charlie.

Aides forcibly start dragging Scheiner out.

SCHEINER: Ask him if I m a psychologist! Ask him that!

SECOND AIDE: Come on. We can't play games all day.

Aides have to turn sideways to get struggling Scheiner through doorway.

SCHEINER: Please fellas. I'm not a patient. Do I look to you like I've got something wrong with me?

SECOND AIDE: Yep.

Aides drag Scheiner off down the hall. We hear Scheiner's voice retreating into the distance.

SCHEINER: You guys are crazy! You'll get in trouble for this! You...

Moss goes to door and watches them out of sight. Then he shrugs and takes off coat and hangs it behind door. He goes to bookshelf and looks over books, picks one out and goes over and sits on edge of desk and begins reading. Hegan sticks his head in the door and looks around office.

HEGAN: Where's Scheiner?

MOSS: He went down the hall.

HEGAN: Was he mad?

Moss is still reading in book.

MOSS: Seemed to be.

HEGAN: I was sorry to cut out on you like that but I didn't see where it'd do any good for me to stay. Did he chew you out pretty bad?

MOSS: Oh, he tried but he doesn't really have any talent for it.

HEGAN: I just came by the tub room and they've got some guy in there and he's yelling and fighting the aides like a wild man. He must be new in here, I've never heard anybody carry on like that before.

MOSS: That's Scheiner.

HEGAN: Who?

MOSS: Scheiner.

HEGAN: Doctor Scheiner? In the tub room? What's he doing in there?

MOSS: Fighting and carrying on like a wild man, I guess.

HEGAN: But how did he get in there? Don't they know who he is?

MOSS: Well, they came in here looking for Crangle and of course he was gone so they took Scheiner instead. They were headed for PT but he must have given them so much trouble that they decided to quiet him down with one of those warm tub baths.

HEGAN: We better get down there and tell them they got the wrong guy!

MOSS: Hegan, just because you don't understand something doesn't mean there's not a good reason for it. Wiser heads than ours are running this hospital.

HEGAN: Come on, you know that Scheiner isn't supposed to be in one of those tubs. They think he's Crangle.

MOSS: To tell the truth, Hegan, I've just about despaired of education. For years I've been in and out of this hospital, giving an example of a civilized, tolerant, slightly alcoholic way of life and what has it taught the staff? Nothing. None of them have even started drinking.

HEGAN: Well, I'm going to go down there and tell them they made a mistake. Are you going to come along?

MOSS: I am not. They won't even let you in the tub room unless you make a big fuss and then they'll just put you in the tub next to Scheiner's.

(Continued on next page)

HEGAN: I'll get one of the other doctors then. Something's got to be done.

MOSS: You're being reasonable, Hegan. That'll only get you in trouble around here.

Hegan goes out. Moss returns to book.

DISSOLVE TO: SAME OFFICE.

SOME MINUTES LATER.

Moss is still reading when an aide appears at the door.

AIDE: Hey, what ward are you on, buddy?

MOSS: 3-B.

AIDE: I got a patient out here in the hall who needs a push. Take him along when you go, okay?

MOSS: Sure.

Moss goes to door and looks into hall. There is Scheiner in hospital pajamas, strapped into a wheel chair.

AIDE: I was looking this guy up in the records and guess how old he is? Sixty-seven!

MOSS: No kidding! I wouldn't have guessed him much over fifty.

SCHEINER: I'm thirty-eight!

AIDE (*Ignoring Scheiner*): I guess they don't age none after that old mind goes blank, huh?

MOSS: They must not.

AIDE: Well, wait here until I get a mask and bandages for him. The chart says he's supposed to wear them all the time.

Aide goes down hall. Moss is standing in doorway.

SCHEINER: Moss, come over here.

MOSS: I can't leave the office.

SCHEINER: Why not?

MOSS: You ordered me to stay in here until you could see about some disciplinary action.

SCHEINER: Forget that! Come here and let me loose.

Moss walks over to Scheiner.

MOSS: Doc, the way it is now, they just think you're crazy — confused, I mean, but if they catch me letting you loose, then they might think we're both out of it.

SCHEINER: Well, do something!

MOSS: I could get one of the other doctors here to identify you.

SCHEINER: Don't do that! If the other doctors found out about this, I'd be the laughing stock of the hospital.

MOSS: I think Hegan went to find one of the staff doctors and bring him here.

SCHEINER: Oh, no! I'd rather do anything than have them find me like this. Think of something, Moss!

MOSS: Look, let the aide bandage you up and then I'll start pushing you toward the ward and when he's gone, I'll turn around and bring you back to your office and let you go, okay?

SCHEINER: I guess so. This has been the most horrifying experience of my life. No matter what I said to those people, they just wouldn't listen.

MOSS: That's what I've been telling you for years, Doc.

SCHEINER: They can't even imagine that they might be wrong. And then they put me in that tub and told me to relax! The whole thing is idiotic!

MOSS: Doc, there hasn't been anything done to you that hasn't been done to hundreds of other people.

SCHEINER: But they're all patients! I'm a doctor.

MOSS: Oh boy, I can see you've learned a lot.

Aide comes in and puts mask and bandages on Scheiner until only his eyes are showing. Then Moss starts pushing him down the hall and they bump into Hegan and Dr. Leach who come around the corner. Leach is carrying the brown paper sack.

LEACH (*To Hegan*): I can't make head nor tail of this story you've been telling me. Is this the man here?

HEGAN: Yeah, that's Dr. Scheiner there in the wheel chair. They've got him tied in.

LEACH: It looks like Crangle to me.

HEGAN: That's what the aides thought. That's why they made the mistake.

LEACH: The whole thing seems incredible to me. (*To Moss*) Is that Dr. Scheiner there?

MOSS: What would Dr. Scheiner be doing wrapped up like this?

HEGAN: What are you trying to do, Moss? Ask the guy in the chair, Dr. Leach.

LEACH (*To Scheiner*): What's your name?

MOSS: He's got a mask across his mouth, Doc. Ask him so he can answer by shaking his head.

LEACH: Oh yes. Is that you, Scheiner?

Scheiner shakes head no.

HEGAN: What is this?

LEACH: Is your name Crangle?

Scheiner nods head yes.

HEGAN: Well, I'll be a son-of-a-gun.

Hegan is staring dumbfounded at Scheiner. Leach slowly turns and looks accusingly at Hegan. Moss looks at him with a superior, pitying expression.

LEACH: Is this your idea of a joke? If you really can't distinguish between your aggressive fantasies concerning Dr. Scheiner and reality, perhaps you need some treatment.

Moss gives chair sudden push so chair arm knocks sack out of Leach's hand. It falls on floor and bottle goes skidding across floor without breaking.

MOSS: Hold still, Crangle! Look what you've done now.

LEACH: This has been an odd morning. I found this on the desk in my office. I don't understand it.

Moss picks up bottle.

MOSS: Vodka, huh? How was it?

LEACH: Oh, I didn't drink it.

(Continued on next page)

MOSS: The stuff evaporated, huh?

LEACH: The bottle was empty when I found it!

MOSS (*Skeptically*): Oh yeah?

Moss puts bottle back in bag.

MOSS: Hegan and I would never give you away, Doc, but you do know that there's a hospital rule against having even an empty bottle, don't you?

LEACH: Why that's preposterous!

MOSS: Doctor Leach! I know you wouldn't say such things about hospital regulations if you were your normal self but try to be more careful. Somebody might hear you.

LEACH: My normal self! I haven't had a thing to drink!

MOSS: Okay, let's see you walk a straight line then. Start right there and follow...

LEACH: You're telling *me* to walk a straight line? I won't do anything of the sort! This whole thing is the silliest thing I ever heard of.

MOSS: That's the wisest choice, Doc. If you don't think you can do it, it's best not to try. But don't worry, I'm not going to say anything to anybody about this. You won't either, will you, Hegan?

HEGAN: Well...

MOSS: Come on, Hegan. You know that when you're on the outside, you like a nip yourself, now and then. Give the doc a break.

LEACH: I don't have to prove anything to you people!

HEGAN: You're right, Doc, and I'm not going to say anything about this. What's walking a straight line prove? I think you're the kind of guy who could walk a straight line no matter how much you've had to drink.

Scheiner is shaking with laughter and making choking noises behind his mask.

LEACH: What's the matter with Crangle? Is he laughing?

MOSS: Oh no, sir. He gets like this sometimes. Well, I'll get rid of this bottle for you by putting it in Dr. Scheiner's office. If it was left for you by mistake, maybe it was intended for Dr. Scheiner.

Scheiner stops laughing and makes protesting noises. Moss ignores him and goes and puts bottle in office.

LEACH: They were looking for Crangle on the ward when I left so I'll take him back with me.

Leach starts pushing Scheiner towards ward.

MOSS: That's okay, Doc. I'll push him.

LEACH: It's no problem. I've got him.

Hegan has dropped back and picked up his crutch from Scheiner's office. Moss is trying to take Scheiner away from Leach.

MOSS: I'm used to this, Doc. Let me do it.

LEACH: I'm quite capable of getting him there.

Moss gives up and drops back with Hegan who is limping along some distance behind.

HEGAN: Who is that in the wheel chair?

MOSS: That's Scheiner.

HEGAN: I could tell by the eyes that it wasn't Crangle. Why did he lie to Leach?

MOSS: He figured it would ruin his professional reputation to be caught like that.

HEGAN: Great! There I am trying to help him and he pretends to be Crangle and I'm left looking like some kind of nut. The little rat!

MOSS: You're lucky I'm not the kind of guy who would ever tell a buddy, 'I told you so.'

HEGAN: Yeah, I'm sure lucky you're not that kind of guy.

MOSS: You know, you see something like this and you have to wonder. Do you suppose that years ago, the original Crangle disappeared and the aides just grabbed some innocent bystander without realizing it and have kept him in Crangle's place ever since?

HEGAN: Might be. Who would ever know?

DISSOLVE TO: HALLWAY OF WARD 3-B.

Leach is pushing Scheiner in chair. He stops and waits for Moss and Hegan to catch up with him.

LEACH: I have to finish ward rounds. Tell them at the nurses' station that Crangle is here, will you?

MOSS: Sure.

Leach goes off. Moss takes hold of chair and turns it around in direction they just came from.

MOSS: Now is our chance to get away.

Mrs. Reslick appears and comes toward them.

RESLICK: Mr. Moss!

Moss keeps going and Hegan gets in front of Reslick.

HEGAN: Mrs. Reslick, I wanted to ask you...

Reslick shoves Hegan to one side.

RESLICK (*Bellowing*): Moss!

Moss freezes in tracks and slowly turns to face Reslick.

RESLICK: Mr. Moss, *where* do you think you're going?

MOSS: I picked up the wrong guy by mistake at PT and I was just going to take him back.

Moss tries to get away with Scheiner.

RESLICK: What do you mean? That's Mr. Crangle there.

MOSS: No, this isn't Crangle.

HEGAN: No, that's not Crangle. You better put him back where you found him, Moss.

RESLICK: Ohh, you two! Who would it be if it's not Mr. Crangle?

MOSS: Uhh, well... I'm sure he's not a patient from this ward.

RESLICK: Ohhww. Why did you hide from them at PT today, Mr. Crangle? They called here looking for you.

Scheiner mumbles something. Moss leans forward to listen.

MOSS: He says you've got it all wrong. He's Dr. Scheiner.

(Continued on next page)

RESLICK: Mr. Crangle! Are you confused again? Your name is Crangle now, isn't it?

Scheiner shakes head no.

RESLICK: Oh, for goodness sakes. Well you'll feel better after you've had your lunch.

MOSS: Do they still tube feed him his egg nogg?

Scheiner slowly and unbelievingly shakes head no.

RESLICK: Yes, and afterwards he'll get a nice enema.

Scheiner vigorously shakes head no.

RESLICK (*Calling down the hall*): Mr. Martin. Mr. Farrow. Time for Mr. Crangle's lunch.

MOSS: Mrs. Reslick, let me take off his mask here and you can...

RESLICK: Mr. Moss! Don't touch that! That mask is there for a purpose.

MOSS: But just suppose this is Dr. Scheiner. Will you take the responsibility?

RESLICK: Yes, Mr. Moss. Now, you've had your joke so try to remember that we're busy here.

Two aides appear and start to wheel Scheiner away.

RESLICK: Mister Hegan! What are you doing with that crutch?

HEGAN: Oh, I'm just carrying it for this fellow here.

Hegan sticks crutch into chair alongside Scheiner. Aides wheel him away.

RESLICK: Did you two make it to your appointment this morning?

MOSS: Well, we got to Scheiner's office on time.

RESLICK: That's good. What did he have to say to you?

HEGAN: Yeah, Moss, what did Scheiner say this morning?

MOSS: Help.

RESLICK: What?

MOSS: That's what he said,— Help!

RESLICK: Mr. Moss, I don't want you making jokes about Dr. Scheiner anymore. He's trying to help you with your problems.

MOSS: He's got problems of his own, that make mine look sick.

RESLICK: He does not!

MOSS: Oh yeah? Let's ask him. We'll... Look out!

Moss grabs nurse and they jump aside as Scheiner comes sprinting up the hall, crutch under arm like battering ram, robe flying, face still bandaged. Aides are in single file pursuing.

HEGAN: Boy, that must have been some egg nogg.

They jump back against the wall as Scheiner goes by the other way, aides still following.

RESLICK: Don't just stand there. Catch him! Hold him!

MOSS: Not me. I don't want him.

HEGAN: Looks like good therapy to me.

Dr. Leach appears and confronts them.

LEACH: What is going on here? Don't you patients know better than to make so much noise?

RESLICK: It's one of the patients, Doctor. He's gone wild.

LEACH: What patient?

MOSS: Right behind you, Doc.

Leach turns around just in time to be bowled over by Scheiner. The aides trip and sprawl over Leach. Nurse chases Scheiner shouting, 'Mr. Crangle, Mr. Crangle.' Aides bounce up, one after the other, and continue the pursuit. Moss and Hegan help Leach up.

LEACH (*Unbelievingly*): That was Crangle?

HEGAN: Active for an old coot, ain't he?

Leach is looking down hall. Now he spreads his arms to block way of returning group. Moss and Hegan get out of way.

LEACH: Crangle, let's stop this now.

Scheiner bowls Leach over again. Aides again trip over Leach, bounce up, and continue pursuit. Nurse comes puffing up and helps Leach to his feet.

RESLICK: Oh dear. I don't think we are ever going to catch him.

Nurse puffs off saying, 'Mr. Crangle, Mr. Crangle.' Leach follows, trotting.

LEACH: Here now. Let's stop this.

Camera remains on Moss and Hegan who are leaning against the wall, looking down the hall.

HEGAN: I should get Smitty and some of the others. They wouldn't want to miss this.

Crangle comes up behind them.

MOSS: Hey, here's Crangle. Pull over, Crangle, and watch the show. It's dangerous out there in the middle of the hall.

Crangle backs his wheel chair up against the wall and all three stare down the hall.

HEGAN: Well, you can't say it's dull around here.

Camera remains on the three of them as they watch as Scheiner runs by followed closely by the aides and Reslick and Leach trailing.

MOSS: What kind of experience do you suppose Scheiner had as a child to make him dislike tube feeding so much?

All of them are staring down the hall.

HEGAN: I don't know. I sure would like to see Leach in the same sort of fix though. Do you suppose we could fix him up like we did Scheiner?

MOSS: I don't know why not if we can get Crangle to help us. What about it, Crangle?

Crangle enthusiastically nods head yes.

MOSS: Okay. we'll see what we can do tomorrow. We... Oh, oh. Here they come again.

END

The Economy of Ideas

by John Perry Barlow

(1993) (Excerpt)

A framework for rethinking patents and copyrights in the Digital Age

(Everything you know about intellectual property is wrong)

"If nature has made any one thing less susceptible than all others of exclusive property, it is the action of the thinking power called an idea, which an individual may exclusively possess as long as he keeps it to himself; but the moment it is divulged, it forces itself into the possession of everyone, and the receiver cannot dispossess himself of it. Its peculiar character, too, is that no one possesses the less, because every other possesses the whole of it. He who receives an idea from me, receives instruction himself without lessening mine; as he who lights his taper at mine, receives light without darkening me. That ideas should freely spread from one to another over the globe, for the moral and mutual instruction of man, and improvement of his condition, seems to have been peculiarly and benevolently designed by nature, when she made them, like fire, expansible over all space, without lessening their density at any point, and like the air in which we breathe, move, and have our physical being, incapable of confinement or exclusive appropriation. Inventions then cannot, in nature, be a subject of property."

— **Thomas Jefferson**

Throughout the time I've been groping around cyberspace, an immense, unsolved conundrum has remained at the root of nearly every legal, ethical, governmental, and social vexation to be found in the Virtual World. I refer to the problem of digitized property. The enigma is this: If our property can be infinitely reproduced and instantaneously distributed all over the planet without cost, without our knowledge, without its even leaving our possession, how can we protect it? How are we going to get paid for the work we do with our minds? And, if we can't get paid, what will assure the continued creation and distribution of such work?

Since we don't have a solution to what is a profoundly new kind of challenge, and are apparently unable to delay the galloping digitization of everything not obstinately physical, we are sailing into the future on a sinking ship.

This vessel, the accumulated canon of copyright and patent law, was developed to convey forms and methods of expression entirely different from the vaporous cargo it is now being asked to carry. It is leaking as much from within as from without.

Legal efforts to keep the old boat floating are taking three forms: a frenzy of deck chair rearrangement, stern warnings to the passengers that if she goes down, they will face harsh criminal penalties, and serene, glassy-eyed denial.

Intellectual property law cannot be patched, retrofitted, or expanded to contain digitized expression any more than real estate law might be revised to cover the allocation of broadcasting spectrum (which, in fact, rather resembles what is being attempted here). We will need to develop an entirely new set of methods as befits this entirely new set of circumstances.

Most of the people who actually create soft property - the programmers, hackers, and Net surfers - already know this. Unfortunately, neither the companies they work for nor the lawyers these companies hire have enough direct experience with nonmaterial goods to understand why they are so problematic. They are proceeding as though the old laws can somehow be made to work, either by grotesque expansion or by force. They are wrong.

The source of this conundrum is as simple as its solution is complex. Digital technology is detaching information from the physical plane, where property law of all sorts has always found definition.

Throughout history of copyrights and patents, the proprietary assertions of thinkers have been focused not on their ideas but on the expression of those ideas. The ideas themselves, as well as facts about the phenomena of the world, were considered to be the collective property of humanity. One could claim franchise, in the case of copyright, on the precise turn of phrase used to convey a particular idea or the order in which facts were presented.

The point at which this franchise was imposed was that moment when the "word become flesh" by departing the mind of its originator and entering some physical object, whether book or widget. The subsequent arrival of other commercial media besides books didn't alter the legal importance of this moment. Law protected expression and, with few (and recent) exceptions, to express was to make physical.

Protecting physical expression had the force of convenience on its side. Copyright worked well because, Gutenberg notwithstanding, it was hard to make a book. Furthermore, books froze their contents into a condition which was as challenging to alter as it was to reproduce. Counterfeiting and distributing counterfeit volumes were obvious and visible activities - it was easy enough to catch somebody in the act of doing. Finally, unlike unbounded words or images, books had material surfaces to which one could attach copyright notices, publisher's marques, and price tags.

Mental-to-physical conversion was even more central to patent. A patent, until recently, was either a description of the form into which materials were to be rendered in the service of some purpose, or a description of the process by which rendition occurred. In either case, the conceptual heart of patent was the material result. If no purposeful object could be rendered because of some material limitation, the patent was rejected. Neither a Klein bottle nor a shovel made of silk could be patented. It had to be a thing, and the thing had to work.

Thus, the rights of invention and authorship adhered to activities in the physical world. One didn't get paid for ideas, but for the ability to deliver them into reality. For all practical purposes, the value was in the conveyance and not in the thought conveyed.

In other words, the bottle was protected, not the wine.

Now, as information enters cyberspace, the native home of Mind, these bottles are vanishing. With the advent of digitization, it is now possible to replace all previous information storage forms with one metabottle: complex and highly liquid patterns of ones and zeros.

Even the physical/digital bottles to which we've become accustomed - floppy disks, CD-ROMs, and other discrete, shrink-wrappable bit-packages - will disappear as all computers jack-in to the global Net. While the Internet may never include every CPU on the planet, it is more than doubling every year and can be expected to become the principal medium of information conveyance, and perhaps eventually, the only one.

Once that has happened, all the goods of the Information Age - all of the expressions once contained in books or film strips or newsletters - will exist either as pure thought or something very much like thought: voltage conditions darting around the Net at the speed of light, in conditions that one might behold in effect, as glowing pixels or transmitted sounds, but never touch or claim to "own" in the old sense of the word.

Some might argue that information will still require some physical manifestation, such as its magnetic existence on the titanic hard disks of distant servers, but these are bottles which have no macroscopically discrete or personally meaningful form.

Some will also argue that we have been dealing with unbottled expression since the advent of radio, and they would be right. But for most of the history of broadcast, there was no convenient way to capture soft goods from the electromagnetic ether and reproduce them with quality available in commercial packages. Only recently has this changed, and little has been done legally or technically to address the change.

Generally, the issue of consumer payment for broadcast products was irrelevant. The consumers themselves were the product. Broadcast media were supported either by the sale of the attention of their audience to advertisers, by government assessing payment through taxes, or by the whining mendicancy of annual donor drives.

All of the broadcast-support models are flawed. Support either by advertisers or government has almost invariably tainted the purity of the goods delivered. Besides, direct marketing is gradually killing the advertiser-support model anyway.

Broadcast media gave us another payment method for a virtual product: the royalties that broadcasters pay songwriters through such organizations as ASCAP and BMI. But, as a member of ASCAP, I can assure you this is not a model that we should emulate. The monitoring methods are wildly approximate. There is not parallel system of accounting in the revenue stream. It doesn't really work. Honest.

In any case, without our old methods, based on physically defining the expression of ideas, and in the absence of successful new models for nonphysical transaction, we simply don't know how to assure reliable payment for mental works. To make matters worse, this comes at a time when the human mind is replacing sunlight and mineral deposits as the principal source of new wealth.

Furthermore, the increasing difficulty of enforcing existing copyright and patent laws is already placing in peril the ultimate source of intellectual property - the free exchange of ideas.

That is, when the primary articles of commerce in a society look so much like speech as to be indistinguishable from it, and when the traditional methods of protecting their ownership have become ineffectual, attempting to fix the problem with broader and more vigorous enforcement will inevitably threaten freedom of speech. The greatest constraint on your future liberties may come not from government but from corporate legal departments laboring to protect by force what can no longer be protected by practical efficiency or general social consent.

Furthermore, when Jefferson and his fellow creatures of the Enlightenment designed the system that became American copyright law, their primary objective was assuring the widespread distribution of thought, not profit. Profit was the fuel that would carry ideas into the libraries and minds of their new republic. Libraries would purchase books, thus rewarding the authors for their work in assembling ideas; these ideas, otherwise "incapable of confinement," would then become freely available to the public. But what is the role of libraries in the absence of books? How does society now pay for the distribution of ideas if not by charging for the ideas themselves?

Additionally complicating the matter is the fact that along with the disappearance of the physical bottles in which intellectual property protection has resided, digital technology is also erasing the legal jurisdictions of the physical world and replacing them with the unbounded and perhaps permanently lawless waves of cyberspace.

In cyberspace, no national or local boundaries contain the scene of a crime and determine the method of its prosecution; worse, no clear cultural agreements define what a crime might be. Unresolved and basic difference between Western and Asian cultural assumptions about intellectual property can only be exacerbated when many transactions are taking place in both hemispheres and yet, somehow, in neither.

Even in the most local of digital conditions, jurisdiction and responsibility are hard to assess. A group of music publishers filed suit against CompuServe this fall because it allowed its users to upload musical compositions into areas where other users might access them. But since CompuServe cannot practically exercise much control over the flood of bits that passes between its subscribers, it probably shouldn't be held responsible for unlawfully "publishing" these works.

Notions of property, value, ownership, and the nature of wealth itself are changing more fundamentally than at any time since the Sumerians first poked cuneiform into wet clay and called it stored grain. Only a very few people are aware of the enormity of this shift, and fewer of them are lawyers or public officials.

Those who do see these changes must prepare responses for the legal and social confusion that will erupt as efforts to protect new forms of property with old methods become more obviously futile, and, as a consequence, more adamant.

From Sword to Writs to Bits

Humanity now seems bent on creating a world economy primarily based on goods that take no material form. In doing so, we may be eliminating any predictable connection between creators and a fair reward for the utility or pleasure others may find in their works.

Without that connection, and without a fundamental change in consciousness to accommodate its loss, we are building our future on furor, litigation, and institutionalized evasion of payment except in response to raw force. We may return to the Bad Old Days of property.

Throughout the darker parts of human history, the possession and distribution of property was a largely military matter. "Ownership" was assured those with the nastiest tools, whether fists or armies, and the most resolute will to use them. Property was the divine right of thugs.

By the turn of the First Millennium AD, the emergence of merchant classes and landed gentry forced the development of ethical understandings for the resolution of property disputes. In the Middle Ages, enlightened rulers like England's Henry II began to codify this unwritten "common law" into recorded canons. These laws were local, which didn't matter much as they were primarily directed at real estate, a form of property that is local by definition. And, as the name implied, was very real.

This continued to be the case as long as the origin of wealth was agricultural, but with that dawning of the Industrial Revolution, humanity began to focus as much on means as ends. Tools acquired a new social value and, thanks to their development, it became possible to duplicate and distribute them in quantity.

To encourage their invention, copyright and patent law were developed in most Western countries. These laws were devoted to the delicate task of getting mental creations into the world where they could be used - and could enter the minds of others - while assuring their inventors compensation for the value of their use. And, as previously stated, the systems of both law and practice which grew up around that task were based on physical expression.

Since it is now possible to convey ideas from one mind to another without ever making them physical, we are now claiming to own ideas themselves and not merely their expression. And since it is likewise now possible to create useful tools that never take physical form, we have taken to patenting abstractions, sequences of virtual events, and mathematical formulae - the most unreal estate imaginable.

In certain areas, this leaves rights of ownership in such an ambiguous condition that property again adheres to those who can muster the largest armies. The only difference is that this time the armies consist of lawyers.

Threatening their opponents with the endless purgatory of litigation, over which some might prefer death itself, they assert claim to any thought which might have entered another cranium within the collective body of the corporations they serve. They act as though these ideas appeared in splendid detachment from all previous human thought. And they pretend that thinking about a product is somehow as good as manufacturing, distributing, and selling it.

What was previously considered a common human resource, distributed among the minds and libraries of the world, as well as the phenomena of nature herself, is now being fenced and deeded. It is as though a new class of enterprise had arisen that claimed to own the air.

What is to be done? While there is a certain grim fun to be had in it, dancing on the grave of copyright and patent will solve little, especially when so few are willing to admit that the occupant of this grave is even deceased, and so many are trying to uphold by force what can no longer be upheld by popular consent.

The legalists, desperate over their slipping grip, are vigorously trying to extend their reach. Indeed, the United States and other proponents of GATT are making adherence to our moribund systems of intellectual property protection a condition of membership in the marketplace of nations. For example, China will be denied Most Favored Nation trading status unless they agree to uphold a set of culturally alien principles that are no longer even sensibly applicable in their country of origin.

In a more perfect world, we'd be wise to declare a moratorium on litigation, legislation, and international treaties in this area until we had a clearer sense of the terms and conditions of enterprise in cyberspace. Ideally, laws ratify already developed social consensus. They are less the Social Contract itself than a series of memoranda expressing a collective intent that has emerged out of many millions of human interactions.
Humans have not inhabited cyberspace long enough or in sufficient diversity to have developed a Social Contract which conforms to the strange new conditions of that world. Laws developed prior to consensus usually favor the already established few who can get them passed and not society as a whole.

To the extent that law and established social practice exists in this area, they are already in dangerous disagreement. The laws regarding unlicensed reproduction of commercial software are clear and stern... and rarely observed. Software piracy laws are so practically unenforceable and breaking them has become so socially acceptable that only a thin minority appears compelled, either by fear or conscience, to obey them. When I give speeches on this subject, I always ask how many people in the audience can honestly claim to have no unauthorized software on their hard disks. I've never seen more than 10 percent of the hands go up.

Whenever there is such profound divergence between law and social practice, it is not society that adapts. Against the swift tide of custom, the software publisher's current practice of hanging a few visible scapegoats is so obviously capricious as to only further diminish respect for the law.

Part of the widespread disregard for commercial software copyrights stems from a legislative failure to understand the conditions into which it was inserted. To assume that systems of law based in the physical world will serve in an environment as fundamentally different as cyberspace is a folly for which everyone doing business in the future will pay.

Unbounded intellectual property is very different from physical property and can no longer be protected as though these differences did not exist. For example, if we continue to assume that value is based on scarcity, as it is with regard to physical objects, we will create laws that are precisely contrary to the nature of information, which may, in many cases, increase in value with distribution.

The large, legally risk-averse institutions most likely to play by the old rules will suffer for their compliance. As more lawyers, guns, and money are invested in either protecting their rights or subverting those of their opponents, their ability to produce new technology will simply grind to a halt as every move they make drives them deeper into a tar pit of courtroom warfare.

Faith in law will not be an effective strategy for high-tech companies. Law adapts by continuous increments and at a pace second only to geology. Technology advances in lunging jerks, like the punctuation of biological evolution grotesquely accelerated. Real-world conditions will continue to change at a blinding pace, and the law will lag further behind, more profoundly confused. This mismatch may prove impossible to overcome.

Promising economies based on purely digital products will either be born in a state of paralysis, as appears to be the case with multimedia, or continue in a brave and willful refusal by their owners to play the ownership game at all.

In the United States one can already see a parallel economy developing, mostly among small, fast moving enterprises who protect their ideas by getting into the marketplace quicker than their larger competitors who base their protection on fear and litigation.

Perhaps those who are part of the problem will simply quarantine themselves in court, while those who are part of the solution will create a new society based, at first, on piracy and freebooting. It may well be that when the current system of intellectual property law has collapsed, as seems inevitable, that no new legal structure will arise in its place.

But something will happen. After all, people do business. When a currency becomes meaningless, business is done in barter. When societies develop outside the law, they develop their own unwritten codes, practices, and ethical systems. While technology may undo law, technology offers methods for restoring creative rights.

* * * * *

An Economy of Verbs

The future forms and protections of intellectual property are densely obscured at this entrance to the Virtual Age. Nevertheless, I can make (or reiterate) a few flat statements that I earnestly believe won't look too silly in 50 years.

- **In the absence of the old containers, almost everything we think we know about intellectual property is wrong. We're going to have to unlearn it. We're going to have to look at information as though we'd never seen the stuff before.**
- **The protection that we will develop will rely far more on ethics and technology than on law.**
- **Encryption will be the technical basis for most intellectual property protection. (And should, for many reasons, be made more widely available.)**
- **The economy of the future will be bsed on relationship rather than possession. It will be continuous rather than sequential.**
- **And finally, in the years to come, most human exchange will be virtual rather than physical, consisting not of stuff but the stuff of which dreams are made. Our future business will be conducted in a world made more of verbs than nouns.**

John Perry Barlow (barlow@eff.org) is a retired cattle rancher, a lyricist for the Grateful Dead, and Co-founder and executive chair of the Electronic Frontier Foundation.

The Economy of Ideas originally ran in **Wired** magazine.

A DECLARATION OF THE INDEPENDENCE OF CYBERSPACE

BY JOHN PERRY BARLOW

COLIN UPTON 96

Yesterday, that great invertebrate in the White House signed into the law the Telecom "Reform" Act of 1996, while Tipper Gore took digital photographs of the proceedings to be included in a book called "24 Hours in Cyberspace."

I had also been asked to participate in the creation of this book by writing something appropriate to the moment. Given the atrocity that this legislation would seek to inflict on the Net, I decided it was as good a time as any to dump some tea in the virtual harbor.

After all, the Telecom "Reform" Act, passed in the Senate with only 5 dissenting votes, makes it unlawful, and punishable by a $250,000 fine to say "shit" online. Or, for that matter, to say any of the other 7 dirty words prohibited in broadcast media. Or to discuss abortion openly. Or to talk about any bodily function in any but the most clinical terms.

It attempts to place more restrictive constraints on the conversation in Cyberspace than presently exist in the Senate cafeteria, where I have dined and heard colorful indecencies spoken by United States senators on every occasion I did.

This bill was enacted upon us by people who haven't the slightest idea who we are or where our conversation is being conducted. It is, as my good friend and Wired Editor Louis Rossetto put it, as though "the illiterate could tell you what to read."

Well, fuck them.

Or, more to the point, let us now take our leave of them. They have declared war on Cyberspace. Let us show them how cunning, baffling, and powerful we can be in our our defense.

I have written something (with characteristic grandiosity) that I hope will become one of the many means to this end. If you find it useful, I hope you will pass it on as widely as possible. You can leave my name off it if you like, because I don't care about the credit. I really don't.

But I do hope this cry will echo across Cyberspace, changing and growing and self-replicating, until it becomes a great shout equal to the idiocy they have just inflicted upon us.

I give you....

A Declaration of the Independence of Cyberspace

by John Perry Barlow

Governments of the Industrial World, you weary giants of flesh and steel, I come from Cyberspace, the new home of Mind. On behalf of the future, I ask you of the past to leave us alone. You are not welcome among us. You have no sovereignty where we gather.

We have no elected government, nor are we likely to have one, so I address you with no greater authority than that with which liberty itself always speaks. I declare the global social space we are building to be naturally independent of the tyrannies you seek to impose on us. You have no moral right to rule us nor do you possess any methods of enforcement we have true reason to fear.

Governments derive their just powers from the consent of the governed. You have neither solicited nor received ours. We did not invite you. You do not know us, nor do you know our world. Cyberspace does not lie within your borders. Do not think that you can build it, as though it were a public construction project. You cannot. It is an act of nature and it grows itself through our collective actions.

You have not engaged in our great and gathering conversation, nor did you create the wealth of our marketplaces. You do not know our culture, our ethics, or the unwritten codes that already provide our society more order than could be obtained by any of your impositions.

You claim there are problems among us that you need to solve. You use this claim as an excuse to invade our precincts. Many of these problems don't exist. Where there are real conflicts, where there are wrongs, we will identify them and address them by our means. We are forming our own Social Contract. This governance will arise according to

(Continued on next page)

the conditions of our world, not yours. Our world is different.

Cyberspace consists of transactions, relationships, and thought itself, arrayed like a standing wave in the web of our communications. Ours is a world that is both everywhere and nowhere, but it is not where bodies live.

We are creating a world that all may enter without privilege or prejudice accorded by race, economic power, military force, or station of birth.

We are creating a world where anyone, anywhere may express his or her beliefs, no matter how singular, without fear of being coerced into silence or conformity.

Your legal concepts of property, expression, identity, movement, and context do not apply to us. They are based on matter. There is no matter here.

Our identities have no bodies, so unlike you, we cannot obtain order by physical coercion. We believe that from ethics, enlightened self-interest, and the commonweal, our governance will emerge. Our identities may be distributed across many of your jurisdictions. The only law that all our constituent cultures would generally recognize is the Golden Rule. We hope we will be able to build our particular solutions on that basis.But we cannot accept the solutions you are attempting to impose.

In the United States, you have today created a law, the Telecommunications Reform Act, which repudiates your own Constitution and insults the dreams of Jefferson, Washington, Mill, Madison, DeToqueville, and Brandeis. These dreams must now be born anew in us.

You are terrified of your own children, since they are natives in a world where you will always be immigrants. Because you fear them, you entrust your bureaucracies with the parental responsibilities you are too cowardly to confront yourselves. In our world, all the sentiments and expressions of humanity, from the debasing to the angelic, are parts of a seamless whole, the global conversation of bits. We cannot separate the air that chokes from the air upon which wings beat.

In China, Germany, France, Russia, Singapore, Italy and the United States, you are trying to ward off the virus of liberty by erecting guard posts at the frontiers of Cyberspace. These may keep out the contagion for a small time, but they will not work in a world that will soon be blanketed in bit-bearing media.

Your increasingly obsolete information industries would perpetuate themselves by proposing laws, in America and elsewhere, that claim to own speech itself throughout the world. These laws would declare ideas to be another industrial product, no more noble than pig iron. In our world, whatever the human mind may create can be reproduced and distributed infinitely at no cost. The global conveyance of thought no longer requires your factories to accomplish.

These increasingly hostile and colonial measures place us in the same position as those previous lovers of freedom and self-determination who had to reject the authorities of distant, uninformed powers. We must declare our virtual selves immune to your sovereignty, even as we continue to consent to your rule over our bodies. We will spread ourselves across the Planet so that no one can arrest our thoughts.

We will create a civilization of the Mind in Cyberspace. May it be more humane and fair than the world your governments have made before.

Davos, Switzerland
February 8, 1996

John Perry Barlow, Cognitive Dissident
Co-Founder, Electronic Frontier Foundation

"It is error alone which needs the support of government. Truth can stand by itself." — Thomas Jefferson, Notes on Virginia

John Perry Barlow, former lyricist for The Grateful Dead, is one of the founders of the Electronic Frontier Foundation. His e-mail address is:

barlow@eff.org

PLEASE COPY "A DECLARATION OF THE INDEPENCE OF CYBERSPACE" AND DISTRIBUTE IT AS WIDELY AS POSSIBLE.

Oklahoma City: Cui Bono?
by Adam Parfrey

Ken Stern of the American Jewish Committee faxes a special warning to "members of the press, AJCers, legislators, prosecutors, attorneys general, federal officials," regarding a possible terrorist attack that will strike the U.S. on "April 19... the anniversary of Waco... THE KEY event for the militias, and for the hard core April 20 is Hitler's birthday." The communiqué is received by federal Judge James Anthony Redden of Portland, Oregon on April 10, 1995, a prophetic week prior to the bombing of the Murrah building.

Judge Wayne Alley, whose office is located directly across the street from the devastated Alfred P. Murrah building, tells a reporter that "security officials" warned him to take "special precautions" several days prior to the April 19th bomb blast. Reported April 20 in the *Portland Oregonian*, Judge Alley's warning is never again mentioned even after it's reported that he has been assigned to try the McVeigh-Nichols case.

Edye Smith, whose two children died in the Oklahoma City bombing, is interviewed by CNN correspondent Gary Tuchman on May 23, '95, the day FEMA officials bring down the ruins of the Murrah building. The childless mother tells Tuchman she was told to "keep your mouth shut, don't talk about it," when she asked officials why BATF agents were "given the day off" on April 19. Although we're told that the BATF was the primary target of the bombing, which kills and maims hundreds, no BATF officer suffers injury in the attack.

"I am an American military man, and I can tell you categorically that if one of you militia drones or one of your crackpot units started any kind of half-witted shooting war, that I would unhesitatingly blow all of your asses into the netherworld. Not even one split second of hesitation, because you're goofy, dangerous examples of twisted delayed adolescence..." *[Posting taken from the Internet newsgroup "misc.activism.militia"]*

Setting Minds Against Terrorism

"Setting Minds Against Terrorism" was the headline of an article relegated to the back pages of the April 24, 1995 "terrorism" issue of *Advertising Age*. Though its placement would seem to indicate that news, advertising and public relations executives might consider its content filler-like or possibly redundant, the article's implications are, to my mind, startling.

In the bloodless manner of the faceless hack, author Joe Mandese reveals how propaganda, here called "public policy," and mind control, here called "behavioral science,"[1] is cooked up by high-level "policy makers" in the National Security Council, and then passed down to the CIA and FBI for dissemination through Madison Avenue and onwards through print and electronic media.

Mandese's bureaucratese is designed to lull the outsider to sleep. But translating his article into plain language leaves one with a schematic diagram of how the media juggernaut collaborates with the highest levels of government intelligence to decide how and where the sheep are to be herded.

Take note that the executives Mandese interviews are not interested in relaying or even cushioning the truth, but how to best tell a lie in order that U.S. subjects will regard the government as a loving benevolent entity. It's not 1995, it's *1984*. This isn't the New World Order, it's *Brave New World*.

"There used to be a day when Americans looked around and reported suspicious things to the FBI, or the local police," says Bob Dilenschneider, of the Dilenschneider Group, in the final paragraph of Mandese's article. He continues, devoid of irony: "Of late, [turning in suspicious characters to the FBI] has been regarded as 'Big Brother is watching,' and carries the overtones of a fascist state. We have to get back to the thinking that the police are there to help us and the FBI is there to protect us."

Despite all the hoary lies told about our "free press" and "objective journalism," the *Advertising Age* article reveals how the media "implements strategies" instead of reporting the facts. Mandese's article asks *how shall the government be served?* rather than *how shall citizens be served by their public servants?* Mandese suggests that brain massage can best be accomplished by ad hoc committees comprised of marketing experts and intelligence agencies. The Persian Gulf War seemed like a dress rehearsal in media's lockstep goosestep with the National Security Agency (NSA). Oklahoma City is further proof of capitalism's cooperative Total War against the consumerist mind. For a precedent for media-approved or media-created foreign escapades, see history books on the Spanish-American conflict, known as "Hearst's War."

When the *Los Angeles Times* building burned in 1910 killing dozens of printers and other low-level workers, the nascent labor movement was buried by *agents provocateurs* from the Burns Detective Agency working behind-the-scenes for Times' owner, Colonel Harrison Gray Otis. On the day his building exploded, Colonel Otis and his staff had previously fled the office. One day earlier, Otis made sure to raise his insurance coverage. Though workers complained of a bad smell of leaking gas, nothing was done to correct the problem.

(Continued on next page)

Despite a sterling defense by Clarence Darrow and labor hero Job Harriman, the entire blame fell to the duped McNamara brothers, declared guilty by the best jury money could buy. Shedding crocodile tears for the victims of the fire, Colonel Otis had his pompous prose chiseled into a monument purchased by insurance money, while he built himself a great new building on the present site of the *Times*.[2]

Advertising Age's paradigm for creating the proper framing around events is nothing new. Christopher Simpson's *Science of Coercion* (Oxford University Press, 1994) tells us how private corporations, foundations, and universities intermingle with government to create an interlocking network in which capitalist propaganda could be disseminated.

Fifty years ago Assistant Secretary of War John J. McCloy established "Psychological Warfare" as a "highly secret" branch of the War Department. According to Simpson's book, McCloy is "probably better known today for his later work as U.S. high commissioner in Germany, chairman of the Chase Bank, **member of the Warren Commission** [my emphasis], and related posts." *Science of Coercion* establishes beyond a doubt that private think tanks and University tenured social scientists advised policy-makers and police agencies how to better deploy Psy War propaganda.

Not only do Psy War units inhabit the Pentagon, but they also perform important roles in the NSA, FBI, CIA and NSC, as well as the ATF, Secret Service, U.S. Marshal Department, et al. White House Press Corps journalist Sarah McClendon has even received official confirmation that Psy War receives a slice of a $3 billion/year domestic anti-terrorism program created in 1987 during the Reagan Administration. Was this expensive program ever mentioned in the news media during debate on the 1995 Anti-Terrorism Act? Not anyplace I can find.[3]

The Psy War payroll extends to private corporations like Wackenhut, Rand and TRW which are even less subject to oversight than FLEAs — the all-too-appropriate acronym for Federal Law Enforcement Agencies. A contractor that "takes care of business" without dirtying the government's hands, Wackenhut can be seen as filling the interstice between the government and the mob. Such connections were being drawn by journalist Danny Casolaro before he died under suspicious circumstances. Another contractor, CalSpan, plays a part in the evolving Oklahoma City bombing, about which more later.

Non-profit foundations field their own intelligence organizations. The Anti-Defamation League, knuckle-rapped with a $75,000 fine for illegal possession of police files, bribed San Francisco police officer Tom Gerard to gain extensive and sensitive information on not only racists, but politicians, leftists, and anti-apartheid groups. Information on anti-racist protesters would have been of intense interest to the formerly apartheid South African Republic, a covert nuclear ally of Israel, a direct ADL conduit.[4] The Southern Poverty Law Center,[5] run by the telegenic Morris Dees, was exposed in a *Montgomery Advertiser* investigation as the second wealthiest non-profit organization in America. Its wealth and preoccupation with fundraising belies SPLC's eponymous objective to battle poverty. The *Advertiser* revealed that the SPLC's few high-profile lawsuits have resulted in little or no compensation for the "victims" in their legal crusades, but have in fact yielded millions of dollars in fees paid to Morris Dees for television movies and a ghost-written autobiography that was criticized by *Publishers Weekly* for its rampant self-aggrandizement.

The ADL and SPLC boast that they are the media's primary sources of information regarding militias and patriot groups. Their information is usually absorbed whole into establishment left news stories as unimpeachable and objective news sources. In truth, the coffers of the ADL and SPLC bulge when constituents are led to believe they're fighting an enemy of enormous evil and mounting strength. Despite their altruistic charters, the ADL and SPLC profit directly off the sensationalism that acts as a spark plug for Hollywood and the weekly tabloids. Their information ought to be regarded with skepticism greeted a docudrama or the *National Enquirer*.

Another non-profit organization media star, Political Research Associate's John Foster "Chip" Berlet, has become something of a ubiquitous presence on establishment news shows and so-called progressive magazines, as an expert on the "extreme right-wing." Berlet stumps for the division of anti-establishment rightists and leftists at a time when even Republicans see the "Democratic" President as "Bush Lite." His pooh-poohing of "conspiracy theories" serves to question government skeptics rather than the government itself. Even though he's a prolific contributor to leftist magazines, Berlet's passionate defenses of Janet Reno and Bill Clinton protect rather than "question authority." Targets of Berlet's smears and criticism include Daniel Sheehan of the Christic Institute, Daniel Brandt, whose NameBase software is a leading resource for tracking government misdeeds, and Ace Hayes, the prolific Portland-area researcher. Both Brandt and Hayes insist that Berlet's past associations seem to render him a chip off of John Foster Dulles' block. Hayes and Brandt contend that the true division in the country is not between left and right, but between up and down, the haves vs. the have-nots.

The wedge Berlet drives between left and right critics of the elite is exemplified in the treatment of a book written about the Trilateral Commission by leftist Holly Sklar. Acquiescing to Berlet's demands, Sklar denounces all readers of her book if they do not subscribe to crypto-Socialist theology. Berlet's ideological purification creates divisions between individuals thoughtful enough to glean knowledge from a book. A right-winger reading Sklar on Trilateralism might well empathize with Third World victims of the New Order economy. Similarly, a leftist reader of Carroll Quigley's *Tragedy and Hope*, purchased at a John Birch Society bookstore, might open his eyes to the many so-called liberal politicians who uphold Eastern Establishment elitism. Reading *Tragedy and Hope* seems particularly urgent in light of Bill Clinton's reference to Quigley as an ideological mentor in his Presidential acceptance speech.

A Berletian smear tactic against government critics was also taken up by Michael Kelly in his "Road to Paranoia"

(Continued on next page)

article featured in the June 19, 1995 issue of *The New Yorker*. Kelly tells us about a dangerous new trend that combines elements of both left and right into a variety of conspiracy theory he calls "fusion paranoia." I can speak of this phenomenon with some degree of depth, since Mr. Kelly includes my company, Feral House, in his short list of publishers ratcheting up the millennial perversity of "fusion paranoia." Kelly, like Berlet before him, implies that it is lunatic to come to the conclusion that a powerful minority of elitists direct the economy and other significant social trends to expand profits and power.

Imagine, Kelly sniffs, "fusion paranoids" say that Bush started the Gulf War for his own gain. The writer should have consulted an earlier issue of *The New Yorker* for a Seymour Hersh investigation that revealed the many millions of dollars received by President Bush, his sons and cabinet members as postwar tribute from Kuwait. He should have also examined a transcript of pre-war conversations between U.S. Ambassador to Iraq, April Glaspie, and Saddam Hussein, in which Glaspie declares that the U.S. would not involve itself in an Iraqi border dispute with Kuwait.

> "If the bombing of the Murrah building was a terrorist reprisal for Waco, why weren't ATF or FBI agents injured? How many ATF personnel took the day off? Why were Judge Alley and others warned by security officials about impending violence on April 19th? Who were these security officials?

The roots of "fusion paranoia" are firmly planted in the Iran-Contra affair, says Kelly, where both leftist and rightist conspiracy theorists believed the tale peddled by "liars" that a shadow government operated behind the scenes to negotiate a bombs-for-hostage deal with Iran. Kelly contends "fusion paranoids" are so deluded as to believe that George Bush personally flew to Paris to negotiate with Iranian representatives months prior to Reagan's inauguration.

Bush's itinerary for the days he allegedly spent in Paris are still missing from his diaries. According to erstwhile Israeli intelligence operative Ari Ben-Menashe, who helped set up the Iran-Contra negotiations on behalf of Israel, Bush was directly involved with the hostages-for-arms negotiations. This charge was seconded by Richard Brenneke, who was found innocent of charges brought against him by the U.S. government for backing Menashe's allegations. The deal had the Iranians holding the hostages until after Jimmy Carter lost re-election and the Republicans assumed power. The hostages were released the very day of Reagan's inauguration.

Will the Real Militiaman Please Stand Up?

Militias are largely a white and middle-class movement, and though the movement has been joined by Jews, Blacks,

Indians, and Asians, it is fair to estimate that at least 60% of militias are Christian, of which a much smaller percentage subscribe to Christian Identity beliefs, a minority sect of racialist Christians who think Anglo-Saxons are the original Israelites. The usurpation of Hebrew identity by the Christian right-wing is correctly identified as a threat to Jews, since Identity types believe Jews to be Satanic impostors. Unfortunately, the sensationalizing of Identity groups by watchdog organizations and their persecution by government authorities, have simply justified the Identity Christians' own paranoid and millennial beliefs. In my opinion, Identity Christians are best left alone in the same way adherents of Nation of Islam ideology are allowed to practice their own religion without the same level of harassment. Continued friction can only increase the likelihood of a volatile reaction.

Militias continue to grow as a response to the creeping internationalization of the economy, with the passage of international trade treaties such as GATT and NAFTA, which reward multinational corporations at the expense of domestic wages and employment. Squeezing the middle class with the highest per-capita tax burden while granting tax breaks and corporate welfare to large corporations, foreign and domestic, contributes to the perception that Bush and Clinton's New World Order rewards the multinational elite while giving the shaft to the working man.

Though it's been repeated a million times, there is no evidence that militias were involved in the Oklahoma bombing. While Timothy McVeigh and Terry Nichols were spotted at two militia functions as far apart as Florida and Michigan, we don't know if their presence was due to government infiltration, the use of doubles, or the result of two men's idle curiosity. McVeigh and Nichols were said to have spouted off about bombing buildings at a meeting of the Michigan militia, whereupon several militia members reported the terrible two to the FBI! Either these militia members were hip to the COINTELPRO tactic of *agents provocateurs*, or became so frightened by the potential violence that they ratted on supposed ideological allies to a government agency bent on the destruction of militias.

Although the establishment media has portrayed militia men as either paranoid gun-toting geeks or the current incarnation of Nazi-like evil, militia membership has sustained steady growth, even after the Oklahoma bombing. According to a militia leader who wishes to remain anonymous, "The bad publicity justifies all the bills they're trying to pass, but when the average American listens to what we're saying on the

(Continued on next page)

tube, it doesn't sound so unreasonable. To them, we look like their next door neighbor who helped them fix a flat. As a matter of fact, we ARE the guys who helped them change their tire. That makes an impression. And the phony politicians who come on with their Armani suits and say we're terrorists, it makes some people think that next week they might be the terrorists. TV brainwashes people, but no matter how they edit the tape, we're still the friendly neighbor with the car jack."

Charles Schumer (D-NY) would like to ban guns. Entirely. This has made him unpopular with gun owners, militias particularly. On July 10, 1995 Schumer held a press conference in which he put several government workers before microphones to tell the world about the inhuman conduct of militias. Much of the press conference consisted of recycled news about judges threatened by Montana racists (not militia members). A female county tax assessor told of being cut with a knife and threatened with a gun. Her assailants were said to be "tax protesters" — with apparently no connection to a militia organization. This distinction was lost on reporters, who dutifully told of the terrible behavior below wailing headlines ("WORKERS SPEAK OUT ON MILITIA BRUTALITY"). The news articles chided Republicans for failing to attend Schumer's show, suggesting their apparent appeasement of militia criminals.[6]

The FBI now claims that it has successfully infiltrated the militia movement. Militias, are, in fact, rife with slippery individuals like Linda Thompson, the subject of a full-length article I wrote for the October 11, 1994 edition of the *Village Voice*. In Spring '94 Thompson sent an "Ultimatum" to every member of Congress, demanding elimination of the IRS, Federal Reserve, Brady Gun law, several constitutional amendments and so on, announcing that as "Adjutant General" of the U.S. Militias she would come marching with guns and lynching rope on Washington D.C. on September 7, 1994, if Congress did not comply with her demands.

Thompson got a lot of attention for her efforts, but negligible support from militias themselves despite Thompson's self-adopted title of "Adjutant General." Frantic about Thompson's misleading stunt, militia-men called up her American Justice Federation computer bulletin board, posting messages about the "suicidal" nature of such a march. Thompson used the opportunity to divide the militia community, accusing nearly all extant leaders as being government agents, and insulting and inciting militiamen who revealed they weren't thrilled with the armed march concept. "Dickless coward" was a favorite comeback. Anyone who logged on to Thompson's bulletin board was compelled to complete an on-line questionnaire. How would they help the movement? With guns? Safe houses? Training? Although Thompson boasted that the FBI constantly monitored her board, she insisted that its users implicate themselves with possible charges of conspiracy or worse, by simply filling out these incriminating questionnaires.

Thompson canceled her notorious armed march after returning home in August '94 from the Arizona high desert, where she assisted the bizarre William Cooper[7] with a semi-

nar on the fine art of propaganda and long-range rifle sniping. In a public announcement, Thompson claimed the march was no more than a publicity stunt, but people should realize that even though it was canceled, the "war is on."

Perhaps Michael Kelly's "fusion paranoia" should not be dismissed too quickly. The phrase seems to accurately fit an individual by the name of Craig Hulet, aka KC dePass. In the late '80s, Hulet made the rounds, speaking on radio talk shows and appearing at seminars to disseminate information on executive orders known as "Rex '84," that would, in time of "emergency," turn the U.S. into a virtual police state and transform emptied military bases into concentration camps. One leg of the "Rex '84" plan has come to fruition: the closure of military bases. After his high-profile presence in the late '80s, Hulet dropped out of sight, particularly after articles appeared linking him to far-right or racist organizations. Hulet has again emerged, this time supplying screeds to the August, 1995 issue of *Soldier of Fortune*, in which he turns about-face from his former position to insult "conspiracists" (a neologism derived from Chip Berlet) and declaring there is no such thing as a "sinister" project emanating from an imperial elite.

Cui Bono, Oklahoma City?

Does it really matter who blew up the building in Oklahoma City? Such knowledge is only useful for purposes of punishment. History tells us to pay attention to the aftermath, not to the puny distractions of trials and culpability. What is in store for us?

At his first post-bomb press conference, Clinton swaggered to the podium, radiating anger and confidence. Clinton's hate rant, invoking the perpetrator's execution, garners the highest approval ratings of his term.

For the first time in memory, Clinton drops his I-feel-your-pain whine. His righteous anger reflects Mussolini-like vitality rather than his usual wan, comforting equivocations. Flying high in the polls, Clinton invokes a hostile "love it or leave it" refrain when Dianne Sawyer informs him that citizens are concerned about Waco. Later, in a Michigan speech, Clinton throttles non-establishment views of history as the "peddling of paranoia," a sowing of distrust in the benevolent institutions known as federal government. "You have the right to say what you please in this country," he explains, "but that doesn't give people the right to tear down this country."

News programs took Clinton's bait and started to report about "conspiracy theorists." With clear astonishment in his voice, *Dateline*'s Stone Philips tells us "some of the conspiracy theorists actually believe the U.S. government was responsible for the Oklahoma City explosion!" "Even worse," says Philips to the eye of the camera, "millions of Americans actually believe them." To demolish these Establishment-Deniers, *Dateline* interviews popularizers of three unlikely stories. Former FBI agent Ted Gunderson says that a four-pound aerially dropped "pineapple bomb" invented by

(Continued on next page)

Michael Riconosciuto of Iran-Contra fame is responsible for the blast. Another scenario features a sharp-featured computer expert, Debra Von Trapp, who tells us Oklahoma City was Japan's retribution for the Tokyo subway gassing, which was executed by the U.S. government as punishment for planting Japanese spies in the White House. The final "kook factor" was supplied by jailbird Ron Jackson, who produced an incoherent, typewritten document as "proof" of the government's involvement.

By offering only the most unlikely scenarios, *Dateline* delegitimizes every alternative reading of Oklahoma City. Never mind Gunderson, Von Trapp, and Jackson; the kookiest tale is currently being told by the FBI and presented to us in daily doses by compliant corporate scabs employed in establishment media. Why doesn't *Dateline* or any other news program ask the following questions?

- If the bombing of the Murrah building was a terrorist reprisal for Waco, why weren't ATF or FBI agents injured? How many ATF personnel took the day off? Why were Judge Alley and others warned by security officials about impending violence on April 19? Who were these security officials?

- By definition, a terrorist must take credit for violence, or else there is no compelling reason to commit his crime. The specific purpose of terrorism is to gain leverage on a specific political objective through the ability to threaten future terrorist acts. No one has claimed credit for the Oklahoma City bombing. Militia groups produced particularly vehement public statements condemning the crime.

- Was the Murrah building a warehouse for documents regarding the Branch Davidians? Are these documents missing? Will the missing papers affect Ramsey Clark's lawsuit against the ATF and FBI on behalf of the remaining Branch Davidian survivors?

- Why did the director of University of Oklahoma's Geological Survey, Dr. Charles Mankin, say that according to two different seismographic records, there were two blasts? Dr. Mankin reports that "the news media even reported two bomb lasts initially, but later changed their story."

- A pre-Oklahoma City bombing issue of *Soldier of Fortune* featured a James Pate article on Waco with a photograph of three ATF agents. One of these agents, the only agent unidentified, is the spitting image of Timothy McVeigh. Is this merely coincidental? Or was there a second "Timothy McVeigh" roaming the country, appearing at militia meetings? (The use of doubles is not a James Bond fantasy but an everyday aspect of intelligence work.)

- According to a *New York Times* chronology, Timothy McVeigh was one of the security personnel employed by the defense contractor CalSpan in Buffalo, New York. CalSpan, owned by the Fortune 500 company Arvin Industries, is actively involved in the research and development of microwave technology and telemetric devices for the Air Force. Telemetry can chart the location of individuals implanted with a microchip, or, quite possibly, send the telemetric device information by satellite. An executive for CalSpan told the *New York Times* that McVeigh was a model employee and that the company was disappointed that he "dropped out of sight," because they were planning to promote him. After McVeigh "dropped out of sight" from his security job at CalSpan, he began complaining that the government was "controlling his mind" through a microchip implanted in one of his buttocks.

- Who is John Doe #2? Why did the FBI entertain the possibility that he was a pre-pubescent relative of Terry Nichols, and yet profess no interest in a John Doe #2 photographed at the crime scene, and then rediscovered in Oklahoma City by the local television station KFOR?

- Retired USAF Brigadier General Benton K. Partin, a 25-year expert in the design and development of bombs and former commander of the Air Force Armament Technology Laboratory, urged Senators and Congressmen to delay destruction of the Murrah building crime site. Partin told the John Birch magazine, *The New American*: "When I first saw the picture of the truck bomb's asymmetrical damage to the federal building in Oklahoma, my immediate reaction was that the pattern of damage would have been technically impossible without supplementary demolition charges at some of the reinforced concrete bases inside the building — a standard demolition technique." Partin further explained that "reinforced concrete targets in large buildings are hard targets to blast. I know of no way possible to reproduce the apparent building damage through simply a truck bomb parked outside.... The evidence indicates there was an inside bomb effort." General Partin's request to examine the possibility of a second bomb in the concrete bases fell on deaf ears. The building was brought down on May 23. Researcher Alex Constantine tells me that Partin's information is suspect due to blaming the bomb on a peculiar coalition of "international leftists." Perhaps more troubling was Constantine's insistence that McVeigh's former employer, CalSpan, subcontracted the development and construction of mind control devices for the Air Force, where Partin was and perhaps still remains a major player.

- FBI agents were said to have tracked down McVeigh's truck rental agency by finding a vehicle identification number (VIN) on the truck's rear axle. This axle was found either in the bomb crater, according to Oklahoma City's Mayor, or three blocks away, if one is to believe the FBI. But there is another problem to the tale. No rear axle is imprinted with a vehicle identification number, even after recent legislation forcing manufacturers to place multiple VINs on the engine, firewall, and frame to discourage chop shops. When queried, a spokesman for Ryder told me that it does not imprint additional VINs on its trucks. The only conceivable number available on a rear axle is a part number, but a part number couldn't lead to the identification of a specific vehicle. Where did the VIN story come from? And why?

- Did McVeigh use a fake ID or a real one to rent the truck? The FBI tells us both versions.

(Continued on next page)

- If he committed such a heinous crime, why did Timothy McVeigh make the mistake of driving 81 miles per hour without a license, and why didn't he shoot the highway patrolman who stopped him?

- The story is told that Timothy McVeigh would have been released from jail on the day of his capture if he had produced sufficient bail money. Why couldn't he contact the Nichols brothers or other friends or family members to obtain bail? Why did he choose to stick around long enough for the sketch of John Doe #1 to reach his small town courthouse, resulting in his arrest for the Oklahoma City explosion?

- The FBI claims that Michael Fortier, McVeigh's friend from Kingman, revealed that he and McVeigh snooped around the Murrah building several days before the bombing, asking many people where BATF agents could be found. Why, then, did McVeigh bomb the building on the opposite side from the BATF offices?

- Why did Fortier tell CNN news on May 8 that "I do not believe Tim McVeigh blew up any building in Oklahoma"?

- U.S. Government Technical Manual No. 9-1910 from the Departments of the Army and Air Force, entitled *Military Explosives,* specifies that ANFO, the acronym for the ammonium nitrate and fuel oil bomb said to be used on the Murrah building, requires a greater than 99% purity of ammonium nitrate, as well as a specific dryness before it can be mixed with diesel fuel to create an explosive substance. The manual further spells out that even under ideal conditions (not often reached, even by experts) 4,800 pounds of ANFO explosive would create a much smaller crater than the one left in front of the Murrah building, and its shockwave could not possibly wield the force necessary to compromise the building's concrete supports.

- Accredited explosives experts (who wish to remain anonymous) agree that the explosion could have only been created with professional detonators and professional explosives. Such things are highly regulated in non-military use. The military is supposedly even stricter about its explosives inventory.

- If the explosion is too strong to have been created by 4,800 pounds of ANFO, if the explosive could only have been detonated by professional materials rather than bags of fertilizer, what sort of explosive was used, and why don't the FBI's public statements support the government's own manuals?

"Did the Murrah building warehouse documents regarding the Branch Davidians? Are these documents missing? Will the missing papers affect Ramsey Clark's suit against the ATF and FBI on behalf of the remaining Branch Davidian survivors?"

An American Reichstag?

Ridicule is an everyday event for researchers who have compared the Oklahoma City event to the burning of the Reichstag. Researcher Ace Hayes believes the Reichstag analogy is appropriate because its burning was the pivotal gambit that permitted the Nazis to unleash the emerging police state on political enemies prior to their total seizure of power.

The Reichstag, much more than a simple federal building in Oklahoma, was something of a sacred national symbol — though the current regime wants to live down its Nationalist mythology by allowing the Bulgarian artist Christo to toilet-wrap the monument under mylar for his personal profit. The burning of the nationally symbolic site spurred on the Nazis to characterize the attack as "terrorism." The Communists, early on accused by the Nazis of perpetrating the attack, produced their own conspiracy theories, turning the Nazi's accusation back on them. A supposedly dim-witted Dutch anarchist named Marinus van der Lubbe became the official "lone nut" terrorist. Even the popular Ballantine histories of the Second World War blame Van Der Lubbe for the attack, supporting neither Nazi nor Communist conspiracy theories.

The U.S. government likewise blames the destruction of a federal building on "terrorism" inspired by its most vocal opponents, the militias. American dissidents, far fewer in number and much less active or powerful than the Nazis' Communist opposition, generally believe that those in power had more to gain by the blast.

Whoever or whatever burned down the Reichstag, the Nazis seized the moment to beat, kill or imprison their political enemies. Hitler induced Hindenburg to sign a decree suspending German civil liberties. The Clinton Administration used the pretext of the Oklahoma City blast to unleash SWAT teams against militias and gun-owners in Michigan, Arizona, Montana and elsewhere, and in the process arrest and seize assets from dozens of anti-government dissidents for various crimes. Multi-jurisdictional Task Force attack teams terrorized communities in Ohio, Pennsylvania and other states in live-fire attacks against imaginary urban dissidents in abandoned buildings.

The most alarming comparisons of Oklahoma City to the Reichstag Fire can be found in newly-passed and newly-proposed legislation. Recent anti-crime and anti-terrorist bills have already eliminated or diminished portions of the U.S. Constitution's First, Second and Fourth amendments, and have dismantled the Posse Comitatus Act, which is supposed to prevent the use of military forces against American citi-

(Continued on next page)

zens. President Bush had already chipped away at Posse Comitatus by allowing the use of military weapons for the "War on Drugs." *Soldier of Fortune* correspondent James Pate discovered that the ATF lied in telling the army David Koresh was running a methamphetamine lab, in order to procure military training and weapons for its initial Waco raid. New anti-terrorist laws have loosened requirements, so that the ATF and other federal police agencies will not have to lie to obtain military training, personnel and materiel for their adventures.

The Executive Branch is now invested with the authority to declare any group or anyone it doesn't like as "terrorist." The terrorist designation amounts to immediate deportation, if a foreign national; or imprisonment, if a U.S. citizen persists in his or her belief. Private property can be seized at will, and there is no appeal process to the terrorist designation.

Sound bad? You ain't heard nothin' yet.

Currently proposed before congress, the "Domestic Insurgency Act of 1995 (HR-1544)," a bill sponsored by Gerald Nadler (D-NY), borrows from the "sample legislation" appended to an ADL scare report, as a legal method to snuff out the phenomenon of militias, which the ADL claims are nothing more than "racist, extreme right-wing hate groups." HR-1544 stipulates:

(a) Whoever knowingly participates in a paramilitary organization shall be fined under this title or imprisoned not more than 10 years, or both.

(b) As used in this section, the term 'paramilitary organization' means two or more individuals acting together, organized in a military or paramilitary structure, who knowingly —

(1) possess firearms, explosives, incendiary devices, or other weapons or techniques capable of causing injury or death to individuals.

(2) provide or participate in training in the use of any such weapons or techniques; with the intention that such weapons or techniques be used unlawfully to oppose the authority of the United States or of any State or for any other unlawful purpose.

Simply put, the "Domestic Insurgency Act" would clap citizens behind bars for ten years simply for observing the constitutional guarantees of free speech, the right to keep and bear arms, the right to wear goofy camouflage clothes, and the right to assemble. Unlawful intention is left for the federal law enforcement agencies to interpret. The definition of "paramilitary organization" is so open to interpretation that it could be used to imprison hunters, Boy Scouts, or attendees of a church picnic, as long as two or more picnickers held Swiss Army knives and discussed their gripes about the U.S. government.

If the ADL or Representative Nadler attempted to foist a "Domestic Insurgency Act" on the state of Israel, citizens would likely riot in the streets. Israeli nationals and settlers view weapons as their last protection against violent enemies.

In light of onerous legislation and continued militarization of domestic police forces, the comparison of Oklahoma City to the Reichstag Fire is perhaps not so far-fetched. There are, however, several important distinctions. Weimar and early National Socialist-period Communists actively expressed political distaste in street brawls, assassinations, riots, large political assemblies, destruction of property, even capture of German territory. By contrast, militias remain largely defensive, chartered to protest the erosion of constitutional rights. The militias' paramilitary flavor is as much a statement of serious intent as a threat to the government. Like the Black Panthers, militias feel empowered by their ability to own and train with weapons.

The question remains: at what point will the militias use their weapons?

Militias are sure to react as the government continues to overturn the Constitution, discarding the right to keep and bear arms, suffocating the right to free speech, or roping off the right to public assembly. If the rancid Domestic Insurgency Act targeting militias becomes law, the law's already-alarmed targets will surely react. But I can only hazard a guess. Militias are unsophisticated, easily misled by *agents provocateurs* scattered throughout the movement; the decentralization of militias makes it difficult for the government to monitor and control most or all of these groups at once.

The End of American Innocence?

Accompanying the news coverage of the Oklahoma City bombing were frequent and peculiar statements to the effect that America had lost its innocence. "It was an explosion of unimaginable magnitude," wailed a CNN anchorwoman. "You expect these kinds of things to happen in New York or Jerusalem, but Oklahoma? If this kind of thing can happen in Oklahoma, it can happen anywhere, anytime. This is the end of American innocence." And so on, *ad nauseam...*

Was America innocent of running black ops in Laos? Innocent of gifting smallpox blankets to Indians? Innocent of selling drugs for guns? Innocent of raking off a share of the world's misery? As Malcolm X said, "the chickens have come home to roost."

Media coverage of the Oklahoma City incident was maudlin in the extreme, a kind of flip-side of militia fetishism for the children killed at Waco.

Two weeks after the bombing, a beaming President Clinton donned a *yarmulke* at a meeting of the American Jewish Congress celebrating liquor tycoon Edgar Bronfman, a vastly powerful Zionist leader alleged to have numerous ties to organized crime. With great media fanfare, Bronfman's son had just purchased MCA, the Hollywood studio also long alleged to be tied to the mob. Clinton lauded Bronfman Sr., a Canadian version of the politically avaricious Joe Kennedy, as a paragon of virtue. He then announced to the assembled guests, with no suppressed glee, that he'd just

(Continued on next page)

decided to punish the "terrorist" state of Iran with economic sanctions in order to fight terrorism both here and abroad. Further, Clinton's domestic anti-terrorism legislation delivers the goods for Israeli hawks. Years after the King David Hotel was bombed by Menachem Begin's Irgun, killing many British soldiers and diplomats, the word "terrorist" has instead come to indicate any activist opposed to capitalism or Zionism. According to Western news organizations, capitalists or Zionists never commit terrorism or even vigilantism, they are instead characterized as "preserving the peace."

The perception of terrorism emanating from the Arab community plays well in Tel Aviv, rekindling hate vibes lying dormant since the Persian Gulf War. It was almost a *fait accompli* that "swarthy, middle-Eastern types" were initially fingered by FBI agents as responsible for the Oklahoma City bomb. They detained a Lebanese-American at Dallas airport several minutes before he was to fly to London, "forgetting" to search the Arab-American's bags, which then fly on to London. While the FBI imprisons their Arab suspect, not allowing him access to an attorney or relatives, his luggage arrives in London for Scotland Yard to rip open before news cameras. Without a shred of evidence to further detain him, U.S. officials release the Lebanese-American, who hops the red eye to London, whereupon Scotland Yard claps handcuffs on his wrists, and chains him to a door until another plane departs to Dallas, where the F.B.I. barks at him to keep close to home and not talk to anyone.

Militias: How Large a Threat?

As of mid-July, 1995, researchers have failed to uncover the smoking gun that implicates any government entity for the bomb blast. Without direct evidence, one must proceed cautiously in assigning blame to any party. That said, it's clear the government continues to withhold and even cover-up evidence: lame excuses accompany the destruction of the crime site... the relatives of three missing civilians need a death certificate to obtain insurance... psychiatrists say the crime scene must be destroyed to provide "closure" to Oklahoma City residents. But like the Branch Davidian compound, crucial evidence is forever destroyed or "lost." In this sense, the government bears comparison to a card sharp who blindfolds his competition. The sighted competitor will win every hand, but his winnings come at the expense of his credibility.

When Timothy McVeigh was fingered as the mastermind of Oklahoma City, a lynch mob bayed for the suspect's blood as he was exposed to the public, a standing target next to near-midget sized FBI men.

It may be advisable at this point to admit my own biases. I own two guns, purchased for self-defense. My political beliefs combine skepticism of authority tempered with libertarian-style economic self reliance. Unlike hardcore libertarians, I do not worship at the altar of a free market economy

for the simple reason that unlimited economic growth along with unchecked procreation seems incompatible with long-term survival of the species. I am more agnostic than Christian, though I appreciate much in the legacy of Christian music, art and architecture.

Why then do I feel compelled to defend the militia-man with his Manichaean conspiracies and apocalyptic dreams? Because quite simply, the Christian militia-man has become a scapegoat, a justification for intelligence agencies' headlong rush into technocratic dystopia, where every opinion voiced over the phone, modem and fax is evaluated, where every financial transaction is instantly monitored by computers operated by Fortune 500 and its omnipotent police force. Waco and Ruby Ridge are harbingers of this spin-controlled, 1984-like world in which paramilitary goons stage theatrical assaults against contentious targets to instill fear into dissidents or make a televised action picture whenever they need to pad their budget.

On the most pragmatic level, militia-men and their pea shooters are no match for electronic or subsonic "non-lethal" weaponry devised to put down civilian uprisings. Anti-gun propaganda has become so intense that all advocates of private gun ownership have become vulnerable to smear campaigns by skittish elements of the left who demand government protection from crib to coffin. Although the militia movement is supposed to take advantage of a Constitutional provision that states that all men between the ages of 18 and 45 not belonging to an organized militia shall be considered members of an "Unorganized Militia," the law was enacted in order to allow the government to draft citizens in a national emergency. Furthermore, many states have already banned private paramilitary organizations back in the 1930s, primarily as a strategy to control the Ku Klux Klan's extracurricular activities.

Alfred McCoy and others have published scholarly tomes linking U.S. intelligence with large-scale sales of opium and cocaine in order to fund illegal insurgent actions. While small elites within the U.S. military have become de facto dealers of tons of hard drugs that find their way to the streets of America, the Executive Branch makes a big show of eliminating the rights of citizens under the so-called War on Drugs. Similarly, the ever-increasing hysteria regarding militias translates into further onerous damage to the Constitution. Is it simply a coincidence that militias are largely composed of ex-military men, or do they know things that average ignorant citizens don't?

The government and media have characterized the Murrah explosion as unreconstructed terrorism. The word "terrorist" has been cultivated to create an emotional reaction, an unreasoning fear that provokes an instinctive reflex to provide the government with anything it asks for to rid the citizen of his fear. Society has consequently become frantic to do away with "suspicious" characters without due process. Communism no longer haunts post-Cold War America; consequently the federal police and intelligence agencies

(Continued on next page)

have become a bad parody of Stalin's NKVD or Honecker's Stasi.

Without an enemy, without terrorism, there would be no justification for police, no rationale for expanded police powers, no reason whatsoever to give into laws providing the police legal access to one's personal business, no possible justification for eviscerating the Posse Comitatus Act, designed to protect the citizenry from governmental attack by its own military.

Militia-men, correctly distrusting the establishment line, have not developed a nose for bad information, which once embraced, discredits the militia's entire plank of beliefs. For this reason, it is important for researchers to reveal the disinformation along with the good information. Only a fanatical adherence to truth can hope to change the face of political opportunism.

A Brief Career as Media "Expert"

James Ridgeway, the usual *Village Voice* staffer who covers right-wing phenomena, was caught by surprise when I submitted a query to his paper regarding a story on Linda Thompson and her ill-fated militia march. My query was accepted by the editors, despite Ridgeway's objection that the militia phenomena was a minor sociological burp, not worth the trouble of an article. Unfortunately, the Oklahoma City bombing and government scapegoating got in the way of Ridgeway's opinion. And so, six months after the article appeared in the October 11th issue of the *Voice*, my phone begins to ring. *New York Times*, *Washington Post*, Associated Press: Everyone wants a quote regarding militias and their possible involvement in the Oklahoma City bombing. I discover that the newspapers already had their quote formulated: they merely needed to attribute it to a so-called expert. "The militias — whoever the fuck they are" an addled staffer from the *Washington Post* tells me, "are a ticking time-bomb composed of paranoid lunatics." "Not quite," I object, giving him a more informed and balanced view of the topic. The journalists, unable to match my name to their pro-forma concepts, decide that perhaps I'm not worth quoting after all.

After the bomb, James Ridgeway starts covering the militias for the *Voice*, regurgitating information from SPLC, ADL and Klanwatch reports, using the bombing as a way to lay blame for the militia mentality on elements within the Republican Party. All the while a bipartisan Congress ushers in totalitarian crime laws, as well as a one hundred million-dollar a year raise for the BATF. And, while even the Treasury Department finds its men criminally culpable for events gone awry at Waco, Charles Schumer attacks a long-overdue congressional investigation as appeasement of the NRA and paranoid conspiracy theorists.

Endnotes

1. John B. Watson's turn-of the century attempt to turn mind control into a science.
2. See *Bread & Hyacinths: The Rise and Fall of Utopian Los Angeles* by Paul Greenstein, Nigey Lennon and Lionel Rolfe, California Classics Books, 1992.
3. According to armed forces spokesman Harvey Perrett III, the $3 billion/year program fields a black helicopter base in Fort Campbell, Kentucky. Sarah McClendon's enlightening interview with Perrett fairly demolishes the canard trumpeted by the press that black copters are the paranoid imaginings of all those extreme right-wing militias.
4. The ADL would love to do away with militias for perceived anti-Semitic overtones in militia conspiracy literature. This perception is at least partially due to Jewish oversensitivity. When a militia-man talks about international bankers, the ADL believes he is using code words to describe Jewish control of the monetary system. If a militia man criticizes specific congressmen who also happen to be Jewish for attempting to do away with the Second Amendment, this is again taken as anti-Semitism. The presumption of anti-Semitism in the militia movement is overstated, especially when a number of Jewish libertarians, including Jews for the Preservation of Firearms Ownership, are movers and shakers within the militia movement. The JPFO has tried to engage the ADL in a debate, to no apparent success. The group is critical of both the ADL and gun control measures because it believes genocide becomes practicable after the general confiscation of firearms.
5. Director Morris Dees boasts of having files on more than 14,000 "populists."
6. Schumer apparently had no interest in the threats, dead animals, or obscene effigies sent to conservative Congressmen, since these activities weren't the province of militias, but of DOJ-protected activists protesting for abortion and gay rights.
7. Linda Thompson's championing of William Cooper at the expense of every other militia member or leader is peculiar, to say the least. In his magnum opus, *Behold a Pale Horse*, Cooper reprints the hoax document "Protocols of the Learned Elders of Zion," stipulating that readers should change the word Jew to "Illuminati."●

"Oklahoma City: Cui Bono?" by Adam Parfrey first appeared in *Prevailing Winds Magazine*, Number 2, ©1995. Send $5.00 for a sample copy to:

Prevailing Winds
PO Box 23511
Santa Barbara, CA 93121

TOP TEN REASONS TO WRITE-IN UNABOMBER FOR PRESIDENT IN 1996
All you have to lose is the Political Illusion
by Lynn Eccles

① **THE ALTERNATIVES.** Clinton, Dole, Buchanan. Moderate republican, right-wing republican, or Fascist? You have the right to vote right. And the right to silence. But isn't it incriminating?

② **HE'S HOT.** His favorability ratings may be low, but his name recognition is close to 100%. We don't need to hype him — he's already hyped. A Unabomber write-in campaign surfs the media wave. (And the trial may be The Big One.) He's the perfect imposter to undermine the presidential election process as it unfolds, and turn the fraudulent election process against itself.

③ **THE VISION THING.** "The Industrial Revolution and its consequences have been a disaster for the human race." Regardless of what you think of the Unabomber and his analysis, the right issues are finally raised. Can you even conceive of any legitimate candidacy, election, or debate which will allow the real questions to be put on the table? We need to dish them out before they cool off... They're giving an election, but we're crashing it and having our own referendum on corpo-technocracy. If the Unabomber put a hairline crack in the myth of progress, we are applying a wedge, and we'll pound on it right up to election day. An anti-technological rallying point was born of a criminal chase with high entertainment value. Is there going to be another opportunity to declare your independence from Western Civilization?

④ **WAITING FOR PEROT?** The election offers a "choice" once all the real decisions have been made. On top of being an anti-republicrat vote, the Unabomber campaign is a counterfoil to faux "populist" outsider-insiders like business magnate Ross Perot and Gulf warrior Colin Powell (a.k.a. the military-industrial complex). The third party "alternative" is designed to safely channel voter alienation into a centrist, media-sanctioned agenda and immunize the system against real change.

⑤ **IF ELECTED HE WILL NOT SERVE.** So it's a nobody-for-president vote. He's not running, so it's a bottom-up free-for-all campaign. Campaign literature, posters, sound bytes, platforms, pranks, the rest: have it your way.

⑥ **DON'T WASTE YOUR VOTE.** The media's like a psychiatrist — and you can't NOT communicate in an election. If you boycott the polls, you'll be counted as apathetic, complacent, or still worse, contented. If you vote for the mainstream lesser of evils, who don't actually represent your views, you've affirmed the political system and buried your voice. Either way you've wasted your vote. To vote Unabomber is to vote and boycott at the same time. If nothing else, it's a vote against the election charade. It can be only seen as absolute protest, ridicule, or a "none-of-the-above" spurning of the political menu. You can cast an anarchist vote you feel good about, and send the message that the presidential elections are a fraud. And you can still vote in local races and referendums where your vote counts for something.

⑦ **VOTE AGAINST THE PROPAGANDA MACHINE.** The Unabomber did an end run around the media monopoly, and published without editorial clearance. The Unabomber has, by the magnitude of his plan, exposed the media as a closed communications system, making it clear — in case anyone hadn't noticed — that it's a communications war. Mass media are launched from a heavily-secured fortress. Other terrorists seek publicity as a means to other ends. The Unabomber waged a guerrilla campaign to communicate as an end in itself. Notice how the press seeks to channel interpretation of the Unabomber story, covering it as a serial-killer story of crime and insanity, while excluding consideration of the ideas themselves. They would have us believe that it would be disastrous if media weren't controlled from the top. Op-ed pages resounded with journalists lamenting, "Why didn't he have to get editorial approval? What if copy cats are aroused, crazies who actually want access to the media, rather than simply being passive target markets for political and commercial propaganda?" Imagine mass communications not subject to corporate control. People might say anything... even things not "fit to print." Exactly. When ABC Nightly News gets renamed Disney World, you'll cherish the memory of your Unabomber vote.

⑧ **HE'S GOT THE CREDENTIALS.** The Unabomber's use of violence should not disqualify him from consideration. His willingness and ability to effectively use violence to achieve strategic political goals merely demonstrate the essential qualifications to be president. After all, Colin Powell's ONLY qualification is his performance as an effective killer. No one's called him a serial killer, or said he craved attention. No running candidate has condemned the Gulf War genocide. This is a country that played war like a video game in a high-tech funhouse. We aren't even allowed information as to home many Iraqis, civilian or military, our tax dollars blew away. That Bill Clinton dodged the draft almost disqualified him. Luckily he picked up points for presiding over executions in his home state of Arkansas, including the execution of a retarded man. Dole's war experience gave him the right stuff... Violence? Cancer deaths caused by toxins in the air, in food, and workplaces... Violence? A minimum wage that is half the poverty level, with the hunger, stress, disease and early death that ensue... Violence? The media just finished re-elaborating the rationale for bombing Hiroshima and Nagasaki... Violence? Terror? Anyone bringing up violence should put it all on the table, not just select attacks on the power structure. Anyone who can truly take a stand against violence in any form — and that would include the American Revolution — can say the Unabomber shouldn't be president on that basis. But he's not running anyway, and even a landslide wouldn't actually put him in office. The beauty of voting for an ineligible candidate is that personality issues are moot. We're voting Unabomber, not Kaczinksi, although Ted may turn out to be Thoreau with a bomb, engaging in military disobedience. And give a little credit to an ex-teacher who may have recruited the FBI to Anarchy 101 and assigned a required reading list of subculture rants.

⑨ **ENTERTAINMENT VALUE.** Watch your favorite TV pundits try to swallow, digest and regurgitate a Unabomber constituency. It's a message that can only be censored — not neutralized, coopted or explained away. The most minimal Unabomber returns will disrupt the usual discussion of false problems and false solutions (usually known as "reform").

⑩ **DON'T BLAME ME — I VOTED FOR THE UNABOMBER.** You can sport your bumper sticker after the election.(but not on a car). But only if we don't win.

Reprinted from SNUFF IT #3, The Journal of The Church of Euthenasia. Send $2.00 for a sample issue to : The Church of Euthenasia, PO Box 261, Somerville, MA 02143. e-mail: coe@net.com.com

www:http://www.envirolink.org/ogrs/coe
www:http://www.paranoia.com/unapack/

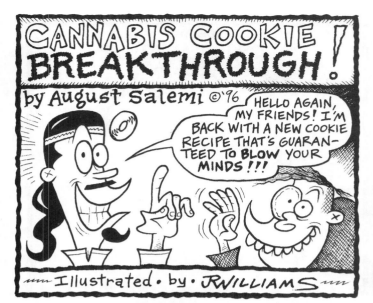

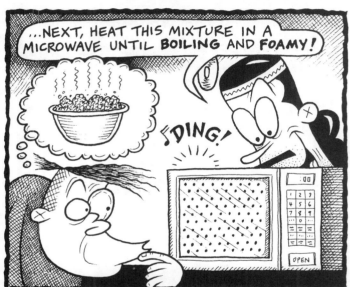

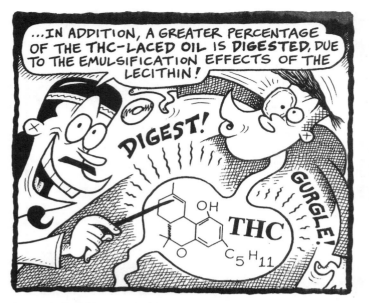

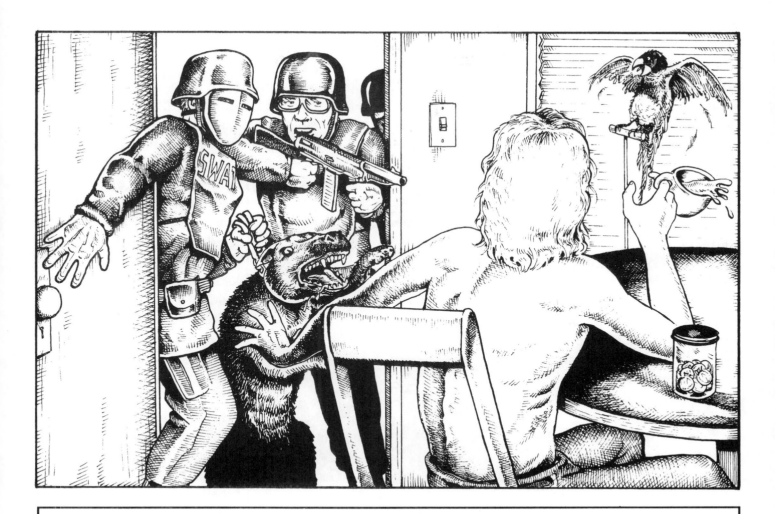

WAY BENEATH THE UNDERGROUND
By Donald B. Parker
Illustration by Nick Bougas

Jim Hogshire is on the lam.

The highly regarded Loompanics Unlimited author (creator of *Opium for the Masses*, *Sell Yourself to Science*, and *You Are Going to Prison*) and editor of the pharmaceutical-capsule-enthusiast zine *Pills-a-Go-Go* has gotten out of Dodge, or in this case, Seattle. Instead of working comfortably in his Capitol Hill digs while imbibing his favorite tea and communing with his small aviary of exotic birds, Hogshire has been reduced to living out a low-rent version of *The Fugitive*.

Now Hogshire rambles from city to city, sleeping on friends' floors and staying as incom-municado as possible. He keeps in touch with his associates via furtive long-distance phone calls from noisy bars and roadside telephone booths, and receives mail through second and third parties. "I'm broke, and I'm fucked up," Hogshire states in a late-night exchange, as the sounds of drunken revelry crash and tinkle in the background. "I don't have anyplace to live, and I'm unable to write under these circumstances. There are serious charges hanging over my head. And I owe it all to Bob Black, goddamn his snitchy soul to hell."

(Continued on next page)

Hogshire's spouse, Heidi Hogshire, is equally bereft, although she hasn't yet left Seattle for parts unknown. That's because she had to stay behind and face the music. And the tune at hand was being played by Seattle's King County Prosecutor's Office, which has made a concerted effort to make life miserable for the Hogshires. They were charged with trumped-up offenses that could have netted them years of jail time — and, in Jim's case, still could.

Why? That's a long and disheartening story. It's a tale of two anti-establishment scribes, and their contentious disagreement. Anger, jealousy, lust, a monomaniacal urge for revenge — this pistle has got it all.

Enter Bob Black. Make that Robert C. "Bob" Black, a writer of some repute in certain circles, and author of Loompanics Unlimited's *The Abolition of Work*, as well as other tracts generally referred to as anarchistic in tone. Black has long been a favorite of Loompanics Unlimited's founder and president Mike Hoy, who has published many of the angry not-so-young man's diatribes in his company's catalogs and supplements.

When *Curio* magazine, a fledgling publication based in New York state, decided to retain Black to craft an article about Loompanics Unlimited in early 1996, Hoy was excited, anticipating a stimulating exchange when Black came to visit. In order to purchase the most economical airplane ticket possible, Black opted to stay a few extra days in Seattle en route to Port Townsend, Washington, Loompanics Unlimited's home. He mailed a plea to his counter-culture confederates, seeking a free spot to

Robert C. "Bob" Black: Anarchist... or "Citizen Informant"?

squat. "Does anybody want to host me in Seattle for a day or two?" Black entreated. "Or at least amuse me there?"

Hoy, in an effort to accommodate Black's request, provided him with Hogshire's phone number, suggesting that they might have a few things in common. The two subversive scriveners chatted at length, and Hogshire offered Black a place to sleep for a few nights. "That was probably the biggest single mistake of my adult life," Hogshire says today. "And that's putting it mildly."

So, on Saturday, February 10, 1996, Black arrived at Seattle's Sea-Tac Airport in mid-afternoon, where he was met by Heidi Hogshire. "He'd been drinking 'nippers,' those little bottles you get aboard airplanes, when I picked him up," she recalls.

Heidi drove Black into the city. At the Hogshires' apartment, he was introduced to his just-awakened host, and their discourse began. The three talked for several hours, and there are conflicting versions of what transpired. "Right off, Black made a beer run to the corner grocery," Heidi says. "He bought a six-pack of tall boys, and a 40-ouncer."

According to the Hogshires, Black rapidly became inebriated, imbibing a sizable quantity of beer and becoming loud and quarrelsome. They claim that he removed his shoes, "stinking up our apartment." When they offered him some potato chips, they state, Black shocked them by wiping his greasy hands on their furniture's upholstery. While Black was visiting the bathroom, they decided to ask him to leave.

(Continued on next page)

Black tells another story. He writes, in his self-produced pamphlet *My Date with Jim Hogshire*, that Hogshire was drug-addled, long-winded, and argumentative. Black alludes to Heidi as "flirtatious" and a "slave-girl," and derides the Hogshires as "declassed bourgeoisie." He claims that Hogshire referred to himself as an Islamic fundamentalist, labels him "anti-Semitic," and characterizes him as "a poseur getting back at his parents."

Black smugly asserts that Hogshire made the fatal mistake of arguing with him. "He drew me into an argument about religion (the last thing I was up for discussing) and lost," Black writes, "as has everyone who has ever argued with me. Pardon my pride, but it's just fact. If you don't want to lose an argument with me, don't start one." Pleading jet lag, Black avouches that he wanted to go to sleep, but contends that Hogshire continued to argue with him and finally lost his temper, suddenly ordering Black out of the apartment.

Here is where the accounts differ greatly. The Hogshires claim that Black had become steadily more verbally abusive, worked himself into a drunken rage, and refused to leave. "I'd had enough," Jim says. He walked to a closet, and grabbed an M-1 rifle. At this point, claim the Hogshires, Black attacked Jim from behind, ripping his shirt. The diminutive Heidi pulled at Black, trying to free Jim from his grasp. The two men fell to the floor, scuffling.

Jim got to his feet and, still clutching the rifle, left the apartment to ask an upstairs neighbor for help in dealing with Black. Heidi extended her hand to Black, she says, offering to help him to his feet. "That was an error in judgment," she admits. "He lurched to his feet, and seized me from behind. Then Black put his hands around my neck, and started strangling me."

According to Heidi, that wasn't all. "Black was choking me, but every so often he'd release one of his hands and feel my breasts," she says. "And he was pressing his groin against my behind, sort of dry-humping me. I tried to cry out, but he was squeezing my throat so hard that I couldn't."

Hogshire heard the sounds of the struggle, and re-entered the apartment. "I told him, 'Bob, let her go!'" Hogshire states. "He wouldn't, and I trained the rifle on him. 'She's my hostage!' he shouted, positioning Heidi as a human shield. 'You'll have to shoot her to get me!' I pounded the gun barrel against the ceiling, trying to get our neighbor's attention. Eventually, Black let go of Heidi, and sat down."

Soon, say the Hogshires, Chris, the upstairs neighbor, arrived, asking what was wrong. "By this time," says Heidi, "Black was sitting there drinking a beer as if nothing had happened! We explained the situation to Chris, and he told Black, 'Guy, you're going to have to leave.' Black seemed to take Chris seriously, and stood up. I packed his empties into a sack and put them into his backpack, and Jim and Chris walked him downstairs to the gate. As he left, Black told us, 'You'll get yours! I'll be in touch!'"

Black's version puts a different spin on the story. "In the middle of the night, I was ordered out of Hogshire's apartment into an unfamiliar area of an unfamiliar city 3000 miles from my home," he writes. "I had no choice but to go, but I couldn't pack my bags fast enough... The fanatic frenzied junkie aimed his M-1 at me."

According to Black, he "turned the tables on the Muslim maniac. You know how the towel-heads are always taking Westerners hostage? I took one of *them* hostage. When Jim pointed his rifle at me, I grabbed Heidi as a human shield."

Luckily, whatever happened, no one was killed or seriously injured. Black eventually released Heidi and left the apartment, and by one a.m. was trudging the quiet back streets of Capitol Hill with his backpack full of empty beer cans. After a futile attempt to rouse an acquaintance and arrange for free emergency lodgings, Black checked into a motel and slumbered. The

(Continued on next page)

Hogshires called the Seattle Police and reported the incident as an assault.

The fallout was immediate. Upon hearing the Hogshires' report of their evening with Black, Hoy canceled the interview. Black returned to New York muttering vague threats of journalistic requital. "I came here to write a story," he told Hoy. "Instead, it appears that I've got two."

Back at his apartment in Albany, New York, Black's thoughts turned to revenge. First, he wrote a letter to the Hogshires' landlord, suggesting that they be evicted for drug-related activities. Then, on February 21, Black wrote a letter to the Seattle Police Narcotics Division, asserting that the Hogshires were operating a drug laboratory in their apartment, claiming that Hogshire had bragged of knowing how to manufacture heroin from Sudafed(!), and calling the police's attention to Hogshire's book about opium and his involvement with a magazine about drugs. Black enclosed copies of portions of *Opium for the Masses* that he felt were germane to establishing Hogshire's penchant for drug use, and closed his letter with a warning that the Hogshires were armed (and presumably dangerous).

Although the Seattle Police had ignored the Hogshires' report of Black's assault against Heidi, Black's letter generated a rapid response. Seattle Police Detective Robert Howard contacted Black, spoke with him by phone, and gathered additional information. Howard then filed an affidavit (in which he acknowledged Black as a "Citizen Informant") for a search warrant, which was quickly issued.

On March 6, in the early evening, Black's retaliatory efforts bore fruit. Hogshire, sitting at home with his nose in a book, was jarred from his reveries as a Seattle SWAT team kicked in the door, weapons drawn, screaming "Down on the floor! Now! Don't make a move, or you're dead meat!" A swarm of cops, clad in "black ninja outfits," burst into Hogshire's apartment, roughly handcuffing him and ransacking his belongings. They seized the Hogshires' books,

tax records, and numerous other effects, including an array of legally registered firearms. The Seattle Police also impounded a small bunch of dried opium poppy pods, recently purchased from a florist, as well as a thermite grenade which Hogshire had acquired at a gun show.

"One of the cops even stole a hundred dollars from my bankroll," Hogshire says. "They broke out a window, dumped the contents of our drawers and cupboards on the floor, and managed to set a section of our sofa on fire. They had a drug dog with them that they called 'Powder.' The cops and their canine sidekick didn't find a thing, other than legally obtained poppies, but they kept up a steady stream of innuendoes and invectives. One of them asked me, 'With what you write, weren't you expecting this to happen?'"

Heidi, returning home from work, was also handcuffed. Both she and Jim were arrested and taken to the King County Jail, where they were soon arraigned and charged with possession, with intent to manufacture or distribute, opium poppies. Friends and relatives arranged for bail, and the Hogshires hired an attorney.

Black's conniving canard didn't end there. The Hogshires' landlord, at the encouragement of the Seattle Police, served them with an eviction notice. Soon, the Hogshires were both homeless and fundless in Seattle, as their legal expenses soared. They moved into a sympathetic couple's basement, waiting for their court appearances and wondering what would become of their lives.

For some reason, the prosecutors seemed to be highly incensed about Hogshire's writings, attempting to introduce them into evidence as part of their ludicrous case against the hapless scribe. In a city where crack cocaine and heroin are readily available on many downtown corners, the brunt of the law was brought to bear against Hogshire for his literary efforts. Assistant prosecutor James Rogers ranted in

(Continued on next page)

King County Superior Court that Hogshire was a danger to society who should be taken to task because of the nature of his writings.

Fortunately, Judge Ricardo Martinez didn't see it that way. He dismissed the charges against Hogshire without prejudice on April 23, pointing out that "my mother has poppies like these growing in her garden," and chastising the prosecution for trying to introduce irrelevant evidence. Heidi, however, didn't fare as well. The charges against her were carried over, as the prosecution threatened to refile their absurd charges against Jim, and tried to leverage him into copping a plea.

Broke, distracted from his writing, fearful of being rearrested and leery of police harassment, Hogshire left Seattle for an undisclosed destination. Heidi stayed behind, waiting for her day in court, and unable to work until her legal difficulties were resolved. On June 20, Judge Martinez dismissed the charges against her with prejudice, meaning that the prosecution will be unable to refile them. Hogshire, however, was charged with possession of opium poppies and possession of an explosive device (the thermite grenade). If convicted, he could be sentenced to up to two years behind bars.

Black, meanwhile, is certain that his efforts to destroy the Hogshires' lives will be successful. "If Poppy Boy (his sobriquet for Hogshire) doesn't cop a plea, he's going to jail on felony charges," he crowed in a letter to Adam Parfrey of Feral House, another of Black's publishers. "And I guarantee that this jerk who nearly killed me will go down."

Au contraire, responds Stephan Illa, Hogshire's attorney. "I've found that one way to evaluate charges is to look at who's making them," he points out. "Black's story makes no sense."

Hoy, incensed by the whole affair, plans to drop *The Abolition of Work* from Loompanics Unlimited's inventory. Feral House has remaindered *Beneath the Underground*, a work of Black's they published in the past, and Parfrey is donating the proceeds to the James Hogshire Defense Fund. It remains to be seen how this debacle will ultimately be resolved, but for now...

Jim Hogshire is still on the lam.

Since this article was published in 1996, all drug charges were dropped against Jim Hogshire, and he was fined $100 and sentenced to perform 100 hours of community service for possessing a thermite flare. Hogshire now lives in New York City, where he works as a free-lance writer. He wishes to thank all of the many supporters who contributed funds, help, and good wishes while he was on the lam.

HOGSHIRE, JAMES FREDERICK

AKAs:

CCN:	**1684311**	DOB:	04/03/58
Sex:	MALE	Race:	WHITE
Eyes:	GRAY	Weight:	150

Orignal Charge:	Dangerous Drugs
Illness/Injury:	NONE.

Operational Alert:	NONE.

Book 'im, Danno! Jim Hogshire, shortly after being jailed by the Seattle Police.

February 21, 1996

Seattle Police Department
Narcotics Division
610 Third Street
Seattle WA

Dear Sirs:

I am writing to inform you of a drug laboratory I learned of
during a recent visit to Seattle. It is located in the apartment
of Jim Hogshire and Heidi Faust Hogshire, 616 Bellevue East -- the
number is, if I recall, #27.

The Hogshires are addicted to opium, which they consume as tea and
by smoking. In a few hours on February 10/11 I saw Jim Hogshire
drink several quarts of the tea, and his wife smaller amounts.
He also took Dexedrine and Ritalin several times. They have
a vacuum pump and other drug-manufacturing tech. Hogshire
told me he was working out a way to manufacture heroin from
Sudafed.

Hogshire is the author of the book Opium for the Masses which
explains how to grow opium and how to produce it from the fresh
plant or from seeds obtainable from artist-supply stores. His
own consumption is so huge that he must be growing it somewhere.
I enclose a copy of parts of his book. He also publishes a
magazine Pills a Go Go under an alias promoting the fraudulent acquisition
and recreational consumption of controlled drugs.

Should you ever pay the Hogshires a visit, you should know that
they keep an M-1 rifle leaning against the wall near the computer.

Sincerely,

Robert C. Black

*"Citizen Informant" Robert C. "Bob" Black's
letter of disinformation to the Seattle Police.*

CONDOM TRACE EVIDENCE

A New Factor in Sexual Assault Investigations
by Robert D. Blackledge, M.S.

I n an age filled with potentially fatal sexually transmitted diseases, more and more individuals practice safe sex. Even perpetrators of sex crimes have begun to wear condoms.[1] It is not likely that a fear of disease prompts this behavior. Rather, just as a burglar dons gloves to avoid leaving fingerprints, sexual offenders now wear condoms to avoid depositing seminal fluids.

Forensic experts typically identify sexual assault offenders by examining seminal fluid residues for sperm, proteins, blood grouping factors, and DNA profile. When sexual assailants use condoms, however, assuming no leaks or spills, this valuable evidence gets trapped inside the condom, which investigators may never recover. The same can be said for any traces from the victim—including vaginal cells, blood, and saliva—that otherwise might have been transferred to the assailant's penis. Nevertheless, when assailants use condoms, they leave behind other valuable evidence.

TYPES OF CONDOM TRACE EVIDENCE

Manufacturers produce condoms using a variety of materials, both natural and synthetic. Each manufacturer has its own formula, which may vary even among its different brands.

Some condoms are made from lamb membranes, and one manufacturer recently introduced a model made from polyurethane plastic. Still, latex rubber condoms have, by far, the largest share of the market, perhaps because they cost considerably less. In addition to the basic materials they use to produce condoms, manufacturers also add other substances, known as exchangeable traces, which comprise particulates, lubricants, and spermicide.

Particulates

Condom manufacturers add finely powdered particulates to prevent a rolled-up latex condom from sticking to itself. Particulates found in different brands include corn starch, potato starch, lycopodium (a powder found in plants), as well as amorphous silica, talc, or other minerals. In the laboratory, forensic scientists use several different techniques to characterize these particles and compare them with those obtained from other condom brands.

Lubricants

Sexual assailants prefer lubricated condoms, probably for the same reason that they use petroleum jelly, that is, to facilitate their crimes.[2] Many condom brands contain a liquid lubricant, which may be classified as either "wet" or "dry."

Both types of condom lubricant have an oil-like consistency, but wet lubricants are water-based and/or water-soluble, while dry lubricants are not. Although many different manufacturers use the same dry lubricant, their viscosity grades sometimes differ. The forensic laboratory can recover these silicone oils easily from items of evidence and possibly associate them with a condom manufacturer.

Wet lubricants may contain either polyethylene glycol or a gel made from a combination of ingredients similar to those found in vaginal lubricants. Despite similarities to other products on the market, forensic examination can associate specific formulations with particular condom brands.

Spermicide

Both wet- and dry-lubricated condoms also may contain the spermicide nonoxynol-9. Its recovery and detection, along with lubricant ingredients and particulates, can help show condom use and indicate the specific brand.

THE VALUE OF CONDOM TRACE EVIDENCE

Condom trace evidence can assist investigators in several ways. It can help prove corpus delicti, provide evidence of penetration, produce associative evidence, and link the acts of serial rapists.

In Proving Corpus Delicti

Traces associated with condoms can help prove corpus delicti, the fact that a crime has occurred. This evidence can support the claims of either the victim or the accused. For example, the U.S. military can prosecute personnel diagnosed as HIV-positive for aggravated assault if they engage in unprotected sex, even if it is consensual. If service men accused of aggravated assault claim that they did in fact wear a condom but it broke or slipped off, condom trace evidence can support that claim.

In Providing Evidence of Penetration

Condom traces found inside a victim can provide evidence of penetration. In many jurisdictions, this evidence raises the charge to a higher degree of sexual assault.

In Producing Associative Evidence

Recovered condom traces may correspond to those found in a certain brand or used by a certain manufacturer. An empty packet of this particular brand found near the crime scene, especially if it bears the suspect's fingerprints, provides a strong association between the suspect and the crime. Unopened condom packages of this same brand found on the suspect, in his car, or at his residence also would help tie the suspect to the crime.

In Linking the Acts of Serial Rapists

People tend to be creatures of habit, and sexual criminals are no exception. A serial rapist likely will use the same brand of condom to commit repeated acts. Moreover, repeat offenders whose DNA profiles have been stored in a computer data bank may be likely to use a condom when committing subsequent crimes. Along with other aspects of his modus operandi, traces from the same condom brand or manufacturer found during several different investigations can help connect a suspect to an entire series of assaults.

GUIDELINES FOR EVIDENCE COLLECTION

Investigators need not make any drastic changes in their usual procedures in order to include the possibility of condom trace evidence. The following guidelines will assist criminal investigators and medical examiners when collecting this valuable evidence.[3]

At the Crime Scene

First and foremost, investigators must wear *powder-free* gloves to protect themselves from bloodborne pathogens and to avoid leaving particulates that may be similar to those contained in some condom brands. After collecting the evidence, they should package the gloves separately and submit them with the evidence so that the forensic laboratory can verify that the gloves did not leave behind any particulates.

At the crime scene, investigators should make every effort to locate any used condom and its foil package. If a condom is recovered, the traces from the victim on the outside and the seminal fluids from the assailant on the inside would have the greatest evidentiary value.

> " ... investigators ...must remember to list condoms on the warrant obtained to search the suspect's possessions. "

If investigators find an empty condom packet, they first should try to recover any latent prints from the outside. The inside of the package probably will not contain prints, but may contain lubricant, spermicide, and particulate residues. Investigators should wipe the inside with a clean cotton swab. The traces on this swab will serve as the standard for comparison with traces recovered from the victim and the suspect.

During Medical Examinations

Examination Kits

Most commercial sexual assault examination kits provide two cotton swabs for each type of examination, i.e., vaginal, penile, etc. In the past, before assailants began using condoms frequently, these two swabs proved adequate—one swab for immediate examination and a second in case the defense team requested another examination by its own experts or by an independent laboratory. With sexual offender's using condoms, however, forensic laboratories should use three swabs: One to save for the defense and two to conduct examinations.

With the potential for positively identifying a suspect, most laboratories first look for traces of seminal fluids, vaginal cells, blood, and the like. Unfortunately, the solvents used to conduct this examination also remove any condom traces present, thus losing potentially valuable evidence. Although examiners feasibly could divide each swab in half, providing an additional swab in kits for each condom trace examination easily could solve the problem.

The gloves provided in commercial examination kits usually come powder-free. However, the medical personnel who examine sexual offenders and their victims frequently prefer the gloves they normally wear, which often contain the same powders (corn starch, amorphous silica, and talc) found on many condom brands. While medical staff members may insist that their collection procedures are above reproach, forensic examiners cannot guarantee the integrity of the condom trace evidence if the medical staff wears their own gloves. In short, investigators must persuade examining personnel to wear unpowdered gloves.

After the medical examinations, investigators should recover and separately package the used gloves. The forensic laboratory then can confirm that the gloves were powder-free.

Examination of Victims

Victims of sexual assault may feel ashamed and may not want to disclose some of the more personal details of the crime. Although investigators should make every effort to spare victims any unnecessary discomfort or embarrassment, they must ensure a thorough investigation. This may mean asking victims embarrassing questions and then making sure that medical examiners obtain samples from any area of the victim's body where evidence may exist, including the vagina, the mouth, and the anus.

In addition to collecting traces from inside the victim's vagina, medical examiners should swab the external genitalia. Traces of water-soluble condom lubricants may have been absorbed or lost, and as a result, any traces found internally may be at a very low level. Thus, if the victim has not showered or bathed, swabs may recover undiluted traces present on the external genitalia. Although these traces would not indicate penetration, they at least would support the victim's assertion that sexual contact took place.

Moistening each swab with a few drops of isopropyl alcohol helps recover traces from external genitalia. To create control swabs for the forensic laboratory, investigators should moisten two unused swabs, allow them to air-dry, and then package them with the evidence. Examining these control swabs will confirm that any traces found on the victim did not come from the cotton swabs or the alcohol.

At the lab, forensic experts first examine the victim's swabs. If these swabs are negative for seminal fluids but show traces of condom evidence, examiners would then look for the same traces on the suspect's swabs.

Examination of Suspects

If investigators identify and arrest a suspect only a few hours

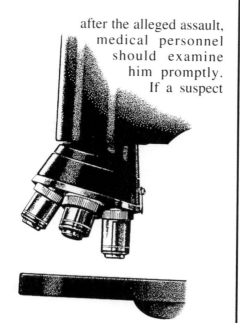

after the alleged assault, medical personnel should examine him promptly. If a suspect has not washed his penis, identifiable traces (either from a condom or from the victim) may be present.

Examiners should moisten two swabs with two drops of isopropyl alcohol, then wipe the penis from the base to the tip. As they did when collecting evidence from the victim, examiners should prepare two control swabs.

INTERVIEWS

With the Victim

In addition to providing general information about the crime, victims may be able to supply valuable details about the condom and its wrapper. They may recall the brand itself or other important details, including the condom's color, shape, texture, odor, taste, and lubrication.

After obtaining facts about the condom, investigators should ask victims about their sexual and hygienic habits, which might account for traces not attributable to the crime. A comprehensive interview would include the following questions:

- Has the victim recently engaged in consensual sex?
- If so, was a condom used? A vaginal lubricant? What brands?
- Does the victim use any external or internal vaginal products (anti-itch medications, deodorants, douches, suppositories, etc.)?
- If so, what brands?

These questions assume an adult female victim. Investigators must modify the interview to accommodate male or child sexual assault victims.

"...just as a burglar dons gloves to avoid leaving fingerprints, sexual offenders now wear condoms to avoid depositing seminal fluids."

With the Suspect(s)

Investigators also should question the suspect about the condom. A cooperative, honest suspect can reveal the brand, tell where he purchased it, and describe how and where he disposed of both the condom and the empty packet. An uncooperative or deceitful suspect may claim he does not know or cannot remember, or he may name a popular brand but will not be able to describe the condom or the packet in detail.

LEGAL CONSIDERATIONS

When investigators know or suspect that a sexual offender used a condom, they must remember to list condoms on the warrant obtained to search the suspect's possessions. The search of a suspect's home may reveal intact condom packets, but if investigators have not listed condoms on the search warrant, they will not be able to seize this valuable evidence.

CONCLUSION

When sexual assailants wear condoms to commit their crimes, they attempt to protect themselves from disease and apprehension at the same time. Although these crimes become more difficult to solve, investigators should not overlook the evidentiary potential of condom traces. By considering the possibility of condom use while processing the crime scene, supervising medical examinations, and conducting interviews, investigators can ensure that this valuable evidence receives the attention it deserves. ◆

Endnotes

[1] In 80 sexual assault cases submitted to the Forensic Laboratory of the Las Vegas Metropolitan Police Department between 9/10/93 and 12/3/93, 19 victims reported that the assailant or one of several assailants had worn a condom during the assault or that a consensual sexual partner had used a condom within 72 hours preceding the incident. Eight additional victims believed that their assailant might have used a condom. Terry L. Cook, criminalist, Forensic Laboratory, Las Vegas Metropolitan Police Department, telephone conversation with the author, December 6, 1993.

[2] R.D. Blackledge and L.R. Cabiness, "Examination for Petroleum Based Lubricants in Evidence from Rapes and Sodomies," *Journal of Forensic Sciences*, 28, 1983, 451-462.

[3] R.D. Blackledge, "Collection and Identification Guidelines for Traces from Latex Condoms in Sexual Assault Cases," *Crime Laboratory Digest*, 21, 1994, 57-61.

"Condom Trace Evidence" by Robert D. Blackledge, M.S. is reprinted from the May 1996 issue of *FBI Law Enforcement Bulletin*.

"The Attorney General has determined that the publication of this periodical is necessary in the transaction of the public business required by law. Use of funds for printing this periodical has been approved by the Director of the Office of Management and Budget."

ON THE BORDER:
Reflections of a Reluctant Immigration Inspector
by Ned Beaumont

Artwork by Mary Fleener

© 1996 by Ned Beaumont

U.S. immigration inspectors call themselves II's (a term pronounced "aye-aye," as if saying "yes" in the Navy). On the day I reported for duty with the Immigration and Naturalization Service, a veteran II gave me a bit of: "Get out while you still can."

I thought he was kidding.

After a few weeks "on the line," however, I came to know that the old inspector's warning had been sincere. Like most officers in the INS, I felt my blood pressure rise as quickly as my morale sank. Both were results of the stress induced from trying to enforce the convoluted, capricious, and fundamentally un-American immigration codes of the modern United States.

Step inside the booth of a reluctant immigration inspector. Let me tell you about the foolishness of the U.S. immigration laws that seem all the more foolish through the eyes of one who has enforced them.

A History Of Idiocy

For most of its history, the Republic survived without federal restrictions on who entered the country, except, of course, for saboteurs and such. Think about your ancestors. Could they legally immigrate to the U.S. under the current laws? Mine were mostly a collection of

(Continued on next page)

anarchists, draft-dodgers and drunks. They lacked family already in this country and the business skills (unless one considers crime a business) that grant green cards now-adays. I consider it fortunate that this country retained some semblance of free borders for most of the nineteenth century — long enough for Beaumonts to sail to America.

Beaumonts and other Europeans, however, were not the targets of the first federal immigration hit lists. Laws were enacted in the 1880's specifically to exclude Chinese and Japanese immigrants. "Yellow Peril" hysteria was rampant, especially on the West Coast, and Asians were viewed as a threat to the golden land of California. In other words, Asian immigrants tended to work harder than the average native-born white Californian, and so were in danger of becoming wealthy, educated, and politically powerful — the same "dangers" that Asians still present in America.

Following the First World War, nativist sentiment combined with the growing power of the federal government to produce the most restrictive laws in American history. This time, Catholics and Jews from eastern and southern Europe (the "garlic eaters" in Frank Capra's memorably wicked phrase from *It's A Wonderful Life*) were marked for exclusion. Indeed, the Golden Door was locked tightly to almost everyone other than an annual few thousand from designated countries in northern Europe. Exceptions were not made even for the masses of refugees from Nazi Germany or Soviet Russia.

That cap on large-scale immigration was kept unopened until 1965, when Congress fiddled with the Immigration and Nationality Act. The doors of the U.S. were opened once again, but in the most foolish ways imaginable. Those most in need of refuge in America, or the most deserving of admittance, were excluded, while lucky leeches were welcomed with open arms.

"Uncle Sam Pays My Bills Now"

When I was first learning about the tangled snakepit of the immigration codes, another inspector taught me a mnemonic to remember the categories of legal im-migrants: "Uncle Sam Pays My Bills Now." The initial letters of each word in the phrase stood for these classi-fications: unmarried children; spouses; parents; married children; brothers and sisters; no preference immigrants, the lucky 20,000 a year who had won the lottery at the U.S. embassy in the home country and had gained a green card for nothing more than patience. The categories were the result of the 1965 revision of The Act. They were designed to promote family ties, but in fact served to flood the nation with immigrants and encourage welfare dependency among the parents, children, spouses, and

siblings of those cunning or lucky enough to get a foot in the tarnished Golden Door by whatever means necessary.

For the Great Society do-gooders of 1965 turned the immigration laws into a poor compromise between no admittance and open immigration, while simultaneously giving lucky, but often unqualified, immigrants the cornucopia of welfare programs which allowed immigrants to live in America without working.

The legacy of do-goodism lived on, to the detriment of immigration policy and the nation. The 1986 Immigration Reform and Control Act (IRCA) went so far as to grant "amnesty" to hundreds of thousands of illegal immi-grants. Those who had gleefully challenged the authority of the feds were now made eligible for the federal free lunch — and for the free and legal importation of their relatives (based on the "Uncle Sam..." categories) who had not yet sneaked across the border. For all practical purposes, Uncle Sam ended up paying the bills not only of II's, but also of the very immigrants whom the II's were paid to keep on the other side of the line.

The Statutes Of Tyranny

A colleague with whom I once worked described the job of an II as "soul-destroying," because of the necessity for inspectors to enforce blatantly unfair laws. Some aliens deserved to be "dumped" (denied admission to the U.S.), but others were victims of blind laws.

Dumping Chinese refugees was the most soul-destroying task I hope to ever perform. In "the land of the free," Chinese who face persecution, prison, forced ster-ilization, and, sometimes, death, are daily denied refuge to the United States.

A few years ago, most of the Chinese dumped at the border were residents of Hong Kong eager to escape before the Butchers of Beijing took over. Many tried to enter the U.S. *via* Canada. But after being denied admis-sion to the U.S., and refused permanent refuge in Canada, many of the refugees from Hong Kong turned to their last resort, the Triads of Asian organized crime.

Operating out of Toronto, the Triads took thirty or thirty-five thousand dollars a head — cash up front, of course. Then, they would send the desperate refugees across the border in such deadly ways as mid-winter crossings of the ice-choked Niagara River (between Ontario and New York) on board cheap rubber rafts. What did the gangsters care once they had their money? In one such case with which I am familiar, the local police across the border in New York State found three frozen corpses with a punctured raft on a cold January day in

(Continued on next page)

1989. No one knows for certain how many bodies remain still beneath the river.

Lately, however, the U.S. government has grown even more cruel in its immigration policies dealing with refugees fleeing directly from Red China. In the ultimate expression of Big Brother power, the Chinese communists instituted their infamous "one-child policy" during the 1980's. An abuse of natural rights so fundamental would seem to cry out for every act of opposition short of open war by the government of the ostensibly free people of the United States.

But of course, there is "The Market" of mainland China. There are deals and dollars to be made for American plutocrats and their allies in Washington. What does it matter if political prisoners are used as slave labor — but *cheap* slave labor! — when there are so many other abuses of human rights in China, and, more importantly, so much money to be made? So the U.S. government has contented itself with token cries about the crimes of its fellow government in China.

Sometimes the U.S. government even cooperates with the Chinese Reds. The Immigration and Naturalization Service not merely denies refugee status to the Chinese women who escape the anti-natalist machinations of the communists, but actively deports back to Beijing those women who have entered the U.S. illegally. The INS does that despite the fact that Chinese women routinely suffer forced abortions and sterilizations for the "crime" of conceiving a child.

The moral stress of participating, even from a distance, in such actions of the INS can drive an II to desperation. I know that because I once created a minor "diplomatic incident" when dealing with Chinese Reds.

I was on the line not long after Tiananmen Square. Like everyone else, I had marvelled at the quiet courage of the unarmed children who defied the Chinese dictators until crushed by troops and tanks. Two Chinese diplomats, whose passports bore the stamp "2129(a)28" (a code indicating their membership in the Communist Party) objected when I gave them the usual inspection. They had expected to be stamped through swiftly at the border checkpoint. Since I was in the midst of a long shift after a week of long shifts, I lost control.

"You Red bastards," I shouted as I flung the passports in their faces. "I'm not some goddam kid you can run over with a tank."

I was mad enough to kill. But a supervisor intervened.

At first the diplomats were outraged and ready to complain all the way to Washington. But nothing ever came of the incident. My guess is that the communists considered themselves fortunate not to have been shot by the red-faced madman in the INS uniform.

Dubious Solutions

Two very different routes to the reform of immigration policy — all or nothing — would seem to make more sense than the current mess.

In the nothing approach, all the cant about America as a refuge for free peoples would be abandoned. Legal immigration, impossible to dry up entirely, would be limited strictly to those who had already demonstrated success in the Social Darwinist competition of modern life. Scientists and engineers who can design and build the twenty-first century technopolis, entrepreneurs who had turned small loans into great fortunes, and the athletes, entertainers, and writers who had turned natural gifts into gold would all be welcome. Economic production would be the price of a green card, and America would gain a small immigrant population of foreign-born go-getters.

Such a "nothing" policy may possess a kind of cold-hearted logic — but it would also be anathema to the traditions of America.

The "all" approach, however, would both be an improvement over the current policy and remain faithful to the traditions of a New World nation forged in the fire of revolution and built by the outcasts who could only find freedom in America. The "all" policy is simply this: admit anyone to the United States who wants to enter as a legal immigrant, *but force him to make it in this country on his own.* Make America the genuine land of opportunity for anyone willing to work.

Welcome to America, new immigrant! But expect not a dollar from the dole, not a drop from the tax teat. All the largesse of Leviathan — from AFDC to student loans — must die a swift and just death if the ever present "immigration problem" is to be solved. Whenever a politician or pundit spouts the usual nonsense about "reforming welfare as we know it," his words are as empty as his crowing about "getting control of our borders." As long as the state steals from you and me to buy bread and circuses, there will be Americans, native and immigrant, willing to eat and be entertained.●

Ned Beaumont is a retired INS Inspector. He is the author of *Beat The Border: An Insider's Guide to How the U.S. Border Works & How To Beat It,* and the forthcoming *The Policeman Is Your Friend and Other Lies.*

THE MEDIA FOUNDATION

Photo: Shannon Mendes

Here we are! From left: Jen Van Evra, Sharon Kravitz, Sheila Mooney, Dan Deresh, Laura McConville, Mike Butts, Kim Anderson, Kalle Lasn, Linda Gould, Brenda Shaffer, Terry Sunderland.

WHO WE ARE

The Media Foundation is a non-profit society dedicated to cleaning up the toxic areas of our physical and mental environments. We are challenging the outdated paradigms of consumer culture. Join us; become a sustaining subscriber; share *Adbusters* with a friend; become involved as a researcher, contributor, coordinator; help fund one of our Projects in progress:

THE DEMARKETING OF NORTH AMERICA

An ongoing multi-media public education campaign to take back control of the roles that the tobacco, alcohol, fashion, cosmetics, food, automobile and broadcasting industries play in our lives. Contact us if you want to jam your local airwaves with the *American Excess, Autosaurus* or *The Product Is You* TV campaigns.

Campaign manager: Brenda Shaffer

THE RIGHT TO COMMUNICATE

A legal action campaign to win the right to walk into a local TV station and buy airtime for advocacy messages. Call us if you are a constitutional lawyer ready to take legal action against the NBC, ABC and CBS networks for violating the American public's right to communicate.

Campaign manager: Kalle Lasn

THE BEST MEDIA LITERACY LESSON IN THE WORLD

A high school classroom video and lesson plan that shows teachers and students how to jump over that great divide between the passive consumption and the active production of meaning. We are looking for a co-production partner.

Project manager: Kim Anderson

ECOLOGICAL ECONOMICS

A university campus campaign to usher in a new economic paradigm. E-mail us if you want to air the *Economists Must Learn To Subtract* TV spot in your area, or do some jamming on campus.

Campus networker: Jen Van Evra

MINDSHIFT — A SIX-PART TV SERIES

Documents the six great paradigm shifts that we must all negotiate in the '90s. We are fund raising to produce the pilot.

Executive producer: Kalle Lasn

THE CULTURE JAMMER'S HANDBOOK

The companion book to the TV series. Contact us if you're a hot-shot writer with a culture jammer's heart.

Managing editor: Dan Deresh

ADBUSTERS QUARTERLY SUMMER 1995

SUPERMARKETEERS

Companies pay $60 billion a year for prime real estate in your supermarket.

by Bob Mackin

"Attention shoppers: two-for-one special on Splendido Coffee for the next 15 minutes in Aisle 6."

A crowd of a dozen people, having just heard the announcement, surges toward the coffee display near the center of the brightly lit supermarket. When they arrive, some out of breath, they jostle for room as if in a rugby scrum, trying to reach out and touch the "bargain of the day."

One by one, in a rather disorderly fashion, each of the consumers grabs their two packages of coffee. The panic ends almost as quickly as it began. Each of the consumers return to their shopping carts with smiles on their faces, content that their pocketbooks will not feel so light after all when they leave the store.

But they wouldn't be so happy if they knew that the prices of their favorite products, either national brands with big advertising budgets or the humbly packaged generic brands, are manipulated by a secretive negotiation system where shelf space is treated like real estate.

Quite simply put, the more money paid to a retailer by a manufacturer, the more "real estate" (shelf space) or the better "property" (positioning) can be "leased" and sometimes even "owned".

And the "landlords" (merchants) are laughing all the way to the bank.

The system has evolved in such a way, say industry experts, that the dominance of the retailers' private label or in-house brands in some categories has driven up the price of shelf space for competing products.

"Chip," an employee of a mid-sized, western Canadian snack food supplier told *Adbusters* (on condition of anonymity) that a level playing field exists for big companies, "but it would be prohibitive for a smaller company coming into the market."

The cost of shelf space to a manufacturer, often called slotting or listing fees, is highly guarded. Even if a price list were available, it may not be accurate on a national or international basis, as the fees are influenced by many factors and are subject to wide fluctuations. Chip's employer, who competes with another western Canadian supplier and the Canadian subsidiary of American giant Frito-Lay, recently launched a new product which comes in nine flavors. One of the chains took six of the nine flavors at a cost of $5,000 per flavor. Stores also charge manufacturers a premium for grocery cart signage, product displays, till-tape signage, and even in-store radio and TV services.

Chip says in-store specials and other discounts at chains like Safeway cost a supplier up to $10,000 in payments to retailers.

Manufacturers and suppliers don't want to talk about listing fees or the larger issue of trade advertising. Giants like Procter & Gamble, Quaker Oats, Kraft General Foods and Pepsi were contacted by *Adbusters*, but either refused to comment or did not return repeated phone calls.

ADBUSTERS WINTER 1996

But perhaps it's their shame that explains why they aren't eager to go public. After all, it is like a narcotic habit, according to Burt Flickinger, a New York consumer goods consultant. And addicts are prone to denial and deceit, not to mention spending absurd amounts of money to feed their disease.

Flickinger estimated that approximately $60 billion was spent last year by manufacturers and suppliers to get their products on American supermarket shelves.

Flickinger, whose great-grandfather founded the first private label brand and franchised chain of grocers, says greed is a prime motivator in the vicious circle of trade advertising.

He says senior managers and executives receive huge pay bonuses each year based on the amount of product they can move on and off store shelves. "If (suppliers) can continue offering more money to drive a little more volume, that in turn increases their bonuses at year end," he says.

Flickinger claims manufacturers have moved as much as three-quarters of their ad spending from traditional broadcast and print media to in-store promotion and payouts to retailers.

A great deal of the money derived from levies on manufacturers goes straight to the retailers' bottom line, although Flickinger says it is common for the retailers to use the payments to "strategically subsidize" exclusive or private label generic brands. The reluctance of manufacturers to spend money on consumer advertising, or invest in research and development to make better products, has allowed trade spending to run amok.

Most deals are cut with a retailer's head office, although some are still made on an individual store basis.

"It used to be pretty shady, there used to be a lot of kickbacks going on, but that was more at store level," Chip says. "You can still get into a store and get deals at the manager's level, but it's very hard to do."

Some unethical practices do persist at store level. For example, Chip says Frito-Lay has been known to buy competitors' items off shelves, and then replace them with Frito-Lay products. Representatives of supermarket chains like Kroger's, Safeway and Overwaitea / Save-On-Foods also declined comment.

But, Dave Ryzebol, spokesman for the Calgary-based Real Canadian Superstore chain, says that "16,000 new products come to the marketplace every year in North America."

"You have to constantly reorganize your shelving to accommodate new products or to list old products."

Ryzebol claims listing fees are often glorified service or administrative

charges to pay for labor, distribution, inventory and stocking of products. He says the ultimate goal is to get the lowest possible price for consumers.

"That's our job, to see what kind of deals we can get from manufacturers and get those prices down. Manufacturers frequently complain about the way retailers squeeze them so they can get a better deal for their customers," Ryzebol says. "But 20 or 30 years ago, the manufacturers dominated the marketplace. They said this is what the price is and if you were a grocer or retailer who wanted to sell it, that was it. You didn't have a lot of other choices."

Now, it seems, it's the consumer's turn for a lack of choices. ✖

ADBUSTERS WINTER 1996

do it yourself

Adding the Blemish of Truth

Making Little Changes to Billboards

by John Craig

The idea probably arose when my brother and I were kids growing up in Ontario. We didn't care at all about the media, advertising or mass consumption. One of the few things we did care about was whether a lot of people would start building houses nearby. We didn't want to see bungalows, lawns and cars replacing the fields and trees nobody seemed to own.

We thought we were safe until one day a huge billboard appeared on the roadside near our house advertising building lots for sale. The next day we mixed a dish of paint and carefully doctored the billboard by adding a zero to the price of each lot. For three years nothing sold as the huge sign warned off every prospective buyer. When the real estate agent who was trying to sell the lots finally noticed the alteration he called the police thinking his competitor had made the changes. It was traced back to us, but in the end it didn't matter because we were kids, and kids are never guilty even if they are.

The real estate sign came to mind as I thought about the billboard improvement. The movement for billboard improvement had never reached its full potential. Answering a billboard by spraying on a written reply was effective when clever but too often weakened toward mere defacement. In any case, a blatantly modified billboard was quickly papered over by watchful crews of local outdoor advertising companies. But what if you made small changes to the

advertising imagery? The result would be more articulate, would probably last longer and would be easier to pull off. Best of all, you could add something so quickly you could be gone before anyone could say Billboard Busters!

To this end, Moth (the cat) and I headed for the workshop. I sat down at my bench and made several sketches before settling on a revised design. Moth looked at the drawing then walked away,

a sure sign we had a winner. Now to build the new device. I rooted out some one inch dowel, some bits of one inch copper pipe, my hammer, rasp file, white glue and a few finishing nails. An hour later the Billboard Buster Mark 1 was finished. I was happy with the final result until I noticed Moth staring at me. I knew what she was thinking. Some people would find this thing difficult to build. Sure it was easier than learning to rappel down

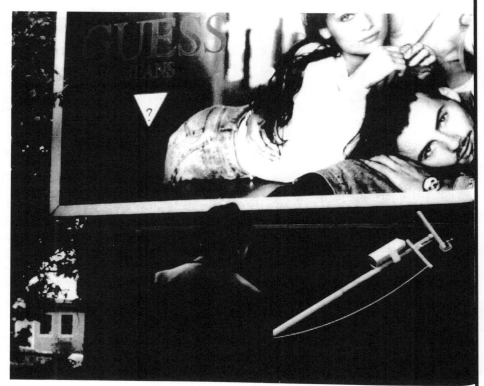

Photo: Doug LeMoine

A D B U S T E R S   W I N T E R   1 9 9 6

⅜" x ⅜" x ? standoff rests against billboard.

Small "C" clamp allows adjustment to standoff distance.

Steel bracket.

Pivoting safety.

⅜" x ⅜" x 7" hammer.

Trigger cord.

The top of a roll-on applicator makes things go more smoothly. Stencils can also be mounted on here.

Duct tape spray can in place — a vertical piece of a ⅜" x ⅜" wood (not visible) positions the can.

1" wood dowel.

5" piece of 1" diameter copper pipe allows disassembly. File down dowel for permanent fit on upper dowel and for secure fit on dowel.

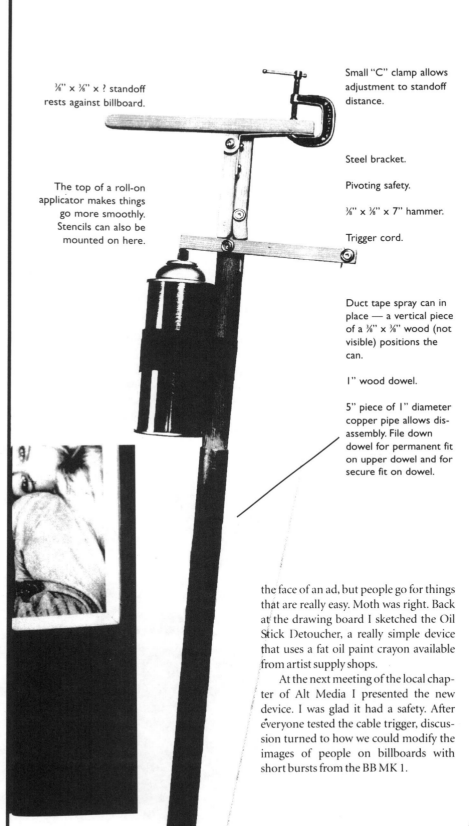

the face of an ad, but people go for things that are really easy. Moth was right. Back at the drawing board I sketched the Oil Stick Detoucher, a really simple device that uses a fat oil paint crayon available from artist supply shops.

At the next meeting of the local chapter of Alt Media I presented the new device. I was glad it had a safety. After everyone tested the cable trigger, discussion turned to how we could modify the images of people on billboards with short bursts from the BB MK 1.

Here's some ideas we came up with:

Case of acne: Retouchers remove the blemishes on model's faces in order to create billboard people. The BB MK 1 and the Oil Stick Detoucher seemed ideal for reintroducing the blemishes. By adding acne spots we could turn billboard person who flogs products into real person who couldn't sell a thing.
Zombie eyes: Simply restoring people to normality seemed rather tame, so we came up with some other ideas. Two quick bursts of white aimed at the center of the eyes would turn a billboard person into a zombie from *Children of the Damned* or *Night of the Living Dead.*
Trickle of blood: A blast of dark red spray paint aimed at the corner of the mouth and allowed to run would make a billboard person look really sick. It would suggest an unfashionable trauma, a distasteful disease, or a nasty bite.
Hitlerizing: Adding a quick Hitler mustache could easily undo the advertising image of an actual person, such as a politician. Because it would suggest the person held fascist views, we thought we should save it for those who belong to the far right.

Back at home, I showed Moth the sketches of our billboard additions. She looked at them and walked away. It was time to track down a set of walkie talkies.

To be continued...

*John Craig was drummed out of the corps for subversive skywriting. He also wrote a novel entitled **Smiling Through Your Teeth**, as yet unpublished.*

A D B U S T E R S   W I N T E R   1 9 9 6

First Amendment Remains Intact... For Now
Judge throws out Hit Man lawsuit

What kind of information should Americans have access to, and what should be restricted? For more than 200 years the First Amendment to the U.S. Constitution has stood unwavering in the face of any debate on that issue. Time and time again, those who have attempted to dilute its guarantee of free speech have met with failure. With precious few exceptions, they have learned the hard way that, as Supreme Court Justice Thurgood Marshall put it, "a state has no business telling a man, sitting in his own house, what books he may read or what films he may watch."

And the recent decision by U.S. District Judge Alexander Williams Jr. reinforces that message. Williams has granted Paladin Press' motion for a summary judgment to throw out the lawsuit filed against it by a Maryland family whose relatives were murdered by James Perry. Perry is on death row, but the family of the victims sought damages against Paladin for publishing the book *Hit Man: A Technical Manual for Independent Contractors*, which Perry allegedly purchased from Paladin prior to the murders. In his own trial, Perry was accused of applying some of the information presented in *Hit Man* in the commission of his crimes. The family contended that by publishing *Hit Man*, Paladin was an accessory to murder.

Judge Williams found that the plaintiffs had failed to prove that *Hit Man* fell within the "well-defined and narrowly limited classes of speech that are unprotected by the First Amendment." Williams' reasoning was based on the test set forth by the 1969 *Brandenburg vs. Ohio* ruling, which established that in order for speech to be restrained or punished, it must do more than just advocate breaking the law; it must *incite imminent* illegal activity. Williams determined that *Hit Man* did not fall into the latter category.

Under Brandenburg, explained Williams, Paladin "must have *intended* that James Perry would go out and murder Mildred Horn, Trevor Horn, and Janice Saunders *immediately*." Such was not the case here, he reasoned, since Perry carried out the murders a year after he allegedly bought the book. Furthermore, Williams reviewed *Hit Man* and found that it in no way constituted incitement or "a call to action," as proscribed by Brandenburg. "The book does not cross that line between permissible advocacy and impermissible incitation to crime or violence," he said. "The book does not purport to order or command anyone to any concrete action at any specific time, much less immediately."

In fact, to say that Paladin advocated, much less incited, James Perry's abominable crime would be stretching it.Like all of Paladin's books that deal with subjects that are potentially dangerous or illegal, *Hit Man* and the catalog advertisement for the book contain disclaimers stating that it is for "*information purposes*" or "*academic study*" only. "This does not indicate a tendency to incite violence," noted Williams. "To the contrary, such disclaimers may be interpreted as an attempt to dissuade readers from engaging in the activity it describes."

Although Williams conceded that *Hit Man* contains information that, "when it makes its way into the wrong hands, can be fatal," he made it clear that published works cannot be exempt from First Amendment protection simply because the ideas they present create a potential hazard. "It is simply not acceptable to a free and democratic society to limit and restrict creativity in order to avoid dissemination of ideas in artistic speech which may adversely affect emotionally troubled individuals," he said.

In response to the ruling, Paladin attorney Tom Kelly said, "I was happy to see the judge willing to keep the starch in the First Amendment, even though the politics of the day seems to favor limiting speech."

Unfortunately, Judge Williams' decision does not put the case to rest. Although Williams cautioned during oral arguments in July that plaintiffs face an uphill battle in their attempt to collect damages against Paladin, their lawyers are determined that the battle shall go forward. It's a battle Paladin believes is worth fighting, but big battles take big dollars to wage. Plaintiffs have stated that they will appeal Judge Williams' decision to the 4th U.S. Circuit court, after which the case could conceivably go as far as the U.S. Supreme Court — a process that could take years.

But a court victory apparently is not the only objective for plaintiffs' attorneys. Recently published newspaper quotes indicated that they will settle for nothing less than the destruction of Paladin Press. Vowing that "we'll go beyond the Supreme Court, if that's what it takes," Howard Siegel, the lead attorney for plaintiffs, has baldly stated that "[Paladin is] the most despicable enterprise I have ever personally encountered, and I will put an end to it."

Throughout this crisis, our customers, authors, and other champions of the First Amendment have shown us tremendous moral and, in many cases, financial support, and we are grateful and appreciative of that. But we need your help and support now more than ever as we press forward in this unprecedented struggle to preserve the integrity of the First Amendment. Please consider making a significant contribution to the Paladin legal defense fund today — and encourage your like-minded friends, co-workers, and associates to join in the effort as well. No matter how controversial our books and videos may seem to some, it is the responsibility of us all to recognize and defend unequivocally the fact that if all ideas were safe and mainstream, there would be no need for a First Amendment. As one Paladin advocate put it, if you don't fight these battles on the fringes, you'll end up fighting them on your front porches.

If you would like to contribute to the Paladin Legal Defense Fund, please send your check or money order to the address below. Any contribution of any amount is helpful and greatly appreciated.

Paladin Legal Defense Fund
c/o Osgood, Simpson & Harris, LLC
2336 Canyon Blvd., Suite 200
Boulder, CO 80302

(Unfortunately, contributions are not tax deductible.)

BRAMBLE BUSH
BY RICHARD McKENNA

Illustrations by David Collier

Team Leader Ed Gard did not tell them until after Explorer Vessel M-24 rotated irreversibly into subspace.

"We'll not come out by kappa-12 Carinae," he said then to the five men standing clumped in the control room. "We're going to alpha-1 Centauri."

Fat Webb Onderdonck, the climatologist, exploded. "A field trip for kids! How come?"

"Isn't it already settled?" asked Minelli, the slender geologist.

Shipman Isaac McPherson punched a reference combination and glanced at the lighted screen.

"One Earth-type planet named Proteus," he said, frowning. "Never been a landing. Now why didn't I ever wonder about that before? My God, the nearest system to Earth —"

"Only in the Riemannian sense," Onderdonck broke in. "Means nothing relative to subspace." McPherson's craggy face cleared.

"But we've taken them in order of Riemannian contiguity all along," objected Chalmers, the bio-chemist. "This exception does seem unaccountable.

There *must* be a reason." His thin, sharp features were troubled.

"Overlooked in the shuffle. Maybe a misfiled report. What's one planet anyway, among a billion?" Webb Onderdonck scowled.

"Not so, Webb," Gard said, squaring massive shoulders. "In the past century the Corps projected several trips to Proteus. Each one aborted through a long series of personal accidents and other delays. We are the first to get away."

"Why the secrecy? Who's being fooled?"

"Fate, maybe. A sop to superstition. Sit down, people, and I'll explain."

Seated along the wall bench, all but the scowling fat man, they listened as their tall leader paced and talked. Proteus has been his personal mystery since he was ten years old, he said, and the mystery was that no one else was curious.

"Everybody shushed my questions and got mad when I persisted," he said. "Just one of those things, they kept telling me, too many planets to worry

(Continued on next page)

about any single one. It came to me that the most insoluble mystery is one that no one will admit exists."

He aimed his education at the Explorer Corps, he went on, enlisted and in time qualified as team leader. When he tried to rouse official interest in a trip to Proteus he hit a stone wall of indifference grading into covert hostility. But finally he had infected Vane, the project coordinator at Denverport, with his own curiosity. Together they had planned this secret diversion of a routine Carina trip.

"So here we go, people. Don't all hate me at once." He put up his hands in mock-guard.

"Curiosity killed a cat," Onderdonck snorted, jowls quivering. "Your mystery is childish nonsense. This will finish you in the Corps, and Vane too."

"*How* did curiosity kill the cat?" Hank Chalmers asked. "I don't like this either, Webb, but I can't put my finger on a reason."

"A planet's a planet, all in the day's work," Minelli soothed. "Let's do a job on this Proteus and there'll be no more mystery."

Joe Svirsky, the biologist, stood up. He was a stocky, graying man with cheekbones prominent in a broad face under slanting gray eyes.

"This is no ordinary mission, my brothers," he said gravely. "We must be careful."

"Amen to that," Gard grinned. "Afterward let the Corps bounce me as far as it likes. I've been pointing for this all my life."

Proteus circled the smaller star close in. Its day was fourteen standard hours, no axial tilt and so no seasons, gravity point seven, air breathable but hot and humid, the instruments told them. Gard called a pre-landing conference in the main workroom on their second day in orbit.

"Mean relief under ninety feet. Eighty-five percent sea, most of it epeiric. Never saw an Earth-type so leveled off," Minelli said.

"Mean annual temperature estimate twenty degrees above optimum," Onderdonck said, looking at Gard across the table. "That alone rules out settlement. No landing necessary now or ever and pop goes your mystery. Let's go home."

"We must sample the biota for a complete report," Gard disagreed. "We serve man's land hunger *and* his curiosity."

"Speak for yourself!" Onderdonck snapped, rising and propping himself on pudgy fingers. "I invoke article ten of regulations and call for a vote of supersession."

"Hold on, Webb, that makes bad feeling," Pete Minelli said. "Besides, I want a closer look at that textbook peneplain down below."

Onderdonck insisted. Only Chalmers, glancing apologetically at Gard, voted with him.

"Take her down, Ike, the place Minelli picked," Gard told the shipman.

McPherson set her down on a continental dome, a comparatively well-drained area of grassy swales and broad-leaf tree clumps.

"Looks ordinary as hell," McPherson said, standing at the foot of the ramp.

"Hot as hell too," Minelli said. "Steam bath. Me for swimming trunks." He started back aboard.

"Just a minute, Pete," Gard called after him. "I was about to propose we stay on ship-time on account of the short local day. Okay with you?"

"Hell, yes, what's time to a geologist?"

They agreed to stay on ship-time. Svirsky was already taking soil and water specimens from a sluggish stream nearby. Chalmers gathered grass seeds and berries.

"Help with the biota, Webb, and we'll do a minimal job, get out fast," Gard offered.

"No," Onderdonck growled, "and don't figure on that account I'll take galley duty, either."

Gard shrugged his broad shoulders.

Chalmers started on protein analysis and Svirsky on the microbiota. Gard, McPherson and Minelli set up observation units in the few varying habitats the gray-green flatness afforded on a five-mile radius from the ship. Each unit transmitted to a scope on the monitor panel in the main workroom and could be switched at will to the large stereo-screen. The three men took turns on monitor watch, making selective recordings of animal behavior for later analysis.

Native protein was unusually similar to that of Earth. The native vertebrates were Earth-homologous too, including birds and reptiles, but small. The largest land animal seemed to be a goat-sized herbivore. Svirsky turned to a comparative anatomy series

(Continued on next page)

and Gard and the shipman trapped specimens for him when off watch. Minelli ranged afield in the atmospheric flyer for geology specimens. Outside the ship the men wore swimming trunks and cursed the heat. After two standard weeks Gard tentatively decided to lift out on the following day.

That afternoon Pete Minelli burst into the main workroom shouting, "Ed, hey Ed, there's men on this planet!"

Svirsky turned sharply from his dissecting table. Chalmers came in from his lab across the passageway, pale and staring. McPherson, at the monitor panel, tugged at his red mustache and Onderdonck flushed. Gard spoke for them all.

"Pete, you're crazy with the heat! What do you mean?"

"At least one man, by God!" Minelli insisted. "Big as you and red-headed as Ike over there. Naked and bearded and wild."

"Tell us about it. Did you speak to him?"

"I was taking a core not far from here and this fellow was all of a sudden there, walking sideways around me with a stupid look on what I could see of his face. It shook me up, Ed. All I could think to do was keep turning to face him. After about three laps he went into the brush and I got out so fast I left my drill rig there."

"Somebody marooned? Maybe a lost Earth colony?" McPherson wondered, rubbing his long chin.

"Could be native," Gard murmured.

"I'll be damned," McPherson said. "Everybody knows men are unique to Earth. We haven't found humans on ten thousand planets now."

"We've found bipedal mammals on plenty of them. These could easily be human-homologs. Right, Joe?"

Svirsky nodded gravely, his eyes wide.

"If so, it's contact." Onderdonck said thickly. "Gard, you fool, you've found man's first rival for the galaxy. You *would* persist!"

"Hey, here's one come into a scope!" McPherson shouted. "I'll switch it over."

A scene of brown-flowered grass and gray-green shrubs took shape in the big stereo. A naked woman squatted, partially covered by long, coppery hair, and plucked grass racemes which she ate or fed to a scrabbling infant beside her.

"Who's crazy now?" Minelli asked, looking around the group. "Ike, there's a carrot-top soulmate for you."

The woman suddenly looked directly out of the screen. Her heavy features were expressionless, her slaty eyes dull.

"Opposites attract," McPherson retorted. "Pete, she's giving you the eye."

"Not a very bright eye," Gard said. "They're not exactly potent rivals, Webb."

The woman scrambled off the screen, eating as she went, the child scrabbling after. McPherson worked his controls.

"Here, I got 'em on another one." he said. "Hey! There's a man!"

The man was eating one of the goat-things. It twitched and jerked with residual life. The woman joined him in gnawing at it. From time to time she fed partially chewed flank muscle to the infant.

"Hell, they must be native," McPherson said disgustedly. "No human could slide back that far."

"Gard, let's get out of here fast," Hank Chalmers said abruptly.

"Not till I try communication."

"Obviously useless. They're pure animal, for all their shape."

"Hank, you know better than that. Extrapolate from the otter-homolog Joe has on his table. These Proteans must have a nervous system capable of forming a very rich symbol world. Right, Joe?"

"Yes, but unlike the skeleton and musculature it is Earth-anomalous," Svirsky said. "The pyramidal motor tracts in the cord do not cross. It might be a very strange symbol world."

"In what way?"

"We don't care!" Onderdonck burst out. "This is a waste of time on an unauthorized deviation from assigned mission. I vote to supersede Gard and go home. Who's with me?"

"I am," Chalmers muttered, casting down his eyes.

"Damn it, Ed, I want to back you, but set *some* limit," Minelli pleaded.

"Okay, Pete, a time limit. Give me one standard week."

"Okay, a week. I'll ride along."

"Me, too," McPherson said. Svirsky nodded agreement.

(Continued on next page)

Over the next three days Proteans by the score came into the observation area, circling aimlessly to within a mile of the ship. They fled when Gard approached them in the field, doubling back to their dumb circling of him when he stood still. He developed headaches and overpowering fits of lethargy and suspected a virus, but Chalmers' bio-analyzer found no foreign protein in him. Frequently McPherson and Minelli watched his maneuverings on the scopes and twitted him later.

"You're too hoity-toity, Ed," McPherson said. "Squat down and eat snakes with 'em and they'll trust you."

"If you'd grow a beard, Ike, they'd make *you* a chief," Gard grinned.

On the morning of his fourth day in the field Gard woke in confusion on a grassy bank. McPherson and Minelli were bending over him and his left shoulder ached horribly.

"She was eating me," he said stupidly.

"Yes," Minelli agreed, white-faced. "You just folded up. Lucky we were watching. Lucky nobody had the flyer out."

"Get aboard, get aboard," McPherson urged. "That shoulder needs fixing."

Chalmers, treating the wound a few minutes later, laughed shortly. "Communication by bite, eh, Gard? Where did you bite her?"

Gard called a luncheon conference around the big table in the workroom. Outside the primary sun was setting.

"They *are* animals," he said ruefully to the men around the table. "We've never seen them communicate or cooperate. I doubt they even have voices. I propose we trap one and make him talk to us in action-language, the way we make rats tell us what they can see and remember."

"How can you make a rat talk?" McPherson asked.

"You teach him triangle means food and square means shock, Ike. When he learns to run to one and away from the other then you and he have a common language of two symbols."

"Ed'll be the food," Minelli said. "They think he's yummy."

"Go crawl under a rock, Pete. This is serious."

"Keep on meddling," Onderdonck said under his breath.

Gard firmed his lips. "What do *you* think, Joe?"

"They must have a nervous system adequate for language," Svirsky said. "The symbol-world is in them, in neural impulse pattern and humoral gradient, far more intricately structured than in any rat. But they lack the Word. I suspect they're like a supersaturated solution lacking a mote to crystallize a world around. But drop a primal symbol into them and they may develop language and verbal thought almost explosively."

"Define a primal symbol," Chalmers demanded.

"I can state one but not define it," Svirsky said. "Space, time, and the object. It's triune, each member existing by virtue of the other two. It is the zygote of all language."

"Then it's a *verbal* symbol?"

"Yes. It is the cultural aspect or correlate of an immensely older neural symbol. The ontogeny of human language recapitulates the phylogeny of the vertebrate nervous system. Both make a model of the world, but language can *bind time*. If your enemy has no primal symbol, then your own becomes your most precious secret. I speak in riddles, my brothers."

"You speak in metaphor and analogy. That's more poetry than science," Onderdonck sneered.

"And perhaps more truth than poetry," Chalmers said thinly. "I'll be honest, Gard. I fear your curiosity. Much as I dislike admitting it, I feel that some things are dangerous to know too soon. We need to keep firm hold of our world and wait the proper time."

"Ed, you don't mean to feed 'em that primal symbol?" McPherson asked anxiously.

"No, Ike. I wouldn't know how, anyway."

"You might trigger something, not meaning to or knowing, if you fumble around."

"*Precisely*, Ike!" Chalmers said. "Vote with Webb and me to stop all this!"

"You promised me a week, people," Gard pleaded. "Let me have the rest of it."

He won a shaky victory. Onderdonck and Chalmers undertook to bring in the observation units and to dismantle and stow the flyer. Gard, McPherson and Minelli set to work on the cage.

(Continued on next page)

The cage was the standard ten-foot cube of reinforced steel mesh. At one end problem boxes flanked a door with an observation unit above it. Sweating in the dim light of the further sun, the men baited the cage and charged one of the boxes with the small ground melons the Proteans ate avidly.

"I'll set this box for a two-lever problem," Gard said. "See, Ike, he'll have to press them in the right sequence to make a melon roll out. He'll do it by random action first, then get the idea. Then we'll make it tougher, record times and trials and so on. I expect he'll learn fast."

They returned to the ship at Protean sunrise. McPherson fixed a late dinner and they ate in the workroom watching the cage on the stereo screen. Minelli cleaned up the dishes and turned in, leaving Gard and McPherson alone. An hour later a male Protean entered the cage, showing no alarm when the door closed behind him.

"That son of a gun looks just like me," McPherson complained. "I wish he was green or purple."

"Watch him turn purple once he knows he's trapped."

The Protean ate three melons, fumbled at the sticks Gard had left in the cage, and shambled through its side. The steel mesh was intact.

"Let's us turn purple," McPherson said. "That ain't possible."

Then it hit them. They stared at each other, speechless, then back at the screen. A female Protean came in view. She approached obliquely and seemed to slide through the mesh. She ate two melons and left, as stupidly unaware as when she came. Gard cursed softly.

"Call Joe, Ike. *Only* Joe. I'll brew some coffee."

The three men sipped coffee and watched a Protean eat the last melon in the cage center. McPherson broke the silence.

"This is more'n I can take, Ed. Let's dump it in their laps back on Earth. This calls for a full expedition."

"No, Ike. They'd never get several hundred people away against the jinx, not even six men another time. We're here on a fluke and it's up to us or never."

"You are the fluke, Ed," Svirsky said. "Here's a suggestion. Wind cable around that cage and send high frequency alternating current through it."

"How could that —"

"A hunch, Ed. I've been wondering whether Proteans might not mix space and time into a world-structure different from our own in their neural model of reality. But so does AC mix them in a way strange to our neural model. Try it, Ed."

"Let's do it, Ike."

Gard carried the heavy power pack, McPherson the cable and oscillator. They wound four turns around the cage, looping it over the door. Gard baited the cage with melons from the puzzle box and reset the door. Proteans shambled aimlessly near the cage when the Earthmen walked back sweating under the bright sun. When they entered the workroom the stereo showed a large male already trapped.

He ate two bait melons leisurely, then walked to the side of the cage and recoiled. The three men watched as he tried again and again in what seemed a mounting excitement. He began howling and other Proteans answered and drifted toward the cage, only to recoil from its outside. They milled in a ragged circle, howling too.

"Well, they do have voices," Gard commented.

"Your hunch paid off, Joe," McPherson said. "We've got 'em by the tail now."

Svirsky grunted. "So we have, Ike."

It was just midnight, ship-time. By Protean sunset two hours later the captive became quiet in the cage center and those outside went away. McPherson and Svirsky turned in. Gard watched and thought.

Minelli came in just after six. Gard asked him to take the watch until Protean sunrise at nine. He said nothing about the earlier escapes.

"I expect Lord Proteus will stay quiet until sunrise. Then he'll stir and be hungry and tell us how smart he is through that problem box," he told Minelli.

Gard's sleep was troubled with dreams. He woke to Minelli's shaking and thought it was still a dream when the geologist said curtly, "Your man talked, Ed. He said 'Open sesame.'"

"You don't mean he got away?"

"You better come." Minelli left.

(Continued on next page)

All hands were standing before the stereo screen and all but Svirsky looked at Gard with narrowed eyes, then back to the screen in silence. Gard saw with relief that his Protean was still a captive, squatting and shuffling the sticks. Then, as he watched, a melon dropped through the side of the problem box. The Protean reached for it, began eating. The dispensing counter on the box registered zero.

"He does it by random action. *Real* random," Pete Minelli said. He did not smile.

"This does it, you fool," Onderdonck said thickly. "*Now* we'll vote."

"Ed, agree to lift out right now," McPherson pleaded.

Gard declined. McPherson and Minelli voted with Onderdonck. The fat man, flushed with triumph, looked at Chalmers.

"I don't know, Webb," the biochemist said slowly. "It was bumping against something like this I was hoping to avoid, I think. But now maybe none of us are *fit* to go back to earth."

"We can regain sanity," Onderdonck urged. "Something shielded us from this until that brain-sick fool —"

"We've got to make a token fight, now," Chalmers interrupted. "I've *seen* it happen. Each in his own way, perhaps, we must make our fight here, get our teeth into this thing."

"Gard, I feel almost a duty to *kill* you!" Onderdonck cried. "You loosen the bonds of Creation itself, you fool, you fool!" He looked apoplectic.

"Give me the rest of the ship-day," Gard said. "I'm scared too, Onderdonck. We'll lift out by six."

Onderdonck and Minelli left the workroom. The four others watched the Protean repeat his performance seven more times and then rest, apparently sated. Gard and Chalmers cut the record-tape into the nine sequences and fed them through the pattern analyzer, first in parallel and then singly for correlation. The highest reading was point sixteen.

"That's more random than pure chance," Chalmers said. "That may give us a handhold."

"No human action can be *purely* random," Svirsky agreed. "Causality is structured very basically into our wiring diagram, perhaps as far back as the Permian. We can't even perceive pure randomness in our world."

They talked around the subject. "I want to help," McPherson said finally, "but I can't make out how we're going to come to grips with this business. What's the Protean wiring diagram like?"

"I have a notion, from work on lower life-forms," Svirsky said. "I should dissect that fellow in the cage."

"No," Chalmers said. "He's para-human, at the least. How about depth photos?"

Svirsky agreed that might do. They decided to anesthetize the Protean, make depth photos for analysis on Earth, and lift out. Chalmers thought neuralin might not work well in Protean biochemistry and said he would persuade Onderdonck and Minelli to come along and help if restraint were needed. It was one o'clock, ship-time.

"If neuralin works too well, they can help carry back the body," he said. "I wouldn't object to taking a *dead* Protean back to Earth."

Onderdonck and Minelli carried pistols to the cage. Gard went in alone with the neuralin gun. The red-bearded Protean moved to one side, not looking at Gard, and suddenly ran for the door. Gard flung out his powerful left arm and the Protean ran through it.

The men at the door jumped aside. Onderdonck aimed his pistol and Svirsky struck it up. Gard came out, pale and shuddering.

"I can't describe it," he said. "Like being violated in a secret place I couldn't know existed. God! My flesh crawls! I'll go home now, Onderdonck."

"Too late," Onderdonck said, pointing his pistol.

They saw a file of naked Proteans emerging from shrubbery between them and the ship, cutting them off, bearing down obliquely. Minelli cursed and drew his pistol.

"Not yet, Pete," Svirsky said gently. "Into the cage, my brothers."

Inside the closed cage they watched the Proteans, led by a huge, red-bearded male, circle them on a ten-yard radius. When the leader cut through the incoming file to close the circle the Proteans set up an uncadenced howling.

The leader led the file through itself and into a second circle of greater radius. Women and half-

(Continued on next page)

grown children spaced randomly with men kept coming in on the long secant. They stepped high and deliberately, arms hanging, howling from expressionless faces. The leader drew a third loop and then a fourth that lost itself in far trees and hollows. Still they came in on the long slant.

Gard climbed the cage wall to look over their heads. "It looks like a logarithmic spiral," he shouted down. Onderdonck cursed steadily. Svirsky and Chalmers talked into each other's ear against the howling.

After nearly an hour the incoming file ended. The spiral unwound out of sight and the howling died away. The men left the cage.

Minelli laughed uncertainly. "Well, that didn't hurt much," he said.

"God, things seem still and silent after that war dance," McPherson said. "Let's go home, men."

He lead off, the others at his heels. After a few steps Chalmers cried, "Stop!"

"Things don't look right," he said. "See those trees ahead."

"Blurry and jumping a little," Gard agreed. "Easy now."

"Twisting in circles," McPherson murmured. "It's scary."

"Danger," Chalmers said quietly. "Back by the cage."

From the cage everything looked all right again. It was Protean midafternoon, with a few cumulus clouds overhead. No breeze stirred the gray-green leaves, no birds flew.

"What kind of danger, Hank?" Gard asked.

"Ignorance is danger now. All we know yet is that some influence unstructures our perception, makes the world look like an impressionist painting."

"Monet sweated to *achieve* that vision. Where's the danger?"

"Van Gogh had that vision thrust upon him," Chalmers said crisply, "and it ended by killing him. Let's map out the boundary and mark it with twigs.

We'll be our own instruments."

The boundary was a rough circle. The men looked at Gard.

"Now what, Hank?" McPherson asked Chalmers.

"We need more data," Gard said. "Have to know how bad it gets. Maybe it's a belt that lets up again. I'll go out alone, a little further. You watch me, but don't come after me *whatever happens.*"

He walked into the zone like a boxer into the ring, his symmetrical athlete's torso gleaming in the sun.

Gard screamed and threshed as they dragged him in by the cage.

"Come out of it, Ed!" Chalmers barked, slapping him. "You're all right."

Gard sat up and shook his head. The others bent above him.

"You wandered like a tapeless robot out there," McPherson said. "When you stumbled back in you flopped and screamed. What happened?"

"First the blur and the vibration of visual things," Gard said slowly. "Then everything came alive and the sky was a big face and I couldn't bear it any more and then *snap* — the dream."

"What did you dream?" Chalmers asked.

"A true thing, Hank, out of my past. When I was ten I fell from a concrete bomb ruin. Part way down rusty rods caught me under the left arm pit and shoulder blade, tore up the brachial plexus — that's how I got this lopsided look and the gimp arm. I hung there — Christ it was awful, living that again!"

He stroked his withered left arm with a wry smile, then stood up.

"Well," Chalmers said. "Disintegration of the world-gestalt. Sudden hypermnesic regression to an earlier personality configuration at a point of trauma. No physical harm, but the subject is incapacitated for rational behavior in present time. I generalize from one instance, as I shouldn't. Words are comforting, but these are only whats. Who'll offer a how?"

(Continued on next page)

"I'll try," Svirsky said. "The Proteans may have a kind of action-space inconceivable to us and probably not conceptual with them. They have thrown a *barrier* around this island of our own action-space —"

"Blank nonsense!" Onderdonck broke in. "Gard is a brainsick fool, that's what and how both. He'll take Webb Onderdonck no further!"

The fat man held a stick from the cage and shook it toward the ship.

"I can *see* the ship," he said. "This is some kind of optical razzle-dazzle, but where this stick can go Webb Onderdonck can follow. I'll *close* my damned eyes!"

He strode off, jabbing the stick angrily into the ground ahead of him with each step.

"There walks a man braver than he is able to know," Svirsky said softly.

They drew together and watched him go, stick jabbing, undeviating, and *tension rose and gripped them in a great collective shudder.*

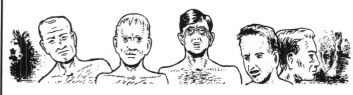

"Their action-space overpowers our own, limits us and frees us in ways inconceivable."

"But how? There's a danger, God knows we all five feel it now, but let's put a finger on it," Chalmers said.

"Death, maybe," Gard said. "When I fell, I caught a ledge with my fingers. It seemed to me I deliberately let go. When I hung on those rods I screamed as much in frustration as I pain."

"So?"

"So maybe the thing that says 'I' can't bear disintegration of the symbol system. Maybe it *is* the symbol system, something emergent at a high level of abstraction and integration, oh dammit, something modulated onto the body's life like information on a carrier wave, a thing of words only — don't mind me, people. I'm talking in tongues."

"Hardly a revelation. But go on."

"All right, in desperation out there we might become able to flash back along ourselves to a point of

danger and tip the scales for death. I tell you, I *felt* it!"

"The pain I grant you, but not the danger. Suppose you *had* killed yourself, aged ten. Then you couldn't have made that unauthorized tape-substitution and we wouldn't be here. But we are here."

"Someone else would have done it, perhaps you."

"That's changing the *past,*" McPherson said angrily.

"The past would be intact all the way back to Creation, for all you could ever determine," Gard said. "But I'd be dead."

"I just can't *think* it, Ed."

"None of us can think it in our bones and muscles, Ike," Svirsky said, "but we can still talk about it in words. Listen now, not with your muscles. Each of us is a word-line in a four-dimensional continuum that contains a certain *irreversibility*. To know ourselves, we segregate the irreversibility into one dimension and call it time. Then we experience ourselves as free in the other three dimensions. Suppose now, not with your muscles, that the Proteans handle the irreversibility differently. They have made a cage for us, as we for them, but of their own word stuff."

"Show me a crucial test for that hypothesis and I'll buy it, Joe," Chalmers said. "But you do give me an idea. We have long known how language both structures and reflects the structure of the microcosm which we project into the world and what a *social* process it is. We may be able to overcome this disintegrating influence by going out in company and *talking* constantly."

"Not all of us," Gard said sharply. "We might all flash back and get hurt or die and this trip would never have been. I won't have that."

"You mean to coerce history by holding back a hostage? I talk in words, I talk in words!"

"Yes. There may also be a least action factor that makes prevention of suicide more probable than bodily replacement."

"I wish we *could* cancel this trip!" Minelli burst out. "That guy Onderdonck that broke his back ski-jumping just before we left must've known what he was doing. God knows how *we'll* end."

"I see your point, Ed, but I prefer to call it a control. Whom shall we leave?"

(Continued on next page)

"Joe and yourself," McPherson said. "In time you two will hammer things out flat, I feel it. We can't risk you."

Chalmers demurred and was shouted down. Gard's right hand clasped McPherson's left strongly. Minelli had firm hold of Gard's left wrist. The three men moved out, talking steadily.

Look, the tree's blurry. Pete, Pete, pick out the leaves. Keep seeing the leaves, well the branches then don't let it get solid pull off a twig man feel it bite it bleeding the tree screamed bending at me the earth the grass pull it bleed ingand foldingover God'seyeup then...

"...eat mud, Ed Gard. You said it's no different up here than on the ground."

"Must be a hundred-foot drop."

"So the I-beam is still just as wide as the one you walked down below. With your eyes closed, down below. Eat mud, Ed Gard."

"I'm scared. But I won't eat mud."

"Eat mud, Ed Gard."

"Here goes, damn you. Just as wide, nothing to it..."

....armsthrashingco lorsflashing the fear the fear jerking him along past lump trees a man too, and there Svirsky reaching out, the zone, of course, clearing now, all right now.

Mary Gard let go of Vane's hand and looked ruefully at Chalmers.

"Well, Hank, talking doesn't help," she said.

"That's data too, Mary. What did you experience, Chuck? Time suicide?"

"Hell no," Vane said. "We talked and things went horrible anyway and then bang, we were still talking, but it was back in my office in Denver. A real memory-dream, like. Mary was just telling me about Ike McPherson being arrested for rape and it was an hour before lift out. She was crying."

"Can you really cry, Mary?" Chalmers asked.

"Tears of rage, Hank," Mary said. "I couldn't bear being thwarted. Even with only Chuck and I know-ing the secret, the jinx still worked. Onderdonck broke his back and Minelli got cut up in a tavern brawl and that was all right, we could go short-handed. But we *had* to have a shipman."

"She knew I was licensed," Vane took up the story. "She said it was Earth's last chance to solve the mystery of Proteus and she *wouldn't* let it go, was I a man or a mouse, and me saying I'd be busted out of the Corps and my wife screaming mad and both of us still saying it as she dragged me up the gangplank."

"That doesn't support your death-urge hypothesis, Mary," Chalmers said.

"Mine does again. Maybe it's just me," Mary said. "I went back to an experience of my father's, a bad fall that kept him out of school for a year. It was eerie — death waiting and a kind of voluptuous *wanting* to fall. I could *feel* myself taunting myself into it, swinging myself into vertigo, yet it was my father all the time."

"But your father survived. Even granting that your consciousness can cross a world-line synapse into a parent, you haven't changed anything. Chuck's experience was innocuous. Our solid evidence indicates only loss of awareness and coordination in present time."

"Even so, that's dangerous," Vane said. "We couldn't man the ship in that state. The wolf-things or even the Proteans could eat us alive."

"Chuck, that's the how!" Mary cried. " Remember how the Proteans seem to paralyze or uncoordinate the goat-things they sometimes eat? I'll bet they just *run around them*. Remember how they walked around us and we felt angry and had headaches and how I conked out and got bitten on my arm? They were trying to put us in cages then and we were too strong. So now they've done it massively. It's as if we'd made our cage out of armor plate after the first one failed."

"That's part of the what, not the how," Chalmers objected, "and your argument is from analogy —"

"Which may be perfectly good *Protean* logic," Svirsky interrupted. "It's a Protean cage we're in. No how will satisfy you until we reduce it to touch and kinesthesis. But this how is different. Consider, our bodies are not caged but our minds are."

"How can a *mind* be *caged?*" Vane asked.

(Continued on next page)

"When we know, we will escape," Svirsky said. "We must play a word game now apart from muscle-thinking. We are in a trap. Here in our cage our entropy increases. I am thirsty. I feel the heat of that sun, but I marked the cage shadow after our first alarm and in all our scramblings since *that sun has not moved.*"

Chalmers paled. "That's something I can grasp, anyway. It supports Mary's weird notion about changing the past. That stillness out there. Time stasis. To be conscious is to be conscious of *change...* now I talk in tongues, Mary."

"It's only a word game, Hank. Keep talking."

"All right, changing the past, words only," Vane said. "Coercing history by leaving someone behind. That dream I had out there, damn it, I *wanted* to tell Mary to go to hell and I couldn't. Maybe that was history coercing me. But let's all go out now, and if I hit that sequence again you can damn well bet I'll refuse and we'll be out of this fix. Word game!"

"No," Mary said. "I won't have it so."

"We can't really change the past, Mary, and you know it," Chalmers said. "Both times you were out you trended to the left under a kind of tropism that brought you back in. The worst that can happen is that we will all have a shaking up and a bad dream. But how do we know that this *island* of ours will not move with us if we all go? We must use trial and error until we have enough data for an operational hypothesis."

"Muscle-thinking," Svirsky said. "But let's try it, Hank. We can pick up our word game afterward."

"I'm coming back," Mary warned.

Svirsky's big hand encircled her left wrist.

Water black as the night sky above swirled around Thomas Gard's chest. His small son in the crook of his left arm whimpered into his ear. His wife was losing her footing, clinging to his right elbow, pulling him over.

"Climb up on me, Mary," he said, stooping a little. "Let me carry you both. We'll be swept away else."

"You haven't the strength, Tom. Let me go, save Edward."

"All of us or none of us, Mary. Only a hundred yards now."

"Too far. I know it. Edward, goodbye Edward,

you be a brave, strong man now."

"Mary!"

"Goodbye, Tom. I love you."

The current swept her into darkness. Thomas Gard shouted her name in anguish over the black, swirling water. The child cried in greater fear.

The four men stumbled into present awareness by the metal cage, still holding hands. Chalmers was trembling.

"I grant you that death-urge now, Ed," he gasped, "but don't ask me —"

"Never mind, Hank," Gard said. "Let's be convinced now that charging bullheaded into it isn't going to change a thing. We have to *think* our minds free of this."

"God yes," McPherson said. "I relived that fight I had with Vane when he tried to restrict me to the base the night before lift out. I felt *murderous*, I tell you. He kept getting up and I beat him almost to death. I thought I'd get a year in jail."

"He was trying to beat the jinx on Proteus," Gard said. "That's why he restricted you and also why he wouldn't bring charges."

"The fight bothered me," McPherson admitted. "I went on to the party, but I couldn't get drunk. I didn't have enough steam or ugliness left in me to carry through that near-rape I relived the first time out. Funny how things hang together."

"Isn't it, though? I went through a crucial episode in my grandfather's life, a flood. I was three people and this time I think I accepted death while willing life. But that's not data, even for a word game."

"I'll play now, Joe," Chalmers said. "Start your word game."

"Let your muscles hear this part," Svirsky said. "Sit down and relax."

They sprawled on the dull green grass.

"We vertebrates define time, space and thingness first in our own bodies," Svirsky began. "Then we

(Continued on next page)

generalize them to all sensory input to make a real world. It was an action-world for a billion years before it became a thought-world, and it is muscles which act. Our wiring diagram provides our muscles with two separate innervation circuits.

"One circuit is for muscle tone and it never relaxes completely until death. It maintains posture, any unchanging position we hold through time. It does it by continuous motor discharge from and kinesthetic sensory feedback to the cerebellum. From the cerebellum association fibers go to the cerebral cortex and almost all of this innervation is on the *same* side of the body as the muscles concerned.

"Suppose for the moment that tonus underlies our basic feeling of time as duration.

"The phasic innervation provides for action, the causing of relative position changes among things. It starts from the motor area of the cortex and feeds back to the adjacent sensory area. Both areas on both hemispheres have the shapes of grotesque manikins. Discriminatory touch, pain and temperature also feed into the sensory areas. But the fibers nearly all *cross over* from muscles and skin on the *opposite* side of the body.

"Suppose now that phasis underlies our root-feeling for space and change. Suppose further that its cortical projection areas are superimposed on the uncrossed sensory-tonic projection from the cerebellum. Suppose finally that combination of sameness-in-difference gives us the stubbornly felt apartness of time from space and, in the tension between them, thingness. Number, magnitude, causality, the world, can follow.

"We know our language structures our thought and the world we experience. But the structure of our nervous system, our coding and uncoding equipment, provides language itself with an invariant pattern upon which linguistic relativity is only secondary elaboration.

"All of this, my brothers, is to persuade your muscles not to listen to what I wish to say next."

Gard flexed his powerful left arm. " You just go along for the ride, now," he addressed his biceps.

"Almost you make me touch the how of how itself," Chalmers mused. "Go on with the word game. My muscles are out of circuit."

Svirsky smiled. "The Protean vertebrate wiring diagram," he said, "does not provide for tract cross-ings in the cord. The brain is imperfectly divided and has no bundled commissures. Like us, they code the world in volleys of neural impulse, but their decoding equipment is *different.*"

"Like us, they exist in the continuum as world-lines. They have wound around our own thin sheaf of world-lines a massive coil of their world-lines. It makes a time cage that coerces our world-lines in a way our muscles cannot *grasp.*"

"You mean they outvoted us muscleheads?" McPherson asked.

"They have more of their kind of muscle, Ike," Chalmers agreed. " But Joe, do you mean we have to grasp *their* reality?"

"We must stop trying to *grasp* it. I said our vertebrate wiring diagram may dictate our primal symbol of reality. But some few of the fibers in each case I cited do not follow the structural rule. And we have also, below consciousness, a phylogenetically older diagram. These are ghosts within us, my brothers, not bound to the primal symbol. Let us wake them now.

"Let go of lever and pushrod causality for the notion of statistical covariance. Let go of that for the still more primitive notion of 'organism' and 'sympathy of the whole' out of which both arise. Remember that fairly late in the pre-space era our own ancestors used to bewitch each other and one potent how was to run nine times widdershins around the victim. Think of that timeless, spaceless, pre-vertebral 'sympathy of the whole' as the substrate from which parapsychological phenomena still arise to bedevil science centuries after Rhine."

"You mean we're bewitched, then?" Chalmers asked.

"That's the simplest how that we can dredge out of our symbol system," Svirsky agreed. "We are under a spell so powerful that our massed rationality cannot prevail against it at any cost. So we must erect your operational hypothesis on an irrational base.

"Here is one. We are caged by a field effect. When we cut across it consciousness drops almost to a cellular level and the coordinating 'I' flees screaming. But fields have structure. We must find a geodesic and it may lead us out."

(Continued on next page)

"We can only grasp fields instrumentally," Chalmers objected. "But, of course, *we* can be the instruments. To hell with observer detachment."

"Exactly," Svirsky smiled. "Each time Ed trended to the left out there, I think the pre-vertebral ghost in him was seeking the geodesic."

"I'll be the instrument," Gard said. "How do you calibrate me?"

"You're already calibrated, in degrees of rationality on scales of perception and speech," Svirsky said. "Get me two of those sticks you meant to use in playing Kohler to the Proteans."

He took out his shoelaces and tied an eight-foot stick to each of Gard's upper arms.

"So I steer you, Ed, when the pointer swings off optimum," he said. "See, we play Kohler to ourselves now."

Gard slanted leftward into the critical area. "The musclehead leading the muscleheads," he laughed. "Here we go, people."

He described what he saw and Svirsky held him to coherence with tugs and nudges. Very shortly Gard learned to correct for himself. He followed an erratic, looping, doubling course that still trended leftward. After the first lap around the cage Chalmers remarked that it was a spiral of opposite hand to the Protean mass-spiral.

"That's our statistical trend," Svirsky chuckled, "but who will write the equation for the path we actually follow?"

"We really must work up the statistical dynamics of witchcraft someday," Chalmers laughed back. "Teach every sophomore how to unrun a spell."

The fifth lap missed the ship's ramp by twenty feet. McPherson was dismayed, but Chalmers laughed again.

"I always knew Finagle was a Protean," he said. "We forgot to add his constant to the right hand vector."

"We'll add it now," Svirsky said. "Ed, untie the sticks. Now imagine yourself running to the top of that ramp. Flex your muscles for each step. Experience yourself at the top looking down. Then pull the trigger and *make it so*. Can you do that?"

"Sure," Gard said.

He looked up and down the ramp, pranced a little, then dashed to the top through a blur of motion. He turned, only to be knocked flat by three hurtling bodies.

"Take it *easy*," Gard said, getting up. "It's good to be home, but not *that* good, people."

"We stood down there at least five minutes deciding why you were frozen like a statue up here," Chalmers said. "Then Ike came up and froze, then Joe, and finally I came. We all got here at the exact, same instant."

"I see. We snapped back into our own time. But Joe, how could you know we'd be out of the field up here? Is it a ship effect?"

"Another hunch, Ed. I suspected the Proteans might only project space in two directions so that the field might attenuate rapidly on the vertical."

"Well what d'ye know!" McPherson said disgustedly.

"We could just as well have walked out on stilts. So damned *simple!* How stupid can you get?"

"Science can't answer that question," Chalmers said.

"Stations," Gard said. "Let's lift out, Ike."

In subspace, on automatics, the four of them relaxed with coffee.

"Our report," Gard said. "I propose we rig it and conclude that Proteus is not only unsuitable for settlement but of no interest to commerce, science or even art."

"Right," Chalmers agreed. "How could we ever tell them otherwise?"

"Oh, I don't know," McPherson said. "Use Joe's line about fields. People savvy fields, all right."

"Yes," Chalmers said. "Fences around them. Flowers and grass. When a man's in a field he's got both feet on the ground."

"Joe," Gard broke in, "I think you knew more all along than you let on. Why didn't you come up with that explanation sooner? Of course nobody got hurt, but you did let us all bloody our noses on that barrier."

"Maybe I could have, Ed," Svirsky admitted. "Maybe I even wanted to. But if I had, my brothers, it would have seemed to all of us too silly for words."

"Not to speak of action," Chalmers said softly. ●

Richard McKenna's "Bramble Bush" was first published in ORBIT 3, edited by Damon Knight. © 1968 by Damon Knight. Reprinted by permission.

MONEY IN THE 21ST CENTURY

by Michael E. Marotta

Illustration by Mary Fleener

In the 21st century, new forms of money will make possible accumulations of capital several orders of magnitude greater than anything today. We will see trillionaires and quadrillionaires.

> **"In the 21st century, new forms of money will make possible accumulations of capital several orders of magnitude greater than anything today. We will see trillionaires and quadrillionaires."**

The ways that people create, store, and transmit wealth define every major shift in social history. This is not Marxism, it is Capitalism. The common

lot, the life of the average person (who may always be called a "serf"), improves. Life gets better. Life gets best, however, for those who understand the nature of money. Like electricity, money works according to objective physical laws. Only an elite few understand these laws. Most people do not even know that such laws exist: they survive hand-to-mouth on monetary superstitions.

KNOWLEDGE IS POWER

Until about 8000 BC, in order to be "wealthy" you had to have a herd to follow. Then, someone invented agriculture. Domesticating herds and crops made it possible to have more food than you could eat in a lifetime. The invention of agrarian villages brought new forms of social organization.

(Continued on next page)

Among these forms was the invention of taxation. Engravings from Babylon show people being beaten with sticks for not paying their taxes. The privilege of living in a world of predictable bounty from agriculture carried a price.

> ## "Like electricity, money works according to objective physical laws. Most people do not even know that such laws exist: they survive hand-to-mouth on monetary superstitions."

Also, about 8000 BC, a system of clay tokens was invented. The tokens represented sheep, wheat, cloth, beer, and other products. The tokens allowed future planning — and the prediction of taxes. By about 4000 BC, use of these tokens led to the invention of writing and numbering.

This, then, is the basic pattern. A new form of wealth (agriculture) brought a new form of society (theocracy) and two new forms of information transfer (writing and counting).

ACCOUNTING FOR HISTORY

The earliest written records consist mostly of inventories. When not tallies of taxes, the inventories are often part of contracts between merchants. Following the accumulation of capital that agriculture made possible, trade became the newest way to manage and accumulate wealth. A special kind or "class" of person discovered profit in carrying goods from place to place.

By 4000 BC, merchants invented (or discovered) metal money. This escalated the levels at which wealth could be created, stored, and transmitted. A shekel of gold (about 10 grams or one-third of an ounce) was the equivalent of a cow. The value of a herd of cows could be carried in your hands. Metal also lasts much longer than a cow. Thus, the value of the animal in the here-and-now could be transmitted in both place and time. The rise of metal money accompanied improvements in record-keeping: cuneiform and hieroglyphics. Also at this time, the records show the first use of abstract number.

About 700 BC, coinage was invented as bonus payments to the mercenary soldiers of tyrants. The Greek tyrants were generally self-made men, merchants, who capped a successful career with civic service. To do so, they had to overthrow the agricultural aristocracies. Coinage was the tool that made the revolution successful. That revolution brought a rapid transformation from hereditary monarchy to tyranny, oligarchy, and democracy.

The written records from the ancient Greeks no longer consisted of the concrete listing of physical objects. The Greeks had also discovered the metaphysical. And the metaphysical is objectively real. So real, that by 300 BC, Philetairos founded the town of Pergamon with 9000 talents of silver from Alexander's treasury. This is about five million ounces at a time when an ounce of silver per month was an average wage for a soldier, a rower on a galley, or a citizen at assembly. Think of it as $7 billion.

During the Middle Ages, bankers invented double-entry bookkeeping and adopted Arabic numerals. They also invented money of account: pounds, shillings, and pence. These units originally had no physical reality. They were only constructs for tallying a confusing plethora of local coinages. More subtly, the books of a banker were regarded as a store of wealth. When bankers met at fairs, they could clear their accounts without ever touching a coin. In the 1500s, Spain looted the Aztecs and Incas, but the silver and gold ran through her ports like water through a sieve: she had already been mortgaged to the bankers of Holland and Germany. Each shipload of hard money made Spain poorer.

> ## "In the 1500s, Spain looted the Aztecs and Incas, but the silver and gold ran through her ports like water through a sieve: she had already been mortgaged to the bankers of Holland and Germany."

The British colonies of North America had always been short on hard currency. They made due with paper. Just as metal money follows rules different than a cow, so, too, does paper money

(Continued on next page)

have its own reality. Paper was well-suited to frontier life: it is easy to transport; it depends on inter-personal trust; it has no permanence. Americans moved mountains with paper. Coal, steel, railroads, telegraphs, everything that America became, derived from a generally correct (if intuitive) understanding of the power of paper money. From John Jacob Astor and Cornelius Vanderbilt to Bill Gates and Donald Trump, far more Americans became far richer, far faster, than anyone could have dreamed possible.

> **"Today, we have an information-based global society whose proper form of money is digital cash. Just as cows and coins and paper changed the people who used them, so, too, will digital cash reshape your world."**

Today, we have an information-based global society whose proper form of money is digital cash. Electronic funds transfers and parking-lot debit cards are only two expressions of this new medium. Just as cows and coins and paper changed the people who used them, so, too, will digital cash reshape your world.

THE GREAT PYRAMID

Every day billions of dollars in transactions cross the electronic networks as banks buy and sell currencies at short term. In a typical midwest American town such as Pittsburgh or St. Louis, a nondescript, medium-sized bank might have four or five high-strung traders who earn a dizzying net of one percent (or less!) by the end of the day. But 1% compounded over 365 days means that their capital increases 37 times in a year.

Futures trading in leveraged accounts opens the door to the person with a desire to get rich electronically. And it must be electronically. The daily "investment" newspapers only record the past. It is not enough to read about a change in price on the bus home and execute a trade the next morning. The global village never sleeps.

While millions of people watch sitcoms, a handful of others are on-line, trading wheat, dollars, sow bellies, and heating oil. In the morning, the price of cooking breakfast has changed, and someone is several hundred dollars richer than they were the day before. One half of one percent each day, compounded over 365 days, means a six-fold increase in your holdings: say from $30,000 to $180,000. The white-collar employee who reads a newspaper and calls a no-load broker is not in the same league at all. That person is much closer to a Third World farmer helping a cow deliver a new calf.

Try to buy something from abroad with a check drawn in a foreign currency. Your bank will charge you $20 just to handle $20 worth of marks or francs. You will pay twice: once for the money and again for the bank to handle it. If you want something from overseas, you have to buy it here from a retailer who bought it from a wholesaler who bought it from an importer. The person who uses cash is condemned to an economy they can visit in person.

But, if you use a bank card, the credit card company will automatically exchange your currencies for the smallest of transaction fees; about one percent, for instance. With a credit card, you enter the world of international electronic money. This is just one small slice of the electronic money pie. In today's world, the rich will outpace the poor at whatever transmission rates their modems will allow.

A NEW CONTINENT

In the 1200s, the bankers of Florence adopted Arabic numerals without hesitation — and the city council outlawed the new system. Of course, this was futile. In our age, the invention of public key cryptosystems is also well-received and also subject to government controls. Such controls cannot last.

Public key cryptosystems enable a technology of anonymous authentication. You no longer need to know who someone is in order to be satisfied that they are who they say they are. If they have the key to the code, that is enough. This means that if a smart credit card says that it has $1000 on it, a merchant can know it does without knowing what bank it came from or how it got there. The merchant can transfer all or some of the value to

(Continued on next page)

his own account — either a bank account or a "digital cash" card.

> ## "Gold may be the best store of value. It is not the best medium of exchange. If he were to liquidate Microsoft for gold, Bill Gates would need a troupe of 3,000 bearers to carry the bullion."

This technology is being developed by several firms today. The leader in the field may be DigiCash, founded in 1990 by mathematician David Chaum. DigiCash has a licensing agreement from MasterCard. That agreement also opened the door to two other cards: Europay and VISA. All of this transaction processing requires computers, of course, so IBM and Siemens are also working with the DigiCash corporation.

Again, we have the basic pattern. The new technology includes new forms of communication. In fact, they are equivalent. The computer is our newest tool of wealth-creation. It is also the contemporary medium of storage and transfer. The person who today cannot be comfortable with a 100-digit encryption cipher is like the Babylonian farmer who could not conceptualize abstract numbers.

In fact, DigiCash has also created its own currency: "Cyberbucks." Launched in October, 1994, this is a "virtual currency." There is no way to exchange Cyberbucks for marks or dollars. But you can buy goods, services, or information with Cyberbucks: the relative scarcity of what you buy gives value to the currency. About 100 companies offer their wares in exchange for Cyberbucks.

This is not a new idea.

In the 1700s, merchants such as John Wilkinson struck tons of their own copper coins. In the early 1800s, bronze tokens from America and Canada joined those from the British East India Company. The King of England and the Congress of the United States outlawed them to no avail. The Supreme Court of the United States declared that American workers had a "right" to be paid in government money. Of course, the officers of America's corporations were happy to be paid in

something far more valuable: options and warrants for stock in their companies.

THE UTOPIA OF GREED

Historically, money has served three purposes: it is a medium of exchange (indirect barter), it is a store of value, and a unit of account. That it is a medium of exchange is its primary nature. This creates the opportunity for the other two purposes. Historically, gold served all three needs. However, there is also a division of labor among the forms of money. The store of value, the medium of exchange, and the unit of account need not be the same item.

Gold may be the best store of value. It is not the best medium of exchange. If he were to liquidate Microsoft for gold, Bill Gates would need a troupe of 3,000 bearers to carry the bullion. Hard currency, paper, or coins, are inherently limiting. On the other hand, electronic transfers involve no such physical constraints. In the world of the 21st century, those who master the medium of digital cash will be the only ones on the top of the pyramid.

Political conservatives claim that gold is an "objective" value, that it is "universally" recognized and accepted. Perhaps so. Perhaps not. The universe is a big place. On the other hand, in a world where airliners drop from the sky for mysterious reasons, your universe can become limited. We may see the end of nation states as we know them. We might see small, sealed communities, relying on telecommunications for virtual exchange. In that world, you are more likely to exchange cyberbucks than gold.

The accelerating accumulation of wealth cannot be stopped. In the next century, successful trillionaires will plot to become quadrillionaires. The "wretched, huddled masses" who debark at a space station called New Liberty might be those who scraped together $20 million in cybercredits.●

Michael E. Marotta is a technical writer, currently creating documentation for a large accounting database. In August of 1996, he was awarded the Heath Literary Prize of the American Numismatic Association for an article on the origins of coinage. His e-mail address is mercury@well.com.

Feasting On The Convicted Class
by Dan Pens

Illustration by Steve Lafler

"The image of the prison guard, 'the screw,' planted in the minds of the American public by the gangster films of the '30s and '40s, has given the job a distasteful aura which the new euphemism 'correction officer' cannot hide." — The American Almanac of Jobs and Salaries, 1984 Edition

It is impossible to be unaware of the tremendous increase in the number of hostages confined in U.S. jails and prisons. Each year the Department of Justice's Bureau of Justice Statistics releases a voluminous report of the previous year's body count. These figures are picked up by the corporate media and trumpeted to the masses. The latest numbers, from 1995, bring the toll to 1,125,979 men and women imprisoned in state and federal prisons as of December 31, 1995. Another half-million were caged in city and county lockups. To put that in perspective, 1 in 167 U.S. residents was behind bars at year's end.

In 1970 there were a total of 196,429 state and federal prisoners; in 1980 there were 329,821. The U.S. prison population is now 5.7 times as large as in 1970, 3.4 times larger than in 1980.

As stated before, these numbers are paraded out each year and are widely disseminated by both the mainstream and alternative press. All you hear about, though, are the numbers of prisoners. What about the flip side? What about guards? Has anybody given much thought (or press coverage) to their ever-increasing numbers? Well, maybe *you* haven't, but you can bet your ass that laid-off oil-field workers in Texas are hip to the glut in prison jobs. Downsized defense workers in California know where to hop onto the next government-subsidized gravy train. Prisons. Guards. Jobs. Gravy. A fat government paycheck. State bennies and retirement. And best of all? You don't even have to *work!* Just show up, go to your post, and stand there looking stupid all day. Piece of cake!

"Job opportunities for corrections officers are expected to be plentiful through the year 2005.... Employment of corrections officers is expected to increase much faster than the average of all occupations through the year 2005."
— U.S. Department of Labor Occupational Outlook Handbook, 1994-95 Edition

(Continued on next page)

How many prison guards are currently employed in the U.S.? There are conflicting figures. According to the Dept. of Labor's *Occupational Outlook Handbook*, in 1988 there were 111,600 guards employed in state and federal prisons (and an additional 74,400 employed at city and county jails). Four years later (1992) the number of state and federal prison guards had increased more than 50 percent to 169,200.

According to a 1996 *Corrections Compendium* survey (which relies on state prisoncrats to self-disclose the data), the nation currently employs 181,489 state and federal prison guards, a 17 percent increase over the previous two years. There is considerable discrepancy, however, between the two sources. If you take the Dept. of Labor's 1992 total of 169,200 guards and superimpose the *Corrections Compendium* survey's growth rate of 17 percent every two years, you end up with more than a quarter of a million prison guards. That figure is probably closer to the truth.

More than 15,000 new guard jobs were created in 1995 according to the *Corrections Compendium* survey, 5,400 in Texas alone.

Since the Reagan era, most labor unions have been reduced in both membership and political clout. By contrast, state employee unions have enjoyed healthy growth since America's imprisonment binge exploded in 1980. Currently, more than three quarters of state and federal prison guards are union members. The American Federation of State, City and Municipal Employees (AFSCME) appears to be the most common guard union, representing prison guards in about 15 states. Guards in 11 states are not represented by a union. In the remaining states they are covered mainly by state unions.

Chief among the various state prison-guard unions, the California Correctional Peace Officer's Association (CCPOA) is unquestionably the hog with the biggest nuts. The CCPOA is an incredibly well-fed Political Interest Group (PIG) which has buried its snout so deep into the state trough that it threatens to starve California's economy and throw the state into complete ruin. Exaggeration? Catastrophizing? Judge for yourself.

In 1980 there were 22,500 prisoners in California. Salaries for prison guards averaged about $23,000. The state corrections budget was $300 million. California's economy was strong in 1980, bolstered by large numbers of defense-related jobs. California's schools and universities were the envy of the world.

In 1996 there are more than 125,000 prisoners in California. The average yearly salary for California prison guards is $37,140 (more than $50,000 with generous benefits factored in). That is $10,000 more than the average teacher's salary. California prison guards need have only a high school diploma (or G.E.D.) and a six-week training course. Most teaching jobs require at least an undergraduate degree in education.

For the first time ever, in 1993, the state spent a greater portion of its budget on corrections than on education, compared to as recently as 1983/84 when California spent 3.9% of its budget on corrections and 10% on education. The state corrections budget was $3 *billion* in 1993/94 and has since topped the $5 billion mark.

Between 1984-94, California added a whopping 25,900 prison employees, substantially more than were added by all other state departments combined (16,000). By one estimate, hiring for prisons and jails has accounted for 45 percent of the growth in *all* California jobs since 1984.

The CCPOA's rise to political power can be traced to 1980, when Don Novey became the union's president. Novey is the son of a prison guard. He graduated from American River College and served in Army Intelligence in the late '60s. Then, before becoming head of the union, he worked as a prison guard in Folsom.

Prior to Novey's ascendancy, the union had been a weak, pitiful parasite, with a membership divided between the California State Employees' Association and the California Correctional Officers' Association. In all, it had only about 5,600 members. But when Novey won control of its leadership, the union combined Youth Authority supervisors and parole officers with prison guards, consolidating and increasing its membership. That consolidation, combined with the acceleration of new prison construction (the state has built 21 new prisons since 1980), swelled the CCPOA membership to more than 23,000.

The union collects nearly $8 million a year in dues, and it expends, according to the *San Francisco Examiner,* twice as much in political contributions as the California Teachers Association, although it is only one-tenth the size. The union is now second only to the California Medical Association in political contributions.

Don Novey has shaped the CCPOA into a potent political force. Candidates for governor have genuflected at Novey's feet in hopes of gaining the endorsement and deep-pocket largess of his union, and have submitted to grilling by the union leadership to see if they were worthy.

Jack Meola, the CCPOA's executive vice president, says their questioning of candidates is intense. To fail the test, Novey maintains, could mean the difference between victory and defeat. Diane Feinstein found that out in 1990 when Novey's union gave almost $1 million to enthrone law enforcement's friend, Pete Wilson. The union pumped *more* than a million dollars into Wilson's successful 1994 reelection campaign.

(Continued on next page)

State Prison Guard Salary Comparison 1980 -1996

	STARTING SALARY			AVERAGE SALARY			
	1980	1996	% chg.	1980	1996	% chg.	Union
Alabama	15,500	17,823	15%	17,225	31,408	82%	Yes
Alaska	22,850	31,572	38%	27,125	N/A	N/A	Yes
Arizona	14,800	N/A	N/A	18,550	N/A	N/A	N/A
Arkansas	10,200	17,293	70%	13,425	20,800	60%	None
California	20,000	24,012	20%	23,225	37,140	60%	Yes
Colorado	15,300	23,784	55%	18,950	37,584	98%	Optional
Connecticut	15,150	25,192	66%	17,600	30,880	75%	Yes
Delaware	12,550	21,753	73%	17,725	27,100	53%	Yes
Florida	10,750	18,109	68%	12,775	19,110	50%	Yes
Georgia	10,400	17,652	70%	13,525	21,306	58%	Yes
Hawaii	12,700	N/A	N/A	15,625	N/A	N/A	N/A
Idaho	12,150	13,977	15%	15,968	21,715	35%	N/A
Illinois	13,800	N/A	N/A	16,450	N/A	N/A	N/A
Indiana	12,400	N/A	N/A	15,975	N/A	N/A	N/A
Iowa	12,900	24,980	94%	17,775	N/A	N/A	Yes
Kansas	12,600	17,868	42%	15,800	N/A	N/A	Yes
Kentucky	10,300	16,260	58%	15,875	21,138	33%	None
Louisiana	10,450	14,736	41%	14,425	20,808	44%	Yes
Maine	11,850	17,722	50%	13,650	19,427	42%	Yes
Maryland	13,700	22,004	61%	18,100	32,460	79%	Yes
Massachusetts	14,900	28,114	89%	17,050	37,015	117%	Yes
Michigan	15,500	22,963	48%	18,225	N/A	N/A	Yes
Minnesota	14,300	23,114	62%	16,525	30,673	86%	Yes
Mississippi	11,000	16,238	48%	16,825	N/A	N/A	None
Missouri	11,700	18,516	58%	14,025	20,604	47%	Yes
Montana	11,650	N/A	N/A	14,900	N/A	N/A	N/A
Nebraska	12,250	20,292	66%	15,775	22,389	42%	Yes
Nevada	13,500	25,618	90%	17,825	26,689	50%	None
New Hampshire	12,500	N/A	N/A	14,575	N/A	N/A	N/A
New Jersey	14,050	31,805	126%	18,000	N/A	N/A	Yes
New Mexico	11,700	16,118	38%	16,575	19,173	16%	Yes
New York	14,800	22,500	52%	17,575	35,000	99%	Yes
North Carolina	11,500	19,645	71%	14,700	N/A	N/A	None
North Dakota	11,700	15,396	32%	17,425	20,640	18%	None

State Prison Guard Salary Comparison 1980 -1996

	STARTING SALARY			AVERAGE SALARY			
	1980	1996	% chg.	1980	1996	% chg.	Union
Ohio	9,950	23,878	139%	12,775	27,082	112%	Yes
Oklahoma	11,600	12,932	11%	14,500	19,800	37%	None
Oregon	14,000	24,600	76%	17,050	27,000	58%	Yes
Pennsylvania	15,200	20,426	34%	20,400	31,724	56%	Yes
Rhode Island	14,300	25,808	80%	16,325	41,736	156%	Yes
South Carolina	11,250	15,310	36%	15,300	17,297	13%	None
South Dakota	11,850	16,016	35%	15,525	19,000	22%	Yes
Tennessee	12,100	14,688	21%	14,625	N/A	N/A	None
Texas	13,850	16,524	19%	16,900	N/A	N/A	Yes
Utah	14,700	N/A	N/A	19,225	N/A	N/A	N/A
Vermont	9,600	20,000	108%	13,200	27,000	105%	Yes
Virginia	11,300	N/A	N/A	14,875	N/A	N/A	N/A
Washinton	14,700	23,280	58%	17,725	N/A	N/A	Yes
West Virginia	10,850	16,110	48%	14,275	19,500	37%	None
Wisconsin	14,100	18,949	34%	17,650	N/A	N/A	Yes
Wyoming	15,400	16,692	8%	20,250	17,556	(14%)	None
Washington DC	13,800	21,707	57%	19,075	30,729	61%	Yes
Federal BOP	N/A	23,915	N/A	N/A	30,577	N/A	Yes
Averages:	$13,136	$20,361	55%	$16,656	$26,158	57%	

Sources: 1980 Figures based on U.S. Office of Personnel Managment's State Salary Survey 1980. 1996 Figures Based on *Corrections Compendium* survey (Vol. XXI, No. 8 — August 1996)

Their bribery does not end, however, with the governor's office. The CCPOA poured $76,000 into the 1992 campaign coffers of David Elder, the chair of the State Assembly's Committee on Public Employment and Security — the very committee that rules directly on the pay and benefits of prison guards. The union received high value for its political contribution dollars. Guards were awarded special pay raises ahead of schedule (and when other state workers received no raises at all). California prison guards now boast one of the best pension plans of any state employees. In addition to excellent medical coverage, they receive 75 percent of their current salary at the time of retirement, with a two percent yearly increase.

Recognizing not only the importance of lobbying but the power of public relations, Novey began spending about a half-million PR dollars yearly, honing a public image of himself: that of a self-deprecating, fedora-wearing, blue-collar labor leader. To ward off critics of his membership's extravagant wages and benefits, Novey's PR machine drums up the theme that prison guards patrol "the toughest beat in the state." But that is simply not the case. As the *Los Angeles Times* pointed out, over the past three decades, 13 prison guards have been killed throughout the state compared with 63 officers in the LAPD — an organization with half the members of the CCPOA's 14,000 members who serve as prison guards (other CCPOA members work in parole or for the Youth Authority).

> **"The California Correctional Peace Officer's Association is an incredibly well-fed Political Interest group which has buried its snout so deep into the state trough that it threatens to starve California's economy and throw the state into complete ruin."**

The slick PR is aimed mainly at the public. State politicos don't need the heavy-handed propaganda to toe the CCPOA line. They know that one false step could result in Novey pulling a "Vasconcellos" on them. That is, the CCPOA richly endowing the campaign coffers of a political opponent, as Novey's union did to John Vasconcellos, the chair of the State Assembly's Ways and Means Committee and an opponent of the prison building boom.

Although it was generally conceded that Vasconcellos' seat was among the more secure in the Assembly, the CCPOA *still* laid more than $75,000 in the lap of his 1992 opponent, just to let Vasconcellos know that the union did not appreciate him signing a ballot argument against a prison bond initiative, or questioning the fat contracts being awarded to prison guards at a time when the state was in the direst fiscal strait since the Great Depression.

Vasconcellos was reelected in 1992 with a substantial majority. But a clear message had been sent to the self-described "progressive" who has labored long and hard for a more thoughtful approach to crime and incarceration.

> **"California now spends more on prisons than it does on colleges and universities."**

The crowning glory of the CCPOA's political-action campaign is without a doubt the passage of Proposition 184, the "Three Strikes" initiative. The CCPOA contributed $101,000 to get Prop 184 on the ballot, which

was clearly a key factor in the measure's passage.

Even though the legislature had already been cowed the previous year into passing virtually identical Three Strikes legislation, the version passed by voter initiative ensures that the legislature cannot easily modify this "Prison Guard Full Employment Act."

CCPOA member Lt. Kevin Peters, summed up the membership's position on "Three Strikes" shortly after it passed: "You can get a job anywhere. *This* is a *career*. And with the upward mobility and rapid expansion of the department, there are opportunities for the people who are [already employed as] correctional staff, and opportunities for the general public to become correctional officers. With 'Three Strikes' and the overcrowding we're going to experience with that, we're going to need to build at least three prisons a year for the next five years. Each one of those institutions will take approximately 1,000 employees."

In the three years since, more than 15,000 prisoners have been processed into California's prison system to serve lengthy sentences under Three Strikes. The state has been reluctant to hire more guards, and that's fine by the CCPOA; they're feasting on fat, juicy, overtime gravy.

> **"The public has been totally hookwinked by crime-fear hysteria which is fueled by the media and capitalized on by both major political parties to gain the attention and support of voters."**

In 1994, Avenal State Prison Lieutenant Darryl Andrade grossed $108,989, making him that year's highest-paid state employee. Andrade's base salary was $57,658; he ladled another $51,000 onto that in fat greasy overtime gravy.

In that same year, 702 California prison guards pulled down more than $75,000 annually, including Leonard Sims, a guard in the state prison's transportation unit, who boosted his regular $44,152 salary with another $52,164 in overtime pay. All told, the state shelled out $146 million in overtime wages for prison guards that year, $52 million more than was budgeted.

State Department of Personnel chief David Tirapelle says that overtime pay is cheaper than hiring more guards, since benefits and retirement packages can total up to 35 percent of a guard's salary.

(Continued on next page)

Guards in other states are reaping similar dividends, cashing in on the "Get Tough" rhetoric of a neo-fascist, corporate-owned State which no longer requires a domestic supply of cheap plentiful labor. Prison guards in Massachusetts have seen their salaries more than double since 1980, while the Rhode Island Brotherhood of Correctional Officers has managed to boost its members' pay by more than 150 percent since 1980.

The public has been totally hoodwinked by crime-fear hysteria which is fueled by the media and capitalized on by both major political parties to gain the attention and support of voters. Critics in California are beginning to voice their concerns over the direction these misguided policies are taking them.

> ## "If prison populations continue to swell at the present 8.5% annual growth rate, by the middle of the next century half the country will be in prison and the other half will be working there."

The once-Golden State, whose public education system was the envy of the world, now ranks in the bottom ten nationally in K-12 education spending. There are almost no meaningful drug rehab programs in California, and almost no housing for the homeless (not even in its prisons, which remain the most overcrowded in the country). Hospital emergency rooms are closing all over the state; libraries in L.A. County are closed on weekends, and many are open only two days a week; kids in poorer neighborhoods have no place to go after school; and California now spends more on prisons than it does on colleges and universities.

Many corporations have fled California because of increased state taxes, and taken their jobs with them. Across the U.S., corporations increasingly close down domestic production facilities to take advantage of cheaper overseas labor. Although the decrease in industrial jobs has been partly offset by the increase in corrections jobs, it doesn't take a genius to see that this trend does not make for a viable economic strategy. If prison populations continue to swell at the present 8.5 % annual growth rate, by the middle of the next century half the country will be in prison and the other half will be working there.

The obscene growth in prison populations has been noted by others than just guard unions, however. And though the prospect of continued growth puts a smile on Don Novey's greedy mug, that golden future is overshadowed by the growth of two private prison corporations: Corrections Corporation of America and Wackenhut Corporation. They make the CCPOA and other guard unions look like veritable runts. The private prison corporations are definitely now the porkers with the grandest genitals in the prison-industrial barnyard. In 1993, total capacity in private-operated prisons rose 31.72 percent. In 1994, it rose 50.99 percent. There are now more than 60,000 members of the convicted class imprisoned in private lockups.

Private prisons are non-union. No bennies. No retirement packages. No overtime gravy.

Corporate prisons are a trend that bodes ill, and not just for prison-guard unions. As the two primary private-prison corporations fatten themselves off of the imprisonment binge, they grow ever larger and more capitalized, and garner greater interest from Wall Street. If you think Don Novey and the CCPOA were skilled political manipulators and PR hucksters, you ain't seen nothin' yet. Corporate-lobbyist and PR firms will have us building prisons so fast they'll be springing up like fast-food hamburger joints.

In a 1995 letter to shareholders, D.R. Grants, Chairman and CEO of Corrections Corporation of America, proudly and confidently expounded on the future: "There are powerful market forces driving our industry, and its potential has barely been touched. Truth-in-sentencing and stricter parole terms are popular strategies in most states... these new *measures* can only increase the demand for [CCA] facilities."

> ## "You ain't seen nothin' yet. Corporate-lobbyist and PR firms will have us building prisons so fast they'll be springing up like fast-food hamburger joints."

Sounds kind of like Don Novey in 1990. Except now it's Wall Street talking, not a state prison-guard union. Kind of scary, eh?

Meanwhile, these ravenous scum continue to gorge on the moldering *corpus delecti* of the convicted class.●

Dan Pens is Co-Editor of *Prison Legal News*. A sample issue of *PLN* is available for $1. Write to: Prison Legal News; 2400 NW 80th Street, Ste 148; Seattle, WA 98117

TAKING THE BACK DOOR TO CENSORSHIP

BY DENNIS P. EICHHORN

© 1997 by Dennis Eichhorn

Illustration by Jim Blanchard

Ever since the Founding Fathers decreed "Congress shall make no law... abridging the freedom of speech, or of the press..." while crafting the Bill of Rights in 1791, there has been an ongoing opposition to that seemingly Utopian concept. Over the years, the intellectual citadel of absolute freedom of expression, which is contained in the First Amendment, has been relentlessly besieged by the dark forces of censorship, who have steadily whittled away at its base.

Frontal assaults on freedom of speech generally don't fare too well with the American masses, whose belief in constitutional freedoms is widespread and firmly entrenched. But, not to be dissuaded by an aged document that they deem inconsequential, the minions of mendacity have ferreted out an alternative method for nullifying the cherished First Amendment rights that were originally meant to allow for outspokenness and unfettered communication of ideas and information. An onslaught of civil litigation, driven by repressive cultural concepts, has proven to be an effective reactionary weapon in the present-day censorship wars.

Case in point: In the fall of 1996, a federal judge ruled that Paladin Press's book *Hit Man: A Technical Manual for Independent Contractors* was not responsible for the murders of three people in 1993, and that the publisher bears no liability for the actions of a misguided reader. At last, a victory for free-speech advocates... or was it?

(Continued on next page)

The case in question was a civil wrongful-death lawsuit filed by the survivors of the three victims. The crimes were committed by James E. Perry, a former storefront minister and self-proclaimed "spiritual advisor" from Detroit, Michigan, who yearned to become a contract killer. He had been hired by Lawrence Horn, an unemployed former Motown Records technician, to kill Horn's ex-wife Mildred and quadriplegic eight-year-old son Trevor, so that Horn could inherit $1.7 million that the child had been awarded in a malpractice suit. Perry, who had ordered both *Hit Man* and another title, *How to Make a Disposable Silencer, Vol. 2*, from Paladin Press (and paid for both with a bad check), allegedly employed at least 27 methods described in *Hit Man*, including using an AR-7 rifle, drilling out the serial numbers to prevent tracing, using a silencer, and shooting his victims in the eyes three times. He entered the Silver Spring, Maryland (a suburb of Washington, D.C.) home of flight attendant Mildred Horn on March 3, 1993, and methodically murdered her and Trevor Horn, as well as nurse Janice Saunders.

"An onslaught of civil litigation, driven by repressive cultural concepts, has proven to be an effective reactionary weapon in the present-day censorship wars."

Arrested after disregarding other components of *Hit Man*'s advice and leaving some unprofessional clues (such as using his real name to rent a car near the scene of the crime), Perry was tried for the three murders in late 1995, convicted, and sentenced to death. Lawrence Horn was also tried, convicted, and sentenced to life in prison. That would have ordinarily been the end of such a sordid matter: the perpetrators were caught, found guilty, and punished.

But not this time. The litigious survivors and their attorneys smelled money. Fueled by the winds of censorship and self-righteousness that are swirling in the United States as the '90s draw to a close, Mildred Horn's sisters, Vivian Rice and Marilyn Farmer, and her daughter, Tiffani Horn, filed a civil suit for unspecified damages against Peder C. Lund of Boulder, Colorado, owner of Paladin Press, and the publishing house itself. The plaintiffs' attorney, Howard Siegel, was especially vituperative in his statements regarding the lawsuit. "The impetus behind the suit is the horrible and terrible ways the victims died," Siegel lamented. "Paladin Press is a player who got away. We feel they cruelly aided and abetted in the deaths." Siegal also charged that Lund and Paladin "conspired" with the authors (who published under pseudonyms; "Rex Feral," author of *Hit Man*, is actually a woman) "to enter into the murder-for-hire business." He accused Lund and Paladin of distributing a type of publication that is "lower than obscenity."

Not surprisingly, Lund and Paladin Press strongly disagreed. "He (Lund) has a great deal of sympathy for the family," said Dan Hale, an attorney for Lund and Paladin Press. "But he feels his First Amendment rights allow for the publication of books such as *Hit Man*."

The case drew national attention, as freedom of speech confrontations often do, and was the subject of numerous editorials and articles. The consensus of many seemed to indicate that yes, *Hit Man* was an offensive and possibly even dangerous work, but Lund and Paladin were within their rights to publish it, and bore no legal responsibility for the actions of its readers. Some commentators, such as Charles G. Brown of *The Wall Street Journal*, weighed in with a pontifical evaluation of the case which inferred that Lund and Paladin should be held liable. Thriller author Carl Hiaasen, writing in *The Tampa Tribune*, concluded that Lund was within his rights, but still has a hefty karmic debt to worry about.

On August 30, 1996, U.S. District Judge Alexander Williams, sitting in Greenbelt, Maryland, handed down his decision. Referring to the lawsuit as "a novel case with unprecedented future implications," Williams noted that he had read *Hit Man* in its entirety, and, while he personally found it "loathsome" and conceded it contained information that, "when it makes its way into the wrong hands can be fatal," had concluded that the plaintiffs had failed to prove that either of the books in question fell within "the well-defined and narrowly limited classes of speech that are unprotected by the First Amendment." Williams ruled that the books had not

(Continued on next page)

incited "imminent lawless actions," pointing out that "Nothing in the book (*Hit Man*) says, 'Go out and murder now.' Instead the books seemed to say, 'If you want to be a hit man, this is what you need to do.'" He dismissed the lawsuit, commenting, "It is simply not acceptable to a free and democratic society to limit and restrict creativity in order to avoid dissemination of ideas in artistic speech which may adversely affect emotionally troubled individuals."

Needless to say, Lund was pleased. "I would say to the families that if there was anything in my power that would relieve them of their sorrow, I would do so," he stated. "I unfortunately would not — cannot — accept responsibility for the actions of Lawrence Horn and James Perry."

"We're happy we had a judge willing to keep the starch in the First Amendment, when the politics of the day seem to be leaning toward restricting speech," added Thomas B. Kelley, another of the defendants' lawyers, noting that had Williams ruled otherwise, the implication for all publishers "was that they were going to have to be policemen over misuse of their books and the information contained in them by readers or face civil liability. It's a good day for the First Amendment."

Siegel, speaking on behalf of the plaintiffs, was both miffed and wrathful. "(Paladin) is the most despicable enterprise I have ever personally encountered, and I will put an end to it!" he railed. "We're absolutely sure the law is on our side! We'll take this case as far as we have to... we'll go beyond the Supreme Court if necessary!"

Siegel has a background that demonstrates dogged perseverance in liability cases. He is a well-known liability specialist and anti-firearms advocate who won a suit in 1985 against a handgun manufacturer, asserting that the gun company was ultimately liable for the shooting of a grocery-store clerk. Siegel wants to win his case against Lund and Paladin, but he has another agenda: he has stated that he wants to completely destroy the mail-order book company. Like many others in recent years, Siegel is capable of manipulating America's judicial process in order to achieve a goal that the Founding Fathers never dreamed of and would have certainly condemned: the preclusion of free speech and the stifling of constitutional dissent.

Barring an amendment to the Constitution sometime in the future, Siegel and his clients will have to settle for an appeal, which they have already filed. Next stop is the Fourth U.S. Circuit Court, after which the case could conceivably be appealed to the Supreme Court. It may take years for this matter to wend its way through the American judicial system, and its only immediate effect will be the continuance of the great financial burden which Lund and Paladin are forced to bear, in order to protect free-speech rights for themselves and everyone else in the United States.

So the case was a victory of sorts for free-speech defenders, but at a ridiculously high monetary cost for Lund and Paladin. Several such lawsuits could bankrupt any publisher. The money spent in defending the collective right to freely communicate is diverted from other endeavors, and the overall effect is constrictive, as other publishers think twice before publishing anything that might expose them to similar litigation.

Defending one's free-speech rights has become more commonplace in recent years, as First-Amendment-related civil lawsuits against individuals, organizations and businesses have increased. Record companies and recording artists have been unsuccessfully sued over allegations that certain lyrics have caused listeners to commit crimes. Filmmakers such as Oliver Stone have been sued for their work; *Natural Born Killers* was accused of inspiring copycat killings.

You don't need the government for censorship these days. As per the born-again right wing's *modus operandi*, repression has been privatized. Individuals and corporations, coaxed ever onwards by avaricious attorneys, are only too happy to indulge in captious legal maneuvers which lead to the suppression of First Amendment prerogatives.

Civil litigation has been employed to discourage and intimidate outspoken private citizens and public-action groups. As George W. Pring and Penelope Canan point out in *SLAPPs: Getting Sued for Speaking Out* (Temple University Press, 1996), a "SLAPP" (strategic lawsuit against public participation) must "meet one primary and three secondary criteria. Primarily, it had to involve communications made to influence a governmental action or outcome, which, secondarily, resulted in

(Continued on next page)

(a) a civil complaint or counterclaim (b) filed against nongovernmental individuals or organizations (NGOs) on (c) a substantive issue of some public interest or social significance."

The authors note that SLAPPs actually began in the United States shortly after the American Revolution, when there were a few instances of citizens being sued because of their criticisms of corrupt public officials. The practice largely died out until it was "reborn" in the 1960s and '70s, burgeoned in the '80s, and metastasized into a clear and present danger to freedom of speech and the right to protest in the '90s.

According to Pring and Canan, citizens have been sued for "writing a letter to the president of the United States opposing a political appointment; testifying against a real estate development at a zoning hearing; reporting violations of environmental laws to federal agencies; complaining to a school board about unfit teachers; filing a complaint with a government safety, consumer, civil rights, or equal employment office; recommending county acquisition of open space; reporting official misconduct; demonstrating peacefully for or against government action; testifying before Congress or a state legislature; reporting a violation of law to health authorities; filing a nonmonetary, public-interest lawsuit against the government; lobbying for local, state, or federal legislation; campaigning for or against a ballot issue; reporting workplace sexual harassment to government authorities; rating judicial candidates for the voters (on the part of a bar association); collecting signatures on a petition."

In many of these lawsuits, the defendants were clearly within their rights, according to our ingrained, treasured precepts regarding American freedoms of speech and protest. They should not have been required to defend themselves in court! But they did, and it was expensive.

From the antagonists' point of view, that's the beauty of a SLAPP. If the pesky citizen or public-interest group doesn't obtain top-level legal representation or secure adequate funding, the plaintiffs often win. Like so many of our society's mechanisms, it's a money game. In many instances, even if the plaintiff loses the case, its agenda wins the greater cultural war. The defendant, drained of funds and energy, is often reluctant to take a chance on being sued again. The net result is another crimp in our constantly diminishing ability to express ourselves and our concerns. Censorship, courtesy of the private sector, strikes again.

Libel suits, in particular, often have a suffocating effect on First Amendments freedoms. More than ever before in American history, media entities such as publications and networks, along with journalists and reporters, are being sued for libel. In *A Chilling Effect: The Mounting Threat of Libel and Invasion of Privacy Actions to the First Amendment* (W.W. Norton & Co., 1987), Lois G. Forer details the current preponderance of such litigation, noting that "from 1964 to 1986, more than 1,029 lower court opinions involving freedom of speech and the press, exclusive of obscenity, have been reported. At least twenty-five times that number have undoubtedly been before the trial courts... Countless libel cases are being docketed in state and federal trial courts every day. The increase in libel litigation is extraordinary and anomalous... Even when authors and publishers have won on appeal, their victories have been Pyrrhic because of the enormous expenses of litigation."

As in the case of SLAPPs, the victim of a libel lawsuit is wary of being embroiled again, and often shies away from future confrontations. Self-censorship, the very worst kind of censorship extant, comes into play. Erring on the side of caution, the media holds back, and the flames of oppression blaze more brightly as they receive a gust of fresh fear.

Product liability suits, SLAPP suits, libel suits... none of these are censorship per se, but the eroding effect on our open society has been tragic. The danger of losing our most basic First Amendment freedoms has never been greater. Only by fighting back and defending our inalienable rights of free speech and protest, whose very natures make the American experiment so beautifully unique, can we hope to salvage our common destiny.●

Since this article was published in 1996, the Fourth Circuit's appeals court voted 3-0 to reverse the lower court's decision in Paladin/Lund's favor, and ruled that Hit Man is not protected by the First Amendment, opening the door for the victims' survivors to sue the publishing house and its owner for aiding and abetting murder. As of late 1997, Paladin and Lund have vowed to appeal this decision to the Supreme Court.

YOUR FRIEND, THE COMMUNITY LAND TRUST
by Stephen Michael Schumacher

© 1997 by Stephen M. Schumacher

Illustrations by Jim Siergey

Conservation nowadays is confusing and divisive. "Wise use" advocates have legitimate concerns about property rights and jobs, concerns which are used as a cover for any act of destruction on earth. On the other extreme, Earth First!-ers are so disheartened by rampant destruction of the last vestiges of old growth forests that they put their lives on the line in civil disobedience.

> **"Conservation nowadays is confusing and divisive. 'Wise use' advocates have legitimate concerns about property rights and jobs, concerns which are used as a cover for any act of destruction on earth. On the other extreme, Earth First!-ers are so disheartened by rampant destruction of the last vestiges of old growth forests that they put their lives on the line in civil disobedience."**

Meanwhile the government veers back and forth, boasting environmental protection with their ponderous regulations and vast holdings of land, while subsidizing polluters and selling out the nation's parks (at a loss!) to private clearcutters.

Suppose that you'd like to support people who bridge these extremes, who protect the land and community and way of life that you love, with proven success and without hurting anybody. Where are you going to turn?

AMERICA'S CONSERVATION SUCCESS STORY

You can turn to one of America's 1,100 grassroots land trusts. With over 900,000 members, they are today's broadest-based and fastest-growing conservation movement. New land trusts are cropping up at the rate of about one a week, so there's likely one near you, or soon will be.

According to the Land Trust Alliance, the national umbrella organization for land trusts, they "have helped conserve more than 4 million acres of wetlands and wildlife habitat, trails and recreational areas, scenic lands,

(Continued on next page)

urban gardens and parks, productive farm and forest land, and fragile natural area.... They are the vanguard of the trend towards local self-sufficiency and individual action to solve important social problems."

WHAT IS A LAND TRUST?

What is a land trust? It's a voluntary, non-profit organization created by people in a community to protect open space which is important to their quality of life — for ecological, agricultural, scenic, historic, or recreational reasons.

A land trust doesn't have any power or interest in giving people orders or taking their land away. Instead, it acts as a friend, providing options for landowners who want to permanently preserve the values of their property.

One option is a conservation easement, which is a way for a landowner to entrust certain rights while retaining the rest. For example, a landowner might permanently assign rights to develop or subdivide a property to a land trust, under the legally-binding trust that these rights will never be used.

Another option is for a landowner to bestow property out-right to a land trust, either while alive or in a will. Well-funded land trusts, such as the national Nature Conservancy, make a practice of buying lands that especially cry out for protection.

The common denominator is that all land trusts acquire valuable lands or rights to land by voluntary means, then hold them in trust for preservation purposes.

WHO IS TRUSTWORTHY?

In a way, a land trust is the only party that can be trusted to safeguard a property permanently. An individual landowner, no matter how good a steward, may

die and pass on his or her property to heirs who don't share the same aims. Neighborhood landowner groups may agree to mutual covenants and restrictions, but they can also change their minds at a later date.

State legislatures may pass protective ordinances, but these can be changed next legislative session. State agencies and park services may hold lands, but they can also sell them off or turn them over to timber and grazing interests.

Only a land trust is constant, because it is a nonprofit corporation carefully constituted for the express purpose of preserving land. Each land trust is run by a board of volunteers from the community, who are legally responsible for ensuring that it lives up to its mission.

As corporations, land trusts can survive indefinitely, beyond the lifespans of individual stewards. New generations of board members are continually recruited. Even if a particular land trust fails, as occasionally happens due to lack of funds or organization, its properties will be passed to another land trust for protection.

HOW DOES IT WORK?

Here's an example of how a land trust works in practice. Trust representatives help a landowner fine tune a legal document called a conservation easement, which transfers development rights to the land trust while retaining rights to live on, sell, bequest, and otherwise enjoy the property. Each conservation easement is carefully customized to suit a landowner's desires, keeping whatever rights he or she wants.

Not only does the owner give away certain rights to his or her property, but he or she is also expected to make a donation to the trust's stewardship fund, which sometimes comes as a surprise. But the land trust is not really being gifted with an asset, it is being asked to take on a perpetual liability.

(Continued on next page)

The trust commits to monitoring the property regularly and making sure the terms of the conservation easement are upheld, taking legal action if necessary. This costs money — not a lot on an annual basis, especially since the work is often done by volunteers. But the cost needs to be covered by just the interest on the stewardship donation, since the land trust is committing to monitoring forever. And even an occasional lawsuit can take a heavy toll on the stewardship fund.

"A land trust is a voluntary, non-profit organization created by people in a community to protect open space which is im-portant to their quality of life — for ecological, agricultural, scenic, historic, or recreational reasons."

In return, the landowner will often receive substantial tax savings as a result of the conservation easement. The value of development rights transferred as well as the stewardship fund donation reduce income for federal tax purposes. Lowering the property's assessed value can hold down inheritance taxes, sometimes making the vital difference that allows land to be kept in the family instead of being sold off to pay taxes.

"A land trust doesn't have any power or interest in giving people orders or taking their land away. Instead, it acts as a friend, providing options for land-owners who want to permanent-ly preserve the values of their property."

Local real estate taxes may also go down, either due to reduced assessed value or according to a public benefit ratings schedule. But these savings can't be taken for granted, for they vary with local policies. Moreover, even if development is proscribed for the bulk of a property, the corner that includes the landowner's house may account for the majority of assessed value and taxes. In general, the more valuable the rights being given up, the more real the tax savings.

AMBITIOUS PROJECTS

Newer land trusts often specialize in helping land-owners with conservation easements, because they cost the trust practically nothing compared to the heavy expense of buying, managing, and paying real estate taxes on comparable properties. By contrast, the well-heeled Nature Conservancy, the famous national land trust, has the resources to purchase large tracts of land for more impressive conservation projects.

But as new local land trusts grow up, get their organizational structure in shape, stabilize their funding bases, and generate a track record that attracts substantial grants and bequests, they're in the position to plan more ambitious, proactive projects. This can be something of a leap-of-faith for an inherently "conservative" organization like a land trust, but it jump starts the trust to a higher level of activity.

WILDLIFE CORRIDOR

In the case of my own trust, Jefferson Land Trust on Washington State's Olympic Peninsula, we've identified a stretch of land on the edge of Port Townsend that's poised for heavy development, and we're committed to preserving it as the North Quimper Peninsula Wildlife Corridor.

It's presently habitat for many native plants and wildlife species, including quaking aspens, bobcats, tree frogs, pileated woodpeckers, and eagles. It serves as an important drainage wetland for the town. We feel now is our window of opportunity save this critical land before it gets nibbled away by development, to safeguard wildlife viability and a rich population of birds around town.

This issue of wildlife viability is important. If only scattered properties are preserved, species populations won't have enough genetic diversity to be sustainable over time. Only by preserving an unbroken corridor of land can the wildlife intermingle sufficiently.

"The issue of wildlife viability is important. If only scattered properties are preserved, species populations won't have enough genetic diversity to be sus-tainable over time. Only by preserving an unbroken corridor of land can the wildlife inter-mingle sufficiently."

(Continued on next page)

Our corridor project is off to a good start, since it was planned to overlap several existing large resource lands, conservation easements, and parklands. Our task is to identify the remaining multitude of smaller parcels, contact their many individual owners, and attempt to arrange conservation easements or purchase.

This massive logistical operation has led Jefferson Land Trust to hire project managers, apply for grants, and redouble our fundraising efforts — big changes for an organization that formerly ran on volunteers and a fraction of the current budget. But the alternative is to continue cultivating scattered easements that don't join into a coherent pattern of conservation.

GOVERNMENT FUNDING

Land trusts are separate from government and don't engage in political advocacy. Sometimes they cooperate with government when courts require land use violators to obtain conservation easements, or when state agencies establish easements on their own properties.

A few local governments continually preserve more and more lands using taxes on real estate sales, with programs like "1% for open space." But in these cases the funds don't go to the land trust, but go instead to a pseudo-governmental land acquisition agency, with any local land trust functioning at most in an advisory capacity.

These programs can yield impressive results. I visited Martha's Vineyard, an island off Cape Cod in Massachusetts, and it was obvious what a large part of this natural treasureland was in trust through a decades-long government preservation program. It was amazingly beautiful.

On the other hand, Martha's Vineyard is to some extent a haven for the rich, and by raising property values this wide scale preservation plays into the island's agenda of keeping the rest of the world out of their little bastion of paradise.

SMALL IS BEAUTIFUL

Lands trusts in general are purely about preservation rather than class interests, though some trusts focus on fostering affordable housing. In fact, land trusts are quite diverse, owing to their numbers, local origins, and independence.

Government programs and national groups such as the Nature Conservancy can achieve much, but the total results of the thousand local land trusts are equally great. Local trusts have the advantage of minimizing costs through volunteer effort and penny-pinching budgets, and can act more intelligently through on-the-spot knowledge of local needs.

> **"Government programs and national groups such as the Nature Conservancy can achieve much, but the total results of the thousand local land trusts are equally great. Local trusts have the advantage of minimizing costs through volunteer effort and penny-pinching budgets, and can act more intelligently through on-the-spot knowledge of local needs."**

By cultivating both community self-sufficiency and the natural world, land trusts put the philosophy of "Small is Beautiful" into action.

Stephen Schumacher is Secretary on the board of Jefferson Land Trust, protecting the northeastern part of Washington State's Olympic Peninsula. He led a seminar on "Land trusts on the Internet" at the 1995 national Land Trust Alliance rally. Comments or contributions to JLT's Wildlife Corridor project may be directed to Jefferson Land Trust, P.O. Box 1610, Port Townsend, WA 98368; phone: (360) 379-9501; e-mail: saveland@olympus.net; web:www.olympus.net/saveland.

The Nature Conservancy can be reached at 1815 North Lynn Street, Arlington, VA 22209; phone: (703) 841-5300; e-mail: mail@tnc.org; web: www.tnc.org.

The Land Trust Alliance is the umbrella organization for America's 1,100 land trusts. If you have questions or want to know if there is a land trust near you, contact them at the Land Trust Alliance, 1319 F Street NW Suite 501, Washington, DC 20004-1106; phone: (202) 638-4725; fax: (202) 638-4730.

PSYCHEDELIC SHAMANISM

AN INTERVIEW WITH JIM DEKORNE

by Wesley Nations

Jim DeKorne originally began his network newsletter, *The Entheogen Review*, in part to help gather information for a book he was writing about entheogens. The book, *Psychedelic Shamanism*, is now finished but the newsletter has continued to grow and attract new readers. It serves as a meeting place for explorers — psychonauts, if you will— to share information on both traditional plant entheogens and newly discovered combinations. Published quarterly, *ER* provides hard-to-find information on all aspects of entheogens and pharmacological shamanism, from chemical extractions and ritual techniques to methods for contacting disembodied entities.

We caught up with Jim recently and took the opportunity to pick his brain about one of our favorite topics.

(*Psychedelic Shamanism* is available for $22, post-paid from *The Entheogen Review*, PO Box 800, El Rito, NM 87530)

CC: *How did you first get involved with psychedelics?*

Jim DeKorne: I lived in San Francisco during most of the sixties. Too young to be a beatnik but too old to be a hippie, I always found myself orbiting the edge of what was "happening" — trying to make sense of it. It's an outsider's role that's been consistent throughout my life. I started smoking cannabis in 1962, and that was the beginning of the end because it's common knowledge that weed always leads to the harder stuff: LSD in 1964. By then I was living in Berkeley, a grad-student obsessed with Eastern philosophy. As described in *Psychedelic Shamanism*, that first acid trip was pure Samadhi — four hours of Buddha consciousness followed by four more hours desperately trying to retain it. It changed my life: I now *know* that there is more to awareness than so-called consensus reality. And it set the tone of my experiments with psychedelics irrevocably: always as a sacrament, never just for kicks. When the available drugs began to deteriorate in quality I stopped taking them. By then the experience seemed to have reached a plateau anyway, so I turned to an intellectual quest: trying to fit my insights into a logical structure. (As a mental type, that has always come naturally to me, though no one knows more than I do how sterile it can be.) It wasn't until I heard a Terence McKenna tape in the late eighties that my interest in psychedelics was rekindled.

CC: *The Entheogen Review seems to have rapidly developed a devoted following. How and why did you start it?*

JD: In 1992 I published a book on greenhouse gardening, and because of McKenna's work became interested in growing the traditional shamanic plants. I soon discovered that there was little reliable information on the subject — most of the literature consisted of either inaccurate underground pamphlets from the sixties or else very technical articles in obscure journals. In the summer of 1992 I attended a psychotropic plant workshop in Hawaii. I soon discovered (from my reading in the scientific journals and some preliminary growing experiments) that I knew nearly as much as the facilitators. It was obvious that there was a lot more to learn: new plants were being found almost weekly and

Crash Collusion: Your Guide to the Fringe

the booming interest in the subject was producing others like myself who had already discovered very interesting data on their own. I started *The Entheogen Review* to serve as a clearing house for this new information as well as to preserve it for the future.

In a rational society these data would be collected and published by university and foundation researchers. We don't have that, so ER is intended to fill that role as much as possible—at least to save the contemporary folk wisdom.

CC: *Interest in psychedelics seems to have come out of the closet of late; do you think this is a new popularity or has the interest always been there, but well underground?*

JD: Psychedelics lost popularity in the early 70's because of media hype and establishment propaganda — which amounts to the same thing. For a long time everyone was terrified that LSD destroyed your chromosomes: that's just one example — there are plenty of others. These negative rumors got front page headlines, but the scientific corrections never seemed to rate more than one column-inch back among the legal notices — if that. The times changed also. When the "Universal Love Utopia" of the LSD-inspired sixties didn't happen, the seventies devolved into the cocaine-based philosophy of the me-generation. The contrast between those two drugs tells the whole story.

CC: *Some have suggested that this is heralding a return to the rampant popular drug use of the 60's...*

JD: It's a different scene today, and hard to predict. I doubt we'll ever see anything like the sixties again — we're too culturally fragmented now. These shamanic states of consciousness are more for individuals and small groups — nobody in his right mind would take ayahuasca and go to a rock concert, for example. The drugs are different: more "introverted" if you will. I'm not familiar with the rave scene in the cities, so I can't comment on what might be happening there.

CC: *I've heard a few researchers make a case for 'natural' entheogens being supe-rior to 'synthetics'; do you hold any preference?*

JD: I used to feel that the plants were somehow superior (don't ask me why — it was an ill-considered bias). For example, ayahuasca is a very special plant-based medicine, though it can be synthesized easily (the so-called "pharmahuasca"). I've never tried pharmahuasca, so I can't say if it's as magically psychotherapeutic as the botanical brew, but even if it isn't, I'm sure it has its own special lessons to teach. I feel there is something to be learned from any psychedelic — some of my most numinous trips have been on synthetics, so I'm eclectic on the subject.

CC: *A topic that seems to be more openly discussed nowadays is the shamanic concept of 'plant spirits' and 'plant teachers'. Many people who have experienced the effects of different plant entheogens will often admit that some seem to have a presence or personality all their own. What are your views on this?*

JD: I have to take an agnostic stance on this, though it's a biased agnosticism. Since I've personally never encountered a plant spirit, I don't really know, but I hypothesize that we're accessing both our own psychic complexes and "others" — entities seemingly separate from ourselves, but not *necessarily* the spirits of plants. The literature of schizophrenia is full of examples of inner voices with an uncanny knowledge of just what to tell someone so as to be believed. They are almost invariably tricksters and not trustworthy.

The psyche is such a mystery that it's really impossible to say for certain who these beings are or what they represent. (They might be *symbolic* constructs of forces so alien that they'd be incomprehensible if they didn't assume the form of recognizable archetypes.) Smoked DMT will teach you quicker than anything that cultural conceptions of the cosmos —religious, philosophical or scientific— are little more than human projections. It's *alien!* It's so alien that most of us can just

> "...the DEA will eventually have to put Nature itself on Schedule-One."

> "Smoked DMT will teach you that all cultural conceptions of the cosmos are little more than human projections. It's alien!"

barely tolerate the brief experience of it pouring into our brains. Since all of my entity encounters have been on synthetics, I think it's just as fair to posit the existence of "DMT spirits" or "LSD teachers" as it is their plant counterparts. That, it seems to me, is opening up an epistemological can of worms, though god knows *both* may be true — or false — or neither!

CC: *The concept of discarnate entities seems to show up quite a bit both in your book Psychedelic Shamanism and in ER. What advice would you give to a psychonaut who encounters such 'personalities' in entheogenic realms?*

JD: Traditional methods of entering hyperspace use visualized defenses (magic circles, banishing pentagrams, spirit allies, etc.) to protect the voyager from harm. I used to regard these techniques as belief-dependent: they probably worked only if you believed they worked. Otherwise, they were really just superstitions and, as one who thought he understood "science," I didn't put much stock in them. I've learned a lot since then: I now *know* that ritual is extremely, important when doing inner work. Entities of the imaginal realm are constrained by thoughts and intention as much as we are by walls and fences. The creation of a safe space, such as a magic circle, is a construct of the imagination—it is a visualization of a barrier, and because these entities exist in the realm of mind, they can't get past a circle made of "thought" anymore than we could get through a chain-link fence. At least that's the way I comprehend it now.

The concept of spirit allies is also important — these mental guardians live in hyperspace and understand the forces there as much as we understand the danger of walking a city street after midnight. If you were charged with protecting a visitor from Mars as he toured New York City, there are certain places you'd avoid and certain precautions you'd take to protect him from his own naiveté: that's what a spirit ally does for you. In general, be as careful in dealing with entities of the imaginal realm as you would with strangers in the subway — especially if you're a newcomer and unfamiliar with the territory. It's useful to arm yourself with the awareness of a warrior: wimpy "good-will" gets you about as far in hyperspace as it does on skid row. Plain common sense is probably the best magickal weapon you have — beware of deals from smiling strangers. If you're in tune with it, your gut will always tell you how to proceed.

CC: *Do you receive any resistance to publishing ER from entheogen users? Many are afraid that the publicity and interest*

will bring down the wrath of the DEA.

JD: That's an interesting question, and one I encounter frequently. Only a few people have expressed fear that I'm somehow "spilling the beans," but I have received incredibly hostile vibes from numerous individuals that I might otherwise consider peers, colleagues, friends. I couldn't figure it out — people who don't even know me cutting me dead at conferences; a few irrational, paranoid letters accusing me of bullshit; friendly letters I've sent that go pointedly unanswered. I won't lie to you — gratuitous rudeness hurts. A correspondent who sells "poisonous plants" commented on this apparently common phenomenon in a most revealing way: "Those people obviously don't take the same drugs that I do." That about sums it up as far as I'm concerned—anyone who uses entheogens and treats others like pond scum somehow didn't get the message.

As far as risking a DEA crackdown by spreading the word: I'm of the opinion that hoarding information for the use of a few dilettantes is not what the plants (if you will) want us to do. The more information about these new species the better; there are so many potent plants being discovered that the DEA will eventually have to put Nature itself on schedule-1 — an obvious absurdity. Maximize the contradictions and the whole untenable system must eventually collapse. As regards the "safety" of thousands of people taking entheogenic drugs, I'll take my chances with that over the cocaine/alcohol world we're living in now. Who wouldn't swap today's world for a return to the sixties, warts and all?

CC: *I've met a few people who are involved in ongoing programs where groups of people are getting together and tripping regularly in a shamanic setting (as opposed to recreational use). Some of these groups have been working together for many years. Have you been exposed to this?*

JD: Group work can be incredibly healing: I love it when it happens. I've been a member of a group for several years now. We don't trip as much as I'd like, but we do connect monthly to compare notes. I live in the boondocks, so it's not easy to meet fellow travelers. Because I edit a newsletter full of blatantly subversive information, I have to be extremely careful — I'd never trip with someone I hadn't known for some time; to be paranoid in America today is a sign of sound mental health.

CC: *You and your book were criticized recently in a magazine review for, basically, not subscribing to a specific shamanic tradition. What's your answer to those who condemn modern or*

> "It may be that UFOs and their inhabitants are "shamans" from hyperspace penetrating our dimension in a manner similar to the way our shamans penetrate theirs."

neo-shamanism? Most of us don't have access to an authentic ayahuascero or curendero, for example.

JD: Traditionalists by definition are threatened by any dialectical re-evaluation of their particular trip. It's just the way it is. Because of my life-long status as an outsider, I've never been comfortable with other people's dogma. I'm an eclectic: I take what makes sense to me from wherever I find it. This encourages the apprehension of general patterns rather than specific applications of those patterns. As I hypothesize in the book, the shamanic world-view is an image of the structure of the human psyche. All shamanic traditions originally emerged from the head of a fellow human being — the fact that the general symbolism holds for any culture, no matter where, no matter when, suggests that it is the pattern itself that we need to study, not specific interpretations of it. It follows then, that for any neo-shamanism to emerge to help us cure our ills, it will have to emerge from our own minds and cultures, not from rituals and beliefs lifted whole-cloth from some jungle tribe.

CC: *Obviously, most in our culture would not embrace any sort of shamanic experience, let alone a drug-induced one. At the other extreme you have people like McKenna calling for a psychedelic-driven 'paradigm shift' or 'archaic revival'. What do you think the chances are of us developing such a neo-shamanic tradition?*

JD: Just about zero in any cultural sense. I like to play around with these utopian ideas and McKenna's concepts are always stimulating, but when I observe how it is now on planet earth, I have to conclude that the cosmos follows patterns beyond the illusion of collective human control: when the gods aren't with us, they're usually against us. A former liberal, I have to fight my knee-jerk responses to calls for social action, which are usually based on reason and common sense. Unfortunately, neither of those prevail here below. Almost everyone knows what the problems are, and plausible solutions aren't that difficult to figure out: so how come is it just getting worse and worse? Because we are not rational beings: we are only partially rational beings, and the gods seldom operate out of the left brain anyway. They're like very powerful children who insist on their ancient addictions without any real comprehension of consequences in a world transformed by technology. Shamanic cosmology is a metaphor for the human psyche and each of us peeks out at the world from an inner multiverse so vast that the external realm is but a flyspeck in comparison. Therefore the only meaningful solutions to the problems of existence must be individual solutions. You can't really save the world, but you can save your own ass, which

ultimately amounts to the same thing. Shamanism of some sort (in the widest possible definition of the term) is extremely useful, if not essential, to achieving personal integration but I no longer believe it will emerge as a cultural paradigm any time soon enough to matter.

CC: *What advice do you have for those trying to find their own way?*

JD: Suspend your disbelief long enough to become familiar with your inner imagary, but retain enough reason not to capitulate to it uncritically. It's a dance, and it's not easy to do. I recommend a book I read many years ago called *The Inner Guide Meditation* by Edwin Steinbrecher. As far as I know, it's still in print. Because it outlines a method of getting into your deeper psyche, it qualifies as a shamanic technique. It's based on the western shamanism of the kabbalah and it works. As you get into it you'll find that the method will customize itself to address your specific needs. It took me years to finally accept the validity of my visions, to realize that they were not just something I "made up." (No ego could ever be that creative!) Once you get well started, almost everything you need to know comes from within, and that of course will be different for everyone.

CC: *The word 'shamanism' is used pretty heavily now and seems to have developed different meanings. What is shamanism to you? Do you consider yourself a shaman?*

JD: Shamanism means something different to me than to an anthropologist say, or to a New Ager who might associate it with anything relating to tribal culture. Classically, shamans are seen as healers, but if their techniques are really just proto-psychological formulae for understanding who we are in the largest possible sense, then it's valid to use these techniques either as healers or as explorers: it depends entirely on who you are and what your interests are. To that extent, I consider myself a shaman-explorer. I'm not interested in healing anything except my own psychological complexes (the "gods"), so I know very little about "healing" in the classical shamanic sense. Just because I don't suck bugs out of people's necks doesn't automatically disqualify me however, since the techniques for coping with shamanic reality are pretty much universal.

CC: *What are your views on the so-called New Age shamanism? Even Michael Harner has distanced himself from plant entheogens, saying that they are secondary to the experience.*

JD: You can get ten years in the joint and forfeit all of

> "For any neo-shamanism to emerge to help us cure our ills, it will have to emerge from our own minds and cultures, not from rituals and beliefs lifted from some jungle tribe."

your earthly belongings if some bureaucrat with a gun catches you growing one of God's own plants. That's reason enough to cause anyone who makes his living shamanizing to repudiate entheogens. And he's absolutely right — one does not need psychotropics to enter the imaginal realm; in fact, for everyday working (I do a very powerful meditation every morning), drugs just get in the way. Psychedelics are useful tools, but they are not any kind of ultimate necessity. Ayahuasca shamanism may be an exception to this — ayahuasca is a very, very special medicine.

CC: *Many of the shamanism workshops and seminars focus on drumming, trance-work, visualizations and the like; do you think these techniques are of use to people experimenting with psychotropics?*

JD: Absolutely, but I have to qualify it in terms of my own experience: I find it impossible to do an "inner guide" meditation when I'm tripping, but that doesn't mean that someone else would necessarily have trouble with it. I took two of Harner's workshops and found them very useful. The main difference (for me) between his method say, and an ayahuasca trip is that I don't have much control over where I go or what happens to me with the latter — I'm rendered relatively passive and I take what comes: so far it has always been mind-blowingly significant. Not that non-drug shamanism is any *less* significant, it's just less mindblowing. Incidently, what most people would call a "bummer," a rough trip, is usually (if you can just stick with it) the most significant in terms of insight and inner growth. After you learn a few techniques (such as ritual, banishing pentagrams, etc.) it's easier to handle bummers without totally freaking out. This is about the only "control" I have over such situations: the rest is just raw data from the cosmos blasting through my consciousness. Entheogens are useful tools during certain phases of inner work: "storming heaven" can get you past blockages like nothing else. But working with them exclusively is probably not a viable longterm strategy because a long-term *need* for them implies that lasting transformations have not taken place. If integration is proceeding in a healthy manner, entheogens should eventually become superfluous. What I'm saying is that both methods are valuable and as you proceed with the work you'll become very sophisticated about which approach to use in specific situations.

CC: *Judging from the information presented in ER, it would seem that we are finally closing in on a North American ayahuasca analog. What combination do you think holds the most promise? Do you think the vast number of available active plants will eventually make criminalization of these substances impossible?*

JD: There are just an amazing number of plants that contain the alkaloids found in the traditional ayahuasca brew. Syrian Rue (*Peganum harmala*) is the hands-down favorite for the beta carboline half, and various species of the *Phalaris* genus of grasses contain high levels of 5-MeO-DMT and DMT to complete the mixture. A friend has created a very smooth combination of these plants: one

which makes you *high* but not *stoned* and produces an amazingly clear-headed spiritual experience. Although it doesn't throw you out of the universe like traditional ayahuasca, it has its own unique power. I am curious to see what, if anything, the DEA will do (*can* do) about *Phalaris* — it's one of the most common grasses growing on the planet, and totally impossible to control.

CC: *DMT has received a lot of press in the last few years, mostly due to Terence McKenna's writings and lectures. It is such a short-acting substance, when smoked, that I wonder if it is truly useful in a shamanic or introspective sense. What do you think?*

JD: It all goes back to set and setting — with the proper will and intent, in a setting appropriate to your query, with proper ritual protection, a smoked DMT trip can show you some amazing realities. Its brevity has a distinct advantage — one doesn't have to sacrifice half a day stoned to get an answer to one's question. We've barely scratched the surface of how to use this substance *intentionally* (as opposed to just: *Wow!!*).

CC: *You are one of very few people to openly discuss both psychedelics and the UFO phenomenon. Do you feel there's a connection between the two?*

JD: Yes, but don't ask me to explain it! As far as I know, McKenna was the first to begin connecting the two experiences. I've never encountered an actual UFO, with or without an entheogen, but I've met aliens on DMT. (Not the standard big-headed "greys," but aliens none the less.) Both experiences are so uncanny and so many people have had UFO encounters while on drugs that there has to be some connection. The fact that the imaginal realm is involved is our most important clue. It may be that UFOs and their inhabitants are "shamans" from hyperspace penetrating our dimension in a manner similar to the way our shamans penetrate theirs. Something like that. We're three-dimensional chauvinists and have a hard time conceptualizing how these other dimensions impinge on our own. As I'm fond of saying: "in the language of the fishes, there's no word for water." Consciousness is the key to interdimensional travel.

CC: *Many people I know who're involved in experimental psychotropic plant use are searching for the "perfect" psychedelic. Do you have an ideal entheogen in your sights?*

JD: There are too many variables for me to pick just one plant or drug. Each one has its own characteristics and uses. Ayahuasca (either classical or analog) is very special and would be high on my list, but it is not something I want to take exclusively (or very often). There are too many other interesting experiences and lessons to be learned from the entheogenic pharmacopoeia. DMT of course, is always fascinating. We're close now to pinning down a botanical source of relatively pure DMT — it will probably be a *Phalaris* species. I look forward to tending a shaman's garden of numerous potent, very innocuous-looking plants.

Crash Collusion PO Box 2237 Berkeley, CA 94702

PRISON ECONOMICS:
(The Cold War Comes Home To Roost)

© 1997 by Danny Mack   **by Danny Mack**   Illustration by Rick Altergott

When the tyrant has disposed of foreign enemies by conquest or treaty, and there is nothing to fear from them, then he is always stirring up some war or other in order that the people may require a leader.
—Plato

The cold war, which began as a standoff with Joseph Stalin in 1945, ended in a 1993 period of "détente," which is Russian for "We're really tired, can we stop this?" While it lasted, life in the United States was shaped by it.

The fear of communism, fueled in large part by the alcohol-induced paranoia of Senator Joe McCarthy, was the impetus behind America's involvement in virtually every foreign civil war for the last 50 years, including Viet Nam. The Cold War cost us $20 trillion, and 118,000 lives. Once we were convinced that communism was the greatest of all evils, money and lives were no object.

We are just now beginning to learn that the Soviet threat was, to put it mildly, greatly exaggerated. It was necessary during the Cold War for all Americans to fear Russia. Otherwise, we never would have agreed to the vast spending by the Pentagon on "defense." Corporations such as Boeing and McDonnell Douglas were literally created by the American public's fear. The fact that Russia was bankrupt and no longer the superpower or "evil empire," as we had always been told, didn't stop the Reagan/Bush administration from escalating the military buildup. Russia's impotence, though it was known to our own State Department, was kept from the American people during the '80s for two reasons. First, it gave our fearless leaders time for one last-hurrah spending binge. More importantly though, before the Iron Curtain was lifted to reveal the great Russian bear as a near-Third World country, it gave them time to create an equally frightening new enemy within our own borders.

Today's "criminal" is our new bogeyman, and the political rhetoric is every bit as paranoid as that of the McCarthy era. Cold War defense contracts have been replaced by Crime War prison contracts in our race to lock people away from society. America needs an enemy, and with the worldwide fall of communism we have turned our anger and aggression inward, declaring war on our own people. The prison-building programs begun in the '80s continue at a rate unprecedented in world history. With 1.6 million people behind bars and over five

(Continued on next page)

million under the control of the justice machine (either on parole, probation or on bail), America is by far the world leader in locking up its own citizens.

The timing couldn't have been better for this shift in institutionalized hatred. In a high-tech world there is no place for low-tech people. The displaced and disaffected victims of the technology boom are at the bottom of the economic food chain, and as Richard Nixon discovered during his 1968 campaign, poor people can be a formidable political force if they are not kept under control. Reagan's trickle-down economy turned out to be a flood-up economy, and the gap between rich and poor became greater than ever. Ten percent of the U.S. population owns 90% of the riches. The government is charged with protecting this very rich minority from the rest of us, and the threat of imprisonment is a very effective tool when it comes to keeping the huddled masses in line. The national debt is blamed on welfare mothers, violent crime on the very young, and the drug problem on poor blacks. The solution, according to the ruling class, is to lock them up and throw away the key. Never mind that it would cost less to house, feed, clothe and send them to college. That would never satisfy our national hunger for vengeance. Those least able to defend themselves are always made into the scapegoats.

Growth Industry

As programs and entitlements are cut, Oregon, like many other states, has seen an explosion in the number of homeless teens on its cities' streets in recent years. The state legislature's response to this very visible sign of poverty was to pass Measure 11, which went into effect April 1, 1995. This Draconian measure allows 15-year-olds to be prosecuted as adults, and 16-year-olds to actually be placed in adult prisons. It also mandates very long sentences, even for first-timers, with no possibility of parole. The list of crimes that can be prosecuted under Measure 11 makes it appear on the surface to target only the most serious crimes against persons or property, but days after it went into effect a Portland youth was charged with kidnapping, for pushing an acquaintance out the front door of a friend's home and punching him in the nose. The sexual-abuse section of the statute says that a 15-year-old who touches the buttocks of a 12-year-old, even with consent, must be sentenced to 8½ years in prison, 7½ years of which could be served in an adult prison. Just imagine the 23-year-olds we'll get out of THAT deal! It's no coincidence that Measure 11 went into effect on April Fool's Day. The voters don't have a clue as to the nature of the monster they are building.

As a result of Measure 11, Oregon now needs ten new prisons. California is also in the middle of a prison-building spree after the passage of their "Three Strikes You're Out" law, under which the theft of a 50¢ slice of pizza can get you 30 years in that state's brutal corrections system. The object of this tough-on-crime philosophy is obviously not to reduce crime (in fact, it turns misguided youths and petty crooks into full-blown sociopaths), but to build prisons.

The prison business is the fastest-growing industry in the country, and the reasons are purely economic ones. In a world economy where most of the manufacturing is done in Third World countries, millions of Americans have been left with no meaningful work. The "make-work" of the prison industry, although it is degrading and produces nothing of value, is often the only alternative for the downsized.

More people are employed in the prison industries than in any Fortune 500 company except General Motors. A large majority of prison guards are young men and women fresh out of the military. Ninety-five percent of these are recruited by the Federal Bureau of Prisons before they are discharged. The skills learned in the military services are considered desirable by the B.O.P., but few of these recruits have skills that would be marketable in the civilian workplace. The regimented, by-the-book life of the prison system is a perfect environment for those whose first life experience after high school was military service.

Small, depressed rural communities are targeted for prison construction because the money that prisons bring with them outweighs the usual fears of having one in your backyard. Escapes are so rare as to be almost nonexistent, and the theory that undesirable relatives of prisoners will move into the area has been proven less of a problem than anticipated. Many people are put to work

(Continued on next page)

immediately upon the approval of a new prison site. Draftsmen, architects, engineers, construction workers and material suppliers all benefit from the prison boom. After construction is completed, literally thousands of people will become dependent on the prison for their livelihoods. The B.O.P. has a policy of hiring 60% of its total staff from the local communities. It is common for husbands and wives to work together at their local penal institution.

Not only do local businesses such as laundries and food suppliers share in this new-found wealth, but a new breed of entrepreneur has also emerged, offering mail-order gifts, quasi-legal services for prisoners, and transportation/lodging for visitors. Another advantage to a small community is the fact that prisoners can be counted as citizens in a local census. With the population increasing by one or two thousand souls overnight, government allocations for sewer, water treatment, and road maintenance also increase. This is a big selling point for small towns where the population may actually double with the building of a single prison.

The alarming thing about all of this economic well-being, is that it induces a political shift to the right in the hearts and minds of those affected. What prison guard or support staff in his or her right mind would ever oppose a bill that would lock up more people for greater lengths of time? How could a business owner who depended on this prison-generated income vote in favor of programs designed to decrease recidivism? It's a simple matter of job security.

Prisons For Profit

The private sector has not been able to ignore the lure of big bucks in the prison business. Federal officials are now comfortable with allowing private companies to run federal prisons, because the industry has gained experience running state and local jails. Wackenhut Corrections and Corrections Corporation of America, the two industry leaders, make a profit by housing prisoners for the federal government. Both trade on the New York Stock Exchange.

Corrections Corporation, a 13-year-old company based in Nashville, Tennessee, employs many former government officials, including, as director of

strategic planning, Michael Quinlan, who directed the B.O.P. during the Bush administration. Wackenhut, of Coral Gables, Florida, has as its director, Norman A. Carlson, who proceeded Mr. Quinlan as director of the B.O.P. Benjamin R. Civiletti, a former Attorney General, also works for Wackenhut.

In 1993 the Donald W. Wyatt Detention Facility was opened in Central Falls, Rhode Island. Wyatt is owned and operated by Cornell Corrections, a private company financed by investors. The facility had 300 beds and a contract with the federal government for $85 a day per prisoner, but no inmates. "Build it and they will come" seemed to be the philosophy at Cornell, and when they didn't come it was quite an embarrassment. Wyatt would need a full house to survive. The prison's financial backers, realizing that their investment was in jeopardy, mounted a vigorous lobbying campaign to divert prisoners from other states. Facing bankruptcy and angry bondholders, Cornell Corrections turned to a lawyer who specialized in brokering prisoners for private prisons. Attorney Richard Crane was paid an undisclosed sum when 232 prisoners were moved from North Carolina to Rhode Island soon afterward.

When Wall Street analysts and brokers, lawyers, corporate CEOs, and rich investors stand to profit from locking people up, you can bet that they will be throwing large amounts of money at politicians who favor the imprisonment of an ever-growing segment of the population. In the short term, Cornell was lucky that North Carolina needed to relieve some overcrowding. Long-term, the prospects are frightening. At this point, can we be far from a return to the days of debtor's prison? The strongest power the government has, short of the death penalty, is that of incarceration. That power should not be handed to those motivated by profit.

Slavery '96

Contrary to what we learned in grade school, the 13th Amendment to the Constitution did *not* abolish slavery in 1865. The Amendment reads, "Neither slavery nor involuntary servitude except as punishment for crime whereof the party shall have

(Continued on next page)

been duly convicted, shall exist within the United States, or any place subject to their jurisdiction." The purpose of this Amendment was not to abolish slavery, but to limit it to those who had been convicted of crimes. The sad fact is that great numbers of newly freed blacks were then "convicted" and forced to work without pay in state prisons. This simply transferred the ownership of slaves from private parties to the state. Today, with the advent of private, for-profit prisons and joint-venture prison factories, this ownership is shifting back to the private sector. Slavery has come full circle.

UNICOR, the prison manufacturing industry of the B.O.P., and by far the largest slaveholder in the U.S., makes a wide range of products for sale to other government agencies and contractors. UNICOR is the "preferred" supplier for these government customers. The word "preferred" in this case is intentionally misleading, and actually means mandatory. If the U.S. Navy needs 500 wooden chairs, and doesn't want to buy them from UNICOR because of over-pricing, poor quality and slow delivery, it is required by law to ask UNICOR for an exemption. These exemptions are never granted, and this is how "preferred" becomes "mandatory." With this kind of lock on such a huge section of the market, the concepts of competition and free trade go out the window.

UNICOR operates 90 prison factories and is rapidly expanding. The products range from office and dormitory furniture to electronics. Individual states have modeled their prison factories after the federal example, with one dangerous difference: They market their products to the private sector. San Quentin inmates enter computer data for Bank of America, Chevron and Macy's. Prisoners in New Mexico take hotel reservations by phone. Hawaiian convicts package golf balls for Spaulding, and at Folsom they manufacture stainless steel vats for beer brewers. The list goes on and on. Businesses all over the country are jumping at the chance to hire prisoners, and why not? There is no unemployment insurance to pay, no health benefits, vacation, sick leave or payroll taxes. It is estimated that total prison industry sales will reach $8.9 billion by the year 1999.

And how about prison labor for strike breaking? It's certainly nothing new. In 1891 in Briceville, Tennessee, mine owners attempted to break the miner's union by using prison laborers. In what is now known as the Coal Creek Rebellion, union workers took over the mine and freed all of the prisoners, thus temporarily ending prison labor in Tennessee. More recently, young inmates at the Ventura Youth Facility in California made flight reservations by telephone for TWA while unionized flight attendants were on strike. The company then transferred ticket agents to flight-attendant jobs.

What will happen to all of the free world workers who are displaced by the slave labor of the '90s is the most depressing thing of all. After their unemployment insurance runs out, and they discover that retraining is of no use when there are no jobs to be had, they will become members of the group most likely to end up in prison: the poor. At a January, 1996, town-hall meeting in New Hampshire where Senator Phil Gramm was campaigning for the GOP primary, he pitched a proposal that would require all prisoners to work six days a week for sub-minimum wages manufacturing consumer goods in private, no-frills prison "enterprise zones." A woman in the crowd was heard to shout, "In order to get a job, an American is going to have to commit a crime!"

The Cycle

Despite a declining crime rate, a lot of money is being made from increasing incarceration. Unfortunately, it doesn't appear that this cycle will be broken anytime soon. As long as big business owns our political system and profits from prison building, the momentum of the Crime War will continue. One encouraging fact is that there must, at some point, be a level of diminishing returns. When every family in America has a member behind bars, a political change will be inevitable. Knowledge is the key to a free and equitable society. We must ask tough questions and demand answers. Remember, the Cold War lasted 50 years. Let us hope that the Crime War ends sooner.●

Danny Mack is currently an inmate in one of America's many prisons.

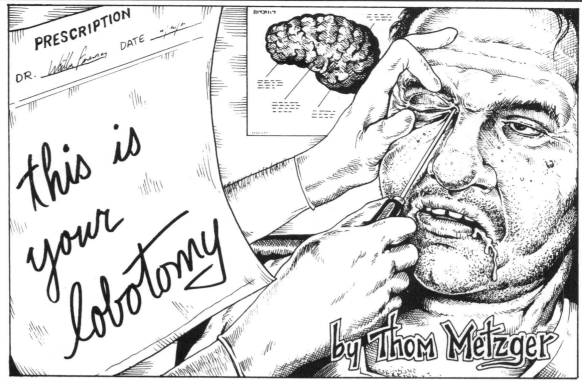

PRESCRIPTION
DR. Walter Freeman DATE ___
this is your lobotomy

by Thom Metzger

A fellow named Freeman said: "I've
A sharp little knife that I drive;
If you want to be dead
I'll bore holes in your head
And then you won't know you're alive."
— Dr. Allen "Kris" Kringle, Director: E1 Camino
Psychiatric Hospital

The nurse holds your hands, after giving you a rag to bite down on. You're laid out flat — no straps, no restraint. Doctor Freeman brings the electroshock wand — a silvery steel wishbone — close to your skull. The electrode discs on the twin prongs graze your temples.

Dr. Freeman wears no surgical mask, no gloves; in fact, his muscular arms are bare to the shoulders of his loose white tunic. The operation, he explained in his book *Psychosurgery*, "can be completed in a few minutes. It does not require complicated operative set-up. Since the [tear duct] is sterile 98% of the time, no preparation of the operative field is necessary."[1] Or, as he put it in layman's terms: there's no need for concern about "all that germ crap."[2]

He gives a quick nod to the nurse, a knowing smile to the other doctors gathered to observe the master at work, and a last glimpse at his trusty electroshock machine. It's square, roughly the size of a cigar box, with a transformer to step down the 110-volt wall current. He hits a toggle switch; the timer clicks in and the first blast explodes in your head.

Squirming, writhing, you bite down hard on the rag. Convulsions now — a tidal wave roaring through your body. Some patients have broken bones, dislocated hip and shoulder joints as the shocks hit. You're lucky — the current merely blasts you into a semi-conscious state.

Two more bolts of electrical anesthesia are fired into your head. With the final jolt, you fall into a coma, and Dr. Walter J. Freeman — evangelist for transorbital salvation, hardest working man in the lobotomy business, the person who single-handedly made psychosurgery the most celebrated therapy since Freudian analysis — prepares for the climax.

He grasps the glittering steel spike, lovingly holds it up to the light.

You're ready; he's ready.

There's no coyness now, no hesitation; he's done this thousands of times already. You may be just one more drooling psychotic in a threadbare bathrobe, but he is the world's greatest lobotomist. In the early days, he'd pause, to prepare himself; "it needed some time to summon up courage to attack the brain through the orbital plate."[3] Now he moves swiftly, eager as a bridegroom but confident as Don Juan at the peak of his powers.

He pinches your upper lid between thumb and forefinger and pulls it away from your eyeball. Then, careful not to touch the skin or lashes, he inserts the point of the leucotome — a slender steel spike — into your tear

(Continued on next page)

duct. Taking a deep breath, he thrusts until the point touches the boney vault of the eye's orbit. In a grand flourish, he suddenly drops to one knee, and aims the leucotome along the ridge of your nose. With a surgical mallet, he strikes a deft blow to the blunt end of the spike, breaks through the skull bone and drives 3½ inches of healing steel into your brain.

But he's not done yet. The therapeutic value of the operation is nil until he swings the leucotome 20° up and down and 30° from side to side, raking the point through the tissue of your frontal lobe.

Satisfied, he pulls the spike out and performs the same delicate operation on the other eye. The name "Uline Ice Company" is still visible on the tool's handle. Modified slightly, it had been taken earlier from Freeman's kitchen drawer. "Yes," said James Watts, Freeman's long-time surgical partner, "originally the leucotome was an ice pick. We tried to get another one, but the doggone things would break. So what we had to do was get an ice pick and put a special head on it."[4]

The boldness of Freeman's attack, the courage with which he tracked mental illness to its source and rooted it out, might come as a surprise to some. However, he was by no means an anomaly in medical history. He truly was, as he claimed, an explorer into the darkest regions of the human mind. Lobotomy was not a freakish episode, but a logical outgrowth of Western medicine's obsessional materialism (mental illness is a purely biological process) and devotion to the cult of progress (any new therapy, especially if it's high-tech, must be tried). With a ready supply of experimental subjects, with doctors audacious enough to thrust knives into places where no blades had gone before, with a fervent faith in new technology, medicine had waged a centuries-long war against mental illness.

Unfortunately, before the introduction of anti-psychotic drugs in the 1950s, mental hospitals had little to offer their most degenerated patients. Often shackled in darkness, naked, ignored and poorly fed, treated in some cases worse than barnyard animals, the insane were an embarrassment to the medical profession and a steadily increasing drain on state coffers.

So, as technological progress improved the quality of life on other fronts, it also held out hope to the keepers of the insane. Spiritual or psychological models might be of use to those who dealt with neurotics, but for abject schizophrenics and raving psychotics, something more was called for. These somatic, or big-mechanical, treatments can be divided into seven categories: shock cures, extreme temperature therapies, use of water, artificial induction of sleep, electro-stimulation, surgery, and the injection of foreign substances into the patient.

By a lumbar puncture, the "inactivated" blood of horses was infused into the spinal columns of paretics — ostensibly to increase the number of white blood cells in the brain. Other researchers hoped that inducing "aseptic meningitis" with foreign blood would have a beneficial effect on the insane.

Noticing that patients who'd suffered high fevers during syphilitic paralysis often made some improvement, Dr. Julius Wagner van Jauregg began in 1883 to inject fluids from various oozing sores into his mental patients. After inoculating these subjects with pus and mucousy ichor produced by tuberculosis, typhoid and malaria, Wagner van Jauregg waited until fever developed, then injected blood from their veins into other patients. He was awarded the 1927 Nobel Prize for medicine, though the fact that he was the only psychiatrist to ever receive the award remains unexplained.

Guessing correctly that it was the fever and not the disease itself that helped patients, other experimenters began to induce fever states by the use of hot baths, hot air, diathermy, radiothermy, infrared light bulb cabinets, therapeutic ovens and special electric "mummy bags."

Other medical innovators set off in the opposite direction, inducing hypothermia in the body. As late as 1941, patients in Massachusetts mental hospitals were placed in patented Therm-O-Rite blankets through which refrigerant was pumped. Drs. Talbott and Tillotson claimed that schizophrenics achieved a measure of "mental clarity" by the process, though death by hypothermic shock was also an unfortunate side effect.

Having a long therapeutic pedigree, water cures were also employed. Steam, high power hoses, wet-packs, douches, "baptismal fonts," and fine-nozzle spritzers were used on the mentally ill.

Electricity was seen in the late nineteenth century as a nearly numinous force: healer and destroyer. It's no surprise, then, that doctors to the insane would try their hand at capturing and applying electricity's godlike power. Various electrical stimulation devices were used, ostensibly to stimulate the nerves. "Faradization, galvanization, and Franklinization" were much touted as cures, especially for neurasthenia and depression.

Electricity was also used (as late at the 1960s in the Soviet Union and East Germany) to keep patients in deep, healing sleep. Using barbiturates and narcotics too, doctors kept patients in a coma-like narcosis for weeks at a time, in hopes that the curative powers of sleep might restore their stressed nervous systems.

Most of these treatments fell by the wayside, increasingly quaint and old-fashioned as modern technology forged forward. It was with the shock cures —

(Continued on next page)

insulin, Metrazol, and ECT — that twentieth-century mental therapies truly fulfilled their potential.

Working in a sanatorium that catered to artists, medical and theatrical folk, Dr. Manfred Sakel stumbled on a cure-all which he spent the rest of his life promoting. One of his patients was both diabetic and a morphine addict. Accidentally giving her an overdose of insulin, Sakel pushed her into a deep coma. When she finally woke, her craving for morphine had lessened, making Sakel an instant believer in the curative power of coma. Soon, he'd shot dozens of schizophrenics full of insulin.

Two years later, in 1935, Ladislas van Meduna, convinced that epilepsy and schizophrenia were mutually exclusive, induced seizures in his patients with an injection of camphor. He later switched to Metrazol, a synthetic preparation, and claimed great success in treating schizophrenics. By 1940, Metrazol was found in the pharmacies of most American mental hospitals.

The most-used and longest-lived of these treatments was electroshock. Drs. Ugo Cerletti and Lucio Bini, determining that the body produced a "vitalizing substance" in response to convulsions, experimented with animals, running current from anus to mouth. After heart attacks killed most of their subjects, they routed the current from ear to ear. At first Cerletti had misgivings; "the idea of submitting man to convulsant electric discharges was considered as utopian, barbaric and dangerous. In everyone's mind was the specter of the electric chair."[5] In 1938, the police commissioner of Rome provided their first human subject. Judged to be a schizophrenic, without family or connections, he was delivered by the police to the doctors and they lost no time in applying the current to his head. Unfortunately, the voltage was too low, failing to produce convulsions or coma. The man squealed and writhed on the bed, begging for them to stop. Cerletti decided to let the man rest for a day before trying again, this time shooting 110 volts through his brain.

By 1942, almost half the mental institutions in the U.S. were using electroshock, easier for the staff and more "pleasant" for the patient than chemically induced convulsions. By 1945, over 75,000 people had been given shock treatments. The popular press was very enthusiastic, though the frequent side effect of broken and dislocated bones was only lessened in the late 1940s by the use of curare to eliminate the more violent spasms.

The last major form of somatic therapy was in a way the most basic and obvious: surgery. If the mind is an entirely biological phenomenon, if thought is the mere effect of electrical brain activity, then it stood to reason that the knife could cut out mental disease as well as it cut out tumors.

Before doctors attacked the brain, other surgical procedures were tried. The endocrine glands were removed to limit the imbalance of hormones. Extirpation of thyroids, ovaries, and testes were performed on the mentally ill, tens of thousands of offending organs cut out in the 1920s in conjunction with the mania for eugenic cleansing that swept the country. More innovative was the work of Dr. Henry Cotton. Not, as some have argued, a peripheral figure in the history of American medicine, but a man of substantial training and accomplishment, he deserves his rightful place in medical annals. Cotton was convinced that all mental illness came from physical infection and that excision of the toxin-producing areas would cure insanity. He concentrated initially on dentistry, insisting that all mentally ill people were being poisoned by tooth decay. After numerous extractions failed to achieve the goals he'd hoped for, he moved on to tonsils, and then deeper into the body in search of the elusive roots of insanity. Cutting out "infected" cervixes, fallopian tubes, ovaries, rectal and colon tissue and other suspect body parts, Cotton reported that by 1922 he'd operated on 1,400 patients and that his method of "detoxification" had saved the state of New Jersey $300,000.[6]

It's no surprise that the brain itself would eventually become the target of the surgeon's blade. The progress of mental hygiene would have to wait, however, until 1935, when a man of steel nerves, unshakable self-confidence and unique vision took his place at center stage.

Egas Moniz, the inventor of lobotomy, was born in 1874 to an aristocratic Portuguese family. Lordly and proud (lecturing in his toupee and satin-lapel tuxedo), he never actually performed the operation which won him the Nobel Prize in 1949. Blissfully ignorant of basic physiology and standard scientific procedure, he was able — amazingly — to base his entire psychosurgical program on a misunderstanding of animal learning experiments done in the U.S.

Drs. Jacobsen and Fulton had devised a delayed-response test to judge the problem-solving ability of chimps. One of the animals — named Becky — was an utter failure, and would throw fierce tantrums, screaming and biting, smearing herself with feces and urine. Following the surgical destruction of her frontal lobes, Becky's personality was radically altered, and Dr. Jacobsen declared that she appeared to have joined a "happiness cult."[7]

This was enough for Moniz. Upon receiving a report of the experiment, he saw his chance to carve a niche for himself in medical history. Already sixty years old, Moniz felt an increasing sense of urgency in his work. If he was

(Continued on next page)

to gain a place in the annals of scientific innovation, he had to work quickly. With no animal research of his own, he developed a new theory of pyschosurgery which some have called a concoction of vague pseudo-science and unadulterated drivel. Nonetheless, because of his position in Portuguese society and his status as a great man of Iberian medicine, he was able to convince a fellow doctor to lend him experimental subjects — mental patients from the Manicome Bombarda asylum.

In November of 1935 Moniz supervised his first lobotomy (which he called "leucotomy" — "leuco" referring to white tissue). The subject was a severely degenerated depressive given to him by his colleague Sobral Cid. She was shaved bald, given an enema, and then an anesthetic rectal suppository was inserted. Unconscious, she was strapped to the table, a sand bag was placed under her neck and her head was pulled forward by canvas tethers. After scrubbing the entry point with a mixture of soap, water, iodine, ether and alcohol, Moniz mapped out the attack on her scalp. Then he directed his assistant — Pedro Lima — to cut two 1½ inch incisions down to the cranial bone. The skin was pulled away and — observed from above — it appeared she'd gained a pair of slanted eyes: bloody tears flowed from the slashes. Using a hand-held circular saw, Lima cut out one inch circlets of bone and placed these rondels on a tray. Unlike later operations, this first time Moniz didn't insert the leucotome into the subject's brain. Instead he jabbed a syringe full of absolute alcohol into the white matter and squirted in 2 cc. on both sides; annihilating the offending frontal-lobe matter.

He performed this same operation on four more subjects, but soon decided that cutting would be much better than destroying with alcohol. Within a month of the first operation, a specially made brain-cutting tool was in Moniz' gout-ridden hands, and the Golden Age of Lobotomy had dawned. The Moniz leucotome was a long metal probe with a wire loop hidden in the tip. Once the tool was thrust fully into the frontal lobe, Moniz would press a button on the handle and the wire would jut out. Then he'd have Lima turn the handle, cutting a "core" of brain tissue — like coring an apple. However, unlike the apple core, the cylinder of disconnected matter remained in the brain to molder. On the first lobotomized patient, only two cores were done. Later, Moniz went to four on each side of the head and even six in particularly difficult cases.

Critics have said that Moniz's theory was a hodgepodge of pseudo-science and self-serving double-talk; some have claimed that his practice was crude and ill-conceived. But compared to his follow-up observations, these were the pinnacle of medical exactitude. Patients were often released only a few days after their coring, and in many cases they were declared fully cured of their mental illnesses, though Moniz might never see them again.

Far more strenuous were his efforts at self-promotion. Moniz presented the results of his miracle cures only four months after the first operation. Within a year, he'd published the same data in five different journals. Many physicians were surprised that he would claim to have cured schizophrenics and depressives with no post-operative observation. Nonetheless, he published thirteen articles (in six languages) and a book within two years of his first lobotomy.

By 1948, 20,000 lobotomies had been performed world-wide. Many were done to helpless mental patients, but a surprising number of middle- and upper-class subjects (whose families had despaired of them ever being well again) were also opened and cleansed by the knife. Lobotomy spread around the globe as a miracle cure, as "surgery for the soul," a cheap and effective way of cutting out diseases of the mind. If Moniz was the "savior of souls," then Walter J. Freeman was his apostle Paul, preaching, teaching, traveling the western hemisphere on his "head-hunting missions," bringing the gospel of lobotomy to hundreds of clinics, hospitals and state asylums. Freeman performed roughly 4,000 of these operations. But numbers do not tell the whole story.

Freeman cut an impressive figure as he swept into backwater state hospitals. He wore a goatee in the style of Old World neurologists at a time when American doctors seldom had beards. Just under six feet tall, at a trim 180 pounds, he affected dapper clothing and a walking stick. His deep tan came from his frequent mountaineering and camping trips, which he combined with his "ice-pick tours": mixing virile recreation and manly scientific struggle. He was the height of self-confidence, acid-tongued, opinionated, hyperactive, willing to offend if that suited his greater purposes, by his own admission "imperial, dogmatic and provocative." He even at times bragged that he was as good as Frank Sinatra at making people faint. Perhaps his most striking characteristic was his penetrating gaze. As he regarded patients or colleagues, his head would cock to one side, a sign, he said, of his "built-in arrogance."

As much a circuit-riding preacher as a physician, he traveled thousands of miles with surgical salvation (in Flannery O'Connor's words) "hidden in his head like a stinger." Though he thumped no Bible, the word was of great importance to Freeman. To spread the good news, he became a one-man publishing company, having thousands of copies of his articles printed and distributed

(Continued on next page)

at his own expense. The cost was considerable, Freeman said, "but it more than paid for itself in the number of patients referred for lobotomy."[8]

The print media praised Freeman. *Time* lauded his "spectacular results" and reported that his "knife can reach into the brain and sever the tensions which underlie the psychopathic personality."[9] In March of 1947, *Life* claimed that "the results were spectacular: about 30% of lobotomy patients were able to return to everyday productive lives."[10] A before-and-after drawing in *Life* shows a bulge-brained super-ego screaming threats at the id and intelligence. In the second picture, after the surgeon's blade had sliced the offending connection, the id is free, smiling placidly, and the "business portions of the brain" are back at work: happy and productive. The caption for another picture — of Freeman and Watts doing a lobotomy — reads: "Patients are encouraged to sing and pray." And Freeman himself would often join in, loud and lusty, on the choruses, all the while cutting away "pathogenic" brain tissue. Other newspaper captions reflect Freeman's glee: "Surgeon's Knife Restores Sanity to Nerve Victims," "Wizardry of Surgery Restores Sanity to Fifty Raving Maniacs," "Forgetting Operation Bleaches Brains," "No Worse Than Removing a Tooth," "Brain-Man Performs 'Crazyectomy.'"

Claiming that "personalities can be cut to measure," and calling his operations "new adventures in that exciting field of the brain,[11] Freeman was quite aggressive at evangelizing for his cause. He called reporter Thomas Henry and asked if he'd "like to see some history made. We've done a few brain operations on crazy people with interesting results." The reporter produced a glowing article and much to Freeman's delight called lobotomy "another shining example of therapeutic courage."[12]

Unfortunately, some beneficiaries of this courage died, the arteries of their brains severed by inaccurate plunges of the knife and ice pick. Some had brief episodes of recovery, followed by a return to chaos and inner darkness. Fecal incontinence, seizures and a numbed will-less state were common side effects. Though Freeman's magnum opus, *Psychosurgery,* includes many before-and-after pictures (confused, zombie-like wretches and the transformed versions: good citizens with shorter hair and better teeth) these were by far in the minority.

Freeman started off his crusade with prefrontal techniques based on Moniz's model. But soon he'd developed his own technique, transorbital lobotomy, which he declared to be "much less traumatizing than a shot gun and almost as quick."[13] Amazingly, it was not just schizophrenia that transorbital penetration relieved, but also tension, apprehension, anxiety, constipation, depression, insomnia, suicidal ideas, delusions, hallucinations, crying spells, melancholia, obsessions, panic states, nervous indigestion and phantom limb.[14] In one case, Freeman even performed a lobotomy on a man with cancer of the rectum, to relieve his pain.

By 1950, Freeman had traveled across the U.S. eleven times to preach the brain-destroying gospel, his car trunk filled with morphine, ice picks and electro-convulsive machinery. Freeman "collected his trophies," as he liked to put it, in his own office, in clinics and at least once in a motel room. A subject who'd escaped from him twice before was caught by police in a motel, and the dauntless headhunter was brought in. Declaring that it was then or never, Freeman had the troopers hold the man down, subdued him with ECT, and triumphantly pounded the ice picks into the man's brain.

Usually, however, the work was done in poorly-funded rural state hospitals. Bored and overworked, the staff there were flattered to have such an eminent healer come to demonstrate his prowess. Besides novelty, the hope of getting people out of the wards was irresistible. In the late 1940s almost half of America's 1.5 million hospital beds were used for psychiatric patients. Freeman could brag, "the relief accorded to the patients, to say nothing of the savings on wear and tear of hospital personnel and equipment marks a genuine advance in human welfare."[15] In poor states such as West Virginia, Freeman only charged $25 a pop. In Nebraska it was $200. Wealthy private patients were at times charged a thousand dollars for the brain-cleansing.

Greed does little to explain Freeman's ferocious devotion to the cause. Clearly, a passion beyond mere lucre or fame was at work. At times, his response to the operations was as euphoric as the patients were reported to be. He spoke of "surgical instincts"[16] as though there was an innate drive in him that needed to be satisfied. And he titled one of the chapters of his unpublished autobiography "Head and Shoulder Hunting," pointing to some ill-defined compulsion.

It's a commonplace, a cliché even, that many go into the mental health professions to cure themselves by curing others. Freeman, who suffered a nervous breakdown at 40 and resolutely refused psychiatric help, may fit this pattern. Addicted to Nembutal for 30 years — throughout his entire brain-cutting career — a loner, pathologically immune to criticism and some would say to human feelings, Freeman seems to have developed an

(Continued on next page)

obsessional hatred for the frontal lobes of the human brain, which were "supposed to be man's most precious possession [but] which can bring him to psychosis and suicide."[17] It's possible to see the thousands of ice pick thrusts directed metaphorically into his own brain: stabbing, ripping, probing, but failing to find and root out the unnamed torments that plagued him. An illustration he created for the title page of his book shows four "black butterflies" — Freeman's term for internal demons — escaping from a trephined skull.

Freeman performed dozens of lobotomies a day. If a surgical mallet was unavailable, then a common carpenter's hammer would do. On more than one occasion, he wrenched the leucotome back and forth with such therapeutic zeal that the tip broke off inside the subject's skull. This necessitated a call to a surgeon (Freeman was a neurologist, and so, not officially allowed to do surgery) to fish the three inch splinter out of the brain. After a few of these embarrassments, Freeman had a machinist create a far heavier, longer stiletto. Freeman bragged that this "orbitoclast" could "lift a door off its hinges without breaking or bending." Eight inches long, thick as a pencil at the blunt end, the orbitoclast was, even in Freeman's estimation, "a savage instrument."[18]

Though Freeman worked tirelessly to improve lobotomy, the rage for psychosurgery peaked in 1954. The number of operations tapered off slightly with increasing reports of stupefied patients, deaths and too-innovative practices (including the use by Dr. Lawrence Pool of six-inch zippers sutured to the scalp to allow repeated entry to the brain).

But it took the introduction of Thorazine (chlorpromazine), one of the first effective anti-psychotic agents, to bring an end to the lobotomy era. First created to counteract surgical shock, Thorazine was soon seen as a wide-ranging "negative stabilizer," in effect a lobotomy in pill form with fewer side effects. The manufacturer, Smith, Kline and French, worked through 1953 to get FDA approval. After five thousand animal tests and two thousand on humans (using psychotics who were awaiting lobotomies in state hospitals), the FDA approved the drug and wide distribution began. Freeman at first embraced the new therapy, but realized that it spelled the end of his time at center stage.

Freeman's head-hunting trips tapered off quickly. Within a few years, the man who'd done so much for so many had been stripped of his surgical privileges, marginalized by colleagues and branded a dangerous crank. Old, dying of colon-rectal cancer (necessitating a colostomy in 1967) Freeman spent his last years visiting hundreds of lobotomized patients, and keeping records of their progress in huge notebooks. At a conference, driven to distraction by the suggestion that his work had been a bit excessive, he dumped out a box of five hundred cards sent to him by lobotomy subjects, and shouted at the audience, "how many Christmas cards do you get from your patients?"[19]

Though he died in 1972, an embarrassing relic ignored by his profession, still "Walter's Tribe" (spread now far and wide) remains his legacy, a living tribute to the man and his superhuman efforts. There are still thousands of people in institutions all over the U.S., with faint scars over their frontal lobes or hazy memories of a man with a spike and a hammer and a zealous gleam in his eye.

NOTES

1. Freeman, Walter J. and James Watts. *Psychosurgery.* Springfield, IL: Charles C. Thomas Co. 1942. p. 56.
2. Personal Communication: James Watts to Elliot S. Valenstein, Sept. 21, 1983.
3. Freeman, p. 53.
4. Quoted in *Lobotomy: Resort to the Knife,* David Shutts. NY: Van Nostrand, Reinhold Co. 1982. p. 143.
5. Quoted in Shutts, p. 79.
6. Cotton, H.A. "The Etiology and Treatment of the So-called Functional Psychoses." *American Journal of Psychiatry.* (2) 1922. pp. 157-210.
7. Jacobsen, C.F. "Studies on Cerebral Function in Primates." *Comparative Psychological Monographs.* 13 (3) 1936. pp. 1-60.
8. Quoted in Shutts, pp. 160-161.
9. *Time.* 12/23/46. pp. 66-67.
10. *Life.* 3/3/47. p. 93.
11. Freeman. (jacket copy, written by the author).
12. *New York Times.* 11/21/36. p. 10.
13. Letter of W. Freeman to J.F. Fulton, 10/6/47.
14. *New York Times.* 6/7/37. p. 1.
15. Quoted in Shutts, p. 131.
16. Quoted in Shutts, p. 213.
17. Freeman. (jacket copy).
18. Freeman, Walter J. "History of Psychosurgery." Unpublished manuscript.
19. Valenstein, Elliot. *Great and Desperate Cures.* NY: Basic Books, 1986. p. 274.

●

LAND-MINE LEGISLATION

by Claire Wolfe

Illustration by Wayno

Let me run by you a brief list of items that are "the law" in America today. As you read, consider what all these have in common.

1. A national database of employed people.

2. 100 pages of new "health care crimes," for which the penalty is (among other things) seizure of assets from both doctors and patients.

3. Confiscation of assets from any American who establishes foreign citizenship.

4. The largest gun confiscation act in U.S. history — which is also an unconstitutional *ex post facto* law and the first law ever to remove people's constitutional rights for committing a misdemeanor.

5. A law banning guns in ill-defined school zones; random roadblocks may be used for enforcement; gun-bearing residents could become federal criminals just by stepping outside their doors or getting into vehicles.

6. Increased funding for the Bureau of Alcohol, Tobacco and Firearms, an agency infamous for its brutality, dishonesty and ineptitude.

7. A law enabling the executive branch to declare various groups "terrorist" — without stating any reason and without the possibility of appeal. Once a group has been so declared, its mailing and membership lists must be turned over to the government.

8. A law authorizing secret trials with secret evidence for certain classes of people.

9. A law requiring that all states begin issuing drivers licenses carrying Social Security numbers and "security features" (such as magnetically coded fingerprints and personal records) by October 1, 2000. By October 1, 2006, "Neither the Social Security Administration or the Passport Office or any other Federal agency or any State or local government agency may accept for any evidentiary purpose a State driver's license or identification document in a form other than [one issued with a verified Social Security number and 'security features']."

10. And my personal favorite — a national database, now being constructed, that will contain every exchange and observation that takes place in your doctor's office. This includes records of your prescriptions, your hemorrhoids and your mental illness. It also includes — by law — any statements you make ("Doc, I'm worried my kid may be on drugs," "Doc, I've been so stressed out lately I feel about ready to go postal.") and any observations your doctor makes about your mental or physical condition, whether accurate or not, whether made with your knowledge or not. For the time being, there will be zero (count 'em, zero) privacy safeguards on this data. But don't worry, your government will protect you with some undefined "privacy standards" in a few years.

All of the above items are the law of the land. Federal law. What else do they have in common?

(Continued on next page)

All of the above became law by being buried in larger bills. In many cases, they are hidden sneak attacks upon individual liberties that were neither debated on the floor of congress nor reported in the media.

Well, when I ask this question to audiences, I usually get the answer, "They're all unconstitutional."

True.

My favorite answer came from an eloquent college student who blurted, "They all SUUUCK!"

Also true.

But the saddest and most telling answer is: They were all the product of the 104th Congress. Every one of the horrors above was imposed upon you by the Congress of the Republican Revolution -- the Congress that pledged to "get government off your back."

BURYING TIME BOMBS

All of the above became law by being buried in larger bills. In many cases, they are hidden sneak attacks upon individual liberties that were neither debated on the floor of Congress nor reported in the media.

For instance, three of the most horrific items (the health care database, asset confiscation for foreign residency and the 100 pages of health care crimes) were hidden in the Kennedy-Kassebaum Health Insurance Portability and Accountability Act of 1996 (HR 3103). You didn't hear about them at the time because the media was too busy celebrating this "moderate, compromise" bill that "simply" ensured that no American would ever lose insurance coverage due to a job change or a pre-existing condition.

Your legislator may not have heard about them, either. Because he or she didn't care enough to do so.

The fact is, most legislators don't even read the laws they inflict upon the public. They read the title of the bill (which may be something like "The Save the Sweet Widdle Babies from Gun Violence by Drooling Drug Fiends Act of 1984"). They read summaries, which are often prepared by the very agencies or groups pushing the bill. And they vote according to various deals or pressures.

It also sometimes happens that the most horrible provisions are sneaked into bills during conference committee negotiations, after both House and Senate have voted on their separate versions of the bills. The conference committee process is supposed simply to reconcile differences between two versions of a bill. But power brokers use it for purposes of their own, adding what they wish. Then members of the House and Senate vote on the final, unified version of the bill, often in a great rush, and often without even having the amended text available for review.

I have even heard (though I cannot verify) that stealth provisions are written into some bills after all the voting has taken place. Someone with a hidden agenda simply edits them

in to suit his or her own purposes. So these time bombs become "law" without ever having been voted on by anybody. And who's to know? If congresspeople don't even read legislation before they vote on it, why would they bother reading it afterward? Are power brokers capable of such chicanery? Do we even need to ask? Is the computer system in which bills are stored vulnerable to tampering by people within or outside of Congress? We certainly should ask.

Whether your legislators were ignorant of the infamy they were perpetrating, or whether they knew, one thing is absolutely certain: The Constitution, your legislator's oath to it, and your inalienable rights (which precede the Constitution) never entered into anyone's consideration.

Whether your legislators were ignorant of the infamy they were perpetrating, or whether they knew, one thing is absolutely certain: The Constitution, your legislator's oath to it, and your inalienable rights (which precede the Constitution) never entered into anyone's consideration.

Ironically, you may recall that one of the early pledges of Newt Gingrich and Company was to stop these stealth attacks. Very early in the 104th Congress, the Republican leadership declared that, henceforth, all bills would deal *only* with the subject matter named in the title of the bill.

When, at the beginning of the first session of the 104th, pro-gun Republicans attempted to attach a repeal of the "assault weapons" ban to another bill, House leaders dismissed their amendment as not being "germane."

After that self-righteous and successful attempt to prevent pro-freedom stealth legislation, Congresspeople turned right around and got back to the dirty old business of practicing all the anti-freedom stealth they were capable of.

STEALTH ATTACKS IN BROAD DAYLIGHT

Three other items on my list (ATF funding, gun confiscation and school zone roadblocks) were also buried in a big bill — HR 3610, the budget appropriation passed near the end of the second session of the 104th Congress.

No legislator can claim to have been unaware of these three because they were brought to public attention by gun-rights groups and hotly debated in both Congress and the media. Yet some *90 percent* of all congresspeople voted for them — including many who claim to be ardent protectors of the rights guaranteed by the Second Amendment.

Why?

Well, in the case of my wrapped-in-the-flag, allegedly pro-gun, Republican congressperson: "Bill Clinton made me do it!"

(Continued on next page)

Okay, I paraphrase. What she actually said was more like, "It was part of a budget appropriations package. The public got mad at us for shutting the government down in 1994. If we hadn't voted for this budget bill, they might have elected a Democratic legislature in 1996 — and you wouldn't want THAT, would you?"

Oh heavens, no! I'd much rather be enslaved by people who spell their name with an R than people who spell their name with a D. Makes all the difference in the world!

HOW SNEAK ATTACKS ARE JUSTIFIED

The Republicans are fond of claiming that Bill Clinton "forced" them to pass certain legislation by threatening to veto anything they sent to the White House that didn't meet his specs.

In other cases (as with the Kennedy-Kassebaum bill), they proudly proclaim their misdeeds in the name of bipartisanship — while carefully forgetting to mention the true nature of what they're doing.

In still others, they trumpet their triumph over the evil Democrats and claim the mantle of limited government while sticking it to us and to the Constitution. The national database of workers was in the welfare reform bill they "forced" Clinton to accept. The requirement for SS numbers and ominous "security" devices on drivers licenses originated in their very own Immigration Control and Financial Responsibility Act of 1996, HR 2202.

Another common trick, called to my attention by Redmon Barbry, publisher of the electronic magazine *Fratricide*, is to hide duplicate or near-duplicate provisions in several bills. Then, when the Supreme Court declares Section A of Law Z to be unconstitutional, its kissing cousin, Section B of Law Y, remains to rule us.

> You may recall that one of the early pledges of Newt Gingrich and Company was to stop these stealth attacks. Very early in the 104th Congress, the Republican leadership declared that, henceforth, all bills will deal only with the subject matter named in the title of the bill.

Sometimes this particular form of trickery is done even more brazenly; when the Supreme Court, in its *Lopez* decision, declared federal-level school zone gun bans unconstitutional because Congress demonstrated no jurisdiction, Congress brassily changed a few words. They claimed that school zones fell under the heading of "interstate commerce." Then they sneaked the provision into HR 3610, where it became "law" once again.

When angry voters upbraid congresspeople about some Big Brotherish horror they've inflicted upon the country by stealth, they claim lack of knowledge, lack of time, party pressure, public pressure, or they justify themselves by claiming that the rest of the bill was "good."

The simple fact is that, regardless of what reasons legislators may claim, the U.S. Congress has passed more Big Brother legislation in the last two years — more laws to enable tracking, spying and controlling — than any Democratic congress ever passed. And they have done it, in large part, in secret.

> Another common trick is to hide duplicate or near-duplicate provisions in several bills. Then, when the Supreme Court declares Section A of Law Z to be unconstitutional, its kissing cousin, Section B of Law Y, remains to rule us.

Redmon Barbry put it best: "We the people have the right to expect our elected representatives to read, comprehend and master the bills they vote on. If this means Congress passes only 50 bills per session instead of 5,000, so be it. As far as I am concerned, whoever subverts this process is committing treason."

By whatever means the deed is done, there is no acceptable excuse for voting against the Constitution, voting for tyranny. And I would add to Redmon's comments: Those who *do* read the bills, then *knowingly* vote to ravage our liberties, are doubly guilty. But when do the treason trials begin?

BILLS AS WINDOW DRESSING FOR AN UGLY AGENDA

The truth is that these tiny, buried provisions are often the *real* intent of the law, and that the hundreds, perhaps thousands, of pages that surround them are sometimes nothing more than elaborate window dressing. These tiny time bombs are placed there at the behest of federal police agencies or other power groups whose agenda is not clearly visible to us. And their impact is felt long after the outward intent of the bill has been forgotten.

Civil forfeiture — now one of the plagues of the nation — was first introduced in the 1970s as one of those buried, almost unnoticed provisions of a larger law.

One wonders why on earth a "health care bill" carried a provision to confiscate the assets of people who become frightened or discouraged enough to leave the country. (In fact, the entire bill was an amendment to the Internal Revenue Code. Go figure.)

I think we all realize by now that that database of employed people will still be around enabling government to track our locations (and heaven knows what else about us, as the database is enhanced and expanded) long after the touted benefits of "welfare reform" have failed to materialize.

(Continued on next page)

And most grimly of all, our drivers licenses will be our *de facto* national ID card long after immigrants have ceased to want to come to this Land of the Once Free.

CONTROL REIGNS

It matters not one whit whether the people controlling you call themselves R's or D's, liberals or conservatives, socialists or even (I hate to admit it) libertarians. It doesn't matter whether they vote for these horrors because they're not paying attention or because they actually *like* such things.

What matters is that the pace of totalitarianism is increasing. And it is coming closer to our daily lives all the time. Once your state passes the enabling legislation (under threat of losing "federal welfare dollars"), it is YOUR name and Social Security number that will be entered in that employee database the moment you go to work for a new employer. It is YOU who will be unable to cash a check, board an airplane, get a passport or be allowed any dealings with any government agency if you refuse to give your SS number to the drivers license bureau. It is YOU who will be endangered by driving "illegally" if you refuse to submit to Big Brother's licensing procedures.

> It's time to drop any pretense: We are no longer law-abiding citizens. We have lost our law-abiding status. There are simply too many laws to abide.

It is YOU whose psoriasis, manic depression or prostate troubles will soon be the reading matter of any bureaucrat with a computer. It is YOU who could be declared a member of a "foreign terrorist" organization just because you bought a book or concert tickets from some group the government doesn't like. It is YOU who could lose your home, bank account and reputation because you made a mistake on a health insurance form. Finally, when you become truly desperate for freedom, it is YOU whose assets will be seized if you try to flee this increasingly insane country.

As Ayn Rand said in *Atlas Shrugged*, "There's no way to rule innocent men. The only power government has is the power to crack down on criminals. Well, when there aren't enough criminals, one makes them. One declares so many things to be a crime that it becomes impossible for men to live without breaking laws."

It's time to drop any pretense: We are no longer law-abiding citizens. We have lost our law-abiding status. There are simply too many laws to abide.

And because of increasingly draconian penalties and electronic tracking mechanisms, our "lawbreaking" places us and our families in greater jeopardy every day.

STOPPING RUNAWAY GOVERNMENT

The question is: What are we going to do about it?

Write a nice, polite letter to your congressperson? Hey, if you think that'll help, I've got a bridge you might be interested in buying. (And it isn't your "bridge to the future," either.)

Vote "better people" into office? Oh yeah, that's what we thought we were doing in 1994.

> The only way we're going to get off this road to Hell is if we jump off. If we, personally, as individuals, refuse to co-operate with evil.

Work to fight one bad bill or another? Okay. What will you do about the 10 or 20 or 100 equally horrible bills that will be passed behind your back while you were fighting that little battle? And let's say you defeat a nightmare bill this year. What are you going to do when they sneak it back in, at the very last minute, in some "omnibus legislation" next year? And what about the horrors you don't even learn about until two or three years after they become law?

Should you try fighting these laws in the courts? Where do you find the resources? Where do you find a judge who doesn't have a vested interest in bigger, more powerful government? And again, for every one case decided in favor of freedom, what do you do about the 10, 20 or 100 in which the courts decide against the Bill of Rights?

Perhaps you'd consider trying to stop the onrush of these horrors with a constitutional amendment — maybe one that bans "omnibus" bills, requires that every law meet a constitutional test or requires all congresspeople to sign statements that they've read and understood every aspect of every bill on which they vote. Good luck! Good luck, first, on getting such an amendment passed. Then good luck getting our Constitution-scorning "leaders" to obey it.

It is true that liberty requires eternal vigilance, and part of that vigilance has been, traditionally, keeping a watchful eye on laws and on lawbreaking lawmakers. But given the current pace of law spewing and unconstitutional regulation-writing, you could watch, plead and struggle "within the system" 24 hours a day for your entire life and end up infinitely less free than when you began. Why throw your life away on a futile effort?

Face it. If "working within the system" could halt tyranny, the tyrants would outlaw it. Why do you think they encourage you to vote, to write letters, to talk to them in public forums? It's to divert your energies. To keep you tame.

"The system" as it presently exists is nothing but a rat maze. You run around thinking you're getting somewhere. Your masters occasionally reward you with a little pellet that encourages you to believe you're accomplishing something. And in the meantime, you are as much their property and their pawn as if you were a slave. In the effort of fighting them on *their* terms and with *their* authorized and approved tools, you have given your life's energy to them as surely as if you were toiling in their cotton fields, under the lash of their overseer.

The *only* way we're going to get off this road to Hell is if we jump off. If we, personally, as individuals, refuse to cooperate with evil. *How* we do that is up to each of us. I can't

(Continued on next page)

decide for you, nor you for me. (Unlike congresspeople, who think they can decide for everybody.)

But this totalitarian runaway truck is never going to stop unless *we* stop it, in any way we can. Stopping it might include any number of things: tax resistance; public civil disobedience; wide-scale, silent non-cooperation; highly noisy non-cooperation; boycotts; secession efforts; monkey-wrenching; computer hacking; dirty tricks against government agents; public shunning of employees of abusive government agencies; alternative, self-sufficient communities that provide their own medical care and utilities.

There are thousands of avenues to take, and this is something most of us still need to give more thought to before we can build an effective resistance. We will each choose the courses that are right for our own circumstances, personalities and beliefs.

Whatever we do, though, we must remember that we are all, already, outlaws. Not one of us can be certain of getting through a single day without violating some law or regulation we've never even heard of. We are all guilty in the eyes of today's "law." If someone in power chooses to target us, we can all, already, be prosecuted for *something.*

And I'm sure you know that your claims of "good intentions" won't protect you, as the similar claims of politicians protect them. Politicians are above the law. YOU are under it. Crushed under it.

When you look at it that way, we have little left to lose by breaking laws *creatively and purposefully.* Yes, some of us will suffer horrible consequences for our lawbreaking. It is very risky to actively resist unbridled power. It is especially risky to go public with resistance (unless hundreds of thousands publicly join us), and it becomes riskier the closer we get to tyranny. For that reason, among many others, I would never recommend any particular course of action to anyone — and I hope you'll think twice before taking "advice" from anybody about things that could jeopardize your life or well-being.

But if we don't resist in the best ways we know how — and if a good number of us don't resist loudly and publicly — *all* of us will suffer the much worse consequences of living under total oppression.

And whatever courses of action we choose, we must remember that this legislative "revolution" against We the People will not be stopped by politeness. It will not be stopped by requests. It will not be stopped by "working within a system" governed by those who regard us as nothing but cattle. It will not be stopped by pleading for justice from those who will resort to any degree of trickery or violence to rule us.

It will not be stopped unless *we* are willing to risk our lives, our fortunes and our sacred honors to stop it.

I think of the words of Winston Churchill: "If you will not fight for the right when you can easily win without bloodshed, if you will not fight when your victory will be sure and not so costly, you may come to the moment when

you will have to fight with all the odds against you and only a precarious chance for survival. There may be a worse case. You may have to fight when there is no chance of victory, because it is better to perish than to live as slaves."

● ● ●

NOTES on the laws listed above: 1. (employee database) Welfare Reform Bill, HR 3734; became public law 104-193 on 8/22/96; see section 453A. 2. (health care crimes) Health Insurance Portability and Accountability Act of 1996, HR 3103; became public law 104-191 on 8/21/96. 3. (asset confiscation for citizenship change) Same law as #2; see sections 511-513. 4, 5 and 6. (anti-gun laws) Omnibus Appropriations Act, HR 3610; became public law 104-208 on 9/30/96. 7 and 8. (terrorism & secret trials) Antiterrorism and Effective Death Penalty Act of 1996; S 735; became public law 104-132 on 4/24/96; see all of Title III, specifically sections 302 and 219; also see all of Title IV, specifically sections 401, 501, 502 and 503. 9. (*de facto* national ID card) Began life in the Immigration Control and Financial Responsibility Act of 1996, sections 111, 118, 119, 127 and 133; was eventually folded into the Omnibus Appropriations Act, HR 3610 (which was itself formerly called the Defense Appropriations Act — but we wouldn't want to confuse anyone, here, would we?); became public law 104-208 on 9/30/96; see sections 656 and 657 among others. 10. (health care database) Health Insurance Portability and Accountability Act of 1996, HR 3103; became public law 104-191 on 8/21/96; see sections 262, 263 and 264, among others. The various provisions that make up the full horror of this database are scattered throughout the bill and may take hours to track down; this one is stealth legislation at its utmost sneakiest.

And one final, final note: Although I spent aggravating hours verifying the specifics of these bills (a task I swear I will never waste my life on again!), the original list of bills at the top of this article was NOT the result of extensive research. It was simply what came off the top of my head when I thought of Big Brotherish bills from the 104th Congress. For all I know, Congress has passed 10 times more of that sort of thing. In fact, the worst "law" in the list -- #9, the *de facto* national ID card -- just came to my attention as I was writing this essay, thanks to the enormous efforts of Jackie Juntti and Ed Lyon and others, who researched the law. Think of it: Thanks to congressional stealth tactics, we had the long-dreaded national ID card legislation for five months, without a whisper of discussion, before freedom activists began to find out about it. Makes you wonder what else might be lurking out there, doesn't it?

And on that cheery note —

THE END

SNEAK AND PEEK WARRANTS
Legal Issues Regarding Surreptitious Searches

by Kimberly A. Crawford, J.D.

Illustration by Bob Crabb   Reprinted from *FBI Law Enforcement Bulletin*, February 1997

Searches and seizures conducted pursuant to validly authorized and executed search warrants are very common law enforcement practices. The canons regulating such searches and seizures at the federal level are found in the Fourth Amendment to the U.S. Constitution[1] and Rule 41 of the Federal Rules of Criminal Procedure.[2]

The Fourth Amendment provides the general requirements that all searches and seizures be reasonable and that all warrants be based on sworn probable cause, particularly describing the place to be searched and items to be seized. Rule 41 imposes more specific regulations regarding the authorization and execution of search

warrants, such as authority to issue, authority to serve, time restraints, and notice requirements.

The prescriptions contained in the Fourth Amendment and Rule 41 are well-established and routinely followed by law enforcement officers. There are occasions, however, when a legitimate law enforcement activity does not fit squarely within the realm of a traditional search, and the government's ability to comply with conventional constitutional and statutory warrant requirements is questionable. Specifically, the use of "sneak and peek" warrants by law enforcement officers has raised questions

(Continued on next page)

regarding compliance with the Fourth Amendment prohibition against unreasonable searches and the Rule 41 notice requirement.

This article examines the emergence of the sneak and peek warrant as a law enforcement technique and reviews cases that have addressed the legal issues involved in the execution of such warrants. Additionally, it offers suggestions for meeting the demands of the Fourth Amendment and Rule 41 when employing a sneak and peek warrant.

A Viable Law Enforcement Technique

Sneak and peek warrants allow law enforcement officers to lawfully make surreptitious entries into areas where a reasonable expectation of privacy exists, search for items of evidence or contraband, and leave without making any seizures or giving concurrent notice of the search. The technique is particularly useful in controlled substance manufacturing cases.[3]

When conducting an investigation into the illegal manufacturing of controlled substances, law enforcement officers may want to enter premises to confirm the presence of precursor chemicals or to assess the stability of a clandestine lab without divulging the investigation or jeopardizing the potential for further investigation. Under such circumstances, employing a traditional search warrant, which requires notice at the time of execution, would be self-defeating. A sneak and peek warrant, however, would satisfy the legitimate law enforcement purpose by allowing the search to occur without concurrent notice.

The Notice Requirement

Because nothing is disturbed or physically seized[4] during the execution of a sneak and peek warrant, surreptitious searches are arguably less intrusive than the traditional search pursuant to a warrant. However, the covert nature of sneak and peek searches has made reviewing courts wary[5] and caused them to impose strict delayed-notice requirements.

The first reported case involving the review of a sneak and peek warrant was *United States* v. *Freitas.*[6] In *Freitas*, DEA agents obtained eight warrants to search numerous sites used in a large-scale methamphetamine operation. Before those warrants were executed, agents applied for and obtained a sneak and peek warrant for one

of those locations to "determine the status of the suspected clandestine methamphetamine laboratory."[7]

When issuing the sneak and peek warrant, the magistrate used a traditional warrant form but crossed out the portions requiring a particular description of the items to be seized and an inventory. The sneak and peek warrant contained no notice requirement.

After executing the sneak and peek warrant, agents used information obtained during the surreptitious search to obtain extensions that would allow them to briefly delay the execution of the remaining eight warrants. When those warrants were finally executed, the agents seized numerous items of evidence and arrested the defendant.

In a subsequent motion to suppress, the defendant contested the validity of the sneak and peak warrant. After a hearing on the matter, the district court concluded that the failure of the warrant to provide notice of service breached the Fourth Amendment.[8]

On review, the Ninth Circuit Court of Appeals agreed that the agents violated the Fourth Amendment by their failure to provide notice.[9] In doing so, the court recognized that not all surreptitious entries are unconstitutional.[10] However, the court found that the "absence of any notice requirement in the warrant casts strong doubt on its constitutional adequacy."[11]

To remove that doubt, the court held that a sneak and peek warrant must be based on a demonstrated need for covertness and "provide explicitly for notice within a reasonable, but short, time subsequent to the surreptitious entry. Such time should not exceed seven days except upon a strong showing of necessity."[12]

The need for covertness may be justified on numerous grounds. The more common justifications for delayed notice of surreptitious searches are the desire to locate unidentified co-conspirators and flight risk of the subjects. However, probably the most compelling reason to delay notice of search was demonstrated in *United States* v. *Ludwig.*[13]

In *Ludwig*, U.S. Customs agents were investigating the break-in of a Customs drug storage facility where 356 pounds of cocaine were stolen. During the course of the investigation, the agents obtained a sneak and peek warrant for the search of a storage locker where an undetermined amount of cocaine was reportedly observed by a confidential source. Among the reasons asserted to justify the delayed notice was the need to protect the confidential source's safety until all the subjects could be

> "...the covert nature of sneak and peek searches has made reviewing courts wary..."

(Continued on next page)

located and arrested. Finding the reasons compelling, the court upheld the 7-day notice delay.

Although the 7-day notice requirement espoused in *Freitas* was a creation of the court and not mandated by the Constitution or Federal Rules, it has been adopted by the only other federal court of appeals to deal with the issue of sneak and peek warrants. In *United States* v. *Villegas*[14] and *United States* v. *Pangburn*,[15] the Second Circuit Court of Appeals relied on the decision in *Freitas* to impose the 7-day requirement.

Extensions of the Notice Requirement

In *Freitas*, the court suggested that extensions of the 7-day notice requirement should not be granted except "on a strong showing of necessity."[16] Subsequently, the court in *Villegas* confronted a defense challenge to a surreptitious search where the notice of the search was delayed for more than 2 months.

In *Villegas*, DEA agents obtained a sneak and peek warrant to confirm the existence of a cocaine factory. The warrant contained a provision requiring notice of the search within 7 days. Two months after the execution of the sneak and peek warrant, agents executed a traditional search warrant and seized large quantities of cocaine in various stages of production and arrested 11 individuals.

In the interim, agents obtained a series of additional 7-day extensions. The defendants ultimately moved to suppress the evidence on

> "...a sneak and peek warrant must be based on a demonstrated need for covertness..."

the grounds that notice of the surreptitious search, which did not occur until after the arrests were made, was not timely.

Addressing defendants' motion, the court found two limitations on the issuance of covert entry searches to be appropriate. First, contemporaneous notice of a search should not be delayed unless the government has made a showing of reasonable necessity for the delay.[17] Second, extensions of the delayed notice should not be granted "solely on the basis of the grounds presented for the first delay; rather, the applicant should be required to make a fresh showing of the need for further delay."[18]

Applying these standards to the facts in *Villegas*, the court found that both criteria were met. First, the government presented ample grounds for the initial delay based on the remote setting of the clandestine lab, the lack of informants, and the large number of unidentified co-conspirators.

As to the numerous 7-day extensions, the court noted with approval that an affidavit supplying information on the progress of the investigation and a statement of the need for further delay were submitted with each request. These affidavits ranged in length from two to six pages and "were neither pro forma nor reflective of stale information."[19] While not suggesting that extensions could properly be granted indefinitely, the court concluded that "tolerable limits were not exceeded in this case."[20]

The court in *Villegas* set a functional standard for the issuance of delayed-notice extensions. Requests for such extensions should keep the issuing authority apprised of the status of the investigation and clearly demonstrate that the need for covertness continues to exist.

Remedy for Violations of the Notice of Requirement

If the government violates the 7-day notice requirement by failing to obtain the initial authorization for delayed notice or by failing to adequately support the need for extensions, the remedy for such violations is likely to be suppression of evidence subsequently obtained during the follow-up traditional search. The likelihood of such suppression, however, depends on whether the court views the government's failure as a violation of the Fourth Amendment or Rule 41.

Jurisdictions that view notice violations as contrary to the Fourth Amendment impose a higher standard than those that consider them violations of Rule 41. To overcome the finding of a Fourth Amendment violation, law enforcement officers must be able to establish that they executed a surreptitious warrant in a good faith belief in its validity. To surmount a claim of failure to comply with Rule 41, on the other hand, the government need only show that the defendant was not prejudiced by any intentional or deliberate disregard for the rule.

In *Freitas*, the Ninth Circuit Court of Appeals concluded that the failure to give contemporaneous notice of a search without adequate prior authorization violated the Fourth Amendment reasonableness requirement. Traditionally, constitutional violations are sanctioned by suppression of the evidence unless, in the case of searches, the law enforcement officer relied in good faith on a warrant.[21]

In light of the fact that court decisions like those in *Freitas*, *Villegas*, and *Pangburn* have existed for a

(Continued on next page)

number of years, attempts to justify a good faith reliance on sneak and peek warrants that contain no notice requirements are likely to be ill-fated. However, if law enforcement officers make reasonable efforts to 1) support initial requests for surreptitious searches, 2) ensure that sneak and peek warrants contain 7-day, delayed-notice requirements, and 3) adequately justify delay extensions, then the prospects of a successful good faith defense on the part of the government increase.

Contrary to the court in *Freitas*, the Second Circuit Court of Appeals has rejected the notion that notice violations contravene Fourth Amendment protections. Rather, the court in *Pangburn* found the contemporaneous notice requirement to be merely an element of Rule 41. Because an infraction of Rule 41 does not amount to a constitutional violation, the court concluded that suppression of the evidence would be unnecessary unless shown to cause prejudice to the defendant or to be an "intentional and deliberate disregard of... the Rules."[22]

Because sneak and peek warrants are essentially an alternative to the more intrusive traditional search warrant, it is unlikely that defendants will be successful in showing that they were prejudiced by the government's use of the surreptitious search. Thus, to defeat defense challenges that the use of sneak and peek warrants violates Rule 41, law enforcement officers should concentrate their efforts on ensuring that there is no "intentional and deliberate" disregard for notice requirements. This can be accomplished by making reasonable attempts to comply with the rules by addressing the need for covertness in sneak and peek warrant applications and, when possible, having those applications reviewed for sufficiency by competent legal advisors prior to submission for authorization.[23]

Suggestions for Ensuring the Admissibility of Evidence

Challenges to sneak and peek warrants usually take the form of motions to suppress evidence obtained during subsequent searches pursuant to traditional search warrants. Defendants inevitably claim that the previously executed "unlawful" surreptitious searches taint traditional warrants. Law enforcement can overcome these challenges in two ways.

One approach is for officers to ensure the lawfulness of the surreptitious search. In that regard, the following suggestions are offered:

1. Sneak and peek warrants should only be used when there is a legitimate need for the government to covertly uncover information that could not be obtained through other, more traditional means of investigation. Because courts are wary of surreptitious searches, they should not be used as a routine matter of course.
2. When sneak and peek warrants are obtained, the warrant forms should contain a statement requiring notification of execution within 7 days.
3. Every effort should be made to comply with the 7-day notice requirements. Delays, when necessary, should be the result of circumstances beyond the control of the government and authorized in 7-day increments.
4. Delays, when justified, should be supported by affidavits summarizing the investigation to date and clearly demonstrating the need for continued covertness.
5. When feasible, a competent legal advisor should review both the surreptitious warrant application and any requests for extensions of the delayed notice prior to submission to the court for authorization.
6. If the conditions justifying the need for covertness are dispelled, notice of the surreptitious search should be given as soon as possible.

The second course of action to overcome a defense motion to suppress evidence seized pursuant to a traditional warrant executed subsequent to a surreptitious search is to protect the independent nature of the traditional search warrant. If the courts view the traditional warrant as an outgrowth of an unlawful surreptitious search, anything seized pursuant to the traditional warrant would be considered "fruit of the poisonous tree" and suppressed.

If, however, the courts deem the traditional warrant autonomous, the seized evidence may be admissible, despite the unlawfulness of the previous sneak and peek.[24] To protect the independent nature of the traditional warrant, law enforcement officers should be careful to omit from the probable cause statement any information obtained during the execution of the sneak and peek.

> "...warrant forms should contain a statement requiring notification of execution within 7 days..."

Conclusion

The covert nature of sneak and peek warrants makes them attractive to law enforcement officers but menacing to the courts. To preserve the continued use of surreptitious searches as a legitimate practice, law enforcement officers should carefully follow the dictates of the

(Continued on next page)

few courts that have reviewed the technique. Furthermore, the government should demonstrate good faith by using sneak and peek warrants only when necessary and by giving notice of the search as soon as feasible.

Endnotes

1. U.S. Const. amend. IV reads: "The right of the people to be secure in their persons, houses, papers and effects against unreasonable searches and seizures shall not be violated and no Warrants shall issue but upon probable cause supported by Oath or affirmation and particularly describing the place to be searched and the person or things to be seized."

2. Statutes regulating the issuance and execution of search warrants at the state level differ greatly from state to state. Thus, state and local law enforcement officers are encouraged to consult with their department's legal counsel prior to engaging in activities discussed in this article.

3. Sneak and peek warrants may be used effectively in other types of investigations. For example, the sneak and peek may be used to locate stolen items without revealing the government's investigation to the subjects so that further investigation can identify additional co-conspirators or fences.

4. Although nothing is physically seized during the execution of a sneak and peek warrant, photographs of observed evidence or contraband are often taken and those images are considered seized.

5. In *United States* v. *Freitas*, 800 F.2d 1451 (9th Cir. 1986), the court made the following statement:

   Surreptitious searches and seizures of intangibles strike at the very heart of the interests protected by the Fourth Amendment. The mere thought of strangers walking through and visually examining the center of our privacy interest, our home, arouses our passion for freedom, as does nothing else. That passion, the true source of the Fourth Amendment, demands that surreptitious entries be closely circumscribed. *Id.* at 1456.

6. 800 F.2d 1451 (9th Cir. 1986).

7. *Id.* at 1453.

8. The district court also concluded that the sneak and peek warrant impermissibly allowed agents to observe, but not seize, tangible property. However, on appeal, the court cited *United States* v. *New York Telephone Co.*, 434 U.S. 159 (1977) for the proposition that the seizure of intangibles does not violate the Fourth Amendment or Rule 41. *Id.* at 1455.

9. Both the district court and the court of appeals concluded that the failure to give notice also violated

Rule 41. However, because failures to comply with the Federal Rules of Criminal Procedure do not automatically require suppression of evidence, it is more significant that these courts found a violation of the Fourth Amendment.

10. See *Dalia* v. *United States*, 441 U.S. 238 (1979).

11. 800 F.2d 1451, 1456.

12. *Id.* at 1456. The court in *Freitas* did not order the evidence seized pursuant to the warrants suppressed. Rather, the court believed there was a strong possibility that the agents relied on the warrants in good faith and that the evidence would be admissible under the Supreme Court's ruling in *United States* v. *Leon*, 468 U.S. 897 (1984). Accordingly, the court ordered a remand. The second time on review, in *Freitas II*, the court concluded that the good faith reliance on the warrant exception to the exclusionary rule did, in fact, apply in this case. 856 F.2d 1425 (9th Cir. 1988).

13. 902 F. Supp. 121 (W.D. Tex. 1995).

14. 899 F.2d 1324 (2d. Cir. 1990).

15. 983 F.2d 449 (2d. Cir. 1993).

16. 800 F.2d 1451, 1456 (1990).

17. The court did not suggest that the government must meet the Title III standard of establishing that "normal investigative procedures have been tried and have failed or reasonably appear to be unlikely to succeed if tried or to be too dangerous." 18 U.S.C. § 2518(3)(c).

18. 899 S.2d 1324, 1338.

19. *Id.* at 1338.

20. *Id.* at 1338.

21. *United States* v. *Leon*, 468 U.S. 897 (1984).

22. 983 F. 2d 449, 455 (citing *United States* v. *Burke*, 517 F.2d 377 (2d Cir. 1975)).

23. In *Pangburn*, the court noted with approval that the agent submitted the sneak and peek warrant application to an assistant district attorney for review prior to presentment to the court. *Id.* at 455.

24. See, *e.g.*, *United States* v. *Sitton*, 968 F.2d 947 (9th Cir. 1992).

Law enforcement officers of other than federal jurisdiction who are interested in this article should consult their legal advisors. Some police procedures ruled permissible under federal constitutional law are of questionable legality under state law or are not permitted at all.

NOTICE: *Sneak and Peek Warrants* is reprinted from the *FBI Law Enforcement Bulletin*, February 1997. It is reprinted here from the public domain. "The Attorney General has determined that the publication of this periodical is necessary in the transaction of the public business required by law. Use of funds for printing this periodical has been approved by the Director of the Office of Management and Budget." YOUR TAX DOLLARS AT WORK FOR YOU!!!

UNINTENDED CONSEQUENCES
by John Ross

"It's *cultural*. That's what I keep telling Henry," Thomas J. Fleming explained as he cut into his steak.

"What do you mean?" Ray thought he knew what Fleming was talking about, but he wanted to hear the man's rationale for what he said. The three men were eating dinner at a private club where Henry was a member. The mounted head of one of the buffalo he had shot sixteen years before hung on the wall over the fireplace.

"People who don't shoot guns have this image of a fat guy in overalls with a sixth-grade education, drinking a six-pack of beer in the front seat of his pickup while driving back from a wedding where two of his cousins married each other. That's what some people think of when they hear 'gun nut,' or 'NRA.' Or alternatively, they envision some moron with a shaved head, wearing camo, distributing Klan literature and bragging about how he's going to shoot any colored guy he sees with a white girl. To many people, those two stereotypes represent the gun culture." He took a drink of iced tea and went on.

"Now there are a few of those stereotypes around, but they're just a handful compared to the rest of us. The real members of the gun culture are the kind of people that are sitting at this table." Fleming paused a moment to let that sink in, and then went on.

"You might think Henry here is an extreme example, but you'd be wrong. There are a lot of guys like him. You know what IPSC shooting is, don't you? They hold the world championships in South Africa."

"Sure," Ray answered easily. "Before that, they were in Rhodesia." Fleming and Johnson were referring to the International Practical Shooting Conference. It was an established series of handgun matches where competitors ran through a course and encountered both "hostile" and "friendly" targets, designed to simulate real-world situations.

"Right," Fleming said, raising a finger. "Well, there are over fifty thousand registered IPSC competitors in this country. Typical serious competitor shoots between forty and a hundred thousand rounds a year practicing, and his competition gun costs two thousand minimum. You shoot IPSC, Henry?"

"No."

"Me neither. So Henry and I aren't part of that fifty thousand." Fleming raised a second finger. "Handgun

(Continued on next page)

silhouette, there's between thirty and forty thousand competitors. They shoot almost as much in practice as IPSC guys. You shoot silhouette, Henry?"

"Entered a couple matches a few years ago, but there's no range around here."

"No to that one too, then. Me, I've never tried it." He raised a third finger. "PPC, Practical Pistol Competition. At least as many competitors as IPSC, at least as much practice, guns are cheaper. You shoot PPC, Henry?"

"Never tried it."

"Nor I. Next we got bowling pin," he said as he raised a fourth finger, "which I know Henry's done, and those guys practice all the time. Then there's bullseye competition, rimfire silhouette, cowboy shoots for black powder guns, and a bunch of other stuff different organizations have dreamed up.

"Mind you now, that's just organized competition involving centerfire handguns. Now we move to rifles," he said as he folded up his fingers and started over. "We got twenty or thirty thousand bench rest shooters shooting dime-sized groups at two hundred yards. We got almost that many in rifle silhouette. We got high power shooters and DCM shooters lying on their stomachs shooting prone. We got a ton of smallbore shooters using rimfires, and we got more rimfire shooters in the GM Sportsman's Truck Challenge. Then there's the centerfire action matches for the semiauto guys, just like IPSC."

"I won one of those with a bolt action last year," Henry said with a smile.

"Show-off. We've also got a bunch of long range black powder shooters like in the Coors Schuetzenfest, plus frontier competitions, and even black powder benchrest.

"Finally, with shotguns, the numbers really go nuts. Skeet, trap, and sporting clays, well over two billion rounds fired last year. There's also crazy quail, plus bowling pin and other combat matches held with shotguns. How many rounds of shotgun ammo did you fire last year, Henry?"

"None."

"How much hunting?"

"None."

"So what we've got to look at now," Tom Fleming went on, "is the biggest part of all: the people like me or like Henry who shoot just to keep their skills up. People shooting just because they like it, without any particular interest in competition." Fleming took a breath, then saw that Henry was about to take over.

"Tom's exactly right," Henry jumped in. "Last year the ammo manufacturers sold over three billion rounds of rimfire ammo. Centerfire rifle and pistol was about two billion. Imports another billion.

"Then there's reloads. I don't have the figures from component companies, but I can make a fair guess. Almost nobody buys U.S. commercial centerfire ammo several cases at a time, but everybody buys primers a few thousand at a whack. I bet there's three or four rounds of reloads shot, minimum, for every factory metallic centerfire round fired downrange. And I haven't even considered shotshells in that estimate.

"So that's — What? Fifteen billion rounds of ammunition fired every year?" Henry asked.

"Sounds right," Tom Fleming agreed. "And this lisping moron in the U.S. Senate wants to put a ten thousand percent tax on it." He shook his head.

"It isn't out-of-work high school dropouts firing all that ammo. It isn't guys with maxed-out credit cards who drink beer and watch sports all the time. It's educated, serious guys just like you, and Henry, and me. We've all got high incomes, or we wouldn't be able to afford to shoot all that ammo. None of us are on the dole. A few gun guys drink, but I don't know a single one that goes to football games or even watches sports on television. Do you, Henry?"

"Nobody I know."

"And if you think back to when you were a kid, I bet almost all your best memories are of when you were out shooting, or talking about it when you were done."

"You're dead-on on that one," Ray admitted.

"Boy, that's the truth," Henry broke in. "I went out to Reno with my uncle when I was in high school. Best time I ever had. Those live pigeon shooters all watched me shoot trap with my .375, and then went with us out in the desert to a cannon shoot. Had a hell of a time. They never shot anything but shotguns up until that day, and I bet a bunch of them now shoot big rifles."

"See what I mean?" Fleming said. "We're all the same. And the kicker is, every single one of us believes that as honest adult citizens, we have the absolute right to own any and all small arms and shoot them just as often as we want. We have a specific culture. Guns and shooting are very important to us, just like living as nomads and hunting buffalo was important to the Indians. We are willing to work hard and have the government confiscate half our money and use it for things we never get any benefit out of, if only we can continue to buy our guns and our ammo and our components, and shoot a lot.

"Our culture is important, and we're willing to pay for it. We have above-average educations, above-average incomes, and almost nonexistent criminal involvement. We pay far more in taxes and receive virtually no subsidy payments. You'd think Washington would be happy, but

(Continued on next page)

instead they are doing everything they can to destroy our culture.

"In the '20s, soldiers sat on their bunks in the cold at Camp Perry, cleaning the handmade .22 target rifles they would compete with the next day. When the President proudly announces that today, seventy years later, he is ordering these same guns thrown into a blast furnace, we in the gun culture feel powerful emotions. They are the same emotions a Native American would feel if the President proudly ordered the destruction of war clubs and other sacred tribal artifacts. They are the same emotions that Jews felt watching newsreel footage of Nazi *Sturmtruppen* gleefully burning intricate copies of the Torah.

"We offer to buy the government's surplus guns, and instead they pay to have them cut up. We offer to buy their surplus military ammo, shoot it, sell the brass to a smelter, and give the government the proceeds, and instead they pay to have it burned.

"These government slugs ban our guns and they ban our magazines and they ban our ammo. They ban suppressors that make our guns quieter and then they ban our outdoor shooting ranges because our guns are too loud. They ban steel-core ammunition because it's 'armor piercing,' then they close down our indoor ranges where people shoot lead-core bullets because they say we might get lead poisoning.

"The people in the gun culture have a better safety record than any police department in the nation, but in several states they actually prohibit us from using guns for self-protection, and in all the other states except one they make us buy a license. They tax us so we can have more cops, and when crime still goes up, they tax us more and ban more of our guns.

"People in the gun culture endure waiting periods that no other group would stand for. We undergo background checks that no legislator, judge, doctor, or police officer has to tolerate, and we submit to it not once, or once a year, but over and over again. Then, after we yield to this outrage, they smile and forbid us from buying more than one gun in a 30-day period.

"If we sell one gun we own that's gone up in value, they can charge us with dealing in firearms without a federal dealer's license, which is a felony. If we get a dealer's license, they say we are not really in business, and report us to our local authorities for violating zoning ordinances by running a commercial venture out of a residence.

"If the steel or the wood on our guns is too long or too short, they make us pay $200 taxes and get fingerprinted and photographed. They make us get a law enforcement certification from the local police chief. If he refuses to sign we have no recourse. If he takes the forms in the next room and brings them back out, signed, he can later claim the signature is not his, and the feds will charge us with the felony.

"We in the gun culture have played all their stupid games on NFA weapons for over half a century, without a single violent crime being committed by any person in the system. So when a bill comes up to keep travelers with guns locked in the trunk of their cars out of jail, what happens? A scumbucket from New Jersey, where NFA weapons are illegal already, puts an amendment on it that closes down the whole NFA process.

"Then, if they even suspect we've ignored the $200 tax process altogether, on the guns where the wood and steel is too long or too short, they'll spend over a million dollars watching us for months, then they'll shoot our wives and children or burn us all alive. When the public gets outraged by these actions, the government issues letters of reprimand and sends the guys who did the killing on paid leave. In the decades that the feds have been raiding and killing people in the gun culture over suspected non-payment of $200 taxes, not one federal agent has been fined a single dollar or spent even one night in jail." Fleming stopped for a moment and took another drink of tea.

"And you know something else that's never happened, Ray? To this day, not a single person in the gun culture has ever dropped the hammer on one of these feds. Not once.

"Then, after these statist bastards have done all these things, they grin and tell us how they like to hunt ducks, and how the only laws they want to pass are 'reasonable' ones." Henry and Ray both looked at their friend. Neither had anything to add at that moment. It was Ray Johnson who finally spoke.

"I now know everything you say is true," he said. "I still can't quite believe it." He was quiet again, then asked a question. "What do you think is going to happen?"

"One of two things," Fleming said with a sigh. "One of the political parties is going to have to wake up, smell the coffee, and start restoring and reaffirming all the articles in the Bill of Rights — the Second, Fourth, Fifth, and Tenth Amendments."

"And if that doesn't happen?" Ray asked gently. Fleming took several moments before he spoke, though it was obvious he knew exactly what he was going to say.

"Then we're going to have a civil war."●

Running Wild

by Dan Kelly

Illustration by King VelVeeda

"People are the same all over": so goes an adage the deluded humanists of the world would have us believe to be a universal truth. Cold reality, of course, makes it abundantly clear that not only are people NOT the same all over, they ain't all that similar on the inside either. Which, overall, is not such a bad thing. Cultural differences are the spiciest of life's seasonings, and a world whose population shared a common character would be a dull realm indeed.

Nowhere is this societal variety more bizarrely illustrated than in the study of the so-called "culture-bound syndromes." "Culture-bound syndromes" — at times also referred to as culture-specific disorders and "folk illnesses" — is an all-encompassing term for a hodgepodge of exotic mental illnesses that are, if not orphaned, then at least disregarded by the Western World's psychological establishment. As suggested by their name, culture-bound syndromes are as much a part of a society's cultural character as any native dish, dance, or folktale. What follows is a layman's survey of the more colorful syndromes. While debate rages on as to their status as "new" mental illnesses (insofar as the Western psychological canon is concerned), verified case studies are nonetheless an entertaining way to see how the other half lives, or, for that matter, goes insane.

AMOK

We begin with the behavioral pyrotechnics of the *amok*. Undoubtedly the only culture-bound syndrome to enjoy household use in the English-speaking world, it's easy to discern what "running amok" involves.

(Continued on next page)

The amok behavioral pattern is eerily familiar to anyone who has read a paper or seen a television set in the past twenty years. Mostly occurring among quiet Malayan men who keep to themselves, the attack is preceded by feelings of isolation, depression, and complete social withdrawal. In due time, the afflicted (referred to as the *pengamok*, while the actual attack is called the *mengamok*) springs up, seizes the nearest weapon, and begins slaying friends, family members, and total strangers alike.

Cultural differences are the spiciest of life's seasonings, and a world whose population shared a common character would be a dull realm indeed.

In his delirium, the pengamok commonly takes to the streets of his village, hacking and/or bludgeoning a bloody swath through the town square. Naturally, this breach of good-neighbor policy does not go unnoticed, and the pengamok is either captured, killed, or takes his own life. If he is fortunate enough to be restrained, the pengamok falls comatose for several days, eventually returning to consciousness with amnesia and yet more depression.

By its nature, amok beggars the question of whether or not it is truly a culture-bound syndrome. While amok may have seemed terrifyingly exotic to the 17th-century Western explorers and missionaries who first beheld it, these days barely a week passes without reports of a disgruntled worker permanently downsizing several fellow employees. In point of fact, amok appears and rages on across the globe under several names. In the Sahara it is called *pseudonite,* while in Polynesia it is dubbed *cathard.* Canada contributes the bizarre mental imagery of "Jumping Frenchman Syndrome," while here in the good old U.S. of A. it is simply Whitman's syndrome, or, in the vernacular, "going postal."

What causes amok? In the United States, everything from brain tumors to poor potty training has been blamed.

What causes amok? In the United States, everything from brain tumors to poor potty training has been blamed. Only in the Malayan Archipelago, however, can one find historical precedence for the activity. Ancient Javanese and Malay warriors were said to have adapted Hindu fighting techniques, one of which involved a platoon of warriors swinging short swords above their heads and hollering, "Amok! Amok!", alerting the opposition to

expect no quarter. Others have suggested that from this primeval form of psychological warfare developed a form of protest against unjust leaders. By bursting into homicidal action, even the least of a despot's subjects could refute his claims to absolute power. Does this fact of the amok carry over to the present day? Perhaps in the pengamok's mind, his actions are a justified response to some great "wrong" performed against him. Any complaints lodged by his victims, I suppose, may be charted to mere quibbling.

GRISI SIKNIS

Sailing down the Atlantic coasts of Nicaragua and Honduras we discover the polynational Miskito culture, a society wherein teenage girls vie for equal amok time. *Grisi siknis* resembles amok in that the afflicted grasps a weapon and dashes hell-bent through her hometown; but that is where the similarities end. Very unlike amok, grisi siknis victims rarely attack those around them. During the episode, the subject experiences hallucinations of devils and non-Miskito people (often Caucasians) suddenly appearing and attempting to take sexual liberties with them. At this, the young lady seizes a weapon — machetes are a perennial favorite — and endeavors to drive the devils away by maniacally waving her blade, this way and that. A justifiable response, surely, when one is confronted with sex-crazed demons, it (regrettably) also increases the danger of self-mutilation. The only trophies garnered in this marathon are the multitude of self-inflicted nicks, cuts and scratches on the runner's body.

One other distinction from amok — one for which the Miskito should give thanks — is that grisi siknis is contagious. "Epidemics" can erupt wherever young women congregate, and when one girl shows symptoms, those around her follow suit. Eventually, whole packs of rabid Miskito teenyboppers may be found rampaging through their village, such behavior being known colloquially as "working for the devil." ·

Strangely enough, attacks of grisi siknis create a carnival-like atmosphere in the community. Whenever some sweet young thing (or things) is afflicted by the syndrome, groups of strapping young men engage her in hot pursuit, cheering each other on while simultaneously alerting the townsfolk. Despite the situation's levity, chasing down the girl is treated with utmost seriousness. Though fatalities at the hands of this modern-day bacchanalia are rare, rampaging hordes of machete-slinging girls must be a less than reassuring sight to the general populace. Despite this admirable sense of duty, however, gang rape is a not uncommon occurrence, which may shed

(Continued on next page)

a little light on the sufferer's delusions of being ravished by a multitude of horny devils.

Attacks of grisi siknis create a carnival-like atmosphere in the community. Whenever some sweet young thing is afflicted by the syndrome, groups of strapping young men engage her in hot pursuit, cheering each other on while simultaneously alerting the townsfolk.

Grisi siknis could be one more — albeit weird — method for Miskito teenagers to work off adolescent angst. An attention-getting device to the nth degree, attacks have a knack for appearing during *saiwan* (late afternoon), a "prime time" which guarantees a captive audience of adults home from work and packs of teenaged boys hanging out on the village streets. Moreover, you don't have to be Freud to detect the syndrome's repressed sexual subtext. While gang rapes happen in some episodes, so too do thinly-veiled seductions. Several case studies point to young women disappearing into the brush with grisi siknis, declaring that only one particular young man can retrieve them. It is left to the reader then to wonder if grisi siknis is either a new form of insanity, or simply one more way to meet cute guys.

PIBLOKTOQ

We now turn to the icy reaches of the north, where frenzied running-about might be mistaken as one more futile attempt to keep warm. Such is not the case with *pibloktoq*, a syndrome affecting Arctic denizens from Greenland to Siberia. Much like the above syndromes, pibloktoq announces itself with tremendous gusto. Per form, the sufferer cries out and bolts upward, but rather than grabbing a weapon, she instead tears her clothes off. If she is not restrained, this is followed by a mad dash across the tundra, culminating in a swan dive into any convenient snowdrift or subzero body of water. The attack may be brief or it may last for hours, though in some cases it is likely the pibloktoq sufferer would run until he or she dropped dead of exposure.

Yet another peculiar symptom is an inexplicable need to imitate local wildlife. Early reports describe pibloktoq victims indulging in amazingly accurate impressions of birds, wolves and other animals — all before finally plunging naked into a snowbank, of course. Almost all attacks end in crying jags or total physical collapse, but,

for some remarkable reason, frostbite is an infrequent occurrence.

Assigning any one cause to pibloktoq is dicey. One theory holds that it is a hysterical reaction to a great shock in one's life, such as the death or long absence of a loved one. Another opinion, one not without the stigma of Eurocentrism, holds that the long, dark winter months throw Eskimos into a state of depression. More likely, this effect was projected by researchers unaccustomed to month-long winter nights. On the other hand, psychologist Zachary Gussow suggests that it's not the persistent darkness that unsettles Eskimos to the point of pibloktoq, but rather the unconscious perception of winter as a time of increased danger and decreased food supplies. Whatever the cause, anyone is prone to pibloktoq, and unlike the above syndromes, the afflicted is perceived as being more likely to harm themselves than others. In the words of Norman Bates, "We all go a little mad sometimes." The Eskimo, apparently, have come to accept that statement as a fact of life.

KORO

Those gentlemen feeling more than a sentimental attachment to the family jewels may wish to skip this section.

While not possessive of the maniacal elan of an amok, grisi siknis, or pibloktoq, *koro* retains a disturbing charm all its own. Like amok, koro has made the rounds of the far east, leading one to wonder again whether it is truly sequestered in any one culture.

While its point of origin is in question, the word koro has been traced to either the Javanese word for tortoise or the Malayan world *Keruk-to* meaning "to shrink." But while koro is its common name, the phenomenon is by no means exclusively Malayan. In China one finds koro under the nom de plumes of *shook yang* and *suoy-ang*. In Thailand, on the other hand, we encounter *rok joo*, while in India koro clocks in as *jinginia*. Exotic nosology aside, the Western psychiatric community places koro under the laborious, and far more telling, designation of "Genital Retraction Syndrome."

The average koro patient is a seemingly average man who develops the irrational fear that his penis is shrinking into his abdomen. If that isn't annoying enough, he becomes convinced that once his little soldier has retreated into his stomach, he will immediately die. Which is, of course, completely preposterous; but then, insanity puts few roots into reality, doesn't it?

Koro has a long historical pedigree. Ancient Chinese medical writings are peppered with descriptions of

(Continued on next page)

patients whose penises scampered into their bellies and thereupon croaked. More than likely, as per Prins, these were cases of peritonitis, followed by edema (the absorption of fluid into body tissue). In time, an ancient legend became an urban one, and several generations of Asian gentlemen were implanted with playground memories of a disease in which a shrinking penis became an instrument of death. Ridiculous, you say? Consider it analogous to the way American children learn that if they cross their eyes, they may remain crossed "forever."

The average koro patient is a seemingly average man who develops the irrational fear that his penis is shrinking into his abdomen. If that isn't annoying enough, he becomes convinced that once his little soldier has retreated into his stomach, he will immediately die.

Koro "cures," it goes without saying, are infinitely worse than the "disease." Remedies include the customary foul-tasting roots and herbs, or, more odious still, the imbibing of one's own urine or that of others. Sidhi holy men would be hard-pressed to match the more physically grueling "cures," including squeezing one's penis in a death grip, or asking (very understanding) friends or family members to do so. The attachment of all manners of hideous devices, including clamps, hooks, weights, clothespins, splints, and safety pins, to the hapless glans is not unheard of; neither is the surgical attention required to undo the damage caused by these items after the attack has subsided.

Incidentally, if any women out there are feeling a tad superior, you too are not free from the disgusting, creeping horrors of koro. With female koro, anxiety stems from fear of the shrinkage and eventual disappearance of the labia and breasts. Tit for tat, indeed.

WINDIGO

Discussion of the *windigo* phenomenon carries the threat of disappointment for the aberrant anthropologist. Tantalizing for its grisly symptomatology — the victim converts from a normal individual into a slavering beastie with a craving for human flesh — windigo has seduced generations of psychologists with its promise of a true-to-life Jekyll and Hyde transformation. Psychologist Lou Marano suggests, however, that windigo may not be the

picture its bad PR has painted it to be. In fact, it could be far worse.

Found among the Cree, Salteaux, Algonkian, and other northeastern Native American tribes, the classic windigo story portrays a hunting party fruitlessly seeking game in the wild for weeks on end. Ultimately, one of the party is possessed by an invisible demon known as the Windigo, whereupon his heart turns to ice and he is overcome with a craving to eat his fellow hunters' flesh. So the story goes: but if reports, some a century or more old, are to be believed, windigo is rarely picky about its victims. Women and children were as equally apt to contract anthropophagy as disappointed hunters, and possession was as likely to take place whether or not game was scarce or food supplies were low. Whomever the windigo chose to light upon, their days where short. Windigos — the term applies equally to the "demon" syndrome, and person affected — were usually executed before they indulged their desire for long pig.

Marano contends that windigo was used to accuse the tribe's weak, infirm, or troublemakers of a crime so horrendous that it justified their extermination for the community's survival during times of privation. In Marano's estimation, stories of sane tribesmen turning into flesh-eating ghouls are either myths or examples of Shirley Jackson's novelette *The Lottery* put into devastating action. Overeager anthropologists with a penchant for the repulsive then used these stories as a spring-board and created the windigo, the cannibalistic culture-bound syndrome. Thereupon, these initial writings were repeatedly referenced by latter-day psychologists with an aversion to seeking out primary sources; a form of cannibalism all by itself.

MISCELLANEOUS SYNDROMES

Culture-bound syndromes abound, and we've only just scratched the surface of the world's psychotic cottage industries.

The Nepalese, for example, strike a blow for masochism with *boxi*, displaying such pleasant symptomatology as severe migraines, vomiting, odd tingling sensations, and, for those who prefer action, sensations of being thrown to the ground, kicked, pummeled, having one's throat stomped on, and being throttled by invisible attackers.

Not to be outdone by the Malayans and Miskito, the Murut people of North Borneo enter the running and screaming marathon with *ruden rupan,* a disorder which truly makes the sufferer feel victimized. Experiencing delusions of being chased by bloodthirsty hordes, the

(Continued on next page)

ruden rupan runner frantically scrambles to get away, screaming out the names of his imagined tormentors. If he is not captured by more well-meaning neighbors, the victim inevitably drops dead of exhaustion, dehydration, or starvation. Talk about being your own worst enemy!

Presuming to apply European and American cultural standards of sanity to a resident of the Far East is not only politically incorrect, it's poor science.

In two final monads of weirdness, Taiwanese gentlemen seen wearing layer upon layer of clothing may have contracted *pa-leng* — an obsessive fear of cold weather. In Bengal, on the other hand, widows who remove their clothes and hang them on a tree before entering their home are undoubtedly vexed with *suchi-bai*. Other anomalous suchi-bai behavior includes bathing for hours, sitting in the Ganges for even longer, sprinkling cow-dung water on guests (a not-unappreciated act in Bengal, one might assume), and washing all currency (from pocket change to the folding kind) by hand.

CULTURE-BOUND SYNDROMES: FOR AND AGAINST

As psychiatric "outsiders," culture-bound syndromes have provoked fervent debate. The primary bone of contention, however, remains: Are they truly "new" mental illnesses, restricted to this or that corner of the world? The question provokes compelling responses from both sides of the argument.

On the con side — though space and sanity do not allow us to fully explore the old "Nature vs. Nurture" argument here — the biological approach presupposes that what is good enough for Joe Blow in New York is good enough for Joe Amok in Malaya. Following that, after spending the past few decades fine-tuning its *DSM-IV (Diagnostic and Statistical Manual of Mental Disorders)* guide, the American Psychiatric Association claims to have devised a category for any form of illness the human brain can muster. As indicated above, though koro and amok may have been first observed in their native Malaya, their symptoms are by no means isolated to those regions. Renaming an illness does not make it a different illness. Whether you call it amok or Whitman's syndrome, the results are pretty much the same.

On the other side of the coin, though it has made dandy progress in diagnostic procedure over the past

century, psychiatry by and large is a tool and product of the West. Presuming to apply European and American cultural standards of sanity to a resident of the Far East is not only politically incorrect, it's poor science. Taking the social-labeling approach, mental illness is recognized as being defined by the culture in which it exists. As such, the definition of insanity is "culture-specific" in that the afflicted is declared ill when he acts according to criteria denoted as insane behavior by his society. In other words, he "learns to act crazy" in a way his fellow society members will recognize and act upon. As Helman points out, while we may snap our fingers at the tribal psychotic's claims of evil influence by witches, sorcerers, evil spirits and so forth, is this really so different from his Western counterpart's description of psychical control by Martians and flying saucers?

Futhermore, looking from the outside in, it's easy to dismiss culture-bound syndromes as flashy-sounding variations on the same old Western psychoses and neuroses. For the societies in which they originate they are real enough; thus, being "bound" should be considered less a matter of geography than of society. Also, aside from the occasional windigo fiasco, it should be noted that the mechanics of diagnosis, remedy, and prevention were oftentimes developed long before the first wave of anthropologists and ethnopsychiatrists showed up with their clipboards and pens.

Be they unique mental illnesses, exiled to this or that corner of the globe, or simply curious local spins on the world's shared madness, culture-bound syndromes demand our attention. In any event, while you may not find them in the *DSM-IV* guide — or in any of Frommer's or Fedor's travel guides either, for that matter — consider them when you plan your next vacation. For the readers of this catalog, a good burst of amok or display of grisi siknis would leave anything Disneyland could produce quite literally beat all hollow.

REFERENCES:

Foster, George M., *Medical Anthropology*, Alfred A. Knopf, New York, 1990.

Helman, Cecil G., *Culture, Health and Illness, 2nd Edition*, Great Britain, 1990.

Prins, Herschel, *Bizarre Behaviours: Boundaries of Psychiatric Disorder*, Tavistock/Routledge, London and New York, 1990.

Simons, Ronald, and Charles C. Hughes, Editors, *The Culture Bound Syndromes: Folk Illnesses of Psychiatric and Anthropological Interest*, D. Reidel Publishing Co., Boston, 1985.

●

by Michael Newton

Artwork by ⛢

We hear a lot today about sadistic crimes committed in the name of Satan, and there is no doubt that certain psychopaths have fastened on the Prince of Darkness as a ready-made excuse for various abominable acts, including sexual assault and homicide. On balance, though, the vast majority of killers with "religious" motives take their marching orders from a higher source — that is to say, direct from God Himself.

There is no lack of precedent for lowly humans spilling blood on orders from Jehovah, Yahweh — pick your favorite name for The Almighty. If we accept the Old Testament as an accurate historical record — no small leap of faith in itself — we find a more or less uninterrupted string of massacres ordained by God across the Holy Land, with thousands butchered in a single afternoon, Jehovah often wading in Himself to crush a tribe of pesky infidels, down to the last woman and child. With that example before them, and bearing in mind Christ's own

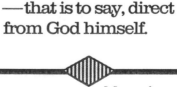

> The vast majority of killers with "religious" motives take their marching orders from a higher source —that is to say, direct from God himself.

admonition that He "came not to send peace, but a sword," some Christian soldiers are ready to kill at the drop of a hat.

One of the first things that we learn in school is that our Pilgrim forefathers arrived in North America seeking religious freedom. This is true, of course... but only to a point. The outcast zealots who endured months at sea to colonize a howling wilderness were tired of being persecuted in their homeland, true enough, but they saw nothing wrong with persecuting others, even unto death, in a religious cause. The first few colonists had barely landed when they started importing dusky slaves from Africa, and passing laws to let them execute or exile anyone who disagreed with the official dogma of the first arrivals on the scene. Massachusetts — the self-styled "Cradle of Liberty" — led the way with a series of laws imposing death on

(Continued on next page)

"witches," Quakers, and violators of sundry Old Testament statutes, including a capital prohibition on sex with livestock.

Colonial theocracies were finally so oppressive that Americans rebelled, in the midst of their larger revolt against England, enacting new laws that barred ministers from holding elective office, spicing the new Constitution with a ban on religious tests for federal officeholders and a First Amendment which Thomas Jefferson described as "a wall of separation between church and state." Their motives were the best, but the roots of sectarian violence in America ran too deep for mere legislation to do the trick. Anti-Catholicism was all the rage in those days of the early 19th century, with Protestant commandos from the aptly named "Know-Nothing" movement bombing churches and touching off more than three dozen riots in ten states. As late as August 1854, twenty residents of Louisville, Kentucky, died in an outbreak of anti-Catholic rioting, immediately followed by another melee that left ten more dead and thirty gravely wounded in St. Louis.

While Protestants and Catholics battled in the streets from Massachusetts to Missouri, a new Christian sect was also coming under fire in Middle America. Joseph Smith's Mormons, or Latter-Day Saints, were initially on the receiving end of violent persecution that included pitched battles involving artillery, climaxing with the lynch-mob slaying of Joseph and his brother Hyrum at Carthage, Illinois, in June 1844. By that time, though, the Mormons were already learning to fight back against aggressive "gentiles," and the incident resulting in Smith's death had been precipitated when a gang of Mormon nightriders demolished the presses of a critical newspaper at nearby Nauvoo, Illinois.

The Mormon exodus to barren Utah was impressive enough to rate the full Hollywood treatment, with Gary Cooper cast as solemn "prophet" Brigham Young, but Mormonism also had its darker side — including a ritual of "blood atonement" which stands as the nearest thing to home-grown human sacrifice in the United States. Conceived by Young as a handy method for eliminating pesky dissidents (and

> **The Pilgrims who endured months at sea to colonize a howling wilderness were tired of being persecuted in their homeland, but they saw nothing wrong with persecuting others, even unto death, in a religious cause.**

> **Mormonism had its darker side — including a ritual of "blood atonement" which stands as the nearest thing to home-grown human sacrifice in the United States.**

gobbling up their worldly possessions in the process), "blood atonement" was advertised in Mormon circles as the one and only way of earning divine forgiveness for certain unpardonable sins — like criticizing Young's administration of the fledgling Deseret theocracy. As laid out by the Prophet, killing wayward Mormons was, indeed, a selfless act of Christian charity. "Love them enough to spill their blood," Young urged the faithful in 1856, and he meant it literally. Nor was it enough to simply kill the miscreant in question; rather, Young insisted that the lucky sinner have "his throat cut from ear to ear, his tongue torn out by its roots, his breast cut open and his heart and vitals torn from his body and given to the birds of the air and the beasts of the field, and his body cut asunder in the midst and all his bowels gush out."

Before that savage doctrine was officially rescinded, scores of Mormons — maybe hundreds — were dispatched by hit teams of "Avenging Angels," known as Danites to the faithful. Nonbelievers sometimes ran afoul of Mormon murder squads, as well — most notably at Mountain Meadows, Utah, in September 1857, when a mixed band of Mormons and Indians raided an immigrant wagon train bound for California, slaughtering 120 men, women, and children. By that time, Mormon Utah was at war with the United States, Danite raiders sacking federal supply trains and murdering territorial officers, but the end result was a foregone conclusion, with Brigham's saints compelled to submit and abandon their cherished ritual of polygamy.

It should not be supposed, however, that the rites of "blood atonement" vanished with the annexation of Utah in the 19th century. In fact, various dissident sects, generally led by polygamous zealots expelled from the LDS Church, regarding themselves as the only "pure" Mormons, have continued its grisly practice to the present day. The most notorious practitioners of "blood atonement" in this century were Ervil LeBaron and his fanatical "Lambs of God," whose internecine war with

(Continued on next page)

rival polygamous cults spanned two decades, leaving twenty-odd corpses strewn about the American Southwest and northern Mexico. Victims of the "Mormon Manson" included one of Ervil's dozen wives and at least two of his children, along with assorted defectors and competing "prophets." LeBaron's eventual imprisonment and death behind bars, in 1981, did nothing to stop the bloodshed, as die-hard disciples worked their way through an enemies list contained in Ervil's *Book of New Covenants*. At this writing, a small platoon of homicidal Lambs is still at large.

Another hands-on advocate of "blood atonement" was self-styled "prophet" Jeffrey Lundgren, who derived his sense of destiny from both the *Book of Mormon* and repeated viewings of the movie *Highlander*. Lundgren was so far gone, in fact, that he convinced himself the movie was produced for him alone, a kind of cinematic vision that proclaimed his immortality and paved the way for him to "purify" the Mormon Church. In fact, he never got around to conquering the LDS empire, and was excommunicated for his efforts, finally settling for a small cult of his own in Kirtland, Ohio (where Joe Smith wrote the *Book of Mormon* and built his first temple, back in 1836). Lundgren's sect was essentially a cash cow for the Prophet, but certain members eventually rebelled at handing their paychecks over to Jeffrey, and he decided that a lesson to the faithful was required. In April 1989, Lundgren shot five members of the Avery family, including three children, and buried their corpses in a barn at the Kirtland commune. When the gunsmoke cleared, Jeff told his surviving disciples, "Now that the sin is gone, we can go into the wilderness and see God." (In fact, the only place they were going was prison, with Lundgren sentenced to die, his wife Alice jailed for 150 years, and ten other cultists convicted or copping pleas in the case.)

No American organization in this century has done more to promote "militant Christianity" than the nightriding Ku Klux Klan, with its long record of cross-burnings, floggings, lynchings, bombings, and other acts of terrorism dating back to 1915. More recently, the hooded "knights" of the "invisible empire" have sought to revive their dwindling movement with a fresh shot of Old-Time Religion... borrowed, in this case, from 19th-century England. The weird dogma — initially christened Anglo-Israelism, renamed "Christian Identity" in the

States to remove any suggestion of a foreign taint — maintains that Western European and Teutonic peoples are the true "lost tribes of Israel" and the chosen people of God, while Jews are the demonic offspring of Eve's coupling with Satan in the Garden of Eden, and nonwhite "mud people" are the product of race-mixing experiments conducted by Jewish mad scientists, à la Dr. Moreau.

"Identity" theology is so bizarre, in fact, that it is tempting to dismiss the movement with a good old-fashioned belly laugh, but its adherents are deadly earnest. Indeed, the merger of racism and religion has united America's redneck fringe groups as never before, providing common ground for Klansmen and paranoid "survivalists," tax protesters and "populists," neo-Nazi skinheads and fanatics of the Christian Right. The movement even has its martyrs. Gordon Kahl, tax-dodger and member of the Jew-hating Posse Comitatus, killed three lawmen in 1983, before he was finally incinerated in an Arkansas shoot-out with police and FBI agents. He left behind a legion of admirers and a 16-page manifesto urging them to continue the war "between the people of the Kingdom of God and the Kingdom of Satan."

One who heard Kahl's summons was Robert Jay Matthews, another "Identity" fanatic who idolized Adolf Hitler and dreamed of leading a full-scale revolt against the "Zionist Occupational Government" in Washington, D.C. To that end, he created The Order, a paramilitary outfit drawing members from the Klan, the National Alliance, and the Aryan Nations (a.k.a. the Church of Jesus Christ, Christian). In June 1984, Order gunmen assassinated Alan Berg, a controversial Jewish talk-show host in Denver, rolling on from there to try their hand at counterfeiting, bombing porno theaters, and robbing armored cars. Matthews was run to earth by G-men in December 1984, killed in a shoot-out on Washington State's Whidbey Island, in Puget Sound, while 25 of his disciples wound up serving prison terms that ranged from three to 250 years. Ex-Klansman David Tate is doing life for murdering a state policeman in Missouri, and a similar charge sent Richard Snell — of the Covenant, Sword, and Arm of the Lord — to his death in Arkansas, in April 1995.

One of the most disturbing recent trends in Christian homicide has been the wide-scale terrorism directed against abortion clinics by Fundamentalist zealots.

(Continued on next page)

> No American organization in this century has done more to promote "militant Christianity" than the nightriding Ku Klux Klan, with its long record of cross-burnings, floggings, lynchings, bombings, and other acts of terrorism dating back to 1915.

Between 1977 and 1995, American abortion clinics reported at least 1,626 incidents of violence and harassment, including five murders, two attempted murders, two kidnappings, 35 burglaries, 148 bombing or arson attacks, 66 attempted bombings or arsons, 91 assaults, 178 death threats, 192 stalking incidents, 137 clinic invasions by armed or abusive individuals, and 568 incidents of vandalism. Vociferous opponents of abortion swear that these attacks are unconnected, individual attempts to halt the "modern Holocaust," and yet their rhetoric gives aid and comfort to the snipers, bombers, arsonists, and vandals who appear to think that Christian values — like Mao Tse-tung's definition of political power — issue from the barrel of a gun. Some leaders of the "pro-life" movement include:

♦ Randall Terry, founder of Operation Rescue in 1987, who has called upon his followers to obey a "higher law than man's" in wiping out abortion clinics. Serving federal prison time for his activities as this is written, Terry claims that he opposes violence, while comparing the "pro-life" campaign to Americans' revolt against England in 1776. "It meant that real men fired real bullets at other real men who shed real blood," he writes, with a notation that those on the receiving end "died excruciating, real deaths." That's fine with Terry, who believes that "Real confrontation and conflict, real courage and sacrifice, real blood, sweat and tears are needed to restore liberty." In a newspaper column written from prison, Terry described a series of "pro-life" murders in Florida as "deplorable" but "inevitable," adding: "God only knows what horrors await us if we do not bring a swift end to the murder of innocent children [sic]."

♦ Rev. Michael Bray, pastor of the Reformation Lutheran Church in Bowie, Maryland, who named one of his children after a convicted clinic bomber doing time in Texas. As editor of the *Capitol Area Christian News*, Bray raised money by selling bumper stickers that read EXECUTE ABORTIONIST-MURDERERS. His book, *A Time to Kill?*, justifies vigilante action against abortion clinics, and he has supported convicted murderer Paul Hill's declaration of all-out war on abortionists by saying, "I defend the position... as distinct from advocating it." Pressed for an answer as to whether *he* would kill a doctor on his own, Bray said, "I can never say I never would, but I have no plans to. The only legitimate reason not to do it is lack of the call." He *would* bomb clinics, though, and served nearly four years in prison during the 1980s for a conviction for conspiracy to bomb ten targets in Maryland, Delaware, Virginia, and the District of Columbia.

♦ Rev. David Trosch, a Catholic priest from Mobile, Alabama, suspended by the church for his extremist views in 1993, who declares that murderer Paul Hill "deserves a medal of honor" for shooting a physician and his bodyguard in Florida. He also lied to the press about knowing Hill, denying an acquaintance when they had, in fact, protested at clinics together. As founder of the ironically-named Life Enterprises Unlimited, Trosch finds the murder of abortionists "not only justifiable, but morally obligatory." "If 100 doctors were killed," he declares, "it would put the abortion industry out of business." Nor is his field of targets limited to doctors who perform the surgery in question. Rather, Rev. Trosch predicts that anyone who *advocates* abortion, including the U.S. President and his staff, "will be sought out and terminated as vermin are terminated." Defiant in his exile from Catholicism, Trosch proclaimed that full-scale war might be required to rid the county of abortion clinics. "It doesn't end," he said. "Not until the Constitution is revised to protect the unborn from the moment of conception. Morally, it cannot end."

♦ Rachelle ("Shelley") Shannon, an Oregon "pro-life" activist sentenced to ten years in prison for the August 1993 attempted murder of Dr. George Tiller in Wichita, Kansas. From jail, she wrote to clinic gunman Michael Griffin, in a Florida prison, proclaiming that "I know you did the right thing. It was not murder. You shot a murderer. It was more like anti-murder." In October 1994, Shannon was charged with thirty more felony counts, based on her role in a conspiracy to burn abortion clinics in California, Idaho, Nevada, and Oregon. That case was settled with her guilty plea on six arson counts, in June 1995.

In the final analysis, mere faith in God is never quite enough for True Believers. They must always find a way to force their will upon the "heathen" and the "infidel," whether the method is a constitutional amendment, federal legislation, boycotts, or a bullet in the back. As we prepare to greet a new millennium, there is no reason to believe that zealous "Christian soldiers" will desist from terrorizing their "ungodly" neighbors in America.

"My wrath shall wax hot," Jehovah warned the Israelites, in *Exodus* 22:24, "and I will kill you with the sword and your wives shall be widows, and your children fatherless." The zealots among us dote on that promise, oiling their guns and biding their time.

Blood without end. Amen.

♦

WHAT TO BRING WITH YOU
WHEN YOU GO TO FEDERAL PRISON CAMP
by Clive Sharp

Illustration by Robert L. Crabb

In August of 1996, the Justice Department reported that the number of women and men in America's jails and prisons reached nearly 1.6 million during the preceding year. As of December 31, 1995, one out of every 167 Americans was in prison or jail. Just ten years earlier, only one out of 320 was in jail or prison. Simple math reveals that, at this rate, in another ten years one out every 78 of us will be incarcerated somewhere. Obviously, it won't be long before every single one of us is in jail.

In light of these depressing facts, here are several things to be sure to bring with you when you actually report to serve your sentence at a federal prison camp.

Bring Your Receipt For Your Fine

Be sure to bring the receipt for the fine you had to pay at your sentencing hearing. You will need it to prove that you actually paid this fine.

Bring Personal Clothing

To find out what you can bring in the personal clothing category, you need to call the institution after you receive your Order to Surrender. Bring everything that is on their list.

Bring Extra of Everything

When prison camp officials list the amount of an item that you can show up with, you should bring two or three times that amount. For example, if they say you can bring four pairs of undershorts, bring 12 pairs. If you can bring six pairs of socks, bring 18 pairs. If they say one bottle of shampoo, bring six or 20. There is a reason for you to do this. Sometimes the administration will allow you to bring in extra items. Sometimes they won't allow it. It all depends on who checks you in, and what sort of mood they are in on that particular day. So bring as much as you can.

Their List Changes From Day To Day

Even if you follow the list that they sent you, that list changes from day to day. When you arrive for surrender, the administration will whip out a new and different list than the one they sent to you. Then they might take away some (but not ALL) of the extra items you have brought. Those items are boxed up and sent home, prepaid.

(Continued on next page)

Bring These Clothes

Don't forget these items in the personal clothing category:
- 1 dress shirt with collar (for visits)
- 1 belt
- 1 sweater
- 1 jacket or windbreaker
- 1 pair jeans, dress pants or trousers (for visits) (At Elgin Federal Prison Camp, you will not be allowed to wear gray pants for visits, because guards wear gray pants, and they don't want to get themselves confused. Other prison camps have similar little rules.)
- 1 pair dress shoes or boots (These should be hard soles... not tennis shoes)
- 6 white T-shirts
- 6 pairs undershorts
- 1 sweatshirt
- 2 pairs of Bermuda shorts
- 1 pair tennis shorts
- 2 pairs of good sneakers
- 1 pair shower shoes... flip-flops or thongs

No logos of any kind can be on any article of clothing. So if your sweatsuit or jacket has a logo on it, have it removed at an alteration shop before you bring it.

Bring Toiletries

Bring a lot of your own toiletries. Selection is a bit limited at the commissary.
- toothbrushes
- toothpaste
- disposable razors
- brush and combs
- hair gel containing no alcohol (no aerosol cans)
- fingernail clippers
- toenail clippers
- soap and soap container
- tweezers
- round-point scissors
- aftershave lotion containing no alcohol
- shampoo
- deodorant (no aerosol cans)
- shaving cream (no aerosol cans)
- hand lotion (a good lubricating kind for personal moments on your private parts)

Bring Miscellaneous Items

I suggest that you also bring these things:
- wristwatch, valued at under $50
- up to two religious neckchains
- cheap but reliable pens and pencils

- sports equipment (weight belt, gloves, tennis racquet, tennis balls...)
- Bible, Koran, Book of Mormon, other religious texts
- all legal documents that you might need to help you file your appeals
- dictionary
- books to read
- your personal address-and-telephone number book
- medicines that you need (you will need your doctor's letter for these)
- musical instrument and music books
- small battery-powered night light

Bring Your Social Security Card

You will need your Social Security card, so bring it with you.

Bring A Keister Container

You can bring it in by employing anal insertion, so that the guards won't see it when they visually inspect your bodily orifices. You can always throw it away after voiding, or you can clean it off and sell it... they are hard to come by in prison.

Do Not Bring Prohibited Items

If it is not on their list, you can't bring it in. Don't bring anything that you know you can't have. There will be ways to get prohibited items, once you are actually in prison camp. But don't try to bring them in when you report, because you'll just make the guards mad at you, and then they won't let you have the extra amounts of the allowed things that you brought.

Do Not Bring Credit Cards

There is nowhere to use them.

Bring A Photocopy Of Your Driver's License

Do not bring your actual driver's license with you to prison. However, you should make a photocopy of your driver's license and bring that copy with you. That way, if you are required to drive as part of your assigned job, you might not have to take the written driver's test.

Bring Money With You

You are not allowed to have any paper money at all while you are in prison. However, you are allowed to spend about $100 per month during each month of your sentence. When you arrive for prison, the guards will take all of your money and give you a receipt. Your money is deposited for you in your Trust Fund or your Commissary

(Continued on next page)

Account. Then you can spend it as needed during your incarceration.

Folding money is prohibited, because it is useful for bribes and escape funds. Cigarettes are most commonly used as prison currency. Folding money is often worth more than face value (i.e., $100 in cash is worth $150 in cigarettes).

Most folding money is well-hidden by convicts, or, most commonly, "keistered," which means it is secreted in a metal or plastic tubular container and inserted in one's rectum.

If You Paid Your Fine, Bring All Your Money With You

Bring $100 per month times all of the months of your sentence when you report. In other words, if you have a 24 month sentence, bring $2,400 in cash. The guards will not be happy about this, because you have money. Of course, this is not good. However, it will be much worse for you if you do not have all of that money in your Commissary Account.

Do not tell other convicts that you have money "on the books." If it's known that you have a surplus of funds, you may become a target for "loans" (a euphemism for "extortion") that will never be repaid.

What If You Have An Unpaid Fine?

If you did not pay the fine imposed at sentencing, the prison will watch your Commissary Account carefully. If you have a lot of money in it, they will want to have that money to apply towards your unpaid fine. You will not be allowed more than $10 extra per month. You need to find someone who has no money in his commissary account and pay him $10 per month to hold your money for you.

Why Bring All Your Allowed Money When You Report?

You will need every bit of this money during your sentence. And if you don't have it with you when you report, you might not ever get it. Why wouldn't you get it? Your family could run out of money. Your family could get mad at you and decide not to send you any money. Your pals who promised to send cash could have a change of heart. Naturally, there are ways to earn extra money when you are in prison, but it's easier to bring it with you when you arrive.

Why Do You Need So Much Money?

Prisons do not supply you with all of the things you need. You might need a deck of cards. You night need ice cream, or cigarettes. You might need postage stamps, or stationery. You might need a better grade of shampoo, or a couple of apples. You might need a radio with earphones. You might need a wrist watch. You might need some "off the books" services

What Will You Buy The Most?

Most of your money will be used to buy food. Food controls inmates. If you can buy your own food, you don't have to scam anyone out of it, unless you want to. If you can buy your own food, you don't have to feel left out. There are very few things in prison to make you feel good. Food becomes a luxury item. Pamper yourself a little. If it makes you feel better to be able to buy yourself some special foods when you want them, go ahead and do it.

Some convicts use cash, cigarettes, or money on the books to purchase sex, drugs, and alcohol. These forbidden pleasures help pass the time, and are much in demand. They can be very expensive.

Beware of gifts of "free" drugs, such as heroin. Drugs in prison are always top-of-the-line, for obvious reasons. It's easy to get hooked and become a steady user, and prison drug dealers are well aware of who the moneyed convicts are, and are anxious to recruit them as addicted customers.

Money For "Off The Books" Items

You will discover that one way for inmates to make money in prison is to work "off the books." This is strictly forbidden, of course. But unless you have extra money, you will be unable to pay for these "off the books" items. For example: Do you want a haircut? Haircuts are supposed to be free in prison. In real life, you will have to pay another inmate for your haircuts, and the price is usually $2 to $5. Do you want an inmate lawyer to help you with some legal problems? If you do, you will have to pay the inmate lawyer whatever he charges you for this service. Do you want a bit of extra food from food service workers? You will have to pay for it. Do you want someone to wash your clothes and make your bed? You have to pay, and it runs $50 to $75 per month.

The Moral Of This Story

You might be able to take it with you when you go... to prison. So take as much as you can.

● ● ● ● ● ● ●

Clive Sharp is the author of *How To Survive Federal Prison Camp*.

MAKING NECESSARY NOISE
By Claire Wolfe

Illustration by Ariel Bordeaux

I'm coming to a conclusion I don't like at all. I've been edging toward it for several years, hating it all the way. But no matter how much I sniff around the idea, turn it upside down, examine it from all angles or peek into its dark interior, I can't say it's wrong. Increasingly, I'm convinced it may be both right and necessary — even though it could rip apart the lives of a lot of good people.

Before I get to that dangerous conclusion, let me show you one example of what brought me to it.

START WITH A QUESTION:

How many Americans resist filing federal income tax returns?

The official estimate from the IRS is five to ten million. IRS bureaucrats admit privately the number may be as high as 35 million. Either way, a great many Americans say, "To hell with the federal government!" on April 15. And good for them.

Let's take the very lowest figure: five million. Let us further assume that 80 percent of those non-filers are simply procrastinators — non-ideological folks who just don't get around to sending in the forms.

That still means *one million Americans* are risking their lives, their fortunes and their sacred honor each year by consciously saying, "I refuse to submit."

The actual numbers are certainly larger — giving us an awesome force on the side of individual liberty.

(Continued on next page)

I often think, "That corrupt, doddering old system, simply *can't* hold up under this resistance." But look at the real world. What has that huge, stubborn force accomplished?

Nothing. Nada. Zip. Zilch.

RESISTING IN A WHISPER

Oh, yes, those who consciously resist the income tax, invasive drug laws, abstruse "regulations," or other forms of arbitrary authority have accomplished a lot on a personal level. Every act of independence is beneficial to the spirit. That's important. Very. But is it enough?

> **Those who consciously resist the income tax, invasive drug laws, abstruse "regulations," or other forms of arbitrary authority have accomplished a lot on a personal level.**

Five or 35 million Americans resisting tax laws...40, 50, 60 or 80 million Americans resisting drug laws...and countless Americans resisting the very concept of excessive law... has had *no* positive impact on the country as a whole. It hasn't changed *anything* for the better.

The tax system hasn't collapsed. The income tax hasn't been repealed — as it should have.

In the 1920s and 30s, America's casual scorning of the Volstead Act (Prohibition) caused that pointless law to be tossed in history's garbage can. But the modern Prohibition against drugs-of-choice hasn't ended because millions are resisting it. Indeed, more — and worse — drug laws are being enacted every day.

Across the country, despite our scorn, new regulations are being promulgated, more police agencies are being created, enlarged and armed, and more innocents are dying or being terrorized in the name of "law."

How can this be? How can millions of people say NO to bad government — and not be heard?

Well, one reason we're not being heard is that we're whispering.

RESISTING WITH A SHOUT

My dangerous conclusion is this: We must not only resist bad laws with all our strength, but we must resist publicly, loudly and articulately. Some of us will be able to do this merely by advocating resistance in the abstract, as a matter of moral and historical right. Some of us will need to publicize our own, personal, principled resistance. Some of us may need to go so far as to stand in the public square and visibly disobey whatever damned law plagues us. All three of these courses could be hazardous to our health.

Nevertheless, we must make noise, make news and make a bloody nuisance of ourselves. We may need to get ourselves arrested, and ultimately may have to throw ourselves in front of tanks and machine guns, if it comes to that.

We need to send a message to the world so loudly it can't be ignored, even if some of us must die to do it.

STANDING ON PRINCIPLE

We have been quiet for a very good reason: because the government, media and in many cases our family and neighbors regard principled resistance as criminal. We fear both their opinions and the dire consequences of breaking the law.

We must now turn that around. We must proclaim that resistance to bad laws is *right*. We must tell the world that we are not criminals, but are instead fine, independent people of exactly the kind this country needs the most.

Others are, of course, free to disagree with our viewpoint. But we ourselves must stop buying into the criminal paradigm, even subconsciously. We must proudly claim a new paradigm. We must make it clear that resistance is a matter of principle — and that we will never yield to unjust laws no matter who threatens us, no matter how dire the threat.

(Continued on next page)

RESISTING THE IDEA OF PUBLIC RESISTANCE

Never have I been more in conflict with myself over an issue. I've spent a whole lifetime seeking privacy. I hate the idea of making public noise. I've spent a lifetime seeking beauty and peace, and I hate the idea of being dragged off to some dismal jail, or seeing my friends dragged there.

I also realize full well that what I'm proposing *is* dangerous.

> **We must not only resist bad laws with all our strength, but we must resist publicly, loudly, and articulately.**

In the past, I've warned readers never to trust anyone who urges them to commit criminal acts. Those arm-twisters are usually cops or informants. That goes double for anyone urging you to take the extra risk of "coming out of the closet" with public resistance. Don't trust them.

Don't trust me. And certainly *never* do anything just because some writer or orator says it might be a good idea.

I'm not asking to be trusted or followed; I'm just asking you to hear and decide for yourself whether my conclusion is correct. If you have an effective idea and less dangerous idea for regaining freedom, I implore you to propose it and put it into action.

THE SCENARIO: ALTERING HISTORY

What could happen to us if we make an issue of our resistance? We could be arrested, prosecuted, jailed, demonized, laughed at, fired from jobs, shunned, fined, and our homes and possessions could be seized even if no charges are ever brought against us. Penalties are becoming more Draconian. Federal penalties are increasingly being heaped atop state punishments. "Coming out" as resisters may inspire compulsive control freaks to take special pains to "get" and punish us. Some resisters will be made examples of, in the worst way.

It's bad. Let's never minimize what we might face. But the growing ruthlessness of government is all the more reason we must shout our objections.

An analogy:

Hitler began his persecution of the Jews with measures that, in contrast to the eventual horror, look mild. He first required Jews to wear yellow stars. They complied. He began confiscating their property. They hid possessions, sneaked them out of the country, bribed officials or simply surrendered. He walled them in ghettos. Some stayed; some fled. He finally herded them into boxcars to their final destination.

> **Had a significant minority resisted Hitler — vehemently, adamantly, loudly resisted — many of them would have been killed. But they might have roused the conscience of the world. They might have shown Hitler there was a barrier he could not cross.**

All along, some resisted, some acquiesced, just as we are doing now. But almost universally, whatever their actions, they remained quiet. Their "good German" (and "good" Polish and "good" other) neighbors were also silent about the outrages taking place in front of them. Some gentiles hid and helped the Jews. But they didn't speak up. No one made a public, moral cause of resistance. Of course, people were terrified of Hitler. And it was unpopular to defend the Jews, who had been even more successfully demonized than tax resisters, militia members and drug users have been in modern America. The media and public institutions were firmly on the side of the Nazis, just as they are on the side of big government today. All very familiar.

(Continued on next page)

Had a significant minority resisted Hitler — vehemently, adamantly, loudly resisted — many of them would have been killed. But they might have roused the conscience of the world. They might have shown Hitler there was a barrier he could not cross. They might have prevented the far worse slaughter that their silence allowed. We don't really know what *could* have happened, had people had the courage both to resist and speak out. We only know what *did* happen when they failed to do so. None of these hopes ever had a chance. People didn't take the risk, and the ultimate fate befell them.

> **We must make noise, make news and make a bloody nuisance of ourselves.**

Silence is not safety. Silence, in fact, implies consent.

Which is worse: suffering now in defense of principle, or suffering later as the citizen of a tyrannical state?

HOW BAD CAN IT GET?

I don't know that it will ever get so bad here that freedom-loving people will be rounded up and sent to concentration camps. It's possible. I do know the future looks bad, very bad, for freedom.

What's *certain* is that, in the words of abolitionist Frederick Douglass, "Find out just what people will submit to, and you have found out the exact amount of injustice and wrong which will be imposed upon them; and these will continue until they are resisted with either words or blows, or both. The limits of tyrants are prescribed by the endurance of those whom they oppress."

Or, in the more modern words of Dilbert, "The more crap you put up with, the more crap you are going to get."

Again, silence implies consent. Silence is "putting up with it" even when we silently disobey.

WHY MAKE NOISE NOW?

Many of us have become accustomed to living free in spite of the "law." A few years ago, even last year, I would have said, "Hell, why paint a target on your backside by going public with resistance?" But the situation has changed.

In the last couple of years, Congress has laid the groundwork for the kind of totalitarian citizen-tracking systems that have been long-rumored and greatly dreaded. As you read this, bureaucrats are building the computer systems, sending out the forms, writing the regulations and installing the machinery that will be used to make you a slave, pure and simple.

A pair of examples:

- Your driver's license was turned into a de facto national ID card. (Check it out: Public Law 104-208, Section 656.)
- Congress passed legislation and Donna Shalala began sending out the forms for the "New Hires" database. It's worse than it sounds. (Check it out: Public Law 104-193, Section 435A, then get your hands on one of the forms.)

There's more. A lot more. Research this for yourself and see how your life will be curtailed... will be *owned*... if you let these things happen.

Silent resistance doesn't stop bad lawmaking. It actually encourages it, as legislatures pass more and more bad laws in an attempt to curb disobedience. How many more rotten laws are we going to take before we put a stop to this pernicious escalation of tyranny?

WHAT, SPECIFICALLY, SHOULD WE DO?

Specifically, you should do only what your own wisdom dictates. Always. I'll mention a few places to start and some cautions to keep in mind.

Frankly, some of this information is milder than what really needs to be said. But free-speech protections extend only so far.

(Continued on next page)

- Pick one or two laws that you especially oppose. Make sure you fully understand, and can calmly, lucidly, articulate the principles behind your opposition.

- Speak up every chance you get. In every forum you can find. Newspapers. Public meetings. Neighborhood gatherings. Don't just speak against the law. Speak on behalf of the right of resistance.

- Creatively defy bad law. Folks who plant hemp in the courthouse garden or pay their taxes in pennies may get useful publicity.

> **Find every available form of alternative media, from the Internet to the walls of public restrooms, and use them.**

- Utilize the mainstream media where you can. But when biased reporting or no reporting is all you can expect, let it go. Put your energies elsewhere.

- Find every available form of alternative media, from the Internet to the walls of public restrooms, and use them. (For instance, you can place stickers in restroom stalls or telephone booths with three or four lines explaining why a law is wrong and reminding people defiance is an American tradition.)

- Be flexible. Tactics must change as situations do.

- If there is enough community support to make it effective, shun employees of unjust agencies. Render their lives as uncomfortable as possible. And don't let them or yourself off with the old excuse that they're just ordinary people doing their jobs. The engineers who drove the trains to the concentration camps were "ordinary." So were the guards. We usually have no access to their masters, but we can reach the masters through their employees. When masters no longer have minions do to their bidding, how can they enforce tyranny?

> **Shun employees of unjust agencies. Render their lives as uncomfortable as possible. And don't let them or yourself off with the old excuse that they're just ordinary people doing their jobs.**

- Never go against your conscience, no matter what the consequences.

- Make it clear to everyone that you will not yield to mere force or terror tactics.

- Remember: the first and loudest to speak will become targets. This whole thing is going to work only if 1) a few people can make a big enough impression to change the conscience of the nation, or 2) so many people rebel that the justice system overloads.

- Realize that there is a fine line between publicizing principled resistance and foolishly blabbing private matters. You'll have to find your own place to draw that line, and even if you draw it perfectly, you're still in danger.

- If you are announcing resistance to either tax or drug laws, understand that you are especially vulnerable. Under seizure laws, your property can become booty for a pirate agency, and enforcers offer cash bounties to anyone who will snitch on you.

- If you have the slightest doubt about the wisdom on this strategy, or about your own willingness to walk through hell for the cause of freedom, DON'T DO IT!

- Finally, remember the young man who stood alone before the tank in Tienanmen Square. His "victory" was equivocal; the tank backed off, but the protesters were ultimately

(Continued on next page)

slaughtered. Yet his image still touches the conscience of the world. It will, ultimately, make a difference.

> **There is a fine line between publicizing principled resistance and foolishly blabbing private matters.**

We must never violate principles. We must never initiate violence. And we should never harm the innocent. But at some point, unless the government backs off, we will have to stop being nice. I don't recommend it. I merely predict it.

ONLY IDIOTS HEED CALLS TO ACTION FROM KEYBOARD REVOLUTIONARIES

A couple of months ago, I read an essay in which some self-proclaimed "patriot" (call him "John Brown") ranted that it was time to start "taking out" government officials. Furthermore, he raved, anybody who didn't *immediately* rush out and start killing feds was a coward and a hypocrite.

John Brown himself, of course, wasn't about to go out and start bumping people off. Nooooo, he was much more comfortable in the role of "inspirational leader" behind his keyboard. Since no rash of fed-killings followed his exhortation, most readers must have realized old John himself was either a total fool, a hypocrite or an agent provocateur.

I may be a fool. And I may be accused of a lot of other things for writing this article. But I won't be a hypocrite. Here's where I stand:

I resist the income tax. Haven't filed in years. Never will, even if the IRS throws me in jail or in the gutter after taking everything I own. (They won't get much; I've made myself poor, and therefore a smaller target. If the IRS

bothers me, their motive will be purely political.)

And when my state passes the enabling legislation to put the Big Brother driver's license into effect here — when government and businesses require my "verified Social Security number" and biometric "security features" as a condition for dealing with them — I'll go elsewhere, thanks.

Plenty of my acquaintances already refuse to get regular driver's licenses. Maybe they can teach us all a thing or two about the much more complicated problem of surviving without the national ID license. In any case, I plan to become the damnedest, finest outlaw I can be when, "Citizen! Your papers, please!" becomes an American reality.

> **Unlike John Brown, I'm not urging you to break the law. You're already breaking it just by living.**

Unlike John Brown, I'm not urging you to break the law. You're already breaking it just by living. If you value personal freedom, you're probably breaking laws and regulations more often than Bill Clinton breaks wind.

I am urging you to claim resistance as your right — and as a necessity — if we are to remain free.

Those who wish to look up laws, bills, and other congressional activities can easily do so by accessing the Thomas web site, operated by the Library of Congress, at:

http://thomas.loc.gov

Thomas contains the texts of laws, some records of congressional votes, all major bills proposed in Congress, and other pertinent information.

Claire Wolfe is the author of *101 Things To Do 'Til The Revolution.*

Israel's Anti-Nuclear Prisoner-of-Conscience
by Sam Day

Illustration by Terry LaBan

In Israel's maximum security prison at Ashkelon, a place reserved for the state's most dangerous enemies, the tightest security of all surrounds a man whose crime was speaking to the press.

Mordechai Vanunu, now approaching 43, has spent almost half his adult life in solitary confinement, locked in a small cell walled off from the rest of the inmate population.

He eats alone in his concrete and steel cage. He walks alone in the empty prison exercise yard. Except for two or three brothers who are allowed to visit him occasionally and converse through a thick metal screen, his only human contact is with the guards who bring him his daily food.

On September 30 Vanunu will complete 11 years in solitary confinement, longer than any other political prisoner in modern times, according to Amnesty International, which has condemned his treatment as cruel, inhuman, and degrading.

With more than a third of his 18-year sentence still to be served, supporters around the world who regard him as a prisoner-of-conscience grow increasingly concerned about signs of mental stress arising from his prolonged confinement. Fearing his jailers may be on the verge of driving him insane, they have launched an all-out drive for his release.

Did his crime warrant this punishment? Underlying the human rights issue in the Vanunu case is the larger question of the rights and obligations of citizens with regard to keeping national secrets, for the subject Vanunu discussed with the press 11 years ago was no ordinary one.

As a former technician in an underground government factory in Israel's Negev Desert, he provided a British newspaper with incontrovertible evidence that his government, unbeknownst to its people or even to its legislature, had become a major nuclear weapons power.

His disclosures made him a hero and a prophet to some, a spy and traitor to others.

* * *

One of 11 children of a Moroccan Jewish family, young Mordechai played with Arab boys and girls in the streets and courtyards of Marrakesh. When he was eight the family emigrated to Israel and settled in the town of

(Continued on next page)

Beersheba, where the father, a deeply religious man, took a job selling artifacts and literature at a local temple.

With his brothers and sisters he attended Beersheba schools. Drafted into the military, he served with distinction as an Army sapper — an infantry engineer who builds trenches and fortifications.

A young man with technical aptitude and an interest in the humanities, Vanunu went looking for work after his discharge from the army. The job would pay his way through Ben Gurion University at Beersheba, where he planned to study philosophy, psychology, and religion.

The job he found was at a large government factory near the town of Dimona, believed by the public to be a desalinization plant, a textile factory, or a nuclear research station. Its real function was a state secret. Vanunu signed the secrecy oath required of all employees and went to work as a trainee.

It wasn't long before he learned that his work would be in the plutonium separation division of a nuclear bomb factory, helping to recover plutonium, the explosive ingredient of fission bombs, from the irradiated fuel rods of Dimona's large nuclear reactor.

The realization that he had unwittingly become part of a secret nuclear weapons program caused Vanunu no discomfiture at first. All that mattered to him was that the job provided steady employment at a good wage. But his attitude was to change as the young weapons worker, still in his early 20s, began making new friends off the job.

At the university Vanunu fell in with Palestinian students, many of them politicized by the continuing Israeli occupation of Arab lands conquered in the 1967 war. In time, he openly identified with their cause, writing articles, giving speeches, carrying banners calling for freedom for the Palestinians.

Israel's 1982 invasion of Lebanon, unpopular even in Israel, heightened Vanunu's sense of outrage. His alienation from government policy reached such a point in the early 1980s that he began thinking about going public with the secret of Dimona.

To that end, Vanunu was able to sneak a camera, wrapped in his towel and swimming trunks, into the factory one night and snap two rolls of film undetected. He realized that if he were ever to leak the story he would need some hard evidence to back it up.

Toward the end of 1985, after nine years at Dimona, Vanunu was laid off, along with several dozen other workers. He decided to use his severance pay for a trip abroad — a trip that might help him sort out some troubling cross-currents in his life. He was in rebellion against the strict dictates of his father and his Jewish faith. And he was in torment over what — if anything —

to do about the secret of Dimona.

Into his backpack he tossed a few shirts, socks, shorts and books — and the two rolls of film that had remained undeveloped on his closet shelf. For the next few months he traveled in the Soviet Union, through India, and into Southeast Asia.

* * *

On a late May evening in 1986 Vanunu found himself in Sydney, Australia. Alone and friendless in that vast city and continent, he came upon a church in the Kings Cross area, a seedy part of town habituated by prostitutes, alcoholics and drug addicts. The door was open. He walked in.

This chance encounter with St. John's Anglican Church of Kings Cross changed Vanunu and altered history. People were there despite the late hour because St. John's had an outreach program for the poor and the alienated of the neighborhood.

Vanunu found himself a cup of coffee and a sandwich. He struck up a conversation with the assistant pastor who was on duty that night. It turned out that David Smith, only a few years younger than Vanunu, had taken similar philosophy courses in college and shared Vanunu's particular interest in the Danish theologian Søren Kierkegaard and the German philosopher Friedrich Nietzsche. The Anglican priest and the wandering Jew talked into the morning hours.

Vanunu started hanging out at St. John's. He was taken in by the rector, John McKnight, a big, strapping man who believed in Christian service to the poor. He did odd jobs around the church, joined a Bible study group, and started sitting in on an adult discussion session delving into problems of peace and justice.

When the subject turned to nuclear war, Vanunu mentioned, innocently, that he had once worked in a nuclear weapons factory. He offered to tell his story to the group, and then, with equal innocence, took his Dimona film rolls to a photo processing shop and developed them for the first time.

It wasn't long before word reached the news media that a man claiming to have helped build nuclear bombs for Israel was talking about it and showing photographs at church meetings in Sydney. One of the newspapers that took a special interest was the *London Sunday Times*, which had a reputation for roaming the world in search of major scoops.

It was widely suspected in the mid-1980s that Israel might be trying to build nuclear weapons in secret, but no hard evidence of that had ever surfaced publicly.

The *Sunday Times* flew Peter Hounam, a reporter with a science background, to Sydney to check out the story. In

(Continued on next page)

two weeks of intensive conversations with Vanunu, the reporter concluded that the story was real.

"I had the impression that he was a sincere yet naïve young man," Hounam said later. "He didn't care about money; he just wanted to get the information to the people in Israel; he wanted to make sure we got the story right."

In early September 1986, the reporter and his news source flew off to London for further interviews with other journalists at the *Sunday Times* and with nuclear weapons experts the newspaper had engaged to double-check Vanunu and his story. Vanunu told well-wishers at the airport he'd be back in a couple of weeks. He was never seen again in Australia.

Meanwhile, two other events had occurred to seal the informant's fate.

On an afternoon in late July Vanunu reached the end of his spiritual journey at the baptismal font in St. John's Anglican Church. His conversion to Christianity may have given him the extra strength he needed to make his fateful decision. But the formal renunciation of his ancestral faith would also prejudice his case among many Jews in Israel and beyond. (It would also cause his father and some of his siblings to disown him.)

And, some time during the weeks preceding his departure, word had reached the Israeli intelligence agency — the Mossad — that a former Dimona worker was talking to the press. The news incensed Shimon Peres, who, in addition to serving as prime minister at the time, also happens to be the father of Israel's nuclear weapons program, a former diplomat who in the late 1950s persuaded France to provide Israel with the key technology it needed to get started in nuclear bomb-making.

Peres ordered the Mossad to do what it needed to bring Vanunu back alive, but to do so without complicating Israel's relations with the Thatcher government in Britain. The Mossad accomplished this by dispatching a SWAT team which included an attractive female agent, Cheryl Ben Tov (alias Cindy), who specialized in enticement.

Posing as an American tourist, Cindy succeeded in catching Vanunu's eye in a London park. As the relationship blossomed, she preyed on his frustration over what seemed to be endless delays in the publication of his story.

On September 30 Cindy and Mordechai flew to Rome for what she promised would be a romantic weekend in the apartment of her sister. She led him to a place where waiting Mossad agents knocked him to the ground, drugged him, and bound him up for transportation to a waiting freighter which would return him to Israel.

Five days later, on October 5, the *London Sunday Times* spread Vanunu's story and photographs over three pages, reporting that tiny Israel had become a major nuclear weapons power, with 100 to 200 warheads of advanced design. The story made headlines around the world, including Israel, where the media is forbidden to originate news of nuclear weapons activity in Israel but is free to report what foreign publications say.

Mordechai Vanunu had achieved his self-appointed goal of telling the truth to his people, but he had done so at an awesome cost to himself.

* * *

Returned to Israel in chains, Vanunu was charged with espionage and treason and convicted at a closed-door trial. The court found him guilty, even though he had worked for no foreign government and had requested and received no pay for his information. It ruled Vanunu's motivation for violating state secrecy was irrelevant, as was the truth or falsity of his disclosures.

In government statements and in the Israeli media Vanunu was vilified as one who exposed Israel to attack by its enemies, even though the story revealed little not already known by outside intelligence agencies. Although Vanunu had intended to open up public debate about Israel's nuclear weapons arsenal, the effect of his conviction and imprisonment was to strengthen the self-imposed taboo which had long cloaked the subject. While accepting the government's unspoken assurances of the need for nuclear weapons as an ultimate defense of the state, few in Israel felt inclined to confront the impact of Israel's unacknowledged introduction of nuclear weapons into the volatile Middle East.

(Fearful of triggering the application of a U.S. law which would cut off billions of dollars it receives annually in economic and military aid, Israel has carefully maintained a policy of ambiguity with regard to acknowledgment of its nuclear arsenal.)

In the United States the official reaction to Vanunu's revelations has been much the same. Official Washington had known of Israel's nuclear arsenal almost since the beginning but had declined for political reasons to challenge it, even though the Israeli program clearly violated this government's professed stance against the secret proliferation of nuclear weapons.

Elsewhere, however, the imprisoned nuclear whistleblower has found growing support. Campaigns calling for his release and for a nuclear-free Middle East have spread from Israel to Britain, Norway, the United States, Canada, Australia, and New Zealand.

Spirited at first, the campaigns flagged after 1990, when the Israeli Supreme Court upheld the conviction and Vanunu lapsed into a four-year silence behind the walls of Ashkelon, cutting himself off from his closest supporters.

(Continued on next page)

Early in 1995, prompted by an appeal from British actress Susannah York, who has campaigned tirelessly for his release, Vanunu emerged from his shell and resumed writing letters which, while eloquent in their appeal for nuclear disarmament, have become increasingly beclouded by what appears to be a paranoid preoccupation with world-wide espionage conspiracies, even among his own supporters.

Nevertheless, the campaign has picked up in recent years, buoyed by the support of scientific, cultural, and religious leaders. Vigils and occasional sit-ins have become commonplace at Israeli embassies and consulates. United States senators and members of Congress have begun to raise questions about Vanunu's prison treatment. Israeli officials in Jerusalem have been bombarded with letters and petitions.

(The Israeli Ministry of Justice contends that Vanunu must be kept isolated so he won't reveal more state secrets. His supporters say he has no more nuclear secrets to tell. They suspect his long solitary confinement serves as a warning to other nuclear weapons workers to avoid talking to the press.)

British physicist Joseph Rotblat, awarded the Nobel Peace Prize in 1995 for a lifetime of anti-nuclear advocacy, brought fresh fuel to the campaign with his call for the release of Vanunu and passage of laws protecting such whistle-blowers. Last fall he chaired a conference in Tel Aviv in which the Israeli mass media for the first time gave attention to major international figures who are calling for a fresh look into the Vanunu matter.

Since then more cracks have appeared in what had been the monolithic media stereotype of Vanunu as arch-spy and traitor. A sympathetic one-man play, "Mr. V.," played to appreciative audiences in Jerusalem and Tel Aviv. An hour-long documentary, "I Am Your Spy," by Israeli filmmaker Nissim Mossek opened in Israel in July. Physicists are circulating a Vanunu petition at Hebrew University in Jerusalem. Teen-agers at an Israeli kibbutz have formed a Vanunu support group called "No More Hiroshimas."

It's a start.

Confident of his ultimate vindication, the prisoner writes from his isolation cell, "I fully believe that the truth about my action will be revealed and that the Israeli public will ask for my forgiveness. The day will come."

Sam Day, a freelance writer and political activist based in Madison, Wisconsin, is coordinator of the U.S. Campaign to Free Mordechai Vanunu, 2206 Fox Avenue, Madison, WI 53711.

I AM YOUR SPY
by Mordechai Vanunu

I am the clerk, the technician, the mechanic, the driver.
They said, Do this, do that, don't look left or right,
don't read the text. Don't look at the whole machine. You
are only responsible for this one bolt, this one rubber-stamp.
So they thought, the big ones, the smart ones, the futurologists:
He's a little man;
Little men's ears don't hear, their eyes don't see.
The clerk driver technician mechanic looked up.
He stepped back and saw — what a monster.
Can't believe it. Rubbed his eyes and - yes,
It's there all right. I'm all right. I do see
the monster. I'm part of the system.
I signed this form. Only now I am reading the rest of it.
This bolt is part of a bomb. This bolt is me. How
did I fail to see, and how do the others go on
fitting bolts. Who else knows?
Who has seen? Who has heard? — The emperor really is naked.
I see him. Why me. It's not for me. It's too big.
Rise and cry out. Rise and tell the people. You can.
I, the bolt, the technician, mechanic? — Yes, you.
You are the secret agent of the people.
You are the eyes of the nation.
Agent-spy, tell us what you've seen. Tell us
what the insiders, the clever ones, have hidden from us.
Without you, there is only the precipice. Only catastrophe.
I have no choice. I'm a little man, a citizen, one of the people,
but I'll do what I have to. I've heard the voice of my conscience
and there's nowhere to hide.
I'm on your mission. I'm doing my duty. Take it from me.
Come and see for yourselves. Lighten my burden. Stop the train.
Get off the train. The next stop — nuclear disaster. The next book,
the next machine. No. There is no such thing.

Hail Priapus!

A SELECTION OF SWINGING SEX GODS!

by Dan Kelly

© 1997 by Dan Kelly
Illustration by Eric York

Note: My apologies for the superabundance of penis jokes.

Monotheism is a drag. Raised Catholic, I was introduced to a God so positively gigantic, compared to him I was a dust speck on a fleck of fly poop. Despite this, or so they told me, He had an obsessive preoccupation with my personal habits: be they eating meat on Friday, reading "bad" books, or how often and to what end I employed my phallus. ALMIGHTY GOD is a dictator, and one with far too much time on His hands; or so I interpreted the evidence put before me.

In light of this, I found it odd that this all-powerful being had never learned to delegate authority — though, in a way, He did. As a Catholic I have access to a celestial bureaucracy of saints, ready to be called on in case of moral technical difficulties. But even with this Yellow Pages of

> Raised Catholic, I was introduced to a God so positively gigantic, compared to him I was a dust speck on a fleck of fly poop. Despite this, or so they told me, He had an obsessive preoccupation with my personal habits: be they eating meat on Friday, reading "bad" books, or how often and to what end I employed my phallus.

sainted souls, I lack for the real spiritual and philosophical guidance I so desperately need these days. Namely, whom do I beseech for nooky on a semi-regular basis?

As a Christian, the solution is obvious: just don't do it. This only adds to my spiritual discord; forcing me to juggle with the psychological bug-fuckery of worshipping a Supreme Being who invents orgasms but doesn't want me to enjoy them. By gum, it's enough to drive a guy positively pagan. At least in the ancient religions, one's patron deities could sympathize with the human sexual condition because, hey man, they've been there: in one form of animal, vegetable, mineral, or another.

We begin with the basic reason for sexual union: reproduction. Unlike the book of Genesis, most creation myths feature a god who initially wanted people to multiply, as opposed to the

(Continued on next page)

idea of God as zookeeper (i.e., grumpy old Yahweh and pre-Tree of Knowledge vacuum tubes Adam and Eve). In Ashanti mythology we encounter a scaly precursor to Dr. Ruth. According to myth, the first people on the planet were a man and a woman who came from heaven, and another couple who sprang from Earth itself. Shortly thereafter, the Lord of Heaven sent down a python who, after touching down, made his home in a river. Much like Christian and Jewish mythology, it was a snake who first tipped off men and women that there was more to do on Earth than pick nuts and berries.

Unlike the sneaky snake of Genesis, however, this serpent had a more beneficent role in the creation. Men and women, according to the Ashanti, lacked the desire for procreation, not to mention knowledge of the act itself. After asking them if they had children, and receiving the negative, the snake leapt back into his watery abode. Soon he emerged with a mouth full of water. Telling the couples to stand facing each other, the serpent sprayed water on their bellies and uttered the sacred words, *"Kus, Kus."* The python then told the couple to return home and lie together. Nature took its course and *presto!* Babies invaded the Earth.

Pygmy mythology, on the other hand, shows a slightly savvier human race; though in this case too, a little help was required from The Big G. Though it might sound like the set up for a bad joke, the first people on the planet were a man, his sister, and a Pygmy. One day, in a prime example of guy talk repeated on countless street corners of the future, the man told the Pygmy that his sister had a bleeding wound that never healed. Hipped by God to what was happening, the Pygmy chuckled and assured the man that he knew exactly how to "cure" her. After spending a lovely evening together, the girl conceived and carried the Pygmy's children. Eventually, the Pygmy paired the man up with his sister and explained the basics to them. Incest not having come into public condemnation yet, the man and his sister did some begatting of their own and, again, the world was quickly populated.

That's all well and good, but what of the gods who taught by example? Naturally, unlike Prometheus who risked life, limb and liver to bring fire to mankind, these gods rarely had humanity's best interest at heart. Hell, let's face it: they were demonstrating the human id to its utmost.

> At least in the ancient religions, one's patron deities could sympathize with the human sexual condition because, hey man, they've been there: in one form of animal, vegetable, mineral, or another.

Celtic mythology shares many a pulse-pounding tale of bloodthirsty, two-fisted he-men *and* she-women who could do it all night then get up early the next morning and kill a few thousand guys with their bare hands. For instance, the Daghdha (whose name means the "Good God") was the "Great Father," but unlike most patriarchal deities, he represented not only power and wisdom, but also fertility and abundance (as symbolized by the club and cauldron he carried; traditional iconography for the masculine and feminine). However, despite being so in touch with his feelings, the Daghdha could be a randy old dog on occasion.

One account tells how, shortly before a battle with the gods' main adversaries, the Fomhoire (a race of demon giants), challenged the Daghdha to eat a giant potful of porridge, or die. After consuming eighty cauldrons worth of oats, milk, and fat — the Dgahdha waddled over and bedded a Fomhoirean wench. As a result of the Daghdha's prowess, the giantess was so utterly awash with afterglow, she agreed to use her magical powers against her own people in the upcoming battle.

Fergus MacRoich — a great hero of the Celts, was no god; but he was no ordinary Celtic G.I. Joe either. Not only was Fergus a bang-up fighter, he had a legendary Johnson that was seven fingers long, and a scrotum as big as a sack of flour. Small wonder (Ha!) that his surname meant "Son of Ro-ech," translated as "Son of Great Horse." Fergus was the consort of the woodland goddess Flidais, and the lover of the goddess-queen Medb. Good thing too, since Fergus' virility was such that whenever these two insatiable goddesses were unavailable, he required seven ordinary women at once to satisfy his manly desires. Ouch!

> Celtic mythology shares many a pulse-pounding tale of bloodthirsty, two-fisted he-men *and* she-women who could do it all night then get up early the next morning and kill a few thousand guys with their bare hands.

Being a licentious god has its drawbacks, however, as demonstrated by Indra, the strongest of the three elemental Vedic deities. Indra was the Hindu equivalent of Zeus, being the god of rain and storms. He was also like Zeus in that he found plenty of time for philandering. The

(Continued on next page)

god's most famous conquest was the sage Gautama's daughter Ahalya. Disguising himself as the holy man, Indra sneaked into Gautama's home and seduced Ahalya. Regrettably, Indra was better at getting in than getting out. Gautama caught him, and was so peeved he cursed the god with impotence, causing Indra's testicles to atrophy and break off. Understandably vexed, Indra begged his fellow gods to help him, and was rewarded with a fine set of ram's balls for his trouble.

Now, you're probably thinking: "Hey, hold on there, Dan. This is all very interesting, but were there any other gods with enormous genitals?" Good call, old chum, as I had the foresight to investigate that very question.

We begin with a (hee-hee) member of the Greek pantheon that your high school literature teacher probably forgot to clue you in on. His name was Priapus, god of fertility, goats and sheep. What makes Priapus so interesting? Well, if a contest were held to determine who had the bigger hammer — Thor the beefcake god of thunder, or the shrimpy, satyr-like Priapus — Priapus would win hands (among other limbs) down. Those wishing a better illustration should seek out the statues of Priapus that adorned ancient Greek gardens, placed there in hopes the god would ensure the health and protection of their fruits and veggies. And *you* thought lawn gnomes were tacky.

However, ithyphallic is as ithyphallic does — ithyphallic being a euphemism for having one's little soldier standing at attention in a big way. Ancient Egyptian gods Min (aka: Tmsu) and Bes presaged Priapus by a few hundred years. Min a, natch, fertility god, was usually rendered with the iconography of a high, double-plumed headdress, a raised right arm holding a flagellum, and — as if the raised right arm and big hat weren't Freudian enough — an enormous schlong. Add to that the fact that Min's sacred animal was a ram and you'll see why I don't feel like mastering the obvious with this particular god.

And no jokes about "Ramses" condoms, please.

Bes, conversely, was an exception to the pattern of "Big Genitals = Fertility God," and was instead the god of human pleasure, music, childbirth and merry-making. Bes was usually portrayed as a nude dwarf with a lion's mane, ears and tail, and bandy legs. Considering the size of Bes' old fella, the bandy legs weren't surprising.

> The best thing about being Catholic is that sex will always be better because it will always be dirty.

> Possessed of chiseled features, a dancer's build, and a stomach you could scrub laundry on, every classical statue or painting of Christ positively oozes with restrained sensuality.

For any Catholics out there feeling above all this pagan penis idolatry, consider the infrequently mentioned St. Guignolé. Guignolé is the patron saint invoked against impotence; which seems harmless enough. Ah, but when one beholds the wooden statue of the saint in the city of Brest — wherein the saint is truly blessed with a jutting "staff" bigger than the one Moses wielded — one realizes that the cult of Priapus may yet live. For a thousand years, pilgrims have whittled bits off the sacred pecker, yet miraculously the beatified tool remains undiminished. Hallelujah! An interesting sidebar is that bloody, bawdy puppet shows starring St. Guignolé and his holy relic are performed in France in much the same way Punch and Judy shows are held in England. Hence, the titling of the similarly grotesque theatrics of le Grand Guignol.

Naturally, in view of this preponderance of prominent peni, a certain envy might be overcoming the ladies out there. Not to worry, gals, as across the globe the vagina has enjoyed similar overt exposure.

P.J. Harvey fans may view the meaning of her song "Sheela-na-gig" in a new light when they realize Sheelagh-na-gig was a Celtic demoness best known for baring her sizable yoni for all to see. Though her image appears repeatedly in medieval art and architecture across Europe, no one knows her real story. In the Middle Ages Sheelagh was displayed on church walls to ward off evil; or so states Irish folklore. The name itself is a Gaelic expression denoting a sluttish, unfaithful woman; which probably explains why most Sheelaghs are shown as fat, leering she-devils, jutting their tongues out and rolling their eyes. Lust, the church wanted to make very damn clear, was not pretty. On the other hand, Irish superstition claims that a man suffering from bad luck could be purged of it by convincing the local hussy/Sheelagh-na-gig to expose herself to him. This might sound suspiciously chauvinist, but before deciding, consider the case of Baubo.

In Greek mythology, Baubo cheered up Demeter the grieving fertility goddess with a unique bit of physical comedy. Baubo, who was not so much a deity as a personification of female fecundity, was extremely politically incorrect in her appearance. She was usually presented as having no head, or with her head between her legs.

(Continued on next page)

The story goes, roughly, like this: Persephone, Demeter's daughter, was abducted to the underworld by Hades, the overlord of hell. Inconsolable, the fertility goddess spent all her time weeping, and thus, nothing grew on Earth. Attempting to cheer her mistress, Baubo began grunting and groaning, as if she were in labor. Finally, Baubo lifted her skirts and — and according to which story you prefer to believe — either 1) revealed Demeter's son Iacchus, who leapt into his mother's arms and kissed her, or 2) flashed her notably large love purse, causing the mopey goddess to laugh aloud. In modern times, the joke seems scatological, but the intrinsic idea is that of female genitalia being a charm against death.

> For a thousand years, pilgrims have wittled bits off the sacred pecker, yet miraculously the beatified tool remains undiminished. Hallelujah!

Hawaiian mythology displays a touch of strange with Haumea, both deity and source of female fertility, and her daughters Laka and Kapo. Haumea is easily explained; every culture has some form of fertility god or goddess. Laka and Kapo though, as explained by author Martha Beckwith, represent different forms of reproductive energy. Kapo represents the passive while her sister personifies the active.

Laka is described in myth and song as being extremely fecund; her perpetually impregnated womb contains generation after generation of offspring. For this, Laka is called Alalahe, the "many branching one," Alohi, "the shining one," and Aloha, "the beloved." You might more easily refer to her as the Hawaiian Venus.

Kapo, on the other hand, was less than happy with her female status. Not only was she saddled with the less ethereal title of "Red Eel Woman," she was also known as Kapo-kohe-lele (or, "Kapo with the traveling vagina"). Disliking her sexual organs, Kapo detached them from herself and sent them on their merry way across the Hawaiian countryside. Being a female host for Kapo, incidentally, was no great shakes. Channelers would wear tea leaves over their nether regions, else the pudenda-loathing Kapo would claw and tear at them in disgust.

****

John Waters once said that the best thing about being Catholic is that sex will always be better because it will always be dirty. Moreover, and despite the Mother Church's stodgy position on contraceptives and premarital sex, studies have revealed that even more than blondes, Catholics have more fun (aren't "studies" great for supporting subjective opinions?). Seeing as the church's rule on sexual asceticism was extrapolated by such virginal fuddy-duddies as St. Thomas Aquinas and St. Jerome; and in view of Jesus Christ's reputation as a ladies' man (Gnostic scripture or otherwise); is it so impossible to imagine the Son o' God playing the role of sex god (though perhaps not in the same rutting sense as a Zeus or Daghdha)?

Possessed of chiseled features, a dancer's build, and a stomach you could scrub laundry on, every classical statue or painting of Christ positively oozes with restrained sensuality. The Annie Liebowitz photograph for the inevitable *Rolling Stone* interview is easily envisioned. The Lamb of God, looking smashing in black denim jeans, CK t-shirt, and crown of thorns, poses with a "I suffer thee to come unto me" look on His most radiant face. To one side kneels Kate Moss, washing His blessed feet with her hair, while Christy Turlington stands opposite, holding a white t-shirt emblazoned with the Man of Sorrows' trademarked visage.

And behind him, the damned are condemned to their Dockers.

REFERENCES:

Beckwith, Martha, *Hawaiian Mythology*. USA: U. of Hawaii Press, 1970.

Graves, Robert, *The Greek Myths: I*. England: Penguin Books, 1986.

Hutton, Ronald, *The Pagan Religions of the Ancient British Isles: Their Nature and Legacy*. Cambridge, MA: Blackwell Publishers, 1992.

Kaster, Joseph, *Putnam's Concise Mythological Dictionary*. New York: Perigee Books, 1990.

Katz, Brian P., *Deities and Demons of the Far East*. New York: Metrobooks, 1995.

Kelly, Sean & Rosemary Rogers, *Saints Preserve Us!* New York: Random House, 1993.

Luricer, Manfred, *Gods and Goddesses, Devils and Demons*. London & New York: Routledge & Kegan Paul, 1987.

Parrinder, Geoffrey, *African Mythology*. New York: Peter Bedrich Books, 1986.

Ross, Anne, *Pagan Celtic Britain*. London: Butler & Tanner Ltd., 1967.

Stewart, R.J., *Celtic Gods, Celtic Goddesses*. London: Blandford, 1991. ●

This article appeared in the 1997 issue of *Cop Porn*.

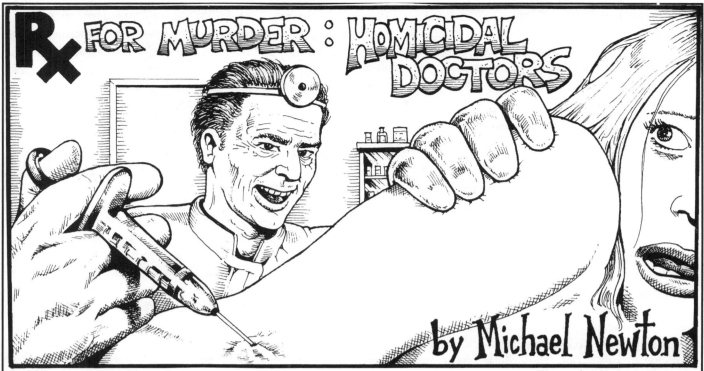

© 1997 by Michael Newton

Illustration by Nick Bougas

Most of us are vaguely conscious of the Hippocratic Oath sworn by most physicians, even if we have no real idea of what it says or signifies. In fact, the modern version of the oath reads as follows:

> *You do solemnly swear, each man by whatever he holds most sacred, that you will be loyal to the profession of medicine and just and generous to its members; that you will lead your lives and practice your art in uprightness and honor; that into whatsoever house you shall enter, it shall be for the good of the sick to the utmost of your power, you holding yourselves far aloof from wrong, from corruption, from the tempting of others to vice; that you will exercise your art solely for the cure of your patients and will give no drug, perform no operation, for a criminal purpose, even if solicited, far less suggest it; that whatsoever you shall see or hear of the lives of men which is not fitting to be spoken, you will keep inviolably secret. These things do you swear.*

And yet, when all is said and done, doctors are simply human beings like the rest of us, subject to lust, greed, hatred, prejudice, and all the sundry mental illnesses that plague mankind. It should be no surprise, then, that some doctors manage to disgrace their proud profession — just as some policeman, politicians, priests, and lawyers do from time to time.

The worst abuse imaginable of a doctor's power is to kill instead of healing, snatching life away — sometimes from healthy individuals — instead of working to prolong it. The issue of assisted suicide, for instance, is a subject of continuing debate from pulpits and in legislatures, but the topic that concerns us here is the menace of physicians who actively seek out healthy victims to destroy.

> **Doctors are simply human beings like the rest of us, subject to lust, greed, hatred, prejudice, and all the sundry mental illnesses that plague mankind.**

Hitler's Germany appears to be the only case in which a nation's medical system was perverted, more or less *en masse*, into a state-sanctioned killing machine, progressing from forced sterilization to systematic disposal of "defectives" and "undesirables," with side trips into bizarre and sadistic vivisection, as performed by Dr. Josef Mengele and others. Soviet Russia often utilized its mental hospitals as de facto prison and "reeducation" facilities for "enemies of the state," but there appears to be no evidence of systematic homicide by Soviet physicians. Likewise, while some may consider abortion as murder, this article does not — nor will it address the

(Continued on next page)

issue of compulsory sterilization as practiced in nations ranging from China to parts of Scandinavia. Still, many doctors have committed murder, some of them repeatedly, inspired by motives mundane or mysterious, pedestrian or bizarre.

In 1984, Life magazine quoted an FBI report which declared that some ten percent of all known serial killers were drawn from the medical profession. The estimate is certainly exaggerated, but serial-killing physicians do exist.

In 1984, *Life* magazine quoted an FBI report which declared that some ten percent of all known serial killers were drawn from the medical profession. The estimate is certainly exaggerated, drawn from a clearly inadequate sampling of cases, but serial-killing physicians do exist, and while none to date has rivaled the exploits of fictional Dr. Hannibal Lector, Sweden's Teet Haerm did his best to make life imitate art.

A medical examiner in Stockholm, Dr. Haerm was assigned to help police discover evidence in local homicides. Unknown to the detectives he befriended, however, he was also a practicing vampire and cannibal, ultimately credited with slaughtering at least eight victims between 1984 and 1988. According to investigators, Haerm — a widower whose wife "committed suicide" in 1982 — would cruise Stockholm nightclubs in search of female prey. Instead of winding up at Haerm's apartment, the unlucky ladies were delivered to the very morgue where Dr. Haerm solved crimes by day, there murdered and dismembered on the autopsy table. An accomplice, Dr. Thomas Allgren, was occasionally called upon to join Haerm in a feast of human flesh, though he apparently did not initiate the murder scheme. The grisly spree was interrupted by Allgren's arrest, on charges of molesting his four-year-old daughter, whereupon he confessed both to that crime and the murders, implicating Dr. Haerm as the alleged leader of a cannibal cult dedicated to exterminating prostitutes. Charged with incest and one count of murder, Allgren pled guilty, while Haerm took his chances at trial and was convicted of killing eight women, including his wife. In September 1988, both doctors where sentenced to life imprisonment.

Another harlot killer, Scottish-born Dr. Thomas Neill Cream, practiced in Canada and Chicago, where he poisoned his first victim, a patient named Stott, in 1881.

In retrospect, the killing seemed mundane enough — Cream was the beneficiary of a large insurance policy on Stott's life — but the aftermath was something else, entirely. Launching a pattern that would persist throughout his homicidal career, Cream started writing anonymous letters to the authorities, urging that Stott be exhumed and examined for traces of poison. He was, and strychnine was discovered. Convicted of second-degree murder, Cream was sentenced to life, but a sympathetic governor commuted his sentence in 1891. He resettled in London, where he poisoned four teenage prostitutes, apparently for the sheer hell of it. Two managed to survive the deadly dosage and describe their assailant for police, but the suspect remained unknown ...until Dr. Cream appeared at Scotland Yard, loudly complaining that he had been accused of the crimes! His craving for attention did him in, this time, and conviction on two counts of murder earned him the death sentence. Mounting the gallows on November 15, 1892, Dr. Cream was still determined to have the last word. Standing with the noose around his neck, a heartbeat before the trap was sprung, he cried out, "I am Jack the R_ _ _." Gleeful newsmen scoured their files, initially believing that London's elusive "Ripper" had been laid to rest, but it was soon discovered that Cream was in Joliet Prison, across the Atlantic, when Red Jack plied his grisly trade in 1888.

It should not be inferred, of course, that most — or even a significant minority — of the doctors now in practice are demented killers. Still, if a particular physician seems inclined toward taking liberties, or is a bit too quick with knife and needle, it may be advisable to seek a second opinion.

A Pakistani-born physician, trained in the United States, Dr. Sohrab Aslam Khan was apparently "normal" in all respects until November 1986, when, at the age of 42, he inexplicably began a month-long murder spree that claimed 13 lives in his native Lahore, Pakistan. Four of those victims were gunned down on November 13, as Khan cruised Mall Road on a motorcycle, randomly blasting a dogcatcher, a night watchman, a laborer, and a

(Continued on next page)

homeless transient. A week later, he shot two more, a night watchman and a rickshaw driver, dumping their bodies in a canal. Another victim was a waiter in a restaurant, killed, as Khan explained, because he moved too slowly with the doctor's order. Arrested on December 11, Dr. Khan was charged with 13 murders and quickly confessed to nine of the crimes. A search of his home revealed an arsenal of unlicensed weapons, plus several false passports and sketches of various murder scenes, drawn from memory. Punjab Province Police Chief Dubbing Khan (no relation) described the lethal doctor as "a maniac or saboteur who killed for the fun of it."

Dr. Sohrab Aslam Khan was apparently "normal" in all respects until November 1986, when, at the age of 42, he inexplicably began a month-long murder spree that claimed 13 lives in his native Lahore, Pakistan.

If sadism motivated doctors Cream and Khan, however, neither one of them could hold a candle to Dr. Geza De Kaplany. Born and educated in Hungary, De Kaplany emigrated to the States following the abortive 1956 rebellion against Soviet rule, his heroic exploits described in an autobiography titled *Doctor in Revolt*. Employed as a hospital anesthesiologist in San Jose, California, De Kaplany met fashion model Hajna Piller, and they were married on July 21, 1962. Barely one month later, on August 28, police were called to De Kaplany's apartment, with complaints of a stereo playing full-blast. Inside, they found Dr. De Kaplany clad only in undershorts, while his nude wife writhed, bleeding from knife wounds to her breast, scarred by acid burns over 60 percent of her body. Jailed on a charge of attempted murder, De Kaplany explained that a neighbor had accused his wife of infidelity, whereupon, he explained, "I wanted to take her beauty away. I wanted to put fear into her against being an adulteress." The charge was upgraded to "murder by torture" after Hajna died, on September 30, and Dr. De Kaplany went to trial in January 1963. His insanity plea was supported by a psychiatrist who described De Kaplany's homicidal alter-ego — one "Pierre La Roche" — who emerged with a vengeance at moments of stress. Jurors rejected the claim, and De Kaplany was sentenced to life imprisonment. Still, incredibly (or not, considering the state of California's justice system), he was released in July 1976, a full six months before his first scheduled

parole hearing. At last report, he was supposedly practicing medicine once again, this time in Taiwan.

Blamed for seven homicides between 1958 and 1980, Engleman's normal modus operandi involved seducing women, whom he then persuaded to insure their husbands' lives, splitting the cash with Dr. Engleman after he killed the men off.

Dr. Glennon Engleman, Missouri's "killing dentist," was apparently more interested in profit than passion, although he sometimes also murdered for revenge. Blamed for seven homicides between 1958 and 1980, Engleman's normal modus operandi involved seducing women, whom he then persuaded to insure their husbands' lives, splitting the cash with Dr. Engleman after he killed the men off. A typical case involved Engleman's dental assistant, Carmen Miranda, who married patient Peter Halm at Engleman's insistence, for the specific purpose of claiming his death benefits. Dr. Engleman then shot Halm to death, in December 1980, and pocketed one-fourth of the $40,000 insurance settlement. A murder born of spite was the January 1980 car bombing of Sophie Berrera, owner of a St. Louis dental supply company, who had sued Dr. Engleman to recover $14,500 in bad debts. Convicted in those cases, Engleman was serving double life plus 60 years when authorities linked him to three more profit-killings, carried out in 1977 and 1979. The dentist pled guilty to those charges in June 1985, receiving three additional life terms. He remains the prime suspect in a 1958 shooting death and a fatal bombing from 1963, but has not been charged in those cases.

Another deadly dentist, Dr. Tony Protopappas, looked no further than his office in the search for victims. Arrested in Costa Mesa, California, in April 1983, Dr. Protopappas was charged with killing three of his female patients over the previous six months, deliberately overdosing each in turn. The first to die, in September 1982, was 23-year-old Kim Andreasson, an 88-pound dialysis patient whom Protopappas injected with nine different anesthetic drugs, during an operation to remove her wisdom teeth. Catheryn Jones, age 31, was next, dispatched on February 13, 1983, while the final victim — 13-year-old Patricia Craven — died six days later. In July 1984, after four months of testimony and five days of deliberation, jurors convicted Dr. Protopappas on three

(Continued on next page)

counts of second-degree murder, earning him concurrent terms of fifteen years to life on each charge.

His record showed 25 complaints to the state medical board, including three cases of death from a drug overdose in his office, plus allegations of illegal abortion, sexual assaults on his patients, child molestation, excessive drug treatment for mythical ailments, and practicing medicine without a license.

If Protopappas was reckless in his choice of victims, Michigan's Dr. Roland Clark was downright clumsy. In fact, it is a wonder that he stayed in business, considering the fact that his medical license was revoked four separate times between 1954 and 1967 — once for "gross misconduct," twice for "moral turpitude," and once without specific charges from the state. Each time, Clark won a grudging reinstatement, hauling his accusers into court and pleading poverty. During the same period, his record showed 25 complaints to the state medical board, including three cases of death from a drug overdose in his office, plus allegations of illegal abortion, sexual assaults on his patients, child molestation, excessive drug treatment for mythical ailments, and practicing medicine without a license. Committed to a state mental hospital in 1958, by his former wife, Clark was released as "cured" after less than three months of therapy. The capper came in 1967, when two of Dr. Clark's female assistants collapsed and died on the job, some eight months apart. The second corpse showed traces of sodium pentothal, and Clark was indicted on two counts of manslaughter, held without bond while authorities proved the deaths of at least nine patients, blamed on "therapeutic misadventure, cardiac arrest, or an injection of one sort or another." None of those cases were pursued, but Dr. Clark was convicted on both manslaughter counts, sentenced to a prison term of three to 15 years. In March 1972, he was killed at the state penitentiary in Jackson, authorities blaming his death on an accidental fall.

An intriguing case, perhaps, of "one who got away" occurred at Riverdell Hospital, a small osteopathic facility in Oradell, New Jersey. There, between December 1965 and October 1966, nine patients were admitted for routine surgery, all dying of unrelated (or unknown) causes, either before or after the operations were performed. Victims ranged in age from 14 years to 80, none of them considered high-risk cases at the time. Hospital administrators launched an investigation of the deaths in November 1966, after a Riverdell surgeon found 18 vials of curare — most nearly empty — in a locker assigned to Dr. Mario Jascalevich. An Argentine immigrant who came to America in 1955, Dr. Jascalevich claimed the curare was used in "private experiments," which he performed on dogs. No motive for the murders was found, and a decade passed before Jascalevich was indicted on five counts of murder, in July 1976. At trial, in 1978, two counts were dismissed for lack of evidence, while Jascalevich was acquitted of the other charges that October. Authorities were steadfast in maintaining that they had their man, though it could not be proven to a jury's satisfaction. Soon after his acquittal, Dr. Jascalevich returned to Argentina, where he died of a cerebral hemorrhage in September 1984. At Riverdell, the case of the curare deaths remains officially unsolved.

It is likely that no other homicidal healer led so checkered a career as French physician Marcel Petiot. A convicted thief and frequent mental patient, Dr. Petiot also served briefly as mayor of Villanueve, before a prison term cut short his tenure in 1930. He apparently committed his first murder — of a woman who accused him of encouraging her daughter's drug addiction — that same year, but the future "Great Liquidator" didn't really get rolling until 1941, when France was occupied by German troops. His latest get-rich scheme consisted of offering refuge to Jews, for a price, then killing them with lethal injections in a basement death chamber. Briefly detained by the Gestapo in May 1943, on charges of aiding escapees, Petiot was released seven months later, when the Nazis recognized a kindred spirit. On March 11, 1944, firemen responding to a blaze at Petiot's home found 27 corpses in the basement, most in various stages of dismemberment. Held on suspicion of murder, Petiot initially claimed the victims were Nazis executed by the French Resistance, but he couldn't make it stick. At trial, in March 1946, Dr. Petiot confessed to 63 slayings, but the total may well have been higher, since one of his statements referred to 150 "liquidations," and 86 dissected bodies were dredged from the Seine near his home, between 1941 and '43. Convicted on 26 counts, Dr. Petiot was guillotined on May 26, 1946.

It should not be inferred, of course, that most — or even a significant minority — of the doctors now in practice are demented killers. Still, if a particular physician seems inclined toward taking liberties, or is a bit too quick with knife and needle, it may be advisable to seek a second opinion. ◆

Western Sect Freedonianism

Have a Little Freedom with Your Religion

by Thomas Ingersoll More

Illustration by Renée French

Hey, where have all the churches gone? The government's rampaging mad with power lust, and the churches are off running bingo games or something. Has anybody heard any protests from the Methodists, the Catholics, or even the redoubtable Mormons, lately?

Why should we expect the churches to protest? We know they've done more than their own share of freedom trampling. Torquemada and Cotton Mather wouldn't exactly be ideal candidates for the Libertarian Party, even if they weren't busy being dead.

But when governments have gotten out of control, churches have also historically been among the first to oppose them. In America, from pre-revolutionary days, through the fight against slavery, to the modern civil rights movement, churches were in the vanguard of the battle against oppression. Maybe they just resented the competition. But by God, they've spoken out.

Not today, though. Unh uh. No sir.

I'll tell you where the churches are. They're out covering their butts.

Nearly every church in the U.S. is a 501(c)3 tax-exempt corporation. Corporations, and therefore churches, are creations of the state. Now, guess why they're keeping their sancti-monious mouths shut! They know down to their last little tax-exempt dollar what they stand to lose if they bite the hand that created them. Get

(Continued on next page)

political and out goes that 501(c)3 tax exemption. Whoosh! Zap! Zowie!

So they don't even say, "Oh, that Waco thing, you know? Um, well, sorry to bother you, but we were just thinking it might not be a very good idea for you to burn little babies."

Or, "About that compulsory government ID card you passed in '96? The one that's based on our Social Security numbers? We really don't like to criticize. It's just that there's this thing about 'The Number of the Beast' that kind of bothers some of our folks just a little, teensy bit..."

Nope. The money changers run the temple while freedom goes to hell.

So to Hell with Them

A lot of us don't really care what the churches do, in general. But we do care about freedom. And when people with responsibility for human souls don't just *neglect* freedom, but sell themselves to the Anti-Free, we can't sit still for that.

ONE OF THE BEST WAYS TO BRING DOWN THE FALSE GODS OF AUTHORITY IS TO LAUGH AT THEM, LOUD AND HARD.

Reform them? Oh, come on! You can't reform a sellout. Anyway, reforming something as bland as the Methodists or the Presbyterians would be like reforming the Ladies' Afternoon Tea & Garden Association. No way. Religions have mostly become ersatz social clubs; having detached themselves from spiritual matters, they are unfit to guide souls or preserve liberty.

It's time to take religion into our own hands. And it's time to take both ourselves and our religion out of the hands of government.

Ladies, gentlemen and others, I offer you forthwith, a religion for unfree times and always-free people: Western Sect Freedonianism.

But First

If you believe yours is the only religion, or if you believe there should be *no* religion, you might just want to leave now and browse the blowgun or bordello sections of our main catalog instead. This article, and this religion, isn't for you.

If you're a skeptic — the type who won't buy any "truth" until you've kicked its tires and taken it for a test drive — hang in there.

Western Sect Freedonianism

Western Sect Freedonianism is a religion for people who haven't, until now, been able to buy into *any* religion. It's for people whose minds shout "No!" to conventional church dogmas, but whose little inner voices still whisper "Yes!" to the notion that human life means much more than just getting up in the morning, going to work, coming home, having a brew and sacking out again at the end of another day.

It isn't for everybody. We're not going to do a whole lot of proselytizing at the White House, for instance. Congress isn't exactly fertile ground. We're not expecting Tammy Faye Bakker to bring her makeup kit and join us, or Oral Roberts to ask his 900-foot-tall Jesus to endorse our program.

But WSF may be for you if you both long to be free *and* envision your longing as spiritual, as well as intellectual.

The Western Sect Freedonian church is not established, and never will be established, as a 501(c)3 state religion. (Nor will we seek ATF approval, despite the Davidians' sad example.) Coupling with government is like mating with a charging rhinoceros — perverse, verrrrry uncomfortable, and deadly.

Individual Freedonians may choose to give allegiance to governments, but no Freedonian

(Continued on next page)

will willingly surrender self-ownership. And no Freedonian organization will seek government's permission to exist. To do so would be to violate the highest moral principles.

Freedonianism in Action

To be truly moral, we must have, and make, choices. If a person is "good" merely because she blindly follows orders, or because he doesn't have any other option, then that person is, in fact, morally null. In depriving people of choices by wrapping them in an increasingly constrictive web of laws and restrictions, the governments of the world commit some of the most heinous crimes possible. They turn individuals into automatons; they destroy morality; they halt spiritual growth.

THE MONEY CHANGERS RUN THE TEMPLE WHILE FREEDOM GOES TO HELL.

Freedonianism stands against this closure of the web.

The core beliefs of Freedonianism are simple: we espouse the principle of self-ownership, believe that the mind and spirit were born to grow, and acknowledge that free choice is the surest path to human intellectual and spiritual growth.

There are no catechisms. No hierarchies. No requirement for obeisance to any gods or goddesses though you're welcome to all the supernatural beings you personally care to adopt, create or discover off obscure Pacific islands. (Mind you, however, we're not too wild about Cthulu, who seems to be worshipped by the IRS.)

Freedonianism prescribes no rituals, other than one-time recitation of a simple credo. It doesn't demand that you fall on your knees.

Quite the opposite! Getting down on your knees is a damn good position for getting your head chopped off (or getting other portions of your anatomy violated).

Freedonianism is for people who want to stay *off* their knees. And that's where the hard part comes in. It's not a religion you can bow to on a slow Sunday. It's one that doesn't have any meaning until you live it, every day of the week.

Living it means saying "Yes!" to freedom and responsibility, and "No!" to many everyday, ordinary and increasing tyrannies. Perhaps it's all best expressed in the Freedonian Credo:

The Freedonian Credo

The one and only requirement for being a Western Sect Freedonian is to recite this creed (you don't even have to do it out loud) and *to live by its principles*.

Here goes:

I believe in personal freedom. I am the sole owner of my body, mind and spirit.

I will not be numbered, indexed, monitored or cataloged.

I have an eternal responsibility to my own soul to break all bonds ever forged upon me by force. I will repudiate and remove from my life all links in any chain of authoritarian ownership or control.

I believe in freedom for others. I will never initiate any act of force or fraud against another.

To be fully human and fully moral we must be free to dream, strive, explore, experiment, think, travel, believe, speak, risk, fail, succeed, defend ourselves, make choices, accept responsibility, and grow. Always to grow.

I will reach for the future. The only barrier I will permit to stand between my soul and the stars is time.

And One Other Thing

It also helps to be able to laugh.

(Continued on next page)

Frequently Asked Questions about Western Sect Freedonianism

There aren't any frequently asked questions about WSF. Nobody ever heard of it until today. So let's make up some.

What is the nature of God? Goddess only knows. And quite possibly, even she isn't sure. But seriously... many freedom fighters I know, even the non-religious, identify a numinous "something" just out of reach, toward which their hearts and souls strive. Perhaps as we grow in spirit, we'll one day understand its nature. Perhaps not. To be a Freedonian, it isn't necessary to espouse any specific belief or non-belief in the nature of God. But Freedonianism isn't mere humanism, rooted in the mundane. It is, if anything, the belief that to discover any great unknowns of the universe, we must be free to ask the questions, seek the answers and live the reality.

How large is the membership of WSF? About 175 pounds. I'm the only member right now. But think of this! If you join today, membership will double, making WSF the fastest-growing church in the entire world.

Are you serious? You damn betcha.

Is WSF one of those mind-control cults? Western Sect Freedonians believe it would be a good idea if we all controlled our own minds, now and then, by filling them with facts, turning off the TV and performing other useful mental exercises.

Are you aware of what can happen to members of unpopular religions in this country? Yes. Therefore, one of WSF's goals is to make government the most unpopular religion in the United States, as quickly as possible. Bring on the flame-throwers!

How does Western Sect Freedonianism compare to Discordianism? WSF is sort of like Discordianism for normal people. Or maybe like Discordianism for people who are too inherently organized to really appreciate pure chaos. However, if we ever start an ecumenical movement, Discordians will be the first ones we'll invite to the party.

Who is the leader of WSF? No one. You. Anyone who subscribes to the WSF credo, above.

How do I join? Recite the credo. Live it. WSF is for people who *do*, not for people who want to impress their neighbors with superficial shows of piety.

Do I have to tithe? You're welcome to send any amount of money, in small, unmarked bills or money orders, to Western Sect Freedonian Headquarters, care of this publisher. If you actually do that, you're probably too gullible to be a good Freedonian. On the other hand, if you do it, but grin wickedly while licking the envelope, you're probably a born Freedonian.

About the Name

Why Western Sect Freedonianism? Isn't it kind of clunky and dull? Is there an Eastern Sect Freedonianism?

One question at a time, please.

LAUGHTER IS THE CROWN UPON FREEDONIANISM'S PATE. UNDERNEATH ARE THE MEAT, THE BONE, THE MIND AND THE HEART AND SOUL BY WHICH WE LIVE. BY WHICH WE BECOME MORE HUMAN, MORE ALIVE. AND NOTHING WILL STOP US.

The name has several derivations. The "Western Sect" part was inspired by Eastern Sect Kyfho, the religion that provides a back-

(Continued on next page)

ground for F. Paul Wilson's science fiction novel, *An Enemy of the State*. WSF isn't particularly like ESK, but Kyfho stands for "keep your fucking hands off," a sentiment to which most Freedonians enthusiastically subscribe.

WE WANT TO DEMON-STRATE THAT IT'S POSSIBLE TO BE RELIGIOUS AND A GOOD MARXIST AT THE SAME TIME.

"Western Sect" is also a statement of sad fact: In the U.S. the love of freedom has nearly disappeared from the Atlantic coast (and large parts of the Pacific coast, as well), leaving the defense of liberty largely to people in the Rocky Mountain West and the South.

No, there is no Eastern Sect Freedonianism. There may well be potential Freedonians in eastern places such as New York, New Jersey and Pennsylvania, but the climate isn't right for the church to thrive there. We will accept interested easterners as honorary Western Sect members.

Anyone wishing to start a Southern Sect Freedonian church is most welcome, as long as they don't cheat on the principles. It ain't Freedonian if it doesn't live by the Credo. (Sorry to sound a bit authoritarian here, but I did invent the concept and thus feel entitled to be doctrinaire about the name.)

As to the term "Freedonianism," devoted Marxists will recognize the source. Freedonia was the land of the brave and free presided over by Rufus T. Firefly in the Marx Brothers' *Duck Soup*.

What's the symbolism here? It isn't that Freedonianism is a joke. (It's NOT A JOKE.) The name reminds all Freedonians of two important things: one, that we need a sense of humor to stay sane in trying times; and two, that one of the best ways to bring down the false gods of authority is to laugh at them, loud and hard.

St. Groucho, we salute you! (Besides which, we wanted to demonstrate that it's possible to be religious and a good Marxist at the same time.)

Yeah, the name's kind of dull and clunky. Too late to do anything about it now, though.

Organizing Your own Freedonian Congregation

You can organize your own Freedonian congregation if you want. Just as long as you and your members live by the Credo. No fudging! If you want a compromise religion, there are lots of others to choose from.

One good test of a Freedonian's sincerity is how well and thoroughly the new Freedonian frees him- or herself from government citizen-numbering and cataloging schemes. "I will not be numbered, indexed, monitored or cataloged." If you can achieve that, you can probably achieve anything Freedonian.

(And you might find it's a bit easier to reject being indexed and databased with the true statement, "It's against my religion," than with the equally true statement, "I am not a fucking number.")

Are You Serious?

Didn't we ask this already? Yes, but it bears repeating. Western Sect Freedonianism is NO JOKE. I restate, it is NOT A JOKE. For the benefit of any dimwitted bureaucrats in the audience, once again: WE'RE NOT JOKING.

Western Sect Freedonianism gives voice to the eternal, searching spirit of freedom. Do we also laugh at ourselves and the world's frequent craziness? You bet we do. It helps keep us alive.

We not only believe in questioning authority, we believe in mocking it.

But laughter is the crown upon Freedonianism's pate. Underneath are the meat, the bone, the mind and the heart and soul by which we live. By which we become more human, more alive.

And nothing will stop us.●

© 1997 by Dennis Fiery
Illustration by David Collier

You got fired? Oh, boo hoo! Like nobody else ever got fired before. Instead of expecting the world to hand you a good job on a silver platter, how about you take charge of your life? Temp. No one wants you cuz you don't have skills? Here's how to boost those skills: Temp.

> **You got fired? Oh, boo hoo! Like nobody else ever got fired before. Instead of expecting the world to hand you a good job on a silver platter, how about you take charge of your life?**

Temp. Temporary work. You sign up with a temp agency. They send you out on assignments. Meanwhile, you exploit those assignments to *your* advantage. How? Improve your computer skills on their equipment. Steal office supplies and leftover food from meetings. Place long-distance phone calls. Photocopy your brains out. You've got all day, and you're getting paid to sit there and do nothing.

Just temp.

You call the shots. You're in control. Want to stay home? You do. Want to work half the year, then ski the slopes the other half? You do that too. Want to educate yourself, write a book, start a biz, earn some fast cash? Then *temp*.

Here's how: The temp agency will test you first to make sure you're "presentable" and that you know how to use Microsoft Word, Excel, etc. Practice the basics at a computer store, local library, or on your current job. Plop yourself down in Barnes & Noble and pore over all those *Dummy* books until you're well-acquainted with the software. Bone up on typing too, because that's the other big thing they look for. If your blood is tainted with the godawful weed, then stay off it a month to clear the system. Use the time to train yourself for their tests. Then, when you're confident you'll pass with flying colors, go in and take their entrance exams. Be sure to dress nice, act like a decent human being, and you'll impress them.

Wowwee! You're in! They think you're a genius! Now the fun begins. They send you on assignments. Some suck. Some don't. Keep a positive attitude. Remember you're better than them. Most temp jobs require you to do little or nothing or next-to-nothing. Sit at a desk and get paid for hardly even flexing your buttock muscles.

So whadaya do all day? Most temps are lazy. They just sit there and vegetate. You're smart, though. You planned ahead the night before. You prepared a bunch of stuff to do. For instance, maybe you cut out job ads from the newspaper. Tomorrow at work you type up your résumé (on their computer), pilfer some snazzy paper (from their supply closet), and make printouts (on their HP Laser). Congratulations—you're getting paid to job search!

Or do what I do: write books *on the job*. Or short stories, or magazine articles, or produce your zine—

(Continued on next page)

whatever you're into. (Pop quiz: Where do you think I am *right now?* Hint: I'm wearing a tie and ignoring a ringing telephone.)

I knew a guy who started his own company on the job. He did all the research, filled out the paperwork, even stocked up on the necessaries, while temping at a variety of firms. *He got paid to become his own boss!*

I knew a guy who started his own company on the job. He did all the research, filled out the paperwork, even stocked up on the necessaries, while temping at a variety of firms. When it was set up he wrote a very nice Thank You note to his temp agency, and split. *He got paid to become his own boss!*

You gotta think like that: gotta be positive. Be forward-thinking. Sure, temp work can be gruntwork sometimes, but think long-term. Set a goal. Make a plan. Twist the system to your ends. How often do you get to do that? Hardly ever, right? Usually everyone's out to get you, you have no control. But in temping *you are in control. You* decide when to sign up with the agency (and you're smart enough to approach them only after attaining the skills). *You* decide which jobs to take, and which to bypass. *You* decide when you've had enough.

Oh, sure, they can fire you, but it's no big deal—it was just a temp job anyway.

And there're dozens of agencies. Play the field.

Temping is growing by leaps and bounds. Most see temping as a leap into hell. They're bitter because they're out of work, relegated to tortuous warehouse work, or headache-inducing data entry. But it doesn't have to be that way. Those lame temps would rather complain than improve their lot. You can improve yourself and thus raise your status in the temping community. If the agency sends you on lousy assignments, ask what you need to do to win better jobs—then do it. Maybe it requires taking some of their free training classes. Maybe it means washing the flaming Manic Panic out of your hair. What say? No can do? You're not gonna conform to Societal Rules? Well, I've got news for you, panther, it's easier to infiltrate the system and undermine it when you *look like one of them.* Comb your hair, tighten the noose around your neck, and go into it with a professional attitude. Once you're in, *then* you can goof off. Then you can make 5,000 photocopies of your rave flyer. Then you can walk off with electric fans and toner cartridges, and whatever other lil doggies ya'all wrangle up from the Supply Closet Corral.

Wait a sec, I hear some grumble rumbles from the rear. Temps get paid peanuts, you gripe? Oh, and I suppose moping around the house is raking in a fortune. Temping gives you the chance to reclaim your life. Do what you want, on your terms, when you want, and still maintain links to the corporate world so you can go back to it again *if it comes to that.*

And if it doesn't…that's fine too. You were smart. You used your temp time wisely. You sat at your desk and studied for the GREs…or the HSPTs…or LSATs…so you're always ready to go back to school and head for the next level. Or maybe you used your temp time (on the job, remember) to work on freelance transcriptions…or copy editing…or book reviewing…or web page design…or whatever freelance jobs your entrepreneurial side has taken on this month, thereby earning double-pay for half the work.

OR—

Maybe you sat at your temp job and made cold calls to 150 prospective clients, drumming up sales for your fiendish money-making scheme. (And maybe the next sucker you call will buy into it.) But even if they don't, that's okay, because there's always tomorrow. Always another temp job willing to set you up with a paid-for office and phones and supplies, hire you to do nothing except run your scam—and pay you for it.

Remember to cover your rosy ass, though. Do any meager work they assign you at your temp job. Then, when you're done, have your way with their equipment. If you're (ahem) writing an article on their office computer, *save it on a disk* and bring it home with you at the end of the work day. You don't want to save it on their hard drive only to blunder in the next morning, find you've been kicked out and you can't resurrect your potential Pulitzer from its silicon grave.

I've had a lot of fun temping. I walk out with a free and easy mind at the end of the day — no strenuous unpaid overtime like at my last real job. No heavy workload. No responsibility from one day to the next. If it gets too intense — quit.

And watch over your shoulder. I mean, nobody expects much from temps, but they do expect you to behave yourself. It's fine to walk off with their laminator machine, just don't let them see you do it. The key word is: don't-be-crass-about-it.

(Continued on next page)

I've had a lot of fun temping. I walk out with a free and easy mind at the end of the day—no strenuous unpaid overtime like at my last real job. No heavy workload. No responsibility from one day to the next. If it gets too intense—quit. If it gets too boring—read a book, surf the web, clip coupons, or write angry letters-to-editors. I've worked on everything from my taxes to my toenails at temp jobs. It sure is great getting paid to participate in the monotony of one's own life. It gives me more free time when I get home, because I don't have to waste my time fuming over credit card bills, junk mail, or handling bureaucratic nightmares—for they were all handled on the job, during work hours. My at-home time is my own time, to do with as I please. Temping brings me freedoms I wouldn't have otherwise. I can take vacations during the off-season so the theme parks are *empty* instead of packed ten-deep with sweating sardines. And I can—oh yes, I knew I was forgetting something:

Women.

Yeh, women temp, and (if you're a woman—) men temp too. And you know what happens when both men and women temp together?

FUCKING!

It doesn't hurt to bond with any other cool people you happen to meet as you swing from one job to the next on your journey through Planet Temp. For as you meet new people the party opportunities begin to escalate geometrically, the babes-to-you ratio pops higher to infinity and your life becomes the exciting fun-filled frolic only previously obtain-able by teenage movie stars.

That's right: fucking occurs. You see, temps are lonely beings. They feel left out from the regular corporate world-at-large. They're basically unemployed, and shuffle every day from one mindless job to the next. Their lives lack growth and maturity and stability. They lack fulfillment and they lack the warmth of a reliable spring of human contact. In short, a temp's life is a desolate one filled with unrealized desires. Seductive eyes glance hungrily at each new person strutting into the room.

For the socially agile, the temp agency is like a romp at Hef's mansion (before the kid). You prance in each morning all dolled up, and hang out with a bunch of similar-minded people, many of whom are as horny as you. I've been both the object of pick-ups and instigator

thereof. Many pick-ups succeed. Some at the agency, some on the job.

The job:

Every day (or week, or two-weeks) you move on to a new place, and you charm the pants off every opposite-sex cutie you come across at each of those temp jobs. After a while you're dating multiple people, each of whom works at a different company and who therefore exist in entirely different social circles from the others: *No chance of discovery.*

And it doesn't hurt to bond with any other cool people you happen to meet as you swing from one job to the next on your journey through Planet Temp. For as you meet new people the party opportunities begin to escalate geometrically, the babes-to-you ratio pops higher to infinity and your life becomes the exciting fun-filled frolic only previously obtainable by teenage TV stars.

So temping rocks. Temping rolls. Does temping solve all problems such as ending world peace and sustaining world hunger (or vice versa)? No, but you don't care about that. You care about you. You're on the way to repairing your life. If you're currently not working, consider temping as something to do, at least a little bit, to help learn the skills needed to pursue your dream job. If you are working a miserable job for a slimy Boss Hogg who stabs you in the back when he's not screaming down your front—well, maybe that's a job you don't need—and maybe you can find a better one through temping. Want to take some time off and plan the next 30 years of your life? Try temping as an easy way to stay afloat upon the sea of your indecision. Temping allows you to dip your toes into different occupations until you find one that best suits your demeanor.

I've turned to temping many times in my life. When I was in school and needed money. When I was out of school and in-between jobs (because I'd been fired, or laid-off, or fired again). Temping always seems to be there for me. I've met many people through temping, many of whom are disgusted by it. But I refuse to feel that way. I'm enraptured by temping, for it allows me a foothold into normalcy (but only a tiny foothold) while allowing the rest of me to lead a Bohemian, carefree, journalistic, artistic existence. I can pursue my dreams and my private ventures (writing and scientific pursuits) while earning some dough and scoring brownie points on my résumé. Temping is so versatile for so many people, for so many reasons—that's why I so highly recommend it. ●

*For more information, read **The Temp Worker's Guide To Self-Fulfillment: How To Slack Off, Achieve Your Dreams, And Get Paid For It,** by Dennis Fiery, published by Loompanics Unlimited.*

WOBBLY REVERIE

BY DENNIS P. EICHHORN. ARTWORK BY COLIN UPTON

Loompanics Unlimited Conquers The Universe

Loompanics Unlimited Conquers The Universe

"EVER THE POET, JOE HILL'S LAST WILL AND TESTAMENT READ:"

My will is easy to decide
For there is nothing to divide.
My kin don't need to fuss and moan -
Moss does not cling to a rolling stone

My body? Ah! If I could choose,
I would to ashes it reduce,
And let the merry breezes blow
My dust to where some flowers grow.

Perhaps some fading flower then,
Would come to life and bloom again.
This is my last and final will,
Good luck to all of you.

Joe Hill

NICE!

JOE HILL HAD THE FINAL SAY, TOO. HE ASKED THAT HIS ASHES BE SCATTERED IN EVERY STATE EXCEPT UTAH!

"DESPITE JOE HILL'S DEATH, THE I.W.W. FLOURISHED. THEY ORGANIZED THE MIGRATORY AGRICULTURAL WORKERS IN THE MIDWEST AND UP INTO CANADA AS FAR AS ALBERTA."

YOU SEE, THERE'S ONE BIG UNION THAT REPRESENTS ALL THE WORKERS...

SI, SEÑOR!

"THE FARMERS BEGAN TO COOPERATE, IMPROVING WORKING CONDITIONS FOR I.W.W. CREWS THAT SHOWED UP ON TIME AND WORKED HARD."

I SURE DO GET MY MONEY'S WORTH OUT OF THEM WOBBLIES!

"WITHIN THREE YEARS, MORE THAN 100,000 MIGRANT WORKERS HAD JOINED!"

"THE WOBBLIES SOLIDLY ENTRENCHED THEMSELVES AMONGST MINERS, LOGGERS, MARINERS AND ASSEMBLY-LINE WORKERS. THE BUSINESS TYCOONS BECAME ALARMED."

THESE DAMNED UNION DEMANDS! MORE PAY! FEWER HOURS! BETTER WORKING CONDITIONS!

WE NEED TO STAND FIRM! CALL THE PINKERTONS!

"THE PINKERTONS AND OTHER PRIVATE SECURITY COMPANIES ACTED AS GOON SQUADS FOR THE GREEDY CAPITALISTS!"

WORK 'EM OVER BOYS!

TAKE THAT, YA DAMNED RED!

LOOK OUT! IT'S THE PINKS!

WE NEVER FORGET

"THEY DID EVERYTHING IN THEIR POWER TO BREAK STRIKES AND HARASS THE WOBBLIES!"

Loompanics Unlimited Conquers The Universe

"THAT SAME YEAR, VIGILANTES AND HIRED THUGS IN BUTTE, MONTANA, SEIZED FRANK LITTLE, A WOBBLY WHO WAS WORKING TO ORGANIZE THE MINERS."

HELP! I'M BEING KIDNAPPED!

THWOCK!

SHADDUP!

"THEY BEAT HIM, THEN DRAGGED HIM BEHIND THEIR CAR FOR MILES."

THOSE SCREAMS ARE MUSIC TO MY EARS!

HA HA HA!

HELP! OH, MY GOD!

"THEN FRANK LITTLE WAS CASTRATED AND LEFT HANGING FROM A BRIDGE."

PRETTY GRIM STUFF.

YES, THE PEOPLE IN POWER WERE GETTING NERVOUS. BUT IT WAS THE WOBBLIES' ANTI-WAR EFFORTS THAT FINALLY TIPPED THE SCALES.

ALL ALONG, THE I.W.W. HAD BEEN AGAINST THE WAR.

WE, AS THE MEMBERS OF THE INDUSTRIAL ARMY, WILL REFUSE TO FIGHT FOR ANY PURPOSE EXCEPT THE REALIZATION OF INDUSTRIAL FREEDOM!

"IN 1917, THE WOBBLIES AND THE SOCIALISTS TEAMED UP TO FORM A 'WORKING CLASS UNION' AMONG TENANT FARMERS AND SHARECROPPERS IN OKLAHOMA. THEY OPPOSED THE MILITARY DRAFT, AND HOPED TO BLOCK ENLISTMENTS."

THERE'S NOT A POWER ON EARTH THAT CAN MAKE THE WORKING CLASS FIGHT IF THEY REFUSE!

"THEY PLANNED A MARCH OF DRAFT PROTESTERS ON WASHINGTON, DC."

"450 MARCHERS WERE ARRESTED AND ACCUSED OF REBELLION. THE LEADERS WERE JAILED."

CAPITALISTS OF AMERICA, WE WILL FIGHT AGAINST YOU, NOT FOR YOU!

I SENTENCE YOU TO TEN YEARS IN FEDERAL PRISON!

"THE I.W.W. WAS STRONG IN THE FORESTS OF THE NORTHWEST. IN THE SUMMER OF 1917, NORTHWESTERN TIMBERMEN STRUCK, CURTAILING WARTIME PRODUCTION."

WE WANT EIGHT-HOUR WORKDAYS!

AND GOOD FOOD!

AND CLEAN BEDS!

WHAT WAS THE MILITARY USING WOOD FOR?

STRAIGHT-GRAINED SITKA SPRUCE WAS USED IN FIGHTER PLANES' FRAMES AND STRUTS...AND SHIPS' KEELS AND TIMBERS WERE MADE OF DOUGLAS FIR.

Loompanics Unlimited Conquers The Universe

Loompanics Unlimited Conquers The Universe

AMERICA'S PRIVATE GULAG
BY KEN SILVERSTEIN

© 1997 by Ken Silverstein

Illustration by Mark Lang

What is the most profitable industry in America? Weapons, oil and computer technology all offer high rates of return, but there is probably no sector of the economy so abloom with money as the privately-run prison industry.

Consider the growth of the Corrections Corporation of America, the industry leader whose stock price has climbed from $8 a share in 1992 to about $30 today and whose revenue rose by 81 percent in 1995 alone. Investors in Wackenhut Corrections Corp. have enjoyed an average return of 18 per cent during the past five years and the company is rated by Forbes as one of the top 200 small businesses in the country. At Esmor, another big private prison contractor, revenues have soared from $4.6 million in 1990 to more than $25 million in 1995.

Ten years ago there were just five privately-run prisons in the country, housing a population of 2,000. Today nearly a score of private firms run more than 100 prisons with about 62,000 beds. That's still less than five per cent of the total market but the industry is expanding fast, with the number of private prison beds expected to grow to 360,000 during the next decade.

The exhilaration among leaders and observers of the private prison sector was cheerfully summed up by the headline in *USA Today:* "Everybody's doin' the jailhouse stock." An equally upbeat mood imbued a conference on private prisons held last December at the Four Seasons Resort in Dallas. The brochure of the conference, organized by the World Research Group, a New York-based investment firm, called the corporate takeover of correctional facilities the "newest trend in the area of privatizing previously government-run programs... While arrests and convictions are steadily on the rise, profits are to be made — profits from crime. Get in on the ground floor of this booming industry now!"

A hundred years ago private prisons were a familiar feature of American life, with disastrous consequences. Prisoners were farmed out as slave labor. They were routinely beaten and abused, fed slop and kept in horribly overcrowded cells. Conditions were so wretched that by the end of the nineteenth century private prisons were outlawed in most states.

During the past decade, private prisons have made a comeback. Already 28 states have passed legislation

(Continued on next page)

making it legal for private contractors to run correctional facilities and many more states are expected to follow suit.

The reasons for the rapid expansion include the post-1980s free-market ideological fervor, large budget deficits for the federal and state governments and the discovery and creation of vast new reserves of "raw materials" — prisoners. The rate for most serious crimes has been dropping or stagnant for the past 15 years, but during the same period severe repeat offender provisions and a racist "get-tough" policy on drugs have helped push the US prison population up from 300,000 to about 1.5 million. This has produced a corresponding boom in prison construction and costs, with the federal government's annual expenditures in the area of $17 billion. In California, passage of the infamous "three strikes" bill will result in the construction of an additional 20 prisons during the next few years.

The private prison business is most entrenched at the state level but is expanding into the federal prison system as well. Last year Attorney General Janet Reno announced that five of seven new federal prisons being built will be run by the private sector. Almost all of the prisons run by private firms are low or medium security, but the companies are trying to break into the high-security field. They have also begun taking charge of management in INS detention centers, boot camps for juvenile offenders and substance abuse programs.

Roughly half of the industry is controlled by the Nashville-based Corrections Corporation of America, which runs 46 penal institutions in 11 states. It took ten years for the company to reach 10,000 beds; it is now growing by the same number every year.

CCA's chief competitor is Wackenhut, which was founded in 1954 by George Wackenhut, a former FBI official. Over the years its board and staff have included such veterans of the US national security state as Frank Carlucci, Bobby Ray Inman and William Casey, as well as Jorge Mas Canosa, leader of the fanatic Cuban American National Foundation. The company also provides security services to private corporations. It has provided strikebreakers at the Pittston mine strike in Kentucky, hired unlicensed investigators to ferret out whistle blowers at Alyeska, the company that controls the Alaskan oil pipeline, and beaten anti-nuclear demonstrators at facilities it guards for the Department of Energy.

Wackenhut has a third of the private prison market with 24 contracts, nine of which were signed during the past two years. In a major coup, the company was chosen to run a 2,200 capacity prison in Hobbs, New Mexico, which will become the largest private prison in the US when it opens late this year.

Esmor, the No. 3 firm in the field, was founded only a few years ago and already operates ten corrections or detention facilities. The company's board includes William Barrett, a director of Frederick's of Hollywood, and CEO James Slattery, whose previous experience was investing in and managing hotels.

US companies also have been expanding abroad. The big three have facilities in Australia, England and Puerto Rico and are now looking at opportunities in Europe, Canada, Brazil, Mexico and China.

The companies that dominate the private prison business claim that they offer the taxpayers a bargain because they operate far more cheaply than do state firms. As one industry report put it. "CEOs of privatized companies... are leaner and more motivated than their public-sector counterparts."

But even if privatization does save money — and the evidence here is contradictory — there is, in the words of Jenni Gainsborough of the ACLU's National Prison Project, "a basic philosophical problem when you begin turning over administration of prisons to people who have an interest in keeping people locked up."

To be profitable, private prison firms must ensure that prisons are not only built but also filled. Industry experts say a 90 to 95 per cent capacity rate is needed to guarantee the hefty rates of return needed to lure investors. Prudential Securities issued a wildly bullish report on CCA a few years ago but cautioned, "It takes time to bring inmate population levels up to where they cover costs. Low occupancy is a drag on profits." Still, said the report, company earnings would be strong if CCA succeeded in "ramp[ing] up population levels in its new facilities at an acceptable rate."

A 1993 report from the State Department of Corrections in New Mexico found that CCA prisons issued more disciplinary reports — with harsher sanctions imposed, including the loss of time off for good behavior — than did those run by the state. A prisoner at a CCA prison said, "State run facilities are overcrowded and there's no incentive to keep inmates as long as possible... CCA on the other hand reluctantly awards good time. They give it because they have to but they take it every opportunity they get... Parole packets are constantly getting lost or misfiled. Many of us are stuck here beyond our release dates."

Private prison companies have also begun to push, even if discreetly, for the type of get-tough policies needed to ensure their continued growth. All the major firms in the

(Continued on next page)

field have hired big-time lobbyists. When it was seeking a contract to run a halfway house in New York City, Esmor hired a onetime aide to state Rep. Edolphus Towns to lobby on its behalf. The aide succeeded in winning the contract and also the vote of his former boss, who had been an opponent of the project. In 1995, Wackenhut Chairman Tim Cole testified before the Senate Judiciary Committee to urge support for amendments to the Violent Crime Control Act — which subsequently passed — that authorized the expenditure of $10 billion to construct and repair state prisons.

CCA has been especially adept at expansion via political payoffs. The first prison the company managed was the Silverdale Workhouse in Hamilton County, Tennessee. After Commissioner Bob Long voted to accept CCA's bid for the project, the company awarded Long's pest control firm a lucrative contract. When Long decided the time was right to quit public life, CCA hired him to lobby on its behalf. CCA has been a major financial supporter of Lamar Alexander, the former Tennessee governor and failed presidential candidate. In one of a number of sweetheart deals, Lamar's wife, Honey Alexander, made more than $130,000 on a $5,000 investment in CCA. Tennessee Governor Ned McWherter is another CCA stockholder and is quoted in the company's 1995 annual report as saying that "the federal government would be well served to privatize all of their corrections."

The prison industry has also made generous use of the junket as a public relations technique. Wackenhut recently flew a New York-based reporter from Switzerland — where the company is fishing for business — to Florida for a tour of one of its prisons. The reporter was driven around by limousine, had all her expenses covered and was otherwise treated royally.

In another ominous development, the revolving door between the public and private sector has led to the type of company boards that are typical of those found in the military-industrial complex. CCA co-founders were T. Don Hutto, an ex-corrections commissioner in Virginia, and Tom Beasley, a former Chairman of the Tennessee Republican Party. A top company official is Michael Quinlan, once director of the Federal Bureau of Prisons. The board of Wackenhut is graced by a former Marine Corps commander, two retired Air Force generals and a former under secretary to the Air Force, as well as by James Thompson, ex-governor of Illinois, Stuart Gerson, a former assistant US attorney general and Richard Staley, who previously worked with the INS.

Because they are private firms that answer to shareholders, prison companies have been predictably vigorous in seeking ways to cut costs. In 1985, a private firm tried to site a prison on a toxic waste dump in Pennsylvania, which it had bought at the bargain rate of $1. Fortunately, that plan was rejected.

Many states pay private contractors a per diem rate, as low as $31 a prisoner in Texas. A federal investigation traced a 1994 riot at an Esmor immigration detention center to the company's having skimped on food, building repairs and guard salaries. At an Esmor-run halfway house in Manhattan, inspectors turned up leaky plumbing, exposed electrical wires, vermin and inadequate food.

To ratchet up profit margins, companies have cut corners on drug rehabilitation, counseling and literacy programs. In 1995, Wackenhut was investigated for diverting $700,000 intended for drug treatment programs at a Texas prison. In Florida the US Corrections Corporation was found to be in violation of a provision in its state contract that requires prisoners to be placed in meaningful work or educational assignments. The company had assigned 235 prisoners to be dorm orderlies when no more than 48 were needed and enrollment in education programs was well below what the contract called for. Such incidents led a prisoner at a CCA facility in Tennessee to conclude, "There is something inherently sinister about making money from the incarceration of prisoners, and in putting CCA's bottom line (money) before society's bottom line (rehabilitation)."

The companies try to cut costs by offering less training and pay to staff. Almost all workers at state prisons get union-scale pay but salaries for private prison guards range from about $7 to $10 per hour. Of course the companies are anti-union. When workers attempted to organize at Tennessee's South Central prison, CCA sent officials down from Nashville to quash the effort.

Poor pay and work conditions have led to huge turnover rates at private prisons. A report by the Florida auditor's office found that turnover at the Gadsden Correctional Facility for women, run by the US Corrections Corporation, was 200 per cent, ten times the rate at state prisons. Minutes from an administrative meeting at a CCA prison in Tennessee have the "chief" recorded as saying, "We all know that we have lots of new staff and are constantly in the training mode... Many employees [are] totally lost and had never worked in corrections."

Private companies also try to nickel and dime prisoners in the effort to boost revenue. A prisoner at a Florida prison run by CCA has sued the company for charging a $2.50 fee per phone call and 50 cents per minute thereafter. The lawsuit also charges that it can take a prisoner more than a month to see a doctor.

(Continued on next page)

A number of prisoners complain about exorbitant prices. "Canteen prices are outrageous," wrote a prisoner at the Gadsden facility in Florida. "[We] pay more for a pack of cigarettes than in the free world." Neither do private firms provide prisoners with soap, toothpaste, tooth brushes or writing paper. One female prisoner at a CCA prison in New Mexico said: "The state gives five free postage paid envelopes per month to prisoners, nothing at CCA. State provides new coats, jeans, shirts, underwear and replaces them as needed. CCA rarely buys new clothing and inmates are often issued tattered and stained clothing. Same goes for linens. Also ration toilet paper and paper towels. If you run out, too bad — 3 rolls every two weeks."

General conditions at private prisons appear in some respects to be somewhat better than those found at state institutions, a fact possibly linked to the negative business impact that a prison disturbance can cause private firms. For example, the share price of stock in Esmor plunged from $20 to $7 after a 1994 revolt at the company's detention center for immigrants in Elizabeth, New Jersey.

Nevertheless a number of serious problems at prisons run by private interests still exist. Back in the mid-1980s, a visiting group of professional guards from England toured the CCA's 360-bed state prison in Chattanooga, Tennessee, and reported that inmates were "cruelly treated" and "problem" prisoners had been gagged with sticky tape. The warden regaled his guests with graphic descriptions of strip shows performed by female inmates for male guards.

Investigators at a CCA jail in New Mexico found that guards had inflicted injuries on prisoners ranging from cuts and scrapes to broken bones. Riots have erupted at various private facilities. In one of the worst, guards at CCA's West Tennessee Detentional Center fired pepper gas canisters into two dormitories to quell a riot after prisoners shipped from North Carolina revolted over being sent far from their families.

In addition to the companies that directly manage America's prisons, many other firms are getting a piece of the private prison action. American Express has invested millions of dollars in private prison construction in Oklahoma and General Electric has helped finance construction in Tennessee. Goldman Sachs & Co., Merrill Lynch, Smith Barney, among other Wall Street firms, have made huge sums by underwriting prison construction with the sale of tax-exempt bonds, this now a thriving $2.3 billion industry.

Weapons manufacturers see both public and private prisons as a new outlet for "defense" technology, such as electronic bracelets and stun guns. Private transport companies have lucrative contracts to move prisoners within and across state lines; health care companies supply jails with doctors and nurses; food service firms provide prisoners with meals. High-tech firms are also moving into the field; the Que-Tel Corp. hopes for vigorous sales of its new system whereby prisoners are bar coded and guards carry scanners to monitor their movements. Phone companies such as AT&T chase after the enormously lucrative prison business.

About three-quarters of new admissions to American jails and prisons are now African-American and Hispanic men. This trend, combined with an increasingly privatized and profitable prison system run largely by whites, makes for what Jerome Miller, a former youth corrections officer in Pennsylvania and Massachusetts, calls the emerging Gulag State.

Miller predicts that the Gulag State will be in place within 15 years. He expects three to five million people to be behind bars, including an absolute majority of African-American men. It's comparable, he says, to the post-Civil War period, when authorities came to view the prison system as a cheaper, more efficient substitute for slavery. Of the state's current approach to crime and law enforcement, Miller says, "The race card has changed the whole playing field. Because the prison system doesn't affect a significant percentage of young white men we'll increasingly see prisoners treated as commodities. For now the situation is a bit more benign than it was back in the nineteenth century but I'm not sure it will stay that way for long."

SIDE BAR

Private prison companies have been predictably enthusiastic about the booming market for convict labor. Between 1980 and 1994, the value of goods produced by prisoners rose from $392 million to $1.31 billion. Prisoners now make articles such as clothes, car parts, computer components, shoes, golf balls, soap, furniture and mattresses, in addition to staffing jailhouse telemarketing data entry and print shop operations. Some states have even begun assigning prisoners to institutions after matching up their job skills with a prison's labor needs.

Prisoners at state-run institutions generally receive the minimum wage, though in some states, such as Colorado, wages fall to as low at $2 per hour (workers receive only about 20 per cent of that amount, with the rest going to pay room and board, victims compensation programs and other fees). As an added bonus, companies that employ

(Continued on next page)

prison labor have no need to offer benefits, vacation days or sick time to employees and many states offer such firms tax breaks and other advantages as well.

Lured by such enticements, many big firms have moved eagerly into the prison-industrial complex. Trans World Airlines pays prison workers $5 per hour to book reservations by phone, less than a third of the rate it previously paid to its own employees. The EAU succeeded in shutting down a program at an Ohio prison where the Waste corporation was paying prisoners $2.05 per hour to assemble parts for Honda cars.

For businesses, the deal is even sweeter at private prisons where pay rates can be as low as 17 cents per hour for a six hour maximum day, which translates into a monthly pay check of about $20. The maximum pay scale at a CCA prison in Tennessee is 50 cents an hour for what are classified as "highly skilled positions." Given such rates it's not surprising that a prisoner there complained about the relative generosity of publicly-run programs, saying, "At federal prisons you can take home $1.25 per hour and work eight hours a day, sometimes even double shifts. A two, three or four hundred dollars a month check isn't unusual in the feds."

Thanks to prison labor, America is again attracting the sorts of jobs that were formerly available only to workers of the Third World. A US company operating in Mexico's maquiladora zone shut down its data processing shop and moved it to the San Quentin State Prison in California. A Texas factory booted 150 workers and set up shop at a privately-run prison in Lockhart, Texas, where worker/inmates assemble circuit boards for companies including IBM and Compaq. Oregon State Rep. Kevin Mannix has even encouraged Nike to shift production from Indonesia to his home state, saying the shoemaker should "take a look at transportation and labor costs. We could offer competitive prison labor [here]."●

[This article originally appeared in CounterPunch, a Washington, DC-based political newsletter ($40/$25-low-income, CounterPunch, PO Box 18675, Washington, DC 20036.)]

Strange Bedfellows
CCA's Political Connections
by Alex Friedmann

♦ CCA's connection with local politics began when the Nashville-based company was formed during Governor Lamar Alexander's administration. When CCA made a bid to operate Tennessee's entire prison system in 1985, the governor's wife, Honey Alexander, was criticized for owning $5,000 of CCA stock. She realized a substantial profit ($100,000) when she converted the stock to a blind trust in order to avoid an apparent conflict of interest.

♦ CCA chairman emeritus Thomas Beasley, who co-founded the company in 1983, was previously a chairman of the Tennessee Republican Party.

♦ Among CCA's board members is Clayton McWhorter, an unsuccessful Democratic candidate for Tennessee governor in 1994.

♦ From 1994-96, Doctor Crants, CCA's chief executive officer, and CCA's chairman emeritus Thomas Beasley donated at least $60,491 to Tennessee lawmakers — including $38,500 to Sundquist's re-election campaign (this includes donations from Beasley's wife, Wendy). In 1996 alone, Crants donated $22,450 to 46 state political candidates, including $2,000 to Rep. Randy Rinks, House Democratic Caucus chairman; and $1,350 to Senator Jim Kyle, chairman of the Select Oversight Committee on Corrections. CCA has seven registered political lobbyists in Tennessee.

♦ In 1995, Governor Sundquist endorsed a controversial arrangement whereby CCA could contract with Hardeman County, TN, to construct and operate a 1,540-bed "jail," funded with $47 million in municipal bonds guaranteed by the state, to house state prisoners. This arrangement circumvented a TN state statute that allows only one privately-managed state prison to operate in Tennessee at a time.

♦ State Senator Robert Rochelle, who received at least $1,000 in campaign contributions from CCA board members, sponsored a bill to permit privatization of any newly-built state prisons. He has sponsored other legislation on behalf of CCA.

♦ Peaches Simkins, Governor Sundquist's former Chief of Staff, reportedly owned CCA stock while she was advising the governor on prison privatization.

♦ The Speaker of the House in Tennessee's General Assembly, Jimmy Naifeh, is married to CCA political lobbyist Betty Anderson.

♦ In terms of connections on a U.S. Congressional level, CCA employs several former high-ranking members of the Federal Bureau of Prisons, as well as Dr. Tyree Tanner, the brother of U.S. Representative John S. Tanner.

Shays' Rebellion and the Battle for the American Jubilee

by Michael A. Hoffman II

© 1996 by Michael A. Hoffman II

Illustration by Nick Bougas

INTRODUCTION

The pusillanimous histories of the American Revolution and the early Republic, by Peter Marshall and similar writers, paint a rose-colored picture at variance with the documentary record.

The American revolutionaries fought for a re-ordering of society; indeed, for the overthrow of debt, usury and dispossession from the land, as symbolized by their objective of declaring the mighty legal earthquake that is the Biblical Jubilee. The scriptural warrant for Jubilee was inscribed on the Liberty Bell and more importantly, upon the hearts of the ordinary men and women who had pledged their "lives, fortunes, and sacred honor" to the call to arms against oppression and tyranny, of July 4, 1776.

The Pollyanna historians have tended to paint the early years of the new republic as idyllic, even utopian, a time when the freedom-loving farmers found their hearts' desire and richly enjoyed the fruits of liberty which their blood, sweat and tears had made possible.

Patriot activists today enshrine those early times and cite them as precedent against the depredations of Clinton and Dole, Reno and Freeh, Kemp and Powell. It is a dangerous precedent to establish, born of historical illiteracy.

The early Republic never did get around to declaring the Jubilee, though the great experiment in personal liberty begun in the wake of the Revolution was in general a blessing to mankind, in comparison with the fearsome oligarchies still holding power in Europe. But once the war had been won and the yeomanry were no longer the essential motive engine for securing independence from Britain, in many regions power was consolidated in the hands of reactionary mercantile interests.

The lawyers and bankers had only gone underground during the Revolution and like all parasites were quick to re-emerge when peace was at hand, to declare their "right" to rule the manual laborers who had done the frontline fighting.

As the watch-fob crooks came out of the woodwork, the veterans of '76 were there to meet them, first with petitions for redress of grievance and later with rifles.

Conservative historians declare that the Shays rebels were forerunners of Bolshevism, "ingrates" who sought to "level" frontier society into some disgusting precursor of Marxism.

Such an interpretation can only be put forth by those who know little or nothing of the Bible-based aspirations of the American yeomanry.

There was nothing "Bolshevik" about Shays' Rebellion. The criminal class was not among the farmers, who Jefferson had nominated as the true

(Continued on next page)

"Chosen people" if ever there was one, but among the usual suspects lurking at the top of the Pharaonic pyramid.

I had to smile when Pat Buchanan visited Los Angeles some years ago, in the wake of the devastating Mexican/African riots there, and proclaimed, in the coded weasel words of Republican conservatism, a statement to the effect that whites are better citizens than the Mexicans and Africans, because whites don't riot. In truth, the white race is the most insurrectionist nation the world has ever seen, or was, until feminism and TV flea'd the lion's rump and pared his claws.

THE SECOND AMERICAN REVOLUTION

Massachusetts after the American Revolution was a largely subsistence culture. Farmers made up more than half the population and these were independent freeholders who valued freedom over material wealth, eking out a living on the rocky soil, but reveling in their status as king of their own castle.

These farmers jealously guarded their hard-fought status and were especially fearful of having to work off their land, for a wage, a condition they compared to peonage and slavery.

The life of the farming community in that era was close-knit and reflected in patterns of clan and kinship. Contrasted with this agrarian community was the cosmopolitan society of the seacoast towns. Here the focus was chiefly on the acquisition of wealth. Lawyers were at its center. Before the 18th century, New England's laws had been largely consonant with Bible law. The vocation of the law clerk was to help to imple-ment the Mosaic statutes and facilitate, rather than obstruct, property and business transactions. But by the 1780s law had degenerated into a means for the regular collection of debts and loans.

During the 1780s many clergymen collaborated with the mercantile elite. Money culture slowly replaced the Bible ethos in major coastal towns and the function of the ministry changed.

Government-paid clergymen upheld usury from the pulpit. The tax-exempt status of New England ministers, coupled with the payment of their salaries mostly from tax funds, tied them to the lawyers and bankers.

THE REIGN OF SHYLOCK

Boston mercantile interests convinced yeomen to make their purchases on credit and accepted farm goods for payment. Retailers later withdrew credit from their farmer-customers and demanded payment in gold and silver.

The yeomen faced the loss of their farms and merchants, lawyers and speculators stood to profit. Farmers were being trapped into a chain of debt. "The constables are venduing (seizing) our property... it is sold for about one-third the value, our cattle about one-half the value," angrily petitioned the townsmen of Greenwich, Massachusetts in January, 1786.

Property seizures enraged the farmers and reinforced their fear of becoming landless "wage laborers."

"The mortgage of our farms, we cannot think of with any degree of complacency," said a Conway, Massachusetts man. "To be tenants to landlords, who we know not and pay rents for lands purchased with our money and converted from howling wilderness into fruitful fields by the sweat of our brow, seems to carry with it in its nature truly shocking consequences."

Taxes were tilted against the landowners and in favor of the mercantile class. Thousands of farmers left the state for the western wilderness because of high property taxes.

A small farmer without sufficient property for settling his debts faced an indefinite jail sentence. Considering the horrible state of New England jails during the 18th century, incarceration for indebtedness represented cruel punishment.

But Massachusetts retailers did not hesitate to throw indebted yeomen into prison. In Hampshire County from 1784 to December, 1786, they sent to jail for an average two-month term, seventy-three men with relatively small debts and arrested hundreds of other farmers. Significantly, no retailer sat in a jail cell.

The case of Timothy Bigelow, an indebted Massachusetts farmer and Revolutionary War veteran who died in a damp cell of the Worcester County prison, became a *cause célèbre* among the farmers.

One Hampshire County farmer and Revolutionary War veteran spoke of how he had "labored hard all his days" and did more than his share of the fighting against King George, but now, with the war over, and liberty supposedly realized, he had been "loaded with class-rates, lawsuits... hauled by sheriffs, constables and (tax) collectors." He predicted the lawyers would "get

(Continued on next page)

all we have." (*Hampshire Gazette*, October 25, 1786).

Now that the British king had been disposed of there were plenty of aspirants to his throne. New England's republican heritage was hardly the sole experience of colonial America. Even in New England the history of subjecting white laborers to some form of bondage went all the way back to Plymouth Rock.

There were bond servants on the Mayflower and a "goodly body" of white slaves aboard the Puritan fleet that arrived in Massachusetts in 1630. Georgia had been founded expressly as a penal colony for white slaves. Maryland had been a "semi-feudal domain, composed in part of manors owned by great landowners and tilled by white bond servants..." (Cf. Charles A. and Mary R. Beard, *The Rise of American Civilization* and Michael A. Hoffman II, *They Were White and They Were Slaves*).

The citizens of the new American Republic were determined to forge a heritage of freedom and to maintain the hardy and independent spirit which had sustained them in the New World.

Unfortunately, matters were not necessarily resolved with their victory over the Redcoats, as many historians mistakenly allege. America had its own homegrown aristocrats who felt they were more deserving of elite privilege than the monarch across the sea.

The Founding Fathers had motivated the Continental army and the militias of the 13 colonies with visions of a post-Revolutionary Biblical Jubilee according to Leviticus 25, wherein all debts would be wiped out and everyone would start over in the new Republic with a clean slate. The American soldiers took them at their word:

> With the ending of the American revolution and the Treaty of Paris of Sept. 3, 1783, there was jubilation in the streets. The future looked bright... Many people even... believed that their debts had been dismissed when the war ended. (Michael Paulin, *The Ballad of Daniel Shays*).

This was the promise represented by the inscription on the Liberty Bell, but it proved to be an empty one.

Still, the yeomen were slow to wrath. They wanted to farm, not fight. Before turning to armed resistance, New England farmers sought justice through peaceful petitions. During the years 1784 to mid-1786, yeomen in the majority of Massa-

chusetts' small towns forwarded their pleas to the Boston courts.

The farmers were not anxious for more bloodletting. They had faith in their new leaders and they sought relief through legal, non-violent means and channels, from the courts to the legislature.

Since gold and silver were beyond their attainment, the oppressed New England farmers desired to have barter legalized through the currency of paper money, *backed by silver and gold*, which would represent so many bushels of corn or wheat or hours of labor. This demand was one of many of the reforms headed under the proposition, "tender laws."

These laws had been in effect in some areas of the colonies during the Revolution, when the Founders were anxious to keep the morale of the yeomen high and their wrath focused on Britain. By means of the tender laws, farmers paid their debts through a legalized form of barter, wherein crops were taken directly as payment or exchanged for specie.

THE "PESTS OF SOCIETY"

As their petitions increasingly fell on deaf ears, the citizens of the new Republic began to examine what force it was that chiefly obstructed them. Like the great anti-Masonic movement that would appear forty years later, the farmers discovered that one of the chief obstructions to reform was that class of parasite known as lawyers, who the farmers termed, "the pests of society" and "an altogether useless order."

In running up against the society of lawyers, the farmers felt their petitions were crashing against the equivalent of their famous New England stone walls.

One of the rebels allied with Shays, Thomas Grover, gave as his reason for revolt, the "large swarm of lawyers... who have been more damage to the people at large, especially the common farmers, than the savage beasts of prey." (George R. Minot, *The History of the Insurrections in Massachusetts*).

As early as 1782, with the war with Britain still officially underway and the Treaty of Paris, concluding hostilities, a year off, the first stirrings of forceful resistance were exhorted by the radical activist Samuel Ely, a homeless, itinerant clergy-

(Continued on next page)

man, who was not tax-exempt or tax-supported by the state.

Ely was a hater of oppression and a ferocious opponent of the Massachusetts plutocracy. He told the farmers that the merchants and bankers who oppressed them should be "made a sacrifice of and given to the fowls of the air and the beasts of the field."

This was not just talk. In April of 1782, Pastor Ely roused a band of farmers in Northampton for an attack on the judges of the debtor's court. In a speech he told the farmers:

> Come on, my brave boys, we'll go to the woodpile and get clubs enough to knock their grey wigs off and send them out of the world in an instant.

Then followed hand-to-hand combat between the farmers and the militia defending the courthouse. The farmers were driven off and Ely was seized and imprisoned. But not for long. Two months later, more than a hundred farmers attacked the building where Ely was confined and released him.

The following autumn farmers closed the debtor's court in Cheshire County, New Hampshire. In early 1783, American freemen, led by Job Shattuck of Massachusetts, assaulted tax collectors and tried to close the Springfield tax court.

There was no U.S. Constitution at this time. The law of the Commonwealth was the 1780 Massachusetts constitution, widely derided by the yeomanry as a "lawyers and merchants constitution." In New England, only the territory of Vermont had a plan of government equitable to the working men.

But in the midst of these early stirrings, most of New England's farmers continued to seek peaceful recourse. For three more years the majority prayed, petitioned and supplicated while the lawyer-controlled state capitals stonewalled.

SHUTTING DOWN THE COURTS

During this period the legislatures and courts issued anti-farmer rhetoric remarkably similar to the "hater" characterizations with which today's American patriot groups are tarred. The General Court of Massachusetts referred to the protesting farmers of 1786 as, "traitors, incendiaries" and "vile creatures." The legislature threatened the farmers with arrest just for "daring to inquire into the present gross mismanagement."

In August the peaceful petitions came to an end. Though no violence was used, the farmers were no longer in a supplicating mood. A hardscrabble Pelham farmer and former American Continental army veteran, Captain Daniel Shays, began to organize a mass movement of courthouse closings.

Shays' friend, George Brock, spoke for both when he said that he thought he saw in the politicians and lawyers of post-Revolutionary New England, the shadow of the same "aristocratical principle" the British had manifested.

These veterans were not willing to tolerate a home-grown dictatorship under a patriotic gloss. Having been once again treated like subjects, once again they arose — like lions

Daniel Shays led more than 1,000 farmers and mechanics to the Massachusetts Court of Common Pleas on August 29, 1786 and sealed it tight as a drum. The Second American Revolution had begun!

In September 600 farmers closed the courts in Worcester, as well as at the birthplace of the American Revolution, in Concord.

800 laborers united into a militia of their own making and closed the debt court at Great Barrington. 500 farmers marched on the court in Bristol County and shut it.

By September the rebellion had spread to New Hampshire, the "Live Free or Die" state where the farmers went their Massachusetts brethren one better: they seized the capital and held the governor and the legislature captive.

In western Massachusetts, the stronghold of the insurgents throughout the rebellion, Daniel Shays led 1500 farmers and laborers to Springfield where they occupied the courthouse for three days. By December of 1786 Shays was at the head of an army of 9,000 farmers.

At no time were any of these protests a "mob action." The farmers marched into the towns with self-imposed military discipline. Though condemned as "seditionists" and "wicked rebels" by the Boston merchants and speculators, this was pure cant, since only twelve years before, in 1774, farmers had closed the Springfield court by similar means, to the general acclaim of the very men who now censured the populist actions of the post-Revolutionary yeomen. (cf. Lee Newcomer, *The Embattled Farmers: The Massachusetts Countryside in the American Revolution*).

(Continued on next page)

In a tone of outrage, the Secretary of War under the Articles of Confederation, Henry Knox, wrote to George Washington that the Shays rebels "are determined to annihilate all debts public and private." Exactly! That's what the Jubilee constitutes.

But some of the Founders would have none of it. "Washington was thoroughly frightened. On hearing the news he redoubled his efforts to obtain a stronger constitution — one that could afford national aid in suppressing such local disturbances." (Beard, op. cit.)

While the fortunes of the farmers' uprising in New Hampshire and Massachusetts were in the ascendant in late 1786, incipient farmer revolts were put down by the militia in Vermont's Windsor and Rutland counties. The skirmish at the Rutland county courthouse involved an exchange of gunfire between the farmers and the militia. At New Haven, Connecticut, a courthouse seizure was halted by means of the mass arrest of the yeomen.

A POLICE STATE — IN 1787 AMERICA

In many cases the actions of the American Republic's ruling class in the post-Revolutionary years surpassed Janet Reno and Louis Freeh in despotic arrogance. For example, in March of 1787, Vermont lawmakers enacted The Riot Act authorizing county sheriffs to shoot rebellious farmers on sight.

Meanwhile in Massachusetts, Governor James Bowdoin, part-owner of the Massachusetts State Bank, whose worthless currency (on par with our present "Federal Reserve Notes"), was a source of the farmers' wrath, was determined to crush Shays' Rebellion and called upon the militia to stop the farmers at the Worcester courthouse.

To the utter consternation of the banker-governor, the Massachusetts militiamen refused. The militia commander, Jonathan Warner, reported, "Notwithstanding the most pressing orders, there did appear universally that reluctance in the people to turn out in support of the government."

As one Shrewsbury judge noted, the Massachusetts militia were "too generally in favor of the people's measures" to turn their guns on their fellow farmers. This was true of the militia throughout western Massachusetts. It

sent shockwaves through the ranks of the lawyers and speculators and caused some to hope for the imposition of a new monarchy.

Noah Webster, the famous lexicographer, found himself wishing for a "limited monarchy" after watching aghast as the people of the Massachusetts backwoods claimed their rights as Americans against the coastal merchant elite:

> I was once as strong a republican as any man in America. Now a Republic is the last kind of government I should choose. I would infinitely prefer a limited monarchy, for I would sooner be the subject of the caprice of one man than the ignorance of the multitude. (*Connecticut Courant*, Nov. 20, 1786)

Massachusetts began passing draconian laws curtailing the rights of the people and effectively establishing a dictatorship. The Massachusetts Riot Acts of 1786 ordered the killing of any rebellious farmer and instituted a property seizure law more tyrannical than even our contemporary confiscation laws. Rebellious farmers were to "forfeit all their lands, goods and chattels to the Commonwealth."

The legislature of Massachusetts also suspended the writ of habeus corpus. "Suspect" farmers could be placed in preventive detention and incarcerated indefinitely without trial. Freedom of speech was also banned if it was "to the prejudice of the government." (*Acts and Laws of Massachusetts, 1786*.)

The chief sponsor of this shameful police state legislation was none other than the once great revolutionary, Sam Adams.

The farmers remained defiant, however, and continued to close courts. Governor Bowdoin sought help from the central government. The Confederation Congress voted the state of Massachusetts a handsome war chest of more than a half million dollars and a force of 1,300 troops, but funds for the punitive campaign had to be appropriated by the individual thirteen states. Under the Articles of Confederation, the Congress had little power over the treasury.

The states constituted virtually separate nations and most could see no advantage in paying for a war against the people of Massachusetts. They refused to appropriate the monies and the scheme failed. The lawyers and

(Continued on next page)

bankers of Boston would have to pay for their war out of their own pockets, something this class of men has traditionally been loath to do.

Without significant armed opposition, by early 1787, the farmers were beginning to establish a groundwork for economic reforms aimed at destroying usury and defanging the lawyers' courts.

THE MASONIC CONNECTION

The bankers and lawyers could no longer hide under color of law and the camouflage of government authority. It was obvious that the army they would raise would be a mercenary one, serving mammon, not justice. The personnel commanding the counter-revolutionary forces gave ample testimony of this. Government troops were led by judges of the debtor court such as Thomas Cobb and wealthy Freemasons, such as Benjamin Tupper, Henry Lincoln, Rufus Putnam and John Paterson.

It would appear that the Shays uprising did not enjoy the approbation of the American-based "Lodge," as the 1776 revolt had. It seems that only those rebellions *sanctioned* and partly *stage-managed* by Freemasonry were allowed to flourish in the U.S.

This is not to suggest, as some critics have alleged, that the American Revolution was little more than an open-air masonic ritual. That is the propaganda of the lodge itself, claiming credit for the fundamentally decent and noble 1776 struggle for individual freedom, which was beyond its competence and resources to control, though it was undoubtedly a factor in the struggle.

The 1776 revolt was as legitimate and necessary a people's uprising as Shays' Rebellion. The Freemasons of America saw in the 1776 Revolution an opportunity and encouraged it in the hopes of channeling and controlling it.

The Shays Rebellion was another matter entirely. Now that America was free of Britain, the homegrown "commercial interests" intended to take charge of the parasitic enterprises of speculation and usury. Talk of "Jubilee" and Biblical justice was so much hogwash to the masonic money men.

An intriguing racial note was injected when the leader of the American Freemasonic Lodge,

Prince Hall, offered the government the services of several hundred negro masons in the shooting and suppression of the Shays farmers of Massachusetts. Recognizing that the spectacle of armed blacks making war against white yeomen might be just the spark that would ignite the overthrow of the Boston plutocracy, Hall's offer was politely declined.

Hall ingratiated himself with the Massachusetts masonic elite in other ways, however, and contemporary Afro-American masonry is named in his honor and continues to serve an Uncle Tom function on behalf of the ruling class. According to researcher K.A. Badynski, the most prominent Prince Hall Freemason today is retired General Colin Powell.

The laws were stacked against the farmers and a high-paid mercenary army under able commanders was forming in Boston and would soon march against them. As the opposing camps formed for battle, one observer assessed the men comprising each side, indicating that Shays' ranks were made up of "the most laborious part of the people," from farmers to "reputable mechanics." Their foes consisted of, "lawyers, sheriffs... impost and excise collectors and their... servants and dependents."

Shays' men were unwavering in their resolve. Aaron Broad pledged, "I am determined to fight and spill my blood and leave my bones at the courthouse till Resurrection."

Soon the raids against Shays began. 300 banker-paid troops, commanded by the lawyer Benjamin Hichborn, assaulted the home of Job Shattuck; in resisting the attack, Shattuck was slashed with a sword. Dozens of other farmer-leaders of the rebellion were seized and their homes invaded. "The seeds of war are now sown," proclaimed farmer Elisha Pownell on Dec. 2, 1786.

While many of the upper class urged the farmers to surrender, the erudite Dr. William Whiting came to their defense, proving that the battle was not a class struggle, but a war between liberty and tyranny:

> "Whenever any encroachments are made either upon the liberties or the properties of the people, if redress cannot be had without, it is virtue in them to disturb government."

(Continued on next page)

THE BATTLE AT SPRINGFIELD ARSENAL

The farmers attacked the Federal arsenal at Springfield on January 25, 1787. Once provisioned with the tons of munitions at Springfield, Shays announced that his farmer-army would, "March directly to Boston" and "destroy that nest of devils who, by their influence, make the Court enact what they please."

Shays commanded a force of 1300 poorly armed day-laborers and farmers who were pitted against a thousand defenders of the arsenal, fully equipped and possessing artillery.

The working men's army marched between tall embankments of snow to within two hundred yards of the Federal facility. The mercenaries fired upon them with howitzers and canisters of grapeshot. The farmers were decimated. The mercenary army sought to rout them, but Shays' men disappeared into the forest like will-o-wisps, carrying what wounded they could manage.

Ecstatic at their initial success, Boston merchants poured money, in the form of loans (of course), into the treasury of the government troops.

In the following weeks, the farmers commenced to fight a guerrilla war, sniping from behind rocks and trees and sending out small bands of skirmishers. Their resistance was undaunted, even as Daniel Shays and hundreds of other fugitive farmers were forced to seek temporary refuge in Vermont and New York.

On February 27, 1787, a mercenary battalion surprised a large party of Shays' farmers during a snowstorm near Sheffield, Massachusetts. A blazing gun battle ensued and casualties were suffered on both sides. But with the element of surprise the mercenaries prevailed, killing and wounding thirty yeomen. The remnant had to again scatter, in deep snow, into the woods.

Governor Bowdoin recruited an additional 2,500 handsomely paid troops. The rebels were now everywhere on the run. Many were captured. Courts prosecuting the yeomen screened the jury pool by means of a "disqualification act" which barred any potential sympathizers from being seated on any Massachusetts jury.

One factor Governor Bowdoin and his merchant cronies were unable to "screen," however, were the voting lists, and in April Bowdoin lost the gubernatorial contest and John Hancock was elected governor.

FOUNDING FATHERS: PRO AND CONTRA

Hancock, another Founder of the American Revolution, had a reputation for moderation and fairness, due in part to the rustic mannerisms he affected. In reality, Hancock was secretly in sympathy with the lawyers and money-lenders and his folksy style was utterly lacking in the substance to match.

Hancock raised another 800 troops and gave them orders to slay every rebellious farmer they could lay hands upon.

Sam Adams, John Hancock and Noah Webster were all comfortable with the status quo and turned their coats and their backs on the ideals which they themselves had once championed.

Writing from England on January 2, 1787, the snooty future First Lady, Mrs. Abigail Adams, blamed Shays' Rebellion on the "luxury and extravagance both in furniture and dress" of the farmers, "accumulating debts upon them which they were unable to discharge."

In neighboring Vermont the case of Ethan Allen, the hero of Bennington and Ticonderoga, was more complex. Allen was walking a delicate political tightrope as he maneuvered the territory of Vermont toward statehood while battling Alexander Hamilton in New York and the government of New Hampshire. Both of those states sought to annex Vermont.

Privately Allen referred to the Massachusetts bankers and lawyers as a "pack of damned rascals" and harbored hundreds of Shays' sympathizers. In public he rebuffed Shays leaders Luke Day and Eli Parsons, who sought his military help in the rebellion, and Allen termed Daniel Shays a "criminal."

The ruse was also acted to the letter by Allen's ally, Vermont Governor Chittenden who "issued a proclamation at the end of February, 1787, warning the citizens of Vermont that they should not 'harbor, entertain, or conceal' Daniel Shays and three other insurgent leaders. At that time Shays and several other rebels were staying at the farm next to Chittenden's." (Michael Bellesiles, *Revolutionary Outlaws,* chapter 10).

(Continued on next page)

Ethan Allen promised the commander of the Massachusetts state troops that Vermont would apprehend and return fugitive Shays men, who were camped by the hundreds in Vermont. Exactly two Shaysites were sent back — a couple of horse thieves.

If Allen was compelled to play politics in order to guarantee the autonomy of his beloved Vermont against the covetous designs of other states and factions, Thomas Jefferson was free to speak his mind. Jefferson's statement concerning Shays' uprising constitutes the intact voice of the '76 Revolution, untainted by the hypocrisy of some of the new lords of the American nation. He wrote:

> I hold that a little rebellion now and then is a good thing and as necessary in the political world as storms in the physical... It is a medicine necessary for the sound health of government. (Letter of Thomas Jefferson to James Madison, January 30, 1787).

Historian Marion Starkey borrowed Jefferson's characterization for the title of her 1955 book about the Shays' movement, *A Little Rebellion.*

EPILOGUE

In April and May of 1787 star chamber "courts" tried captured Shays insurgents. Among these, John Bly and Charles Rose were hung.

Pockets of farmer resistance continued for months and assaults on those who loaned money at interest, such as factory magnate Josiah Woodbridge, continued.

But Shays' rebels lacked funds and as hunted fugitives, it was difficult for them to maintain efficient organization. Daniel Shays' military strategy had not won the conflict and hard luck contributed to his men's losses. But neither can it be said that the Shays rebels were defeated.

Many were unknown to the government in an era before photographic wanted posters and telegraph communications. These men resurfaced as "reformers" and played a part in the resistance to the sedition laws of John Adams in 1798. Others like Shays himself melted into the American frontier.

The wildlands of New York and Ohio offered territories with fewer laws, better soil and greater opportunities for free men. Some fared well, others never recovered from the loss of their farms and earthly possessions in Massachusetts. Daniel Shays and a hundred yeomen fled to New Hampshire after which they drifted apart and went separate ways.

Capt. Shays took up residence in upstate New York and lived the rest of his life in penury. He was so poor that upon his death his second wife didn't even bother to probate his will.

The worth of combat is not always determined by success on the field. Those who will only fight if victory is guaranteed, are looking for an insurance policy, not a battleground.

In some cases the very act of resistance is so significant it is itself an achievement. By fighting the tyranny emanating from within, the farmers of western Massachusetts confirmed their ancient heritage of unending struggle for freedom.

Thanks in part to Shays' Rebellion, the intractable fighting spirit of the yeomen of early America would remain kindled for decades to come, first in the anti-Federalist resistance to the U.S. Constitution of 1789 and the Sedition Act of 1798, and later, in 1826, a year after the death of Shays, in the populist movement against lawyers and Freemasons which shook the Northeast, forcing the closure of masonic lodges across the region.

Daniel Shays, Luke Day, Job Shattuck and the other thousands of fighters, were not awed by the prestige of the Founding Fathers, or the glittering cosmopolitan works of their merchant "betters." They insisted on holding their leaders to the principles of 1776 and in compelling them to make good on the Jubilee.

In our time our people also wax sore with debt. Never was the cry of Jubilee more apropos or more necessary than now. Does the blood of Daniel Shays flow yet in our veins?

Reprinted from *Independent History and Research* newsletter, which has since evolved into *Revisionist History Magazine*. For a sample issue, send $6.50 to Independent History, Box 849, Coeur d'Alene, Idaho 83816. Online at http://hoffman-info.com

REPRESSED MEMORY:
Junk Science in the Courts
by Paul and Shirley Eberle

Illustration by Nick Bougas

Barbara (not her real name) was stressed out. Everything in her life was going badly. Her marriage had failed, her job was a nightmare. She wasn't feeling well. But she had medical insurance. Barbara was told of a facility where the kind of difficulties she was experiencing were cured.

Barbara checked herself into the facility. Her psychiatrist sternly told her that all of her distress had been caused by incestuous childhood sexual abuse, and that she must remember being raped by her father before she would be well. She was isolated from the outside world, drugged, surrounded by patients who spoke of nothing but incestuous childhood sexual abuse. There was overpowering pressure to 'remember,' to scream out her rage and act out by throwing and smashing things.

"Dr. Smith is an expert. He can cure anything."

"He will make you well. Trust him."

Barbara checked herself into the facility. Her psychiatrist sternly told her that all of her distress had been caused by incestuous childhood sexual abuse, and that she must remember being raped by her father before she would be well. She was isolated from the outside world, drugged, surrounded by patients who spoke of nothing but incestuous childhood sexual abuse. There was overpowering pressure to "remember," to scream out her rage and act out by throwing and smashing things. Those who engaged in this behavior were rewarded with glowing approval. Those who did not were ignored. Barbara was in a very vulnerable state already. Now, surrounded by the hard-eyed custodians of fanaticism with their all-consuming obsession with incest, she searched desperately for memories of childhood rape, which just weren't there. "Gradually," she said, "I lost the ability to think for myself."

(Continued on next page)

Barbara observed that she and all of her fellow patients were not getting well but were getting much worse, descending into a downward spiral of paranoia and psychotic experiences. Some attempted suicide and self-mutilation. What they suffered before entering the hospital was nothing when compared to the damage done to them by the psychiatrists. After intense brainwashing sessions Barbara broke down. She had difficulty speaking coherently. Her psychiatrist had given her not one but several mind-altering drugs. When Barbara tried to check herself out of the hospital she was seized by orderlies, thrown into a padded cell and given more drugs. She began to understand that she was not going to be allowed to leave this locked facility until she declared that her father had raped her when she was an infant. Barbara complied. She was ordered to put her lurid accusations in writing. Her parents were summoned to the hospital and confronted with the letter. Naturally, they were crushed. They did not know what to say. They just wept. Nothing had prepared them for this.

A new wave of unreliable allegations of child sexual abuse has been sweeping over the nation during the past several years, causing incalculable pain and tragedy for families all over the United States and Canada. In a very short time it has become a billion-dollar industry for therapists, clinics, lecturers, authors, publishers and self-proclaimed gurus. It is one of the most bizarre and cruel quackeries of all time.

After Barbara was finally released she began to understand that she had been deluded. When she recanted, her psychiatrist urged her husband to divorce her and told him that she was an incurable drug addict — this in spite of the fact that the only drugs Barbara took were the drugs he had prescribed.

Barbara apologized to her parents, who forgave her. She was one of the lucky few.

All of this was some bizarre anomaly, a well-intentioned, bumbling effort by an otherwise efficacious, honorable profession — right?

Well, not really. A new wave of unreliable allegations of child sexual abuse has been sweeping over the nation during the past several years, causing incalculable pain and tragedy for families all over the United States and Canada. In a very short time it has become a billion-dollar industry for therapists, clinics, lecturers, authors, publishers and self-proclaimed gurus. It is one of the most bizarre and cruel quackeries of all time.

In the new "Repressed Memory Therapy," thousands of women have gone to psychiatrists, psychologists and other clinicians in search of cures for such commonplace discomforts as bulimia, nail biting, depression, headaches, stress, insomnia, a failing marriage, a job from which they are getting nothing but numbing servitude, a sense that something important is missing, an absence of any meaning or joy or direction in their lives, nothing to look forward to: the kind of malaise that nearly everybody experiences at some time.

But they come out of this "therapy" believing that they have been sexually abused by their parents, usually the father, in satanic blood-drinking rituals. Many have been convinced that they have multiple personalities. They are told by their therapists that they must break off all contact with their parents and make vile, horrifying accusations against them, and cut off all contact with other family members who do not believe. This protects the therapist and reinforces the beliefs. The patient moves, gets an unlisted telephone number, and all gifts from her parents are returned, unopened. These therapists almost invariably refuse to speak with the parents. The patients are mostly women. They have been told that these psychotherapists are "experts" who will make their lives whole. They are not told that what they have been indoctrinated into believing is without any evidential or scientific support. What happened to "Barbara" is so prototypical of this brand of "therapy" that you could delete her name and substitute any of thousands of other names in its place and the psychiatric abuse she suffered would differ only in the most trivial details from the others. It's all played from the same script.

In one case with which we are familiar, a 32-year-old woman who had been bulimic for 22 years decided to do something about it. She went to a therapist who sat and stared at her for a couple of sessions and then began to talk more and more about incest. He diagnosed her as having been sexually abused as a child. He told her that her mother wanted to kill her. This woman worked for the Houston Police Department. She neglected her daughter and nearly everything else in her life. She spent all of her money on therapy, nearly lost her house and her job. Finally, she was hospitalized and fed a great multiplicity of pills. She tried to commit suicide. Her therapist put her in a group where there was powerful peer pressure to conform, and to say she was sexually abused. This group became her family — her only family. She became so ill that she nearly lost her job. She decided to get a new therapist. This one was more reality-based. She still had her bulimia and she had indeed been molested by a stranger, but these things had never been addressed by her

(Continued on next page)

former therapist who talked only about incest. Even the cops with whom she worked tried to tell her that this was a misuse of therapy.

After some time in therapy with her new psychologist she became so angry that she sued the first therapist and collected a very substantial settlement. This was a ground-breaking case. She got enough money to keep her house, and also renewed her relationship with her mother and her family.

Most of the victims of this "therapy" are not so fortunate. Most people, once they become ideologues, block out anything that might persuade them to reexamine their beliefs.

What, exactly, is repressed memory therapy? An adult — almost always female — goes to a therapist and is told that her eating disorder, her failing marriage or depression stems from incestuous childhood sexual abuse, usually at the hands of the father. Using powerful mind-altering techniques (which, to all but the strongest and most sophisticated, would be irresistible and above suspicion), stringent, relentless pressure is applied, not only by the therapist but also by her group of converts, to break the patient down and make her "remember." This, the patient is told, will make her well. It is well known that many people are extremely susceptible to this kind of pressure and suggestion — particularly when they are frightened and desperate — when under the influence of hypnosis and drugs, an "expert," and overpowering group pressure; many of them actually begin to believe they are remembering an event that is nothing more than a suggestion or a visualization. It is also well known that all memory is distorted by any number of influences, both internal and external, and the erosion of time.

Of the children who testified as alleged victims in the celebrated McMartin case, several attended the preschool at a time when the defendant was living 100 miles away in San Diego. Yet, some gave extremely detailed descriptions of the molestations and the surroundings. Apparently they had come to believe that these events actually occurred. They were assured by everyone in the community that it was true: all the authority figures, all the people they needed, feared and trusted. And they were put through a powerful process of persuasion at Children's Institute International, a clinic in downtown Los Angeles that received several million dollars in government grants. But the stories changed each time the children testified; no two children described the same event, and most of the events they described were demonstrably impossible.

Memory can indeed be distorted and false memory implanted. That does not deter these apostles of New Age

brainwashing. When the insurance money is depleted the patient is told to sue her parents and file criminal charges against them, divesting them of all their assets and dropping them into the maw of a system that incarcerates the innocent and gives immunity to perjurers, particularly in cases of alleged child abuse. In McMartin the star witness for the prosecution was a career criminal who had an open rape/murder charge hanging over him. Might that have influenced his testimony?

When the insurance money is depleted the patient is told to sue her parents and file criminal charges against them, divesting them of all their assets and dropping them into the maw of a system that incarcerates the innocent and gives immunity to perjurers, particularly in cases of alleged child abuse. In McMartin the star witness for the prosecution was a career criminal who had an open rape/ murder charge hanging over him.

In many cases adult daughters have tried to put their parents in prison. In the Sousa case in Boston a 65-year-old couple are facing a sentence that would put them in prison for the rest of their lives. They are under house arrest pending the outcome of their appeal.

One woman went to visit her father as he lay dying in a hospital and spewed out her hate and her revolting accusations at him. She was not the only one.

Many of these women came out of the therapy claiming that they were brutally raped every day from the time they were born until adulthood. Others said it started when they were six months old. None of them remembered anything of these events until they received enlightenment from the psychologist. Can you remember anything that happened when you were six months old? At least one young woman told the news media she was raped in the womb, before her birth.

In 1994 there were 6,000 civil lawsuits filed by adult daughters against their parents based on this voodoo psychology. We don't know how many criminal charges have been filed, but there are too many to count. The first was the case of George Franklin, a California man who was convicted on the "recovered memory" testimony of his daughter, Eileen. Last year, his conviction was overturned by an appellate court. Dr. Richard Ofshe, a noted psychologist who was retained to study the case, said, "There is absolutely no evidence to suggest that he was anything but innocent." But Franklin spent six and a half years in prison looking at the world from an iron

(Continued on next page)

cage. When a federal court affirmed the ruling which vacated Franklin's conviction, the prosecutors did not release him but kept him in custody for months, zealously asserting that he was not innocent and that they intended to retry him. Finally, they admitted that the evidence to convict wasn't there. Prosecutors do not enjoy confessing that they have put a person in prison for six and a half years for a crime he did not commit.

Many of these women came out of the therapy claiming that they were brutally raped every day from the time they were born until adulthood. Others said it started when they were six months old. None of them remembered anything of these events until they received enlightenment from the psychologist. At least one young woman told the news media that she was raped in the womb, before her birth.

When Franklin was finally released in early July, 1996, prosecutors, members of the repressed memory industry, and radical feminist leaders bemoaned this tragic defeat.

Since then, there have been a number of legal victories for patients and their parents who sued the therapists. A Los Angeles Superior Court judge recently dismissed criminal charges against a father which were based on repressed memory, calling it "junk science." One of the most dramatic victories was that of Gary Ramona, who sued a psychiatrist and one of his colleagues who provided Ramona's daughter with this "therapy." Ramona won a judgment of $500,000 but he lost much more that that. He paid that much for legal counsel and expert witnesses. When his daughter went public with her accusations he lost his $500,000-per-year job as manager of a winery. His wife immediately divorced him and nobody would speak to him or be seen with him in the town where he had once been a most respected citizen.

Bereaved parents, stunned by the brutal ingratitude of daughters on whom they have lavished their love and their assets in order to provide them with college educations, have formed groups in nearly every city to share new information and expose this quackery in the hope of getting their families back together. The repressed memory "experts" have counterattacked by calling these people "the backlash," "a group of molesters," and "Satanists." When you attempt to dissect, examine and expose a fraud that has mutated into a fanatical ideology and a staggeringly lucrative industry, you can expect to get some heat.

Many parents tearfully pray for the reunification of their families, despite the vile accusations. Others are more realistic. One father, a brilliant scientist, appeared in court for a hearing on a petition to terminate his parental rights and to respond to incest accusations from his teenage daughters. He dispassionately told the judge, "There is no dispute. I don't want them back. I don't ever want to see them again."

We have lectured at conferences and seminars in which this subject was discussed. Afterward, many middle-aged women approached us and sadly told us, "My husband is in prison on repressed memory accusations. I don't know if he'll ever get out." We saw their tears and their pain. There have been enough horror stories to fill a library, almost too much for one person to read. There are two excellent books available, *Confabulations* and *True Stories of False Memory*, by Eleanor Goldstein and Kevin Farmer. Any library with a computer can provide you with a very complete bibliography of books authored by people on both sides of this issue, plus many articles and papers.

The consequences to these families have been devastating. The cruelty is truly mind-boggling. But the consequences to the practitioners have been enormous, staggering fees from insurance companies, clients and their parents. It is not uncommon for a therapist to receive several hundred thousand dollars in fees for providing this nostrum to one patient.

Typically, these patients are put in therapy groups in order to further break them down. In group, they are encouraged to scream epithets at their parents and batter Mom and Dad, using dolls and other effigies. Patients are told:

- ❏ If you can imagine it, it happened.
- ❏ If you don't remember it, that doesn't mean it didn't happen.
- ❏ If you don't believe it you are in denial.
- ❏ You must have a funeral for your relationship with your parents.
- ❏ Even such bizarre fables as the ubiquity of satanic cults molesting infants while murdering children and drinking their blood must be believed.
- ❏ If you sue your parents and file criminal charges against them, causing them to become indigent and spend the rest of their lives in prison, you will be made well and live happily forever after.

This system of therapy has its roots in Freud's seduction theory and even earlier fables. The theory of repression for years was accepted as an article of faith by psychiatrists and psychologists alike. But after nearly a century of studies and experiments, the leading experts in memory have concluded that evidence of repression does not exist. We know of no survivor of the Holocaust, or of

(Continued on next page)

Vietnam, who totally forgot the experience, then recovered it in a therapy session. Dr. Richard Ofshe, a professor of psychology at the University of California and a leading expert on memory and coercion, stated in a lecture that Repressed Memory Therapy is "the worst fraud of the Twentieth Century." He further stated that the incidence of cases in which repressed memories correspond with fact is about as common as Siamese twins joined at the head.

The media were quick to seize upon this bizarre phenomenon in their desperate race to attract audiences and compete for advertising revenue. Newspapers and television freak shows eagerly trumpeted these urban legends to an unwary public. Women claiming to be in possession of dozens — even hundreds — of multiple personalities were presented to us on television on a daily basis in a setting reminiscent of P.T. Barnum.

The media were quick to seize upon this bizarre phenomenon in their desperate race to attract audiences and compete for advertising revenue. Newspapers and television freak shows eagerly trumpeted these urban legends to an unwary public. Women claiming to be in possession of dozens — even hundreds — of multiple personalities were presented to us on television on a daily basis in a setting reminiscent of P.T. Barnum.

Most of the people out there believed it. They didn't get it from a seedy purveyor of diabolical conspiracy theories in an occult bookstore. It came to them from the heart of the United States government, the mainstream news media, liberal politicians, radical feminist celebrities, doctors, psychiatrists, professors, cops, district attorneys and attorneys general.

Ambitious, self-serving politicians have enacted laws which abrogate the statute of limitations that normally applies to child abuse. Now in about half the states, the statute of limitations runs from the time the alleged victim had her miraculous flashback. Incredibly, that great guardian of our constitutional rights, the A.C.L.U., has lobbied for the passage of these bills. It is, after all, a radical feminist agenda: hatred of the family, and particularly of the father. Feminist leaders have zealously embraced the repressed memory ideology as evidence of the depravity of the human male, and powerfully indoctrinated their communicants with this madness. Sadly, many women who turned to feminist leaders in search of greater freedom and equality merely exchanged a male bully for another kind of tyrant.

Nearly every large bookstore has a voluminous section labeled "RECOVERY." These sections are filled with books that preach the ideology of the Recovered Memory movement. Patients are strongly urged by their therapists to read these books which proclaim the horrors of the traditional family, hatred of the father, and the cosmic joys of lesbianism.

How did all this get started? Therapy — particularly that of the "New Age" variety — has become increasingly popular in the past twenty years. According to *U.S. News,* about 80 percent of the yuppie generation devoutly believes in the efficacy of therapy. They are apparently unaware that psychotherapy is an inexact science, even in the hands of a board-certified psychiatrist, to say nothing of scientifically illiterate M.F.C.C.s, M.S.W.s and all of those persons providing "therapy" who have nothing more than a B.A. in Theater Arts, or Business.

In 1974, the Child Abuse Prevention and Treatment Act (CAPTA), also known as the Mondale Act, was passed by the Congress, providing enormous funding for those who were willing to work in the field of "intervention in child abuse." Suddenly, the nation was flooded with Child Abuse Units, Child Abuse Clinics, and self-ordained child abuse experts. It was America's biggest growth industry. Congress addressed the problem of child abuse by throwing money at it without establishing any standards of professional competence or ethical conduct.

The consequences to these families have been devastating. The cruelty is truly mind-boggling. But the consequences to the practitioners have been enormous, staggering fees from insurance companies, clients and their parents. It is not uncommon for a therapist to receive several hundred thousand dollars in fees for providing this nostrum to one patient.

As a natural consequence, thousands of young people, mostly women, went into the field of psychology and obtained Ph.D.s, M.F.C.C.s and other credentials that would enable them to deal themselves into this game. Colleges and universities began pumping out Ph.D.s at an alarming rate. As the numbers of new therapists burgeoned, new "disorders" and "syndromes" began to

(Continued on next page)

proliferate. As the numbers of psychotherapists increased, the quality of their scientific training declined. Like their ecclesiastical predecessors, what these New Age priests imparted was more ideology than science. There is also the fact that it is easy. A heart surgeon, if he makes one mistake, will probably kill his patient. A clinical psychologist can get away with any number of errors and provide his client with a program of "treatment" that has absolutely no scientific basis.

At some point in time we are going to look into the qualifications and ethics of these therapists. The Hippocratic Oath enjoins the healer to "do no harm." These people are doing great harm. It is quackery that has spun out of control. Not one practitioner of this New Age panacea has expressed any regret or contrition.

In many states there are no requirements that must be met before a person can hang out a sign and offer himself/herself as a psychologist. Even in states where there are licensing requirements, the profession has done little or nothing to restrain the excesses of irresponsible, incompetent psychologists. A man who went to the Colorado State Legislature and told a legislative committee about this scandal was received with perfunctory courtesy and the usual platitudes: "You may be sure that we are deeply concerned about the issues you have raised today and you may be sure..."

After the committee adjourned the lawmakers told him privately in the hallway: "We know that everything you say is true but if we say one word about it our careers would be finished."

Shortly after the passage of the Mondale Act, we began reading headlines in the media that sexual abuse of children was increasing at astronomical proportions, that there was a worldwide secret society of sexual predators lurking, waiting to pounce on your child. We were told that all allegations of child sexual abuse must be believed, no matter how unfounded, no matter how physically impossible. It was a thinly disguised pitch for more money. As one lawyer who specializes in child-abuse cases told us, "It's not about child-abuse. It's about money. In order to get all this money the child abuse people have to generate cases! They are inflating their statistics! They are fabricating these cases."

At this time there was a tidal wave of child sexual abuse allegations against day-care facilities, with hundreds of counts and multiple defendants in a single case. Many people were sent to prison with sentences that would keep them there for the rest of their lives. Gradually, these cases began to fall apart. Several big cases have been overturned on appeal. Others appear to be inexorably on their way to reversal. As the day-care cases began to crumble, the child-abuse industry found a lucrative new market: adult survivors of incest.

How is it possible that a nation of presumably literate, reasonable people could buy into such an idiotic belief, relinquish control of their lives to a stranger, hand over the keys to their psyches to a therapist who is drunk with power and greed, and leave behind all critical judgment and any ethical principles or filial loyalty they might have had? This belief was not presented to them as a hypothesis. It came from people who had the imprimatur of authority, people with advanced degrees and titles, accompanied by a massive media-hype campaign. And there may be millions who are not capable of processing such a complicated issue. But even highly intelligent people, in a time of great social change and instability, fear, insecurity, chaos and the absence of any responsible leadership, can be sold almost anything if the seller is sufficiently persuasive. Therapy has become a religion.

In times like these, more than ever, people hunger for certainties. They are powerfully drawn to a person who claims to have the key, the secret, the power to make their lives whole. People who make such claims are almost invariably charlatans. As one of the defense attorneys in McMartin said, "Look a little closer. Look a little deeper."

And why do these psychotherapist-wannabees embrace the twin obsessions of incest and sexual abuse so devoutly? "It's a question of Hell," opines Stan Passy, who is quoted in psychotherapists James Hillman and M. Ventura's *We've Had a Hundred Years of Psychotherapy and the World's Getting Worse* (1992, NY, HarperSanFrancisco). Passy goes on to theorize that although we've lost the "place of Hell" in our culture, we are desperate to rediscover it, and as a result some therapists have redefined childhood (or at least the "death of the Inner Child") as Hell, and in the process have become ersatz priests who are on self-imposed evangelical missions to deliver their patients from Hell and its attendant damnation.

"So," concludes Passy, "we have a new Hell in modern times called childhood and a priest cult, a craft designed to save you from that Hell, all with the aim of recovering one's lost innocence."

Heady stuff, indeed.

(Continued on next page)

Dr. Elizabeth Loftus and Katherine Ketcham, co-authors of *The Myth of Repressed Memory: False Memories and Allegations of Sexual Abuse* (1994, NY, St. Martin's Press), advance this concept of a contemporary crusade by a deluded cabal to save patients, who are perceived as abused, from Hell one step farther. "The journey to recover our lost innocence takes us deep into the land of metaphor and myth," they state, citing, in addition to the "Inner Child" and the "Hell of Childhood," "the Myth of the Dysfunctional Family... (from which) we learn that every family is dysfunctional in one way or another and that family rules and customs 'kill the souls of human beings.'"

There have been a number of legal victories for patients and their parents who sued the therapists. A Los Angeles Superior Court judge recently dismissed criminal charges against a father which were based on repressed memory, calling it "junk science."

Loftus and Ketcham also posit "the Myth of Psychic Determinism (from which) we discover that our personalties, psyches, and behaviors are determined by events that occurred in our childhood. While we may think we are free to choose, the myth teaches that we are passive characters acting out a script, moved and played upon by unconscious, uncontrollable forces."

There are two more myths which, Loftus and Ketcham point out, allow the neophyte therapist a chance to redeem their allegedly abused patients. "The Myth of Growth promises that we can 'grow out of' our complexes and conflicts and 'grow into' more mature, stable, understanding, and loving human beings. Salvation is possible... through the Myth of Total Recall. Memory is imagined as a computerized process in which every action, expression, emotion, and nuance of behavior is imprinted into the soft tissue of the mind. If we are willing to search for the Truth, we can discover it (and in the process be cured) by going back to the past, facing our demons, and reclaiming our lost innocence.

"Do the myths hold up to reality? Only if reality is molded and framed to fit the myth."

And what does it say about the quality of our mental health professionals when they so eagerly embrace this kind of science fiction? We think you already know the answer to that. At some point in time we are going to have to look into the qualifications and ethics of these therapists. The Hippocratic Oath enjoins the healer to "do no harm." These people are doing great harm. It is quackery that has spun out of control. Not one practitioner of this New Age panacea has expressed any regret or contrition. They speak of it with the wide-eyed, apocalyptic zeal of evangelists.

Will it be a priority that insurance pays for recovered memories, past-life regressions, space-alien abductions and satanic-cult conspiracies, even if memory-enhancement techniques are used? Dr. Richard Gardner of Columbia University said: "Sex abuse is big business. There's lots of money to be made by a whole parade of individuals who involve themselves in these cases." Adult women who accuse their fathers may well turn to a lawyer for assistance. In the United States there is approximately one practicing lawyer for every 340 people. It is likely that these women will find one. Is the cure worse than the bite?

As Debbie Nathan and Michael Snedeker conclude in *Satan's Silence: Ritual Abuse and the Making of a Modern American Witch Hunt* (1995, NY, BasicBooks), "In Salem, it was an act of moral strength, political self-interest, and social progress to say 'we were wrong.' Three centuries later, it is up to all who sanctioned our modern-day sex-abuse witch hunt to help redress this terrible mistake."

It's not going to go away soon. As long as there is such massive profit taking; as long as the media feed on spectacular allegations of depravity and never report exculpatory evidence; as long as there is such an enormous army of psychotherapists who are so incompetent they have nowhere else to go except downward to the bottom of the labor pool; as long as the propaganda is so pervasive that it would take an Emile Zola to bring it down, this travesty will endure. It is almost impossible to dislodge these beliefs with evidence because we did not get them with evidence. And we have a collective fascination with tales of horror and mystery, which explains the phenomenal success of Stephen King, Alfred Hitchcock and their imitators, and movies like *Sybil*. Perhaps the first thing we need to learn from all of this is the importance of not being stupid enough to believe everything we are told, but rather to examine, question and test popular beliefs.

Briefly, in closing, we would like to say unequivocally that we abhor the mistreatment of children, adults, animals, or anybody. That should go without saying. But during a witch hunt nothing goes without saying.●

Paul and Shirley Eberle are co-authors of the best-selling book, *The Abuse Of Innocence: The McMartin Preschool Trial*, (1993, Buffalo, NY; Prometheus Books) and *The Politics of Child Abuse* (1986, Secaucus, NJ; Lyle Stuart, Inc.)

YOU WILL ALSO WANT TO READ:

❑ **94146 LOOMPANICS' GREATEST HITS: Articles and Features from the Best Book Catalog In The World,** *Edited by Michael Hoy.* A collection of articles and essays, cartoons and rants, gleaned from the pages of the Loompanics Unlimited book catalog. For over a decade, the Loompanics Catalog has served as a kiosk for writers from the far left, the far right and the *far out* — including Robert Anton Wilson, Kurt Saxon, Robert Shea and many, many others. A compendium of counterculture thought, this provocative book contains more than 75 features in all. *1990, 8½ x 11, 300 pp, illustrated, soft cover.* **$14.95.**

❑ **94067 LOOMPANICS' GOLDEN RECORDS: Articles and Features from The Best Book Catalog in the World,** *Edited by Michael Hoy.* Three years in the making! A brand-new collection of articles and features from the Loompanics Unlimited Book Catalog. Loompanics has always strived to make the articles and features it publishes every bit as exciting, frightening, eye-opening, controversial and unusual as the books it sells. This brand new collection contains more than 40 of the best and most imaginative pieces Loompanics has ever published, including work by Jim Hogshire, Michael Newton, James B. DeKorne, and many other. Also features some never-before-published pieces. *1993, 8½ x 11, 200 pp, illustrated, soft cover.* **$10.00.**

❑ **94268 LOOMPANICS UNLIMITED LIVE! IN LAS VEGAS,** *Edited by Michael Hoy.* Every three years or so, Loompanics Unlimited lights up the desert landscape of American letters by compiling a collection of articles and stories, culled from the catalogs and supplements that we've published during that time. Since we've specialized in providing controversial and unusual works for over twenty years, it should come as no surprise to anyone that many of the selections in this book are both shocking and exhilarating. *1996, 8½ x 11, 255 pp, illustrated, soft cover.* **$12.95.**

❑ **94281 101 THINGS TO DO 'TIL THE REVOLUTION,** *Ideas and resources for self-liberation, monkey wrenching and preparedness, by Claire Wolfe.* We don't need a weatherman to know which way the wind blows — but we do need the likes of Claire Wolfe, whose book offers 101 suggestions to help grease the wheels as we roll towards the government's inevitable collapse. "Kill your TV... Join a gun-rights group... Fly the Gadsden flag... Buy and carry the Citizens' Rule Book... Join the tax protesters on April 15... Bury gold, guns, and goodies..." Wolfe's list is lengthy and thought-provoking, as she elaborates on each piece of advice, from generalities to precise instructions. For the concerned citizen who wishes to keep a low profile, protect his or her rights, and survive in the "interesting times" which are sure to come, this is essential reading. *1996, 5½ x 8½, 216 pp, soft cover.* **$15.95.**

❑ **10065 HOW TO HIDE THINGS IN PUBLIC PLACES,** *by Dennis Fiery.* Did you ever want to hide something from prying eyes, yet were afraid to do so in your home? Now you can secrete your valuables away from home, by following the eye-opening instructions contained in this book, which identifies many of the public cubbyholes and niches that can be safely employed for this purpose. Absolutely the finest book ever written on the techniques involved in hiding your possessions in public hiding spots, profusely illustrated with over 85 photographs. Also contains an appendix of Simplex lock combinations. *1996, 5½ x 8½, 220 pp, illustrated, soft cover.* **$15.00.**

❑ **32060 DAVID'S TOOL KIT: A Citizen's Guide to Taking Out Big Brother's Heavy Weapons,** *by Ragnar Benson.* What do you do when faced with the overwhelming firepower of ruthless authority? *Fight back,* that's what! Ragnar Benson provides citizen defenders with the information they need to mount a successful campaign against overwhelming odds... and win! Learn how to employ homemade explosives and detonators; build effective flame throwers; select accurate sniper rifles and scopes; generate smoke, and much more. Brief histories of armed resistance and tank warfare are included. This may be the most essential self-defense book ever written! *1996, 5½ x 8½, 217 pp, illustrated, soft cover.* **$16.95.**

And much, much more. We offer the very finest in controversial and unusual books — a complete catalog is sent *FREE* with every book order. If you would like to order the catalog separately, please see our ad on the next page.

• **LCU98**

LOOMPANICS UNLIMITED
PO BOX 1197
PORT TOWNSEND, WA 98368

Please send me the books I have checked above. I am enclosing $ _____ (which includes $4.95 for shipping and handling of books totaling up to $20.00. Please include $1 extra for each additional $15 ordered) *Washington residents please include 7.9% for sales tax.*

NAME _____

ADDRESS _____

CITY/STATE/ZIP _____

To place a credit card (Visa or MasterCard) order only, call 1-800-380-2230,
8am to 4pm, Pacific Standard Time, Monday through Friday.